REGNUM ST

Diaconal Studies

Lived Theology for the Church in North America

Series Preface

Regnum Studies in Mission are born from the lived experience of Christians and Christian communities in mission, especially but not solely in the fast growing churches among the poor of the world. These churches have more to tell than stories of growth. They are making significant impacts on their cultures in the cause of Christ. They are producing 'cultural products' which express the reality of Christian faith, hope and love in their societies.

Regnum Studies in Mission are the fruit often of rigorous research to the highest international standards and always of authentic Christian engagement in the transformation of people and societies. And these are for the world. The formation of Christian theology, missiology and practice in the twenty-first century will depend to a great extent on the active participation of growing churches contributing biblical and culturally appropriate expressions of Christian practice to inform World Christianity.

Series Editors

Marina Behera	Research Tutor, Oxford Centre for Mission Studies
Paul Bendor-Samuel	Director, Oxford Centre for Mission Studies
Bill Dyrness	Former Dean of the School of theology, Fuller Seminary
Tony Gray	Director, Words by Design
Paul Woods	Asia Graduate School of Theology – Alliance

REGNUM STUDIES IN MISSION

Diaconal Studies
Lived Theology for the Church in North America

Edited by
Craig L. Nessan and
Darryl W. Stephens

Copyright © Craig L. Nessan and Darryl W. Stephens 2024

First published 2024 by Regnum Books International

Regnum is an imprint of the Oxford Centre for Mission Studies
St. Philip and St. James Church
Woodstock Road
Oxford, OX2 6HR, UK
www.regnumbooks.net

The right of Craig L. Nessan and Darryl W. Stephens to be identified
as the editors of this work has been asserted by them
in accordance with the Copyright, Designs and Patents Act 1988.

All rights reserved. No part of this publication may be reproduced, stored in a retrieval system, or transmitted, in any form or by any means, electronic, mechanical, photocopying, recording or otherwise, without the prior permission of the publisher or a license permitting restricted copying. In the UK such licenses are issued by the Copyright Licensing Agency, 90 Tottenham Court Road, London W1P 9HE.

British Library Cataloguing in Publication Data
A catalogue record for this book is available from the British Library

ISBN: 979-8-8898-3867-8
eBook ISBN: 979-8-8898-3868-5

Typeset by Words by Design

Cover artwork © Cecily A. Stephens

Scripture quotations from the *New Revised Standard Version of the Bible* are copyright © 1989 by the Division of Christian Education of the National Council of Churches of Christ in the USA. Used by permission. All rights reserved.

Distributed by Fortress Press in the US, Canada, India, and Brazil

Contents

List of Figures	vii
Abbreviations	ix
Foreword by Ted Dodd	xi
Foreword by Jean Berchmans Mweningoma	xiii
Introduction by Craig L. Nessan and Darryl W. Stephens	1

PART 1: *DIAKONIA* FOR THE LIFE OF THE WORLD

1	Establishing Diaconal Studies in North America Craig L. Nessan	15
2	Emergent *Diakonia* in Response to Changing Contexts Sandra Boyce	29
3	Ecumenical Convergence on the Diaconate in North America Mitzi J. Budde	39
4	The Problem and Promise of the Diaconate Benjamin L. Hartley	51
5	Strengthening *Diakonia* for a Thriving Church Margaret Ann Crain	63

PART 2: LIBERATING DIACONAL PRAXIS

6	Christian Diaconal Practice Through the Lens of Human Dignity Ignatius Swart	75
7	Liberating *Diakonia* in a Brazilian Perspective Dionata Rodrigues de Oliveira	89
8	A Theology of *Diakonia* at the Margins Norma Cook Everist	101
9	The Work of *Diakonia* Toward *Koinonia* Among LGBTQIA+ Persons and the Church Leo Yates Jr.	111
10	De-Subjugating the Servant Image as a Theo-Diaconal Intervention Man-Hei Yip	123
11	Developing a Trauma-Informed Diaconal Praxis Darryl W. Stephens	133

PART 3: DIACONAL LEADERSHIP AND SPIRITUALITY

12	The Diaconal Spirituality of Activism in the Philippines Norma P. Dollaga	149
13	Women Shaping Diaconal Theology in The Episcopal Church Valerie Bailey	159
14	Reclaiming the Lessons and Legacies of the Earliest Episcopal Deaconess Daphne B. Noyes	173

15	Imagining the Future of *Diakonia*	
	Jessica Bickford	185
16	Reclaiming Spirituality in Diaconal Work in Germany	
	Johannes Eurich	195

PART 4: DIACONAL STUDIES AND FORMATION

17	Diaconal Studies in an Interdisciplinary PhD Programme in Norway	
	Annette Leis-Peters	207
18	A Norwegian Case for Formation in the *Diakonia* Curriculum	
	Kristin Husby Dyrstad	221
19	Investment in Diaconal Flourishing in The Episcopal Church	
	Lori Mills-Curran	239
20	A Competency-Based, Mentor-Assessed Path for Diaconal Formation	
	Julie Anne Lytle	251
21	Theology of Liberative Service	
	Mary Elizabeth Moore	265

Index of Names	275
Index of Subjects	277
Contributors	285

List of Figures

4.1	Gravitational Centers of Meaning for *Diakonia*	55
4.2	Comparison of Definitions of *Diakoneo* in the New Testament	57
6.1	Pieterse's Classification of Congregational Projects Among the Poor Based on Sermon Analyses	79
6.2	Johnson's Examples of Faith-Based Community Revitalization	82
11.1	Bearing Witness in Four Moments	139
17.1	PhD Dissertations: Diaconia, Values, and Professional Practice	215
20.1	Continuum of Theological Education/Opportunities for Lifelong Learning	256
20.2	The "Yours, Mine, and Ours" Approach for Diaconal Preparation	259
20.3	Signposts Along Student's and Mentor's Paths to Degree	260

Abbreviations

AED	Association for Episcopal Deacons
BIPOC	Black, indigenous, and persons of color
BSSF	Bexley Seabury Seminary Federation
CBE	competency-based education
CBTE	competency-based theological education
COVID-19	coronavirus disease caused by the SARS-CoV-2 virus
CPE	clinical pastoral education
EDOM	Episcopal Diocese of Maryland
EKD	*Evangelische Kirche in Deutschland*
ELCA	Evangelical Lutheran Church in America
HIV/AIDS	Human Immunodeficiency Virus/Acquired Immunodeficiency Syndrome
IECLB	*Igreja Evangélica de Confissão Luterana no Brasil* (The Evangelical Church of the Lutheran Confession in Brazil)
LGBTQIA+	lesbian, gay, bisexual, transgender, queer, intersex, asexual, and others
LWF	Lutheran World Federation
MDA	Mission and Diaconia Archives (at VID Specialized University, Oslo, Norway)
NIV	New International Version
NRSV	New Revised Standard Version
NRSVUE	New Revised Standard Version Updated Edition
SAMHSA	Substance Abuse and Mental Health Services Administration
TEC	The Episcopal Church (US)
UMC	(The) United Methodist Church
US	United States (adjective)
WCC	World Council of Churches

Foreword

Currently, I serve as president of DIAKONIA of the Americas and the Caribbean (DOTAC), an organization composed of twelve diaconal communities and associations within this region. As such, I am positioned as a vice president of DIAKONIA World Federation, the global network. At home, I connect with my own community, Diakonia of The United Church of Canada, locally and nationally. I welcome this effort of the authors and scholars in this edition as a passionate and thoughtful addition to the field of diaconal studies.

Understandings and practices around the diaconate vary among these ecumenical communities and associations. Some members of the diaconate are in lay orders; some are ordained. Some are non-stipendiary; some work for and are paid by the church. Some associations are regulated by the church; some are free-standing organizations. Some operate within a hierarchical structure; others function with more lenient expectations. Some have extensive seminary-based formation programmes; others have less formalized training. And of course, theologies differ. Yet when we are together, sharing in programming and events offered by these alliances, a sense of oneness exists. We feel known and connected in the richness of these diaconal relationships. These ecumenical, international, and denominational ties have broadened my worldview and deepened my sense of diaconal identity.

Diaconal Studies: Lived Theology for the Church in North America captures some of that sacred magic, while intensifying and developing our collective understanding of the theology, practice, formation, and spirituality of *diakonia*. This exciting project covers a lot of diaconal ground, from a variety of perspectives. In the face of ongoing confusion and the church's ambivalence toward *diakonia*, the scope of this volume is to be appreciated. Those who write from the outlook of the academy add a strength of considered thought and fullness of themes pondered. Those who write as diaconal practitioners contribute the intensity of the "front line" and the authenticity of action. Holding action and reflection in tension, balance, and integration belong to the diaconal way of praxis.

The spirituality of *diakonia* needs the attention of our thinkers and actors. Often, those of us committed to *diakonia* are so busy doing that praying and listening to the divine are lost. When soul work is neglected, we lose our way and our heart. Without renewal or deepening, we become empty. Giving and giving, we can forget to receive. Diaconal discernment and wisdom do not dualistically separate temporal and spiritual but incarnate faith and embody compassion and love of the world.

This book offers confirmation and reassurance despite the difficulties and frustrations. Its show of support and rich reflection will encourage those who feel drained or defeated. Our call needs to include joy alongside determination. Some authors write from the viewpoint of those designated (ordained, commissioned, consecrated) to the diaconate. As a minority within the church's ministry, the diaconate has known experiences of patronization and faced obstacles and devaluing. There has even been heartbreak. Other authors, while not officially in the diaconate, share a critique of the church's tendency to sideline the work and mission of *diakonia*. They want that sad neglect to change. Their ecclesiologies plea for the transformation of the church. We are called toward the Gospel vision of Kin-dom – first-last, Samaritan-good, children-as-the-sign-of-the-Realm-of-God – turning the world around. As the church, our diaconal vocation stands with the edges, with those exiled and excluded and estranged. Our prophetic responsibility demands that we address the imbalances and injustices that confront us every day in the news.

Those committed to the diaconal vision attempt to build and foster community wherever we are located. Ministries of welcome and hospitality promote radical inclusion and are dedicated to equality. Everyone needs places to connect and to have companionship and engage in meaningful conversations where we are encouraged, nurtured, and empowered. We are members of circles that provide belonging and trustworthy exchange, belonging to groups both supportive and challenging. Community embraces one with warmth while holding one accountable. Much of North American society is based on individualism. Many of our theologies emphasize personal sin and salvation, without reflecting the log-in-the-eye of corporate and systemic evils and conversion. Being in and creating community are countercultural activities, practices that *diakonia* fosters.

Historically, the basin and towel have been our symbols. The foot washing story from John's Gospel has been held up as our model of service. Yet all too often, this model of service has been interpreted in ways that have slipped into subservient, invisible, humble obedience and limited our imagination to charity models of ministry. Reflecting on other biblical images and aspects of our history, this volume offers welcome alternatives. What is our role as ambassadors, advocates, catalysts, storytellers, messengers, gatekeepers, go-betweens, and bridges between the church and the world? Our work involves transforming the institution (*ecclesia reformata, semper reformanda*) and leading the planet and its people to reclamation, reconciliation, and restoration.

This book, lifting up this sacred vocation and vision, is welcomed as blessing. Diaconal studies is often overlooked in our seminaries and theological enterprises. *Diaconal Studies: Lived Theology for the Church in North America* provides resources for correcting that absence. The inspiring stories presented in this volume tell us about individuals of courage and commitment. The theologies expressed here stretch us intellectually, prayerfully, and emotionally. The writers describe historic and present-day world-changing ministries of liberation and transformation. We need this work to help us reclaim our focus in *diakonia* and to redirect the church and all its people to the "*diakonia* of all believers." The church is not the church without *diakonia*.

Ted Dodd is president of DIAKONIA of the Americas and the Caribbean (DOTAC), a vice president of DIAKONIA World Federation, and a diaconal minister of The United Church of Canada.

Foreword

It is high time if not too late for the church to discover that there are handicaps in the ministry due to the absence of deacons. Jesus wanted people to have life and life in abundance (John 10:10). The ministry of a deacon is faithfully to serve God's people in a holistic way, attending to persons physically, emotionally, socially, and spiritually. This ministry is demonstrated by acts of love, compassion, and commitment to the manifestation and the presence of God among human beings.

For the success of the mission of the church, the role of deacons is essential. Ministry requires a combination of gifts as the members of Christ's body work for the good of the whole. Scriptures tell us that the church is like the body with its different parts, which, though working differently, make a unity (Rom 12:4–8; 1 Cor 12:27–a). The leg cannot see, and the eye cannot walk. They complement each other. Likewise, the church should let Christians and the wider community know that the order of vocational deacons is a divinely instituted reality and be proud of their role in the church's mission.

We realize that the ministry of a deacon is wide because it is not limited only to the church. Deacons are called to deal with issues that arise in the community, like child abuse, gender-based violence, poverty, homelessness, injustice, and oppression. Deacons play a role of lending compassion to improve people's daily lives. In addition to their liturgical service in the church, they are God's representatives in the community. The community constantly needs the church's response whenever living conditions become hard. The church must recognize deacons, treating them as equals to priests.

Within my own tradition, the Anglican Church, deacons are often considered inferior to priests because of the widespread understanding of the diaconate as transitional. Some priests act as if deacons were simple interns. This way of looking down on vocational deacons for not reaching the status of the priesthood is prevalent in the parts of the world where such a permanent ministry is not familiar. We need to make clear that the diaconate as part of the church orders is biblical and so essential for the church as it seeks to offer a holistic ministry to humankind. The church needs the diaconate in its daily action to improve the lives of the people it serves.

It is the responsibility of the church and its educational institutions to recognize the importance of this ministry. The church needs to offer a formal training for deacons and at the same time recognize them as fully called ordained ministers. From my experience in establishing diaconate training in Burundi – though we are still at the beginning – the whole process starts with a commitment from the structures of the church to support deacons in their specific formation. This commitment comes out of a fair discussion on the place of deacons.

Since the diaconate is a special ministry, there is a need for a special curriculum. Deacons should be trained and equipped with appropriate skills. They should also be encouraged to be prayerful persons due to their involvement in communities, being confronted daily with a variety of people with different needs. Prayer is key in the diaconate ministry. However, most theological training institutions are meant to train priests with no attention to the diaconate as a separate ministry requiring special formation. In most Anglican theological institutions worldwide, there are no programmes and no proper trainers for the diaconate. This traditional way of educating ministers misses the opportunity of having well-trained deacons. Consequently, believers who are called to become vocational deacons rather than priests may lack interest and support in pursuing theological formation. Thus, it is important to organize a well-designed curriculum for the diaconate to enable deacons to clearly see the work that lies ahead of them.

This book examines the place of a deacon and why the church needs to encourage believers to join the diaconate. It develops a proposal for the field of diaconal studies and the importance of having a special curriculum and theological training for deacons. I take this opportunity to express my gratitude to all the stakeholders who have been involved in the development of diaconal studies, in particular those who initiated this collaborative project and book and all the contributors to the present work. This joint work has enriched our experiences. We hope it is inspirational for the readers who envision the diaconate as a ministry that needs to be sharpened through a well-organized formation. It is our hope that the church in different traditions will move forward to make the diaconate an essential ministry and to prepare vocational deacons as separate ministers.

Jean Berchmans Mweningoma is bishop of the Anglican diocese of Muyinga, Burundi and founder of Burundi's first school for deacons, located in Buyé.

Introduction

Craig L. Nessan and Darryl W. Stephens

The call to *diakonia* is constitutive of Christian identity and the nature of the church. The church today is navigating complex challenges: cultural divisions, membership declines, and multiple crises – structural racism, xenophobia, endemic poverty, climate collapse, and ongoing traumas from the COVID-19 pandemic. Both church and academy urgently need a constructive diaconal theology to spark revitalization of mission amid these and other emerging crises.

Vibrant diaconal theology can be a catalyst not only for church revitalization but also for cutting-edge theological education. Beyond North America, the diaconate has become an identifiable field of academic study. Theological education in Germany, Scandinavia, South Africa, and other global contexts claim a rich history of diaconal studies. However, churches and theological education institutions in North America have been slow to recognize this advancement. While the practice of *diakonia* has begun to grow here in recent decades, research has not kept pace. In North America, "diaconal studies" has been limited to ecclesial training programmes and manuals, introductory books, and a few specialized studies.

This book aims to accelerate learning between North American and global diaconal educators and reflective practitioners, drawing on ecumenical dialogue and global research over the past three decades. Global collaborators have served as conversation partners and contributors throughout the project, sharing their wisdom to inform the development of diaconal research and study in the North American context. Based on the interactions between these international scholars and reflective practitioners from Australia, Brazil, Canada, Germany, Norway, South Africa, and the United States, this book aims to establish the foundation for diaconal studies in North America. The authors share the common conviction that diaconal studies can explore and create new ways of incarnating the church's ministry. By bringing together contributors from diverse traditions and contexts, we seek to catalyze attention to the promise of an ecumenical, lived diaconal theology for North America. The guiding question among us has been: what shape should diaconal studies take in North America and how can it contribute both to church mission and the academy?

Defining *Diakonia*

The leading edge of ecumenical theology depicts *diakonia* as integral to discipleship, focused on service, justice, and advocacy for the marginalized. Worldwide, diaconal practice is no longer simply associated with alms and palliative ministries. As the chapters of this book demonstrate, there is a lively and fruitful discussion underway to define *diakonia* beyond inherited traditional understandings.

The work of John N. Collins on the meaning of *diakonia* and its cognates in the New Testament has overturned the conventional definition of *diakonia* as "humble service." Instead, Collins argued that *diakonia* involved the role of mediation by a messenger or emissary.[1] The research of Collins authorized critical examination of the limitations of the servant model of leadership that became the standard understanding of *diakonia* in the nineteenth-century retrieval of the diaconate in Germany. Critique of the servant model becomes acute when it valorizes the role of a slave or provides rationale for the inferiority and subservience of deacons in the life of the church.

At the same time, both in the teachings of Jesus and in the practice of *diakonia* in the history of the church, there are strong warrants for understanding *diakonia* as "service" to others, especially service to those experiencing acute need. The New Testament testifies to the servanthood of Jesus: "The greatest among you will be your servant [*diakonos*]" (Matt 23:11, NRSVUE). Jesus ordained his followers to a diaconate of all believers by the washing of feet. The basin and towel are signs of diaconal ministry for the whole church. Throughout church history, the physical, social, political, emotional, and spiritual conditions that cause human suffering have summoned forth a diaconal response from the church and its agents.

Diakonia, as an embodied and lived theology, witnesses to the faithfulness of God in all times and places. *Diakonia* today must encompass the notion of mediation, taking up the challenge of Collins. At the same time, the definition of *diakonia* must be broad enough to honor and include the range of compassionate ministries that have been offered as service to the neighbor throughout Christian history. The meaning of *diakonia* must also embrace the work of advocating for social change and being in solidarity with the oppressed, as expressed by the term "prophetic *diakonia*" developed in response to the challenge of liberation theologies. In addition to mediation, service, and solidarity, *diakonia* encompasses the work of repair and reconciliation (2 Cor 2:18).

The Jewish concept of *tikkun olam* provides a point of departure for defining the work of *diakonia* in an era when other interpretations of Christian mission have become either discredited or shopworn. *Tikkun olam* refers to God's work of repairing the world. Mary Elizabeth Moore described *tikkun olam* as "a vison of social, political, and religious transformation ... grounded in hope for the restoration of the world, or the restoration of justice and righteousness."[2] *Diakonia*, accordingly, becomes *our participation in God's work of repairing creation*. It is liberative and transformative, serving in solidarity in the name of the One who is reconciling and making new all of creation. The diaconate of all believers is constituted of those who are called to mediate God's work of bringing *shalom* to a broken humanity and an endangered creation.

---

[1] John N. Collins, *Diakonia Studies: Critical Issues in Ministry* (Oxford: Oxford University Press, 2014), 3–36.
[2] Mary Elizabeth Moore, *Ministering with the Earth* (St. Louis: Chalice, 1998), 4.

The Value of Diaconal Studies for North America

Revitalization of the church requires strengthening its diaconal identity and capacity. A necessary part of this effort involves the establishment of diaconal studies within theological education. The recent document *Called to Transformation: Ecumenical Diakonia*, from the World Council of Churches, encourages "theological seminaries ... to include *diakonia* in their curricula and training programs ... thereby enhancing the capacity building of churches in *diakonia* and strengthening their work in social services."[3] Establishing diaconal studies within North American theological education promises to enhance connections between doctrine and daily life, service and social critique, and solidarity and transformation. This volume provides impetus to the North American realization of these purposes.

The value of diaconal studies in the academy has implications not only for the preparation of those becoming deacons in the church but also for a wide array of helping professions. There exist several degree programmes that could be enhanced through interaction with a robust diaconal theology in courses of study that are related to other theological studies programmes at their institutions. Schools with counselling programmes, for example, could discover a vibrant theological resource in diaconal studies, such as exists in Germany and Norway. The same is true for professionals who do not intend to enter ordained ministry but who need theological training to enhance their work in nursing, social work, not-for-profit leadership, and many other professions engaging "religion and public life."

There are several existing programmes that deserve such consideration, for example, at Candler School of Theology, Harvard Divinity School, and Boston University School of Theology, among others. Candler offers a Master of Religion and Public Life that is "designed for professionals in law, healthcare, social work, education and other fields whose work requires them to navigate issues of faith on a regular basis."[4] Harvard Divinity School has a Master of Religion and Public Life Program that "provides an opportunity for journalists, government officials, humanitarian aid workers, educators, artists, health care professionals, businesspeople, lawyers, and other practitioners to develop in-depth knowledge of the complex ways religion influences public life relevant to their arenas in ways that will advance their own vocational aims."[5] Boston University School of Theology offers a Master of Arts in Religion and Public Leadership "designed for leaders from diverse vocations who want to enhance

---

[3] World Council of Churches and ACT Alliance, *Called to Transformation: Ecumenical Diakonia* (Geneva: WCC, 2022), 113,
https://www.oikoumene.org/resources/publications/ecumenical-diakonia.
[4] "Master of Religion and Public Life," Candler School of Theology,
https://candler.emory.edu/academic-programs/master-of-religion-and-public-life/.
[5] "Master of Religion and Public Life (MRPL) Program," Harvard Divinity School,
https://hds.harvard.edu/academics/degree-programs/mrpl-program.

their skills through advanced study of religion, leadership, and public life."[6] These and other degree programmes can be deepened and strengthened by engagement with robust diaconal studies oriented toward the significance of religion and ethics in the public world.

The field of diaconal studies also deserves attention at the doctoral level. Currently, a doctoral dissertation with a focus on *diakonia* might be located in one of several disciplines: history, mission, theological studies, or practical theology. The field of diaconal studies, if recognized as such at all, is often relegated to the status of a subdiscipline. The recognition of diaconal studies in the academy globally, based on the integrity of its method and subject matter, warrants its development as a recognized field of study also within theological education in North America.

Diaconal studies, as evidenced in this book, provides a complex and methodologically sophisticated perspective to ground the study of theology at both the master's and doctoral levels. The method of diaconal studies involves the correlation of the resources of the theological tradition with the practical challenges of social service and social advocacy needed for faithful and effective public leadership. The field of diaconal studies advances a perspective that embraces service and advocacy by Christian actors in arenas of public life beyond the traditional parameters of the church. While *diakonia* as an academic paradigm is deeply rooted in the theological tradition, diaconal studies can ground, renew, and invigorate interdisciplinary academic discourse to address the most urgent challenges in the contemporary world.

Structure and Contents

This book is arranged thematically in four parts. Common threads are shared among all parts, stitching the volume together as a coherent whole. Readers are encouraged to choose their entry points based on topical and thematic interests.

Part 1: Diakonia for the Life of the World

In response to global and ecumenical impulses, including *Called to Transformation: Ecumenical Diakonia*, **Craig L. Nessan** contends that it is time to establish diaconal studies in North America as an academic discipline and ecumenical field of research beyond denominational training programmes. This chapter proposes a path toward revitalizing the church through *diakonia*. First, *diakonia* as a guiding theological paradigm turns the church inside out in responding to the needs of the world. The diaconal paradigm has emerged prominently in ecumenical research over recent decades. Second, *diakonia* provides impetus for a transformed theology of ministry that places the diaconate of all believers at the forefront of the church's mission. *Diakonia* by the baptized in daily life orients the ministry of deacons, pastors, and bishops in relation to this universal diaconate. The recovery of *diakonia* as a central paradigm makes

---

[6] "Master of Religion and Public Leadership (MARPL)," Boston University School of Theology, https://www.bu.edu/sth/academics/degree-programs/master-of-arts-in-religion-and-public-leadership-marpl/.

the vocations of deacons and deaconesses, often marginalized by existing church structures, central to a transformed theology of ministry. Third, scholarship on the revitalization of the church in North America can be advanced by the establishment of diaconal studies as a distinctive field of research within the academy, following the pattern in other global contexts and as demonstrated by the chapters of this book.

Sandra Boyce offers a global perspective in demonstrating how diaconal ministry needs to be seen with fresh eyes. Throughout history, diaconal mission and ministry has responded to particular contexts. What form should diaconal ministry take in a post-Christendom, post-pandemic, technological world that is always on the edge of or engaging in conflict and war? What forms of diaconal ministry are needed to respond to this context? Far from being a secondary, subservient ministry – described as a lowly, humble ministry – *diakonia* needs to be seen as core to the church's mission and ministry. This chapter looks at expressions of *diakonia* in four different eras – the early church, nineteenth-century Germany, twentieth-century Australia, and our contemporary era – and the ways that context shapes priorities for mission and ministry. Particular forms of *diakonia* emerged in response to historical and social contexts. This responsiveness suggests a fresh theological framework is needed in our time and place.

Mitzi J. Budde explores a convergence in ecumenical understandings of the diaconate. The chapter begins by examining the 2023 *Proposal for Exchangeability of the Diaconate* between The Episcopal Church (TEC) and the Evangelical Lutheran Church in America (ELCA), which adopted an ordained diaconate in 2019. This ecclesiological change in the ELCA's order of ministry has opened new opportunities for diaconal exchangeability under full communion, establishing a solid precedent for other ecumenical relationships, especially the full communion agreement between the ELCA and The United Methodist Church. This chapter describes theological and ecclesiological similarities and differences in the diaconate of these three denominations, imagining how each church's diaconate might be enhanced by mutual recognition and reciprocity. Finally, the author suggests that ecumenical convergence will offer creative new opportunities for diaconal formation and ministry.

Benjamin L. Hartley engages the World Council of Churches document *Called to Transformation: Ecumenical Diakonia* and the exegetical work of John N. Collins to explore multiple meanings of *diakonia*. This chapter responds to this ecumenical document, first, by placing it in the context of similar documents generated by the World Council of Churches in the recent past, and then by offering biblical reflections on *diakonia* that are germane to the aspirations of the document. *Diakonia* is understood both as religiously motivated social service and as a Greek term in the New Testament for ministry as a go-between or emissarial activity. The author warns that this unresolved tension in the understanding and practice of *diakonia* could be a barrier to ecumenical relations if not recognized and explored.

Margaret Ann Crain asks about the mission of the church and the kind of leadership needed to accomplish its purposes. Central to the issue is ordination: what does it mean, and what difference does it make that deacons are ordained? In 1996, The United Methodist Church created an order of ordained deacons parallel to and distinct from the order of elder, whose focus is building up the church. Diaconal leaders help the church to love the world with the compassionate heart of Jesus and to confront the powers of the world. The ordained deacon particularly challenges the church to undertake the mission of transforming the world. Through denominational documents defining the complementary and distinctive order of deacons and illustrations of ministries by United Methodist deacons, this chapter argues for the centrality of the ordained deacon to the church and its participation in the *missio Dei*.

Part 2: Liberating Diaconal Praxis

Ignatius Swart considers how unequal relationships of power and privilege can faithfully be met by a diaconal practice based on the Gospel values of justice and human dignity. Endemic inequalities and consequent divisions between privileged and disadvantaged communities create an unavoidable tension between members of the "Church for the Poor" as those seeking to do good and members of the "Church of the Poor" as the recipients of such goodwill. This chapter considers inclusive, faith-based community revitalization, the notions of "bridging" and "linking" social capital, and the transformational potential of community development through diaconal practice.

Dionata Rodrigues de Oliveira demonstrates how *diakonia* in the Evangelical Church of the Lutheran Confession in Brazil has always been present, based on the traditional tripartite understandings of communion, ministry, and proclamation. *Diakonia* has suffered, however, the profound impact of this land's exploitation since its invasion in 1500 by the Portuguese and Spanish crowns. Assessing the church's history of mistakes and successes in this work, three key concepts stand out. The first is the necessity of a diaconal theological methodology rooted in practical theology and liberation theology. Diaconal methodology seeks to free both oppressor and oppressed from their yoke of captivity, empower the oppressed, and allow the people served to be active and involved participants in the transformation process. Finally, the purpose of *diakonia* is to transform the reality of pain into abundant life, not merely to assist in the maintenance of suffering.

Norma Cook Everist invites exploration of the theology of *diakonia* and an ecclesiology for a diaconal church. This world is broken by war, inequity, violence, and the climate crisis. In Christ's incarnation, ministry, death, and resurrection and by the power of the Spirit, Christians are called to serve in the world as the real presence of Christ. This chapter presents a theology of marginalization and *diakonia*. Jesus was a diaconal minister. *Diakonia* is not just an optional addition but is essential to the life and work of the church. Central to *diakonia* is ministry among the marginalized. Throughout the ages, diaconal ministers and *diakonia* have often been marginalized by the church because the people served were seen to be of less worth. When the baptized are equipped for *diakonia*, ministry is multiplied. Christians work for justice and reconciliation. The chapter concludes with a Diaconal Litany.

Leo Yates Jr. encourages us to recognize how the Spirit of *diakonia* connects individuals and communities with Christ's ministries. The Spirit also inspires deacons, deaconesses, diaconal ministers, and other ministers to reconcile, heal, affirm, seek justice, empower, support, equip, educate, advocate, and provide care and encouragement to LGBTQIA+ persons, among others, who have been outcast and marginalized. These examples of *diakonia* were modelled by Christ the Servant in his ministry and are leadership gifts to the diaconate for leading and supporting the church. When applied, these activities are diaconal pathways of compassion and justice that can support LGBTQIA+ persons who have been deprived of community (*koinonia*); moreover, these diaconal activities can bridge persons to grace and wholeness. In this chapter, readers will glean from stories of affirming churches who have benefited from these diaconal pathways so relationships among LGBTQIA+ persons can be restored in order for the church to fully experience *koinonia*.

Man-Hei Yip argues that de-subjugating the servant image is both urgent and necessary for the reconceptualization of *diakonia* in the age of the new normal post-COVID-19. Problematizing the concept of servanthood, including the sacrificial language deposited in the *diakonia* of Jesus, entails subverting the narrative of Jesus as a submissive and subservient servant in Christian discourse. Such a process of theological imagination disassociates itself from unrealistic speculation and is attentive to the complexity by which communities continue to be haunted by the history of slavery. The task of theological imagination serves as an intervention that, on the one hand, stops us from making totalizing claims about the particularity of the peoples that perpetuate the subjugation of others and, on the other hand, helps reconceptualize *diakonia* in a broader framework that informs appropriate diaconal practices. Creating sites of memory honors and affirms the humanity of the oppressed that sets forth a path toward healing and reconciliation.

Darryl W. Stephens investigates how those of privilege can participate in a liberative praxis. Contemporary ecumenical *diakonia* is focused on liberation and empowerment of the poor, suffering, and oppressed. Most North American diaconal actors are not poor, however, and attempts at solidarity are laden with power differentials. Exploring points of connection between trauma-informed response and diaconal praxis, this chapter presents a model to assist diaconal workers attempting to serve as ambassadors of God's reconciliation in the world. Through an interdisciplinary approach – drawing on trauma studies, theology, and ethics – the practice of bearing witness becomes a tool for ecumenical *diakonia*, together with responsible interfaith encounter (diapraxis) and community building (conviviality). The resulting trauma-informed ethic provides guidance for diaconal workers bearing witness to individual victim-survivors, equipping both parties to participate in social change movements for justice, healing, and reconciliation.

Part 3: Diaconal Leadership and Spirituality

Norma P. Dollaga, a United Methodist deaconess, advocates for the importance of diaconal ministry during times of economic turmoil and tyranny by witnessing how deaconesses in justice ministries in the Philippines demonstrate a spirituality of activism. This chapter celebrates the lives and commitments of four colleagues in diaconal ministries: one who served as a deaconess for twenty-four years and then became ordained to serve in ministry with the poor; another who first served as a deaconess and later in clergy work that was deeply engaged in ministry with migrants; a deaconess coworker engaged in seeking justice for the victims of the war on drugs of former President Duterte; and a deaconess who was martyred for embracing revolutionary spirituality. Their stories, recorded through personal conversations with the author – together with her own story, provide testimony of relevant, risk-taking diaconal response, manifesting the meaning of church in such a time as this.

Valerie Bailey reflects on how the 1970 Deacons' Canon created an opportunity for both confusion and clarity about diaconal theology in The Episcopal Church (US). Existing deaconesses hoped that the new canon would bring clarity to a diaconal theology of ministry, new possibilities for pension benefits, and access to holy orders. Women ordained under the 1970 Deacons' Canon were adamant about the diaconate as a transition order, as exemplified by the irregular ordination of eleven women deacons to the priesthood in 1974. This chapter examines questions of hierarchical power and service, confusions that still linger within The Episcopal Church's understanding of the diaconate. Influential leaders included Frances Zielinski of the Central House for Deaconesses, who wanted to redefine and strengthen deacons as models of servant leadership; James W. Montgomery, ninth Bishop of Chicago, who favored perpetual deacon status for women; and some of the earliest women ordained under the 1970 Deacons' Canon, whose vocational self-understanding and lived experiences shaped their diaconal theology.

Daphne B. Noyes interprets the life of Adeline Blanchard Tyler (1805–1875), the first deaconess of The Episcopal Church (US), as a model for *diakonia*. Spurred by her life circumstances – a combination of pain and privilege – she used her God-given skills to minister to those in need, bringing into their lives hope that springs from faith and love. Tyler's focus on service and justice parallels the call of today's Episcopal deacons, insofar as it encompassed work in schools, military hospitals, a women's refuge, and a children's hospital. She was sustained by close relationships with supporters of her call and by a determination to serve despite challenges of ill health, Civil War disruptions, and gender bias. Tyler's story illuminates an early chapter in the ongoing challenge to keep *diakonia* central to the church's identity. Her determined commitment overcame embedded institutional barriers in her era and serves as inspiration for deacons who face similar challenges today.

Jessica Bickford recognizes the last 100 years as the most rapidly changing era in history. From technology, medical advances, and cultural and social constructs, today's world is very different than that of previous generations. For some, change is exciting and exhilarating. For others, change evokes anxiety when we are asked to try something new or conceptualize a different method.

When change occurs – whether chosen or imposed – it can feel as if we are Alice falling down the rabbit hole to Wonderland. Things may appear similar to the way they did before, but what was up is now down and what made sense no longer does. With the changing make-up of North America society and the decrease in parochial numbers, the church finds itself in its own version of Wonderland, facing an identity crisis. As the church transitions to find its place within our current societal context, opportunities emerge for new forms of leadership and organizational structure that involve the role of the diaconate in implementing innovations to convert a hierarchal approach to a grassroots methodology.

Johannes Eurich views *diakonia* as the helping care of fellow human beings in the spirit of neighborly love. This involves the professional help, support, and accompaniment of people in emergency situations or with special needs, emphasizing the spiritual motivation of the help. In the beginning of modern *diakonia* in the nineteenth century in Germany, Christian faith played a major role. Since then, professional orientations, which often guide diaconal action without reference to spiritual aspects, have taken hold alongside Christian understandings. Christian faith can still play a formative role in the self-image of employees as well as in the diaconal institutions of Germany, but this is also subject to general social developments. Through diaconal faith formation events (faith courses, religious education, retreats, and so on), attempts are being made to awaken and reclaim a greater awareness of the Christian tradition and to open access to the spiritual dimension of helping.

Part 4: Diaconal Studies and Formation

Annette Leis-Peters describes the development of an interdisciplinary PhD programme in *diakonia*, "Diaconia, Values and Professional Practice," at VID Specialized University in Norway. This programme serves as a platform for communication and collaboration with scholars from other disciplines, enriching practitioners, scholars, and the field of diaconal studies. This chapter: 1) describes the Nordic context for *diakonia* and diaconal studies, 2) looks at the history of the origin of the PhD programme, 3) enquires about decisive preconditions for the emergence of the PhD programme, and 4) gives a short overview of the content and the PhD project of the programme. The chapter concludes by discussing future opportunities and challenges of interdisciplinary PhD programmes related to diaconal studies.

Kristin Husby Dyrstad provides a Scandinavian historical perspective on diaconal studies by investigating curricular changes in Norwegian *diakonia* education in the 1970s and 1980s. The author looks at the case of Diakonhjemmet, the Deacon's Home, in a transition period marked by significant developments within the welfare professions, the higher education system, and the Church of Norway. Exploring archival sources, the author finds that the educational institution terminated traditional formative elements without replacing them with new ones. This Norwegian case study shows that it is important to emphasize programme coherence and to balance intellectual, practical, and formative aims when new deacons are trained and programmes of diaconal studies are developed.

Lori Mills-Curran highlights how The Episcopal Church's denominational practices concerning the (ordained) diaconal order do not fully support the effective realization of the people's *diakonia*. Of most concern are theological assumptions about diaconal identity that undergird diaconal practice: specifically, that this order needs little organized support for its work; that the provision of supports can be left to each diocese; that deacons may be expected to fund their ministry supports from personal wealth; that diaconal support needs are quite similar to those of priests; and that certain social resources on which deacons have relied in the past will remain available to the next generation of deacons. Also of grave concern is a shadow legacy of unexamined racist and sexist influences on diaconal identity, which may extend invisibly to diaconal practice today. This chapter invites The Episcopal Church to consider how these factors influence Episcopal diaconal identity itself and how they continue to be interpreted in ways that subject deacons to unique vocational stresses, attenuate their effectiveness, discourage vocations, and ultimately impede *diakonia*.

Julie Anne Lytle offers a case study of diaconal formation. This chapter describes the contexts influencing theological education and diaconal formation in The Episcopal Church and introduces an innovative competency-based, mentor-assessed model that prepares deacons for the whole church. Four currents within theological education influenced the development of the Deacons Formation Collaborative at Bexley Seabury Seminary: the expansion of competency-based education theological education, the introduction of competencies for ministry and discipleship, shifting diocesan financial and human resources, and the seminary's embrace of a wider understanding of theological education for laity, deacons, priests, and bishops. The goal is to provide a cost-effective, student-directed, time-flexible model that enables students to prepare in their contexts for their contexts. It also encourages a common diaconal theology, consistent formation requirements across The Episcopal Church, and collaboration which responds to the needs of dioceses with few postulants and/or limited resources.

Mary Elizabeth Moore summons us to recognize that the heart of the diaconate is liberative service, a calling for all Christians and a calling for deacons to inspire, lead, and support their service of all. This chapter explores a theology of liberative service, marked by compassion, justice, and peace. These features are not general and vague but far-reaching and particular. To be compassionate is to extend loving attention and care to every being in God's creation through the practice of eco-diakonia. To be just is to ensure thriving for people living in poverty or slavery and those facing mental illness, racial discrimination, and the vulnerabilities of political violence and ecological destruction, as well as to ensure thriving for oceans, forests, and wildlife. To sow peace is to cultivate communities of reconciliation, reparation, and restoration. Through theological analysis and vocational narratives, the chapter offers imaginative theology and missional direction for diaconal ministries, proposing educational approaches for diaconal studies.

Gratitude

This book is intended for church leaders (lay and clergy), seminarians, graduate students of religion and theology, reflective practitioners desiring to integrate their faith into practice, and leaders in all helping professions seeking a deeper understanding of religion and public life.

We would like to thank our steadfast colleagues Man-Hei Yip and Lori Mills-Curran who, with the editors, formed a leadership team that first met in April 2021 and continued to work together steadily to lay groundwork for this three-year collaboration. Together, we invited diverse contributors to join this book project and participate in three virtual conferences. The level of integration in the chapters of this book is a fruit of our engagement with one another throughout the project and the passion of each contributor dedicated to this project. We are also grateful for the many institutions and church bodies represented by the editors and authors of the book. This project is supported by grants from the E. Rhodes and Leona B. Carpenter Foundation and the Oxford Centre for Mission Studies. Administration of the grant funds were handled by Wartburg Theological Seminary.

Craig L. Nessan and Darryl W. Stephens, co-editors
August 2024

Works Cited

Boston University School of Theology. "Master of Religion and Public Leadership (MARPL)." https://www.bu.edu/sth/academics/degree-programs/master-of-arts-in-religion-and-public-leadership-marpl/.

Candler School of Theology. "Master of Religion and Public Life." https://candler.emory.edu/academic-programs/master-of-religion-and-public-life/.

Collins, John N. *Diakonia Studies: Critical Issues in Ministry*. Oxford: Oxford University Press, 2014.

Harvard Divinity School. "Master of Religion and Public Life (MRPL) Program." https://hds.harvard.edu/academics/degree-programs/mrpl-program.

Moore, Mary Elizabeth. *Ministering with the Earth*. St. Louis: Chalice, 1998.

World Council of Churches and ACT Alliance. *Called to Transformation: Ecumenical Diakonia*. Geneva: WCC, 2022. https://www.oikoumene.org/resources/publications/ecumenical-diakonia.

PART 1

Diakonia for the Life of the World

Chapter 1

Establishing Diaconal Studies in North America

Craig L. Nessan

Although the diaconate was established in the New Testament (Acts 6:1–7), *diakonia* as a theological movement and mission focus of the church has had an uneven development in church history.[1] The renewal of the diaconate in the modern period began in nineteenth-century Germany through the initiatives of Johann Hinrich Wichern (1808–1881), Theodor (1800–1864) and Friederike Fliedner (1800–1842), Wilhelm Loehe (1808–1872), and Friedrich Christian Carl von Bodelschwingh (1831–1910).[2] In North America, however, the development of the diaconate has largely been conditioned by the polity of respective denominations, with a plethora of literature supporting denominational training programmes for deacons and deaconesses. In the Lutheran churches, for example, the transfer from Germany and Scandinavia to the United States of the diaconate as the primary agent of social services never took root, despite the best efforts of William Passavant (1821–1894) and the deaconess initiatives he (and others) organized.[3] *Diakonia* in North America became located primarily within the varied orders of ministry in denominations, often in an office of deaconess or deacon, rather than a central theological and missional commitment by the ecumenical church.

This chapter aligns scholarship in North America with the renewal of *diakonia* as a central theological and missional theme that is also unfolding in many other global contexts. First, *diakonia* is reemerging as an organizing theme for the life of the church. How can the churches in North America be revitalized by making *diakonia* central to their calling in service to the world? Second, diaconal ministry is situated within a theology of ministry highlighting their role to accompany the baptized as the primary agents of God's mission as the "diaconate of all believers."[4] How can the ministry of deacons and deaconesses respond to the world's suffering by empowering this "diaconate of all believers" to serve neighbors in their roles and relationships in daily life? Third, the emerging

---

[1] For an overview, see Teresa J. White, "Diakonia," in *Dictionary of the Ecumenical Movement*, ed. Nicholas Lossky et al. (Grand Rapids, MI: Eerdmans, 1991), 275–80.
[2] For a summary of this history, see Craig L. Nessan, "The Transfer of Diakonia from Germany to North America: The Diaconate and Lutheran Social Services in the United States," in *Diaconia in Contexts: Regional Case Studies and Linking Perspectives*, ed. Johannes Eurich, Beate Hofmann, and Thorsten Moos (Oxford: Regnum Books International, 2024).
[3] Nessan, "The Transfer of Diakonia."
[4] Craig L. Nessan, "The Diaconate of All Believers: Theology, Formation, Practice," *Religions* 14, no. 6 (2023): 1–13, https://doi.org/10.3390/rel14060741.

paradigm shift in the church's commitment to *diakonia* and the orientation of theology toward *diakonia* require disciplined reflection and scholarship to place this effort on a solid foundation. How can the development of the field of diaconal studies in North America contribute to this shift?

Diakonia as an Ecumenical Paradigm for Christian Mission at the End of Christendom

The establishment of Christianity as the *de facto* religion of Western countries in Europe and North America disintegrated over the course of the twentieth century.[5] In the wake of two world wars, the Holocaust, controversy over social justice movements, and increasing religious pluralism, the religious hegemony of the church's influence over society inexorably has crumbled.[6] As one response to this development, the emerging church and missional church movements attempted to provoke the churches to transformation.[7] The development of *diakonia* as a central theme of the ecumenical movement from the middle of the twentieth century to the present promises an even more radical paradigm shift.

The retrieval of *diakonia* by the ecumenical church is one of the most significant developments in contemporary theology.[8] In the 1960s, the World Council of Churches (WCC) turned attention both to the role of the deacon/deaconess in the life of the churches and to their relation to *diakonia*: "Church cannot be truly the Church of Jesus Christ without giving itself to such *diakonia*."[9] This view was developed through a series of WCC consultations in the subsequent decades. The theology of ministry presented for ecumenical deliberation in *Baptism, Eucharist, and Ministry* affirms this view of the diaconate: "Deacons represent to the church its calling as servant in the world. By struggling in Christ's name with the myriad needs of societies and persons, deacons exemplify the interdependence of worship and service in the Church's

---

[5] As one example, see the analysis of Douglas John Hall, *The End of Christendom and the Future of the Church* (Eugene, OR: Wipf & Stock, 2002). This text is a companion volume to his three volumes on "Christian Theology in a North American Context." Douglas John Hall, *Thinking the Faith: Christian Theology in a North American Context* (Minneapolis: Fortress, 1991); *Professing the Faith: Christian Theology in a North American Context* (Minneapolis: Fortress, 1996); and *Confessing the Faith: Christian Theology in a North American Context* (Minneapolis: Fortress, 1998).

[6] Pew Research Center, "In US, Decline of Christianity Continues at Rapid Pace," 17 October 2019, https://www.pewresearch.org/religion/2019/10/17/in-u-s-decline-of-christianity-continues-at-rapid-pace/.

[7] As one example of an extensive literature, see Darrell L. Guder, ed., *Missional Church: A Vision for the Sending of the Church in North America* (Grand Rapids, MI: Eerdmans, 1998). See also Nathan C.P. Frambach, ed., "Whither Now Emergence," *Currents in Theology and Mission* 42, no. 2 (April 2015): 91–143, https://www.currentsjournal.org/index.php/currents/issue/view/7/3.

[8] An early and significant instance is Jürgen Moltmann, *Diakonie im Horizont des Reiches Gottes* (Neukirchen-Vluyn: Neukirchener, 1984).

[9] World Council of Churches and ACT Alliance, *Called to Transformation: Ecumenical Diakonia* (Geneva: WCC, 2022), 20.

life."[10] The consultation "Contemporary Understandings of *Diakonia*" at Geneva in 1982, one of a series of WCC meetings on this theme, led to the affirmation of *diakonia* at the WCC Vancouver Assembly in 1983 "as the church's ministry of sharing, healing, and reconciliation."[11] Subsequent to this assembly, regional gatherings and publications contributed to the reception of *diakonia* across the global church.

The Lutheran World Federation (LWF) also carried on deliberations on *diakonia*, leading to the publication of *Diakonia in Context: Transformation, Reconciliation, Empowerment* in 2009.[12] *Diakonia* is an "integral part of being Church" and belongs integrally to the mission of the Triune God in the world, expressed through the work of individuals ("the diaconate of all believers"), congregations, dedicated institutions, and international cooperation.[13] "Prophetic *diakonia*" affirms "that the prophetic task belongs to the mandate and authority that God has given to the Church and its *diakonia*."[14] *Diakonia* has its own distinctive methodology, leading to a "diapraxis" by "diaconal actors" in specific contexts who respond to local challenges.[15] Central themes related to *diakonia* in the work of the WCC and LWF include transformation, reconciliation, and empowerment. These have become formative for the development of "ecumenical *diakonia*," the cutting edge of which seeks to transform society through intersectional analysis and postcolonial critique.[16]

Diakonia is constitutive of the very nature of the church and not merely what the church does. "The concept of *diakonia* thus holds together what the church *is* and what the church *does*, and must be reflected as such."[17] Diaconal action must not be separated from what the church proclaims as its core message. Theological research on *diakonia* focuses on its value for an ecumenical ecclesiology.[18] The WCC at its 10th General Assembly in 2013 embraced the theme that the church is on a "pilgrimage of justice and peace," in which *diakonia* plays a leading part.[19] In 2022, the WCC and ACT Alliance highlighted

---

[10] World Council of Churches, *Baptism, Eucharist and Ministry*, Faith and Order Paper No. 111 (Geneva: WCC, 1982), Ministry § 31.
[11] WCC and ACT Alliance, *Called to Transformation*, 20.
[12] Kjell Nordstokke, ed., *Diakonia in Context: Transformation, Reconciliation, Empowerment: An LWF Contribution to the Understanding and Practice of Diakonia* (Geneva: LWF, 2009).
[13] Nordstokke, 47–58.
[14] Nordstokke, 82.
[15] Nordstokke, 87–90.
[16] WCC, "Diakonia and Ecumenical Solidarity: Understanding of *Diakonia*," https://www.oikoumene.org/what-we-do/diakonia-and-ecumenical-solidarity#understanding-of-diakonia.
[17] Kjell Nordstokke, "Trinitarian Perspectives on Diakonia," in *Evangelism and Diakonia in Context*, ed. Rose Dowsett et al. (Oxford: Regnum Books International, 2015), 145.
[18] Stephanie Dietrich, "Ecclesiology on the Move: Rethinking the Church in Diaconal Perspective," in *The Diaconal Church*, ed. Stephanie Dietrich et al. (Oxford: Regnum Books International, 2019), 18.
[19] Dietrich, 19–21.

three components of ecumenical *diakonia*: 1) "it is action, or performing services, by using words and deeds," 2) "Christian faith motivates this action and views it as an expression of Christian discipleship," and 3) "diaconal intervention reflects social reality and seeks in its performance to alleviate human suffering and promote justice, peace, and human dignity."[20] Each element points to an intentional, embodied, outwardly facing engagement in mission, emphasizing the church as a verb active to transform society.

A comprehensive concept of *diakonia* encompasses five dimensions: care, transformation, empowerment, advocacy, and conviviality.[21] Care involves an orientation to life that issues forth in words and actions of concern for others that affirms their wellbeing. Transformation analyses the causes of suffering and strategizes how these conditions can be changed. Empowerment involves subsidiarity, letting those who are afflicted claim their own dignity, raise their own voices, and exercise their own power. Advocacy involves building coalitions, holding those in authority accountable, and focuses collective action on changing the circumstances and structures under which others are suffering. Conviviality involves building life-giving relationships with others, especially with those different from us, through hospitality, mutuality, and cooperation. "Diaconia is a being-in-the-world, an awareness of what is going on from a personal, interpersonal, communal, and structural perspective. Diaconia is a transforming presence that encompasses the transformation of individuals and communities."[22] This substantial body of research on *diakonia* from the global ecumenical communion and which is informed by diaconal practices in global contexts needs to become the foundation for diaconal studies as a discipline in North America.

The Diaconate in a Theology of the Ministry

The diaconate has had varied and uneven development in North American denominations. There are underlying dynamics of hierarchy, clericalism, and congregation-centered reductionism that affect the standing of diaconal roles in the church. Uncertainty about the vocation of deacons and deaconesses in the life of the church has been unsettling for those called to these offices. The place of deacons and deaconesses within each denomination often has not been clearly defined in terms of polity and standing. Adding to the complexity, judicatory leaders within any given denomination often interpret the standards differently than other judicatory officials in the same church body. Furthermore, when the leaders in those judicatories change positions, so do the binding interpretations of the diaconate.

Diaconal vocations are further complicated by clericalism. Over the centuries, most churches have become defined both in polity and practice by the ministry

---

[20] WCC and ACT Alliance, *Called to Transformation*, 16.
[21] Wanda Diefelt and Beate Hofmann, "Towards a Comprehensive Concept of Diaconia," in *International Handbook on Ecumenical Diakonia*, ed. Ampony et al. (Oxford: Regnum Books International, 2021), 53–61.
[22] Diefelt and Hofmann, "Towards a Comprehensive Concept of Diaconia," 60.

exercised by pastors and priests, giving them power to define the nature of church's mission according to their own exercise of pastoral ministry.[23] The center of power in the organization of the church by definition and precedent is largely located in the office of presbyter (pastors and priests). The weight of history and the homeostasis of existing power relations inhibit momentum for change that would make greater room for the vocations of the baptized, deacons, and other expressions of the diaconate.

At the end of Christendom, the church needs a new theology of ministry to shape ecclesiology. This theology of ministry must focus on both *diakonia* and the mutuality of the gifts of all its ministers. As early as the 1950s, ecumenical and theological literature began to connect the universal priesthood of all believers to the work of *diakonia*. "All the members are baptized, so to speak, into or stamped with this 'diaconal' seal and should acknowledge it with heart and mind."[24] The "diakonia of all believers" originates in baptism, where the baptized person is joined to the death and resurrection of Jesus Christ and bestowed with spiritual gifts.[25]

While the weight of tradition favors a hierarchical understanding of ministry, with bishops at the apex and with pastors and priests at the next level of authority,[26] a new paradigm for ministry places the ministry of the baptized at the forefront with the ministry of the diaconate alongside to equip and accompany their diaconal service to the world. *Diakonia in Context* affirms that these gifts are the grounding for *"the priesthood of all believers,"* which "can also be reformulated as the *diakonia of all believers* to which all baptized are called and equipped, regardless of their apparent status or social condition."[27] The diaconate of all believers is a form of "individual diakonia, which normally is spontaneous in everyday life and expressed through a wide variety of good works."[28] *Diakonia* belongs to all the baptized as "a dimension integral to the nature and mission of the church."[29] *Called to Transformation* gives new attention to

> "the diaconate of all believers," based on the view that God's Spirit graciously empowers and equips for discipleship, from the youngest to the oldest, men and women (Acts 2:17). From this follows that the diaconal vocation in the first place relates to everyday life: the family that cares for its members and in particular children and the elderly, the neighborhood and the workplace, civil society, and other arenas for social action. Diaconal activities organized by local congregations

---

[23] This was not overcome in the churches shaped by the Reformation but rather was perpetuated in new forms. See Hendrik Kraemer, *A Theology of the Laity* (Philadelphia: Westminster, 1958), 62–69.
[24] Kraemer, 153.
[25] The term "diakonia of all believers" is referenced by White, "Diakonia," 275.
[26] Kraemer, *A Theology of the Laity*, 53–55.
[27] Nordstokke, *Diakonia in Context*, 27, original emphasis.
[28] Nordstokke, 47.
[29] WCC and ACT Alliance, *Called to Transformation*, 10.

and other church structures, including professional diaconal agents, depend on and are largely borne by the diaconate of all believers.[30]

Unfortunately, these themes have remained underdeveloped beyond formal acknowledgement.

In North America a deep rift exists between what happens in the name of the institutional church and the rest of people's lives.[31] The homeostasis that strangles the vitality of the institutional church – "churchification"[32] – remains a formidable challenge to reconstituting the church's mission through the service of the baptized diaconate.

In a Trinitarian understanding of *diakonia*, God in Christ by the power of the Holy Spirit is the primary actor sending the church for the life of the world.[33] With primacy of place, this sending belongs to all the baptized. Not since the first three Christian centuries has ecclesiology been focused primarily on the calling and equipping of the baptized for the *diakonia* of daily life. The diaconate of all believers belongs at the forefront of God's mission for the life of the world.

All other church offices only have clarity about their calling and purpose in relation to maximizing the effectiveness of the ministry of the baptized. This was the character of the early church and provides the plumbline for the revitalization of the church today.[34] With this definitive orientation to the ministry of the baptized, the three offices – deacon and deaconess, pastor and priest, and bishop – each discover their proper direction.

The primacy of the diaconate of all believers gives renewed logic to the ministry of deacons, deaconesses, and other set-apart diaconal roles. Deacons and deaconesses accompany and equip the baptized in fulfilling their vocation through all their roles and relationships in daily life. Deacons and deaconesses exercise this ministry in a twofold way. First, according to their charismata and responsibilities, deacons and deaconesses model the movement of the entire church from liturgy to *diakonia*. By call and training, they have distinctive specializations that are exercised through diaconal service to others and for creation. Here the diaconal office exercises the exemplary function of embodying the fundamental ecclesial movement of the church to the world

---

[30] WCC and ACT Alliance, 16–17.

[31] See the Life of Faith Initiative, www.lifeoffaith.info, which has as its purpose: "to stir up a culture change that frees us to make the service by the baptized in the arenas of daily life the central focus of the church's mission." The churches of the North have much to learn from the churches of the South and East about validating and equipping all the baptized for their vocations in daily life. Philip Jenkins, *The New Faces of Christianity: Believing the Bible in the Global South* (New York: Oxford University Press, 2006).

[32] Use of this term occurs, for example, in Kraemer, *A Theology of the Laity*, 176, and Konrad Raiser, "Laity in the Ecumenical Movement: Redefining the Profile," *The Ecumenical Review* 45 (1993): 376.

[33] Catherine Mowry LaCugna, *God for Us: The Trinity and the Christian Life* (New York: HarperCollins, 1992).

[34] See Rodney Stark, *The Rise of Christianity: How the Obscure, Marginal Jesus Movement Became the Dominant Religious Force in the Western World in a Few Centuries* (San Francisco: HarperSanFrancisco, 1997).

through *diakonia*. Second, it is the responsibility of deacons and deaconesses always to intentionally accompany the baptized in exercising the universal diaconate in daily life. This gives deacons and deaconesses a vital role in equipping all the baptized for *diakonia*. The universal diaconate of all believers is inseparable from the ministry of deacons and deaconesses.

The vocation of pastors and priests can also be revitalized in relation to the ministry of all the baptized. This theology of ministry deconstructs the passive dependency of the baptized upon pastors and priests by making the ministry of Word and Sacrament a service for the liberation of the baptized for their callings in daily life. Pastors and priests preach, teach, preside at worship, and exercise pastoral care that through the Gospel of Jesus Christ the baptized are set *free from* all that holds them captive and *free for* serving all the neighbors God gives them in the arenas of daily life. This paradigm does not threaten the value of the pastoral ministry of Word and Sacrament. Rather, it provides a theological framework according to which pastors can serve in life-giving partnership with all members of the body of Christ. Moreover, it reminds pastors of their own roles and responsibilities as baptized persons that they are called to serve in daily life beyond their pastoral service.[35]

Finally, the office of bishop discovers new vitality as an office of support to deacons and deaconesses and to pastors and priests in their ministries of accompanying, equipping, and liberating the baptized for their diaconate. Within this theology of ministry, bishops have a distinctive calling to minister to the whole: "to equip the saints for the work of ministry [*diakonia*], for building up the body of Christ" (Eph 4:12, NRSV). In order that the church "promotes the body's growth in building itself up in love" (Eph 4:16, NRSV), bishops exercise authority as servants of the one, holy, catholic, apostolic church. In relation to the *unity* of the church, the bishop promotes ecumenical relationships and addresses conflicts that undermine the church's unified witness. In relation to the *holiness* of the church, the bishop upholds the centrality of the Gospel of Jesus Christ and high ethical standards for all ministers, including the baptized and specifically for those in professional ministry.[36] In relation to *catholicity*, the bishop tends global relationships and the responsibility of the church for creation care. In relation to *apostolicity*, the bishop cares for the faithfulness of the church's teaching and fulfilling its apostolic mission. In every aspect, this episcopal office of oversight gives attention to the effectiveness of the ministry of the baptized in service to the world.

Establishing Diaconal Studies in North America

Diaconal studies can contribute to revitalizing the church in North America by addressing the contemporary crisis facing the church after the erosion of

---

[35] Craig L. Nessan, "Universal Priesthood of All Believers: Unfulfilled Promise of the Reformation," *Currents in Theology and Mission* 46, no. 1 (January 2019): 12, https://currentsjournal.org/index.php/currents/issue/view/55.

[36] Arden F. Mahlberg and Craig L. Nessan, *The Integrity of the Body of Christ: Boundary Keeping as Shared Responsibility* (Eugene, OR: Cascade, 2016).

Christendom. The earlier cultural supports for Christianity no longer function, and churches are searching for new ways forward. Beyond the obvious declines in church membership and financial support, intersectional challenges raised by society demand the church's attention: institutional racism, xenophobia and exclusion politics, endemic poverty and the wealth gap, growing effects of climate change, challenges of interfaith engagement, and traumas exposed by and resulting from the global pandemic. The diaconal commitment to the interface between church and society can turn the church inside out to address these and other challenges.

Beyond North America, *diakonia* has become an identifiable field of academic study. There exists a burgeoning body of scholarly work, published in English and German languages, that grounds diaconal studies ecumenically and globally as an academic discipline. The growth and expansion of this literature has been hastened by the ecumenical publications already cited, especially the WCC study *Called to Transformation* and the LWF document *Diakonia in Context: Transformation, Reconciliation, Empowerment* that have generated international engagement with *diakonia*. Through these ecumenical processes of the last two decades, a substantial body of published scholarly research has emerged in the English language to provide a platform for diaconal studies in North America.

Two compendiums have been published as handbooks. The *International Handbook on Ecumenical Diakonia* captures the current state of diaconal studies research globally.[37] This volume serves as a reference work for scholars and a text for students of *diakonia*. The entries are organized into four major parts: 1) Theologies of Diakonia in Different Ecclesial and Social Contexts; 2) Concepts and Profiles of Diaconal Ministries in Different World Regions; 3) Trends and Crucial Concerns in Diakonia; and 4) Models and Methods for Competency Building in Diakonia. A second handbook, *International Handbook on Creation Care and Eco-Diakonia: Concepts and Theological Perspectives of Churches from the Global South*, provides a comprehensive account of theological work, advocacy concerns, practical engagement, and educational efforts from churches in the Global South.[38] The book is organized into four sections: 1) Biblical and Theological Foundations for Creation Care and Eco-Diakonia; 2) Concepts and Profiles of Creation Care and Eco-Diakonia in Different Regions and Denominational Traditions; 3) Trends, Key Issues, and Best Practice Models for Creation Care and Eco-Diakonia; and 4) Models and Methods for Training and Competency Building in Creation Care and Eco-Diakonia. Each of the sections is subdivided according to three regions: Africa and the Middle East; Asia and Pacific; and Latin America and the Caribbean. This handbook documents the proliferation of diaconal studies across the Global South.

---

[37] Godwin Ampony et al., eds., *International Handbook on Ecumenical Diakonia* (Oxford: Regnum Books International, 2021).
[38] Daniel Beros et al., eds., *International Handbook on Creation Care and Eco-Diakonia: Concepts and Theological Perspectives of Churches from the Global South* (Oxford: Regnum Books International, 2022).

Regnum Books International has been involved in publishing not only these reference works but also a series of books that build a knowledge base and advance the academic discussion of *diakonia*. The following books on discrete topics have been organized by the respective volume editors to generate an ecumenical and global exchange among diverse authors and readers. *Diakonia as Christian Social Practice: An Introduction* (2014) discusses a paradigm shift away from viewing *diakonia* as primarily related to professional activities by diaconal actors and institutions toward recognizing its ecclesial character and inherent contribution to the mission of the church.[39] *Diakonia* as a holistic undertaking authorizes prophetic diaconal action, not merely humble service. *Diakonia in a Gender Perspective* (2015) examines the critical role played by gender perspectives for the theory and practice of *diakonia*.[40] The diversity among the authors of this book invigorates interdisciplinary engagement with questions about how gender impacts both diaconal method and diaconal practices, while case studies illumine theoretical constructs. *Evangelism and Diakonia in Context* (2015) provides an expansive discussion of the fruitfulness of viewing evangelism and *diakonia* in reciprocal relationship with each other as dimensions of integral mission.[41] Evangelism involves sharing the faith with others to invite them into discipleship, while *diakonia* is faith in action through loving one's neighbors. International and ecumenical authors discuss the inextricable connection whereby evangelism has consequences for social action and *diakonia* has consequences for evangelistic sharing the faith with others.

The Diaconal Church (2019) explores how centering on *diakonia* transforms the fundamental understanding of the church.[42] *Diakonia*, as a biblical call to service, endures as an essential dimension of the church's identity and not merely a matter of church practice. The argument inheres *diakonia* in the very essence of the church, a paradigm shift that redefines church and revises how being a diaconal church informs integral mission. *Developing Just and Inclusive Communities: Challenges for Diakonia/Christian Social Practice and Social Work* (2022) fosters global dialogue about the theoretical and practical implications of *diakonia* for community development.[43] In particular, the authors reference the United Nations Sustainable Development Goals in presenting case

---

[39] Stephanie Dietrich, Knud Jørgensen, Kari Karsrud Korslein, and Kjell Nordstokke, eds., *Diakonia as Christian Social Practice: An Introduction* (Oxford: Regnum Books International, 2014).
[40] Stephanie Dietrich, Knud Jørgensen, Kari Karsrud Korslien, and Kjell Nordstokke, eds., *Diakonia in a Gender Perspective* (Oxford: Regnum Books International, 2015).
[41] Rose Dowsett, Isabel Phiri, Doug Birdsall, Dawit Olika Terfassa, Hwa Yung, and Knud Jørgensen, eds., *Evangelism and Diakonia in Context* (Oxford: Regnum Books International, 2015).
[42] Stephanie Dietrich, Knud Jørgensen, Kari Karsrud Korslein, and Kjell Nordstokke, eds., *The Diaconal Church* (Oxford: Regnum Books International, 2019).
[43] Hans Morten Haugen, Benedicte Tveter Kivle, Tony Addy, Terese Bue Kessel, and John Klaasen, eds., *Developing Just and Inclusive Communities: Challenges for Diakonia/Christian Social Practice and Social Work* (Oxford: Regnum Books International, 2022).

studies from various global regions that promote just, convivial, and inclusive communities that intend to overcome social exclusion.

Two seminal studies by John N. Collins conclude this literature review. Through his lexical scholarship, Collins has dramatically shifted the terrain for interpreting the meaning of *diakonia* based on its cognates in Ancient Greek literature and the New Testament. His two works *Diakonia: Re-Interpreting the Ancient Sources* (1990) and *Diaconal Studies: Critical Issues in Ministry* (2014) challenge the conventional view that *diakonia* refers to humble service and a servant church.[44] Collins concludes instead that *diakonia* refers to a "go-between," messenger, or emissary role that does not inherently involve works of mercy. According to Collins, the *daikon-* word group describes a range of involvements related to Christian existence and living out responsibilities in Christian communities. The findings of Collins have reset the assumption that *diakonia* involves the work of deacons in their service to those in need. This argument demands more thoughtful usage of *diakonia* in theological discussions related to diaconal studies.

While the practice of *diakonia* has continued to grow in North America, research has not kept pace through lack of attention in academic institutions and scholarly guilds. "Diaconal studies" largely has been limited to denominational training materials, survey texts, and a few specialized works. Based on its emerging significance globally, *diakonia* is uniquely capable of opening the church in North America to new understandings as it confronts challenging ecological and social realities. Located in the complex relationship between church and world, the diaconal vocation attends to the cries and responds to the crises of contemporary society. Vibrant diaconal theology can be a catalyst for church revitalization.

The sections of this book provide evidence of the contribution that diaconal studies can make to church and academy. Part 1 demonstrates how the international and ecumenical focus on diaconal studies warrants it a place both in the North American academy as an emerging field of research and in the North American church to transform its theology of ministry and embolden diaconal engagement with the world (Nessan). These chapters establish the contextual (Boyce), ecumenical (Budde), and ecclesial (Crain) dimensions of *diakonia* for the life of the world. *Diakonia* needs to inform and shape the emerging missional paradigm to guide the future diaconal church. On the way, diaconal studies must engage in careful examination of its own definition and focus (Hartley). These chapters provide arguments for how a diaconal paradigm can transform the shape of theology, the church, and its leadership.

Part 2 explores methodological dimensions of diaconal praxis in dialogue with the church in Brazil (Oliveira) and asks about the limitations of the servant model in favor of a more prophetic stance (Swart and Yip). The value of compassionate diaconal praxis to enhance the church's *koinonia* among the marginalized (Everist) is demonstrated through ministry with and among the

---

[44] John N. Collins, *Diakonia: Re-Interpreting the Ancient Sources* (New York: Oxford University Press, 1990) and John N. Collins, *Diakonia Studies: Critical Issues in Ministry* (New York: Oxford University Press, 2014).

LGBTQIA+ community (Yates). Given its concern for the world's suffering, diaconal praxis must become informed by research from trauma studies (Stephens).

Part 3 begins with a case study on the courageous activism of diaconal agents in the Philippines (Dollaga). Two chapters document the history that informs the status of deaconesses in The Episcopal Church (US) (Bailey) and in particular the witness of Adeline Blanchard Tyler in the nineteenth century (Noyes). The future of *diakonia* requires fresh imagination (Bickford), yet without losing its core spiritual identity (Eurich). Diaconal identity and mission require both adaptive leadership and vibrant spirituality.

This book engages in lively dialogue with diaconal studies in other global contexts. Part 4 learns from the development of diaconal studies in Norway about the possibilities of interdisciplinary PhD study (Leis-Peters) and the place of formation in the educational process (Dyrstad). Diaconal studies can clarify denominational misunderstandings about the diaconal office and contribute to a flourishing diaconate (Mills-Curran). The emergence of diaconal studies requires curricular innovation in the educational process for deacons, and this focus also will enhance the preparation of pastoral leaders (Lytle). Finally, Mary Elizabeth Moore makes the case for diaconal studies by affirming that the heart of the diaconate is liberative service, marked by compassion, justice, and peace. Liberative service involves loving attention to every being in God's creation, advocacy for social justice, and the practice of eco-diakonia. Cumulatively, the chapters in this book form a substantial argument for the development of diaconal studies in North America.

Called to Transformation highlighted the need for diaconal studies:

> Diaconal competence requires attention and training. Church leaders in general would benefit from basic knowledge of the nature and practice of *diakonia*, however, most theological seminaries have not included *diakonia* in their study programmes. Equally, few leaders of diaconal activities have had a chance to study *diakonia* and to build their professional competence from its interdisciplinary way of reflecting on praxis.[45]

Establishing diaconal studies in North America can address this deficit.

Revitalization of the church requires strengthening its diaconal capacity. Accomplishing this mandate necessitates the establishment of diaconal studies within theological education. *Called to Transformation* encourages "theological seminaries ... to include *diakonia* in their curricula and training programmes ... thereby enhancing the capacity building of churches in *diakonia* and strengthening their work in social services."[46] Establishing diaconal studies within North American theological education will enhance connections between doctrine and daily life, service and social critique, solidarity, and transformation. This book provides impetus for the North American realization of these purposes.

---

[45] WCC and ACT Alliance, *Called to Transformation*, 76.
[46] WCC and ACT Alliance, *Called to Transformation*, 113.

Works Cited

Ampony, Godwin, Martin Büscher, Beate Hofmann, Félicité Ngnintedem, Dennis Solon, and Dietrich Werner, eds. *International Handbook on Ecumenical Diakonia: Contextual Theologies and Practices of Diakonia and Christian Social Services – Resources for Study and Intercultural Learning*. Oxford: Regnum Books International, 2021.

Beros, Daniel, Eale Bosela, Lesmore Ezekiel, Kambale Kahongya, Ruomin Liu, Grace Moon, Marisa Strizzi, and Dietrich Werner, eds. *International Handbook on Creation Care and Eco-Diakonia: Concepts and Theological Perspectives of Churches from the Global South*. Oxford: Regnum Books International, 2022.

Collins, John N. *Diakonia: Re-Interpreting the Ancient Sources*. New York: Oxford University Press, 1990.

———*Diakonia Studies: Critical Issues in Ministry*. New York: Oxford University Press, 2014.

Diefelt, Wanda, and Beate Hofmann. "Towards a Comprehensive Concept of Diaconia." In *International Handbook on Ecumenical Diakonia*, edited by Ampony et al., 53–61. Oxford: Regnum Books International, 2021.

Dietrich, Stephanie. "Ecclesiology on the Move: Rethinking the Church in Diaconal Perspective." In *The Diaconal Church*, edited by Stephanie Dietrich, Knud Jørgensen, Kari Karsrud Korslein, and Kjell Nordstokke, 15–26. Oxford: Regnum Books International, 2019.

Dietrich, Stephanie, Knud Jørgensen, Kari Karsrud Korslein, and Kjell Nordstokke, eds. *Diakonia as Christian Social Practice: An Introduction*. Oxford: Regnum Books International, 2014.

———. *Diakonia in a Gender Perspective*. Oxford: Regnum Books International, 2015.

Dowsett, Rose, Isabel Phiri, Doug Birdsall, Dawit Olika Terfassa, Hwa Yung, and Knud Jørgensen, eds. *Evangelism and Diakonia in Context*. Oxford: Regnum Books International, 2015.

Frambach, Nathan C.P., ed. "Whither Now Emergence." *Currents in Theology and Mission* 42 (April 2015): 91–143. https://www.currentsjournal.org/index.php/currents/issue/view/7/3.

Guder, Darrell L., ed. *Missional Church: A Vision for the Sending of the Church in North America*. Grand Rapids, MI: Eerdmans, 1998.

Hall, Douglas John. *Confessing the Faith: Christian Theology in a North American Context*. Minneapolis: Fortress, 1998.

———. *The End of Christendom and the Future of the Church*. Eugene, OR: Wipf & Stock, 2002.

———. *Professing the Faith: Christian Theology in a North American Context*. Minneapolis: Fortress, 1996.

———. *Thinking the Faith: Christian Theology in a North American Context*. Minneapolis: Fortress, 1991.

Haugen, Hans Morten, Benedicte Tveter Kivle, Tony Addy, Terese Bue Kessel, and John Klaasen, eds. *Developing Just and Inclusive Communities: Challenges for Diakonia/Christian Social Practice and Social Work*. Oxford: Regnum Books International, 2022.

Jenkins, Philip. *The New Faces of Christianity: Believing the Bible in the Global South*. New York: Oxford University Press, 2006.

Kraemer, Hendrik. *A Theology of the Laity*. Philadelphia: Westminster, 1958.

LaCugna, Catherine Mowry. *God for Us: The Trinity and the Christian Life*. New York: HarperCollins, 1992.

Life of Faith Initiative. "Life of Faith: Trusting Jesus, Serving Our Neighbors." https://lifeoffaith.info/.

Mahlberg, Arden F., and Craig L. Nessan. *The Integrity of the Body of Christ: Boundary Keeping as Shared Responsibility*. Eugene, OR: Cascade, 2016.

Moltmann, Jürgen. *Diakonie im Horizont des Reiches Gottes*. Neukirchen-Vluyn: Neukirchener, 1984.

Nessan, Craig L. "The Diaconate of All Believers: Theology, Formation, Practice," *Religions* 14, no. 6 (2023): 1–13. https://doi.org/10.3390/rel14060741.

———. "The Transfer of Diakonia from Germany to North America: The Diaconate and Lutheran Social Services in the United States." In *Diaconia in Contexts: Regional Case Studies and Linking Perspectives*, edited by Johannes Eurich, Beate Hofmann, and Thorsten Moos. Oxford: Regnum Books International, 2024.

———. "Universal Priesthood of All Believers: Unfulfilled Promise of the Reformation." *Currents in Theology and Mission* 46 (January 2019): 8–15. https://currentsjournal.org/index.php/currents/article/view/155.

Nordstokke, Kjell, ed. *Diakonia in Context: Transformation, Reconciliation, Empowerment: An LWF Contribution to the Understanding and Practice of Diakonia*. Geneva: Lutheran World Federation, 2009. https://www.lutheranworld.org/sites/default/files/DMD-Diakonia-EN-low.pdf.

———. *Liberating Diakonia*. Trondheim: Tapir Akademisk, 2011.

———. "Trinitarian Perspectives on Diakonia." In *Evangelism and Diakonia in Context*, edited by Rose Dowsett, Isabel Phiri, Doug Birdsall, Dawit Olika Terfassa, Hwa Yung, and Knud Jørgensen, 141–52. Oxford: Regnum Books International, 2015.

Pew Research Center. "In US, Decline of Christianity Continues at Rapid Pace." 17 October 2019. https://www.pewresearch.org/religion/2019/10/17/in-u-s-decline-of-christianity-continues-at-rapid-pace/.

Raiser, Konrad. "Laity in the Ecumenical Movement: Redefining the Profile." *The Ecumenical Review* 45 (1993): 375–83.

Stark, Rodney. *The Rise of Christianity: How the Obscure, Marginal Jesus Movement Became the Dominant Religious Force in the Western World in a Few Centuries*. San Francisco: HarperSanFrancisco, 1997.

White, Teresa J. "Diakonia." In *Dictionary of the Ecumenical Movement*, edited by Nicholas Lossky, José Míguez Bonino, John Pobee, Tom Stransky, Geoffrey Wainwright, and Pauline Webb, 275–80. Grand Rapids: Eerdmans, 1991.

World Council of Churches. *Baptism, Eucharist and Ministry*. Faith and Order Paper No. 111. Geneva: WCC, 1982.
https://www.oikoumene.org/sites/default/files/Document/FO1982_111_en.pdf.

———. "Diakonia and Ecumenical Solidarity: Understanding of *Diakonia*."
https://www.oikoumene.org/what-we-do/diakonia-and-ecumenical-solidarity#understanding-of-diakonia.

World Council of Churches and ACT Alliance. *Called to Transformation: Ecumenical Diakonia*. Geneva: WCC, 2022.
https://www.oikoumene.org/resources/publications/ecumenical-diakonia.

Chapter 2

Emergent *Diakonia* in Response to Changing Contexts

Sandra Boyce

Throughout history, diaconal mission and ministry has responded to particular contexts. The obvious question is: what now, in our time and place? We live in a post-Christendom, post-Enlightenment, post-pandemic, "fake news," technological world always on the edge of or engaging in conflict and war. What forms of diaconal ministry are needed to respond to this context? Diaconal ministry needs to be seen with fresh eyes. Far from being a secondary, subservient ministry – described as a lowly, humble ministry – *diakonia* needs to be seen as essential to the church's mission and ministry.

This chapter looks at expressions of *diakonia* in four different eras – the early church, nineteenth-century Germany, twentieth-century Australia, and our contemporary era – and the way that context shapes priorities for mission and ministry. Particular forms of *diakonia* emerged in response to historical and social contexts. This responsiveness suggests a fresh theological framework is needed for our time and place, as well as new forms of diaconal study and formation.

Mission and Ministry (*diakonia*) in the Early Church

Diakonia was expressed in a variety of ways in the early church, including public witness and advocacy, worship and proclamation, and attention to the welfare of others. The significant research by John N. Collins suggests that the *daikon-* words in the biblical record of the early church were neither primarily focused on concern for the welfare of others nor connected with lowly and menial service (such as those who served at tables). Notably, according to Collins, the words did not express the idea of lowliness or humility. Rather, the *diakon-* words indicated one who was a go-between, one who undertook a responsibility to fulfil a task at the direction of another.[1]

This interpretation makes sense when we reflect on Phoebe's role on behalf of the apostle Paul. Her role as a go-between was to take his letter to the church in Rome, read it to the faithful believers, and help interpret it. Paul held her in high esteem as a sister, a *deacon*, and a benefactor (Rom 16:1–2). Jesus undertook a diaconal responsibility received from the Father: "The Son of Man came not to be *served* but to *serve*, and to give his life as a ransom for many"

---

[1] John N. Collins, *Diakonia: Re-Interpreting the Ancient Sources* (Oxford: Oxford University Press, 1990). See also, chapter by Hartley in this volume.

(Mark 10:45, English Standard Version, emphasis added). The focus of the verse is on the task of the go-between.

The early church functioned as a go-between community, fulfilling the tasks they had received from Jesus and modelled on the example of Jesus. The early church practice of hospitality continued the open, inclusive table fellowship Jesus had modelled. With their table fellowship and sharing of goods, the early church reported: "There were no needy persons among them" (Acts 4:34, Common English Bible). The early church groups met in private homes or homes adapted to include a gathering space. Women had a primary role in food preparation and hospitality in their homes, welcoming followers of Jesus and growing the community of faith. It was a vibrant, engaged expression of *diakonia*. Hospitality was offered with no strings attached, in contrast to the Greco-Roman societal expectations which assumed practices of reciprocity and social compensation. *Diakonia* practices served to concretize the inclusive nature of the early church where there was no longer "Jew nor Gentile, neither slave nor free, nor is there male and female, for you are all one in Christ Jesus" (Gal 3:28, New International Version). Through baptism, the early church found their mutual belonging in Christ, transcending the particularity of cultural and ethnic backgrounds.

Diakonia is appreciated but often undervalued. Over the early centuries, the role of deacon slowly gave way to an ecclesiology that focused on the primacy of the priest and bishop; by the seventh century, the role of deacon no longer existed.[2] What remained was the notion of "humble, lowly service" associated with *diakonia* – a legacy that has continued to this day.

Mission and Ministry in the Nineteenth Century

Diaconal ministry re-emerged during the Industrial Revolution, when large numbers of people moved from rural to urban areas hoping to find work and offer their families a better life. At the turn of the nineteenth century, only 17 percent of Europe's population lived in an urban setting; by the mid-nineteenth century, the percentage had doubled. Consequently, there were social and economic challenges with overcrowding, disease, social conflict, malnutrition, insecure housing, and poverty. Living conditions were often miserable for the lower social classes. Many low-wage workers had to give up their own actual trade to work long hours for people from the upper class. Factory owners reduced wages because there were so many people who had come to the cities to find work. Women were considered valuable employees because their wages were so much lower than those of the men.

This was the context for the renewal of diaconal ministry in Germany. Theodor Fliedner (1800–1864), a Lutheran pastor, saw the social and economic impact of industrialization on the urban poor. Appointed to pastor a congregation in Kaiserswerth in 1822, he became engaged in social work in the community, including prison ministry. In 1826 he established the German Prison Association.

---

[2] James Monroe Barnett, *The Diaconate: A Full and Equal Order* (New York: Seabury, 1981), 105–22.

He also recognized education as the key to transformation and therefore established the Kaiserswerther Diakonie school system for poor and disadvantaged children.

In 1836 Fliedner, together with his wife, Friederike Münster (and later his second wife Caroline Bertheau), responded to the desperate need to care for the sick by establishing a hospital and training center. Nursing at the time was considered menial work with no social standing. However, religious communities saw nursing as charitable work and were motivated to care for the sick by the example of Jesus. Fliedner recruited trustworthy women workers who could be trained to provide appropriate nursing care. He drew on what he understood of the early church's model of *diakonia* as well as what he had observed from the Mennonite and the Moravian deaconess order (revived in 1745). He adapted the Roman Catholic model of nuns to establish a modern Protestant movement, establishing the Kaiserswerth Mother House and the Order of Lutheran Deaconesses. The role of deaconess provided a vocation for unmarried young women and a safe environment to live. Over three years, the women were instructed in theology, ethics, and pharmacy to prepare them for teaching or practical nursing. Deaconesses did not receive payment but instead were provided with food and lodging.

A new word in German, *Diakonie*, was coined in the late nineteenth century to express this kind of Christian social work. Other significant people, including Amalie Sieveking and Johann Wichern, were instrumental in renewing the diaconate in Germany at this time. Each of these reformers linked diaconal ministry with Christian social welfare among the poor and disadvantaged. Fliedner opened Deaconess Mother Houses and training centers all over the world. At the time of his death, it is reported that there were thirty Mother Houses and 1600 deaconesses worldwide. By the mid-twentieth century, 35,000 deaconesses were serving in parishes and institutions worldwide. The legacy of "lowly, humble service" continued in the *Diakonie* associated with the Mother House tradition and nursing.

Mission and Ministry in the Church in Australia

The renewal of the diaconate in Australia in the early twentieth century was primarily through the Methodist Church and through the Presbyterian Church of Australia, where women were allowed to engage in ministry through deaconess training at the Deaconess Training Institute. On completion of their formation, they were "set apart ... in a special way for Christian service as the chief object of their life."[3] Those who completed the training were able to continue their calling both within the gathered church and beyond. Diaconal ministry was still seen as a lower form of ministry, sometimes as a support to ministers in a congregational setting. Even so, because deaconesses were trained in theology

---

[3] Alannah Croom, "Presbyterian Deaconess Order in Victoria," *The Australian Women's Register*, 26 August 2009, modified 20 November 2018, https://www.womenaustralia.info/entries/presbyterian-deaconess-order-in-victoria/.

as well as nursing, they could conduct services where there was no congregational minister available. Deaconesses also served as missionaries in the Pacific, Asia, and India. Sometimes they took on placements in remote areas of the Australian outback, a context in which a wave of "second peoples" to Australia grew in the nineteenth century, provoking a great deal of exploration in the harsh inland of the continent.

In 1936, the Presbyterian Deaconess Training Institute was renamed Rolland House Deaconess and Missionary Training College, named in honor of William Stothert Rolland, who helped found the original Deaconess Training Institute. His son, Francis William Rolland, served as agent of the Smith of Dunesk Mission from 1905 to 1908. His role was

> to oversee, alone, an enormous area of country notorious for extreme heat and aridity and the roughest of male subcultures. He drove by horse and buggy where tracks were few and confused, and facilities non-existent, to carry his ministry to mining and railway construction camps, shearing sheds and bore-sinking parties, "where depravity and alcoholic excess were rampant."[4]

His letters at this time contained heart-rending accounts of the suffering of women and children in the outback. The absolute absence of medical care and the grim fatalism of life in the outback led to deep despair at his inability to improve people's lives. He continued to work tirelessly for improvement in the conditions of life for people in the outback and paved the way for the later development of the Royal Flying Doctor Service.[5]

The formation of deaconesses at Rolland House became interwoven with the work of the Mission to outback Australia. In September 1912, the younger Rolland, together with John Flynn, led the public launching in Melbourne of the Australian Inland Mission. Deaconesses were important leaders in the establishment of Flynn's Australian Inland Mission. They were trained in nursing to work in hospitals and with people living in the Australian outback. Some of the first nurses ever seen in the Australian outback were deaconesses, who understood that their ministry was to the body as well as to the soul. In 1980 the Australian Inland Mission became Frontier Services, an agency of the Uniting Church in Australia.

The Case of Betty Matthews[6]

After completing her formation in the Presbyterian Church for the ministry of deaconess in 1954, Betty Matthews was "set apart" and assigned to ministry to

---

[4] B.R. Keith, "Sir Francis William (Frank) Rolland (1878–1965)," *Australian Dictionary of Biography*, National Centre of Biography, Australian National University, published first in hardcopy 1988, https://adb.anu.edu.au/biography/rolland-sir-francis-william-frank-8261.

[5] "Outback Pioneer: Sir Francis Rolland and the Inland Nursing Service," Heritage Guide to the Geelong College, https://gnet.tgc.vic.edu.au/wiki/OUTBACK-PIONEER-Sir-FRANCIS-ROLLAND-and-the-INLAND-NURSING-SERVICE.ashx.

[6] Extracts from Sandy Boyce, "Pathfinder and Pioneer: A Tribute to Betty Matthews, the Uniting Church's First Ordained Deacon," *Uniting Church Studies* 24, no. 2 (December 2022).

establish a church in a developing industrial suburb in Western Australia where an oil refinery was being built and with workers coming from all over the world. Matthews was an early pioneer in church planting. Her role included visiting migrant families in hostels as they moved into new homes.

Matthews wore a distinctive blue and white deaconess uniform. It provided an acceptable way for women in ministry to appear in public as representatives of the church, like the deaconess movements in Germany, England, and the United States. The dress of a deaconess was seen to play a role in how others saw her moral and spiritual standing before God. This publicly subscribed to the church's gendered expectations around restraint and propriety. The aim was simply to be clothed in respectability – inconspicuous yet set apart for work that was lowly.[7]

In 1970, Matthews and her husband, Alan, moved to the Aboriginal community of Yirrkala, the center of the first land rights movement in Australia. On 15 August 1963, representatives of the tribal groups brought a petition – written on a length of stringy bark – to Federal Parliament, protesting the development of a bauxite mine by a private company on land owned by the Yolgnu people and without consultation with them. It was the first traditional document prepared by Aboriginal Australians recognized by the Australian Parliament and today hangs in the Federal Parliament building. In 1971, the year after Matthews and her husband arrived, the court decided that the ordinances and mining leases were valid and that the Yolgnu people were not able to establish their native title through common law. The Gove bauxite mine commenced production in the same year. The family eventually moved to Nhulunbuy, the remote town created for the bauxite mine. They established a congregation, with services first held in a marquee and then in the recreation hall until the church was built.

In October 1974, M.J. Thalheimer became the first woman to be ordained to the Ministry of the Word and Sacraments in the Presbyterian Church in Australia. Matthews chose not to go down that path: "I felt my calling was still to be of service, but not as a Minister of the Word, because of my interests which related to those on the edges of the church and society."[8] Matthews' ministry was focused on building bridges between the Aboriginal and mining communities, helping the newcomers to understand and respect Aboriginal culture.

Meanwhile, the newly formed Uniting Church welcomed both men and women to become ordained ministers of the Word – but there would be no new deaconesses. A renewal of the diaconate would be explored. In 1977, the Presbyterian, Congregational, and Methodist churches in Australia formed the Uniting Church in Australia. The 1977 Statement to the Nation, read at the

---

[7] Pamela E. Klassen, "The Robes of Womanhood: Dress and Authenticity Among African American Methodist Women in the Nineteenth Century," *Religion and American Culture: A Journal of Interpretation* 14, no. 1 (Winter 2004): 40–42, doi.org/10.1525/rac.2004.14.1.39. See also Kerrie Handasyde, "Religious Dress and the Making of Women Preachers in Australia, 1880–1934," *Lilith: A Feminist History Journal* 26 (2020): 103–19, doi.org/10.22459/LFHJ.26.05.

[8] Heather Dowling, "Loving God's Mob," *Revive Magazine* 27 (December 2012): 7.

inauguration of the Uniting Church, defined this new church in a missional context. It identified itself as the kind of church that would be very outward looking, affirming basic rights and freedoms, political participation, religious liberty and personal dignity, and working toward the eradication of poverty and racism, and for the protection of the environment.[9] In many ways the missional context used a diaconal lens. Matthews advocated for a renewal of the diaconate.

Many deaconesses were hurt by the inability of the Assembly to reach agreement on a reshaping of their ministry, especially given that other churches in Australia and overseas were implementing a renewal of diaconal ministry. In 1979, the Second Assembly of the Uniting Church declared its intention to "renew the ministry of the Diaconate," and theological rationale for this ministry were presented to the 1979, 1982, and 1985 triennial Assemblies. In 1988, a report was received "that the work of the committee on the responsibilities and functioning of a renewed diaconate has exposed considerations that render its implementation inappropriate at this stage."[10]

The Sixth Assembly in 1991 finally resolved to renew the diaconate. A report received from the Task Group on the Ministry of the Church stated:

> The deacon is present in the places where people of all sorts live their everyday lives, as a sign of the presence of God there. Particularly among people who are marginalized, oppressed, suffering, the forgotten, the unlovely, the deacon is a sign of the justice and mercy, judgement and forgiveness, compassion and saving grace, the suffering and victory of God.
>
> Moreover, because the deacon works for the most part outside the institutions of the church, the deacon is a sign for the congregation, scattered as they go about their daily work and ordinary lives, of the presence of God in the world ... In response to the deacon's presence the members of the congregation are encouraged to tell their own stories of being God's people at witness, facing the costs and ambiguities, naming the powers and principalities.
>
> Ordained Deacons hold before the church the model of service ... as central to all Christian ministry.[11]

The report identified the distinction between deacons and ministers of the Word in the focus of their ministries and in their training and formation. Furthermore, the report stated, "neither ministry is complete without the other ... Word and Service cannot be separated."[12]

In December 1992, Matthews became the first person in the Uniting Church in Australia to be ordained as a deacon. She had already served as a deaconess

---

[9] Uniting Church in Australia, "Statement to the Nation (First Assembly)," 1977, https://ucaassembly.recollect.net.au/nodes/view/150.

[10] Uniting Church in Australia, "Minutes of the 5th Assembly" (Melbourne: Uniting Church Press, 1988), 88:27:3.

[11] Uniting Church in Australia, "1991 Report of the Task Group on Ministry of the Church to the Sixth Assembly," 40, https://ctm.uca.edu.au/lay-ministries/wp-content/uploads/sites/6/2016/02/UCA-1991-Ministry-in-the-Uniting-Church-in-Australia.pdf.

[12] Uniting Church in Australia, "1991 Report," 37–38.

for thirty-eight years, "one foot in the Church, and one foot in the community."[13] Matthews's ministry involved both acts of compassion as well as advocating for justice. Wherever she was, her deacon heart led her to focus on the outsider, the disadvantaged, the stranger, the isolated, the victims of violence and injustice, those on the edges of church and society. Matthews continued in ministry for sixty-eight years. Deacons around Australia honor her as a pioneer in diaconal ministry.

Mission and Ministry in the Twenty-First Century

In the late twentieth century, *diakonia* began to move from a "subservient" ministry to a more liberating and prophetic ministry. According to one researcher, Alison F. McRae, the ministry of the deacon challenged the Uniting Church in Australia "to move away from understanding diaconal ministry as a ministry of humble servanthood, and to see it as an ecclesial concept that helps us understand more about the nature of the church and what is at the heart of its own diaconal mission."[14] *Diakonia* includes helping the poor and vulnerable and marginalized and more recently has come to be seen as an expression of the radical missionary values of God's reign. The prophetic and liberating work of *diakonia* can challenge systems that perpetuate disadvantage, raise awareness around issues of injustice, champion environmental matters, and actively pursue pathways of peace.

It is the deacon who pronounces the benediction at the end of a service and sends people on their way into the world to encourage them to share in *diakonia* in their communities. As Dorothy McRae-McMahon, a leader in the Uniting Church in Australia, noted: "Unless the diaconate enters into mission and ministry with the church rather than for it, I believe it will fall far short of its calling."[15] In some traditions, the work of deacons and deaconesses is a stand-alone office, working on behalf of the church or a community. In other traditions, like the Uniting Church in Australia, deacons are *representative* of the work of the whole people of God. "Ordained deacons hold before the church the model of service among those who suffer, and call the members to engage in such service."[16] Diaconal ministry of the whole people of God then becomes a visible expression of our baptism as disciples of Jesus Christ.

A sustained reflection on what it means to stand on the margins will enable those engaged in diaconal ministry to bring a renewed understanding of the

---

[13] Wellspring Community, Inc., *Pipeline* (June 2014), 8, http://wellspringcommunity.org.au/documents/pipeline/2014_06_pipeline.pdf.

[14] Alison F. McRae, "De-Centred Ministry: A Diaconal View of Mission and Church," DMin thesis (Melbourne College of Divinity, 2009), 1, https://illuminate.recollect.net.au/nodes/view/940.

[15] Dorothy McRae-McMahon, "Deacons and the Mission of the Church," unpublished paper presented at the Ministerial Education Commission National Consultation on Deacon Education, Mt. Martha, Victoria, Australia, April 1994, cited by McRae, "De-Centred Ministry," 10.

[16] Uniting Church in Australia, "1991 Report," 40.

mission of the church. According to Alan Roxburgh, "The contextualizing congregation must learn to 'listen' and 'see' where God is at work in the midst of secularism, pluralism and technological transformation ... Contextualization requires a dynamic *interaction* in which both sides are changed through dialogue."[17] It invites a posture of respectful listening in the neighborhood, rather than the usual approach of "doing" and then returning to the safe harbor of the church.

The challenge for the church is to recognize mission as God's dynamic calling to be "out there" in the neighborhood, rather than the church being the end point of mission. However, churches in many Western countries are focused on addressing the challenge of decline. Ruth Powell, director of NCLS Research (Australia) said, "The news is not good for churches whose response to major social change is to double down on what hasn't been working for decades ... There are signs that churches are turning inward."[18] Diaconal ministry holds up service as an inescapable response to the Gospel and reminds the church what it is called to be, to move from an inward focus to one that is more intentionally engaged and present in the community.

Implications for Diaconal Studies and Formation

Diaconal studies and formation can resource the church in the task of reimagining mission and ministry and contextualizing missional engagement in our time and place. Diaconal ministry is often offered from the margins, beyond the church walls. It should not equate to "out of sight, out of mind," disconnected from the church. Diaconal ministry is a public expression of the church's mission in the world, reflecting the radical missional values of God's reign. It is the work of *diakonia* to speak less and listen more to the voices of those on the margins and to partner with them to create a more just and peaceful world. This is good news for those absent from the church and who welcome signs of God's presence in the world. Those serving in diaconal ministry become caretakers of the stories and experiences they share back into the life of the church. These stories in turn are a catalyst for reimagining mission and ministry.

Diaconal ministry identifies areas of community life where new needs are emerging, challenging the church to effective action. Alison F. McRae suggested that "[deacons] are amongst those people who 'dare to stand on the margin' and to offer a form of theological leadership which will enable the church to 'lead into a new future.'"[19] Nurturing this diaconal vision will require theological formation informed by praxis. It will involve a capacity to reflect theologically on engagement in the community, connecting Christian faith and values with

---

[17] Alan J. Roxburgh, *Reaching a New Generation: Strategies for Tomorrow's Church* (Downers Grove, IL: InterVarsity, 1993), 69, original emphasis.

[18] "600 Pastors and Teachers Learn about Church Growth, Decline and Planting," NCLS Research, December 2023, https://www.ncls.org.au/articles/600-pastors-and-teachers-learn-about-church-growth-decline-and-planting/.

[19] McRae, "De-Centred Ministry," 25, quoting Dorothy McRae-McMahon, *Daring Leadership for the 21st Century* (Sydney: Australian Broadcasting Commission, 2001), 4.

community issues and social justice. It will demonstrate a capacity for compassionate caring and listening to vulnerable voices. It will also require a commitment to call for better outcomes for people, which may be through peacemaking, community building, resistance and advocacy, partnership building, prophetic imagination, and willingness to address structural and social injustice.

Formation for ministry, and especially formation for diaconal ministry, will benefit from an investment in the development of diaconal studies that responds to the urgent challenges of our times, in dialogue with other academic disciplines. What is required transcends revitalizing formation only for deacon and deaconess candidates. It also requires reimagining formation for *everyone* preparing for ministry, because *diakonia* is at the heart of the mission and ministry of the whole church. For decades, diaconal formation has leaned into the core formation designed for those preparing for ministry within the church and often included "add-ons" for diaconal candidates. Now is the time for *all* those engaged in ministry formation to lean intentionally toward ministry beyond the four walls of the church, to reimagine the locus of mission and ministry as the neighborhood, and – as the church – to seek to discern and join in with the *missio Dei*.

Even so, diaconal formation is to equip not only those on a pathway to a particular ministry in the church. More significantly, a robust theology and praxis of *diakonia* will have a profound impact upon the diaconate that is the responsibility of the whole people of God.

Works Cited

"600 Pastors and Teachers Learn about Church Growth, Decline and Planting." NCLS Research, December 2023. https://www.ncls.org.au/articles/600-pastors-and-teachers-learn-about-church-growth-decline-and-planting/.

Barnett, James Monroe. *The Diaconate: A Full and Equal Order*. New York: Seabury, 1981.

Boyce, Sandy. "Pathfinder and Pioneer: A Tribute to Betty Matthews, the Uniting Church's First Ordained Deacon." *Uniting Church Studies* 24, no. 2 (December 2022).

Collins, John N. *Diakonia: Re-Interpreting the Ancient Sources*. Oxford: Oxford University Press, 1990.

Croom, Alannah. "Presbyterian Deaconess Order in Victoria." *The Australian Women's Register*, 26 August 2009, modified 20 November 2018. https://www.womenaustralia.info/entries/presbyterian-deaconess-order-in-victoria/.

Dowling, Heather. "Loving God's Mob." *Revive Magazine* 27 (December 2012).

Handasyde, Kerrie. "Religious Dress and the Making of Women Preachers in Australia, 1880–1934." *Lilith: A Feminist History Journal* 26 (2020): 103–19. doi.org/10.22459/LFHJ.26.05.

Keith, B.R. "Rolland, Sir Francis William (Frank) (1878–1965)." *Australian Dictionary of Biography*. Published first in hardcopy 1988. National Centre of Biography, Australian National University. https://adb.anu.edu.au/biography/rolland-sir-francis-william-frank-8261/text14469.

Klassen, Pamela E. "The Robes of Womanhood: Dress and Authenticity Among African American Methodist Women in the Nineteenth Century." *Religion and American Culture* 14, no. 1 (Winter 2004): 39–82. doi.org/10.1525/rac.2004.14.1.39.

McRae, Alison F. "De-Centred Ministry: A Diaconal View of Mission and Church." DMin thesis, Melbourne College of Divinity, 2009. https://illuminate.recollect.net.au/nodes/view/940.

McRae-McMahon, Dorothy. *Daring Leadership for the 21st Century*. Sydney: Australian Broadcasting Commission, 2001.

McRae-McMahon, Dorothy. "Deacons and the Mission of the Church." Unpublished paper presented at the Ministerial Education Commission National Consultation on Deacon Education, Mt. Martha, Victoria, Australia, April 1994.

"Outback Pioneer: Sir Francis Rolland and the Inland Nursing Service." Heritage Guide to the Geelong College. https://gnet.tgc.vic.edu.au/wiki/OUTBACK-PIONEER-Sir-FRANCIS-ROLLAND-and-the-INLAND-NURSING-SERVICE.ashx.

Roxburgh, Alan J. *Reaching a New Generation: Strategies for Tomorrow's Church*. Downers Grove, IL: InterVarsity, 1993.

Uniting Church in Australia. "1991 Report of the Task Group on Ministry of the Church to the Sixth Assembly." https://ctm.uca.edu.au/lay-ministries/wp-content/uploads/sites/6/2016/02/UCA-1991-Ministry-in-the-Uniting-Church-in-Australia.pdf.

———. "Minutes of the 5th Assembly." Melbourne: Uniting Church Press, 1988.

———. "Statement to the Nation (First Assembly)." 1977. https://ucaassembly.recollect.net.au/nodes/view/150.

Wellspring Community, Inc. *Pipeline*, June 2014. http://wellspringcommunity.org.au/documents/pipeline/2014_06_pipeline.pdf.

Chapter 3

Ecumenical Convergence on the Diaconate in North America

Mitzi J. Budde

Many denominations in North America have discovered, or reclaimed, the gifts of the vocational diaconate as part of the latter-twentieth-century liturgical renewal movement. As deacons encounter and engage expanding expressions of *diakonia*, the Spirit is also leading the church to an enriched and expansive understanding of the diaconal identity of all the baptized in Christ.

Decades of ecumenical progress on the theology of the diaconate have brought us to this liminal moment. The Roman Catholic Church revitalized its permanent diaconate after the Second Vatican Council, and The Episcopal Church (TEC) reinvigorated its vocational diaconate in 1970 through canonical changes that were then incorporated into the new *Book of Common Prayer* in 1979. In 1982, the first convergence document of the World Council of Churches (WCC), *Baptism, Eucharist, and Ministry*, called the churches to recover the ordained diaconate.[1] The United Methodist Church (UMC) instituted an order of permanent ordained deacons in 1996. The Evangelical Lutheran Church in America (ELCA) created an order of deacons in 2016 and established ordination as the entrance rite in 2019. "*Diakonia* belongs to the very essence of being church and is an integral part of its mission," the WCC asserted in 2022.[2]

In this chapter, I explore this convergence in ecumenical understandings of the diaconate. I begin by examining the 2023 *Proposal for Exchangeability of the Diaconate* between The Episcopal Church and the Evangelical Lutheran Church in America. Next, I suggest that this approach to diaconal exchangeability establishes a solid precedent for other ecumenical relationships, especially the full communion agreement between the ELCA and The United Methodist Church. Finally, I discuss theological and ecclesiological similarities and differences in the diaconate of these three denominations.

---

[1] World Council of Churches, *Baptism, Eucharist, and Ministry*, Faith and Order Paper No. 111 (Geneva: WCC, 1982), Ministry ¶31, https://www.oikoumene.org/sites/default/files/Document/FO1982_111_en.pdf.

[2] World Council of Churches and ACT Alliance, *Called to Transformation: Ecumenical Diakonia* (Geneva: WCC, 2022), § 6.3, p. 70, https://www.oikoumene.org/sites/default/files/2023-02/Called%20to%20Transformation%20Ecumenical%20Diakonia_webMedRes.pdf.

An Ecumenical View of Deacons

Deacons are bearers of the Word and witnesses to the Holy Spirit at work in the church and the world. Denominational voices describe deacons in complementary terms. For Episcopalians, deacons are "animators and leaders,"[3] "grass roots change agents,"[4] "wise fools, … and agents of hope."[5] Lutheran deacons are "catalysts … equipping the baptized people for service, in order that the church becomes a diaconal church at the heart of its identity and mission."[6] United Methodists describe deacons as "emissary-servants,"[7] "entrepreneurs, enfleshed representatives of Christ … and embodied mission."[8] For the Greek Orthodox, a deacon is "herald, mediator, minister, prophet."[9]

Ecumenical dialogues also reflect this convergence in the diaconate. The proposed full communion agreement between Episcopalians and United Methodists says deacons are "icons of the servant ministry of Jesus Christ,"[10] while the Episcopal–Lutheran full communion relationship describes deacons as "participants in and means for God's mission of hope, healing, and reconciliation in God's beloved world."[11]

The diaconate in all denominational expressions calls the church to address issues of power and privilege. The deacon is one called to serve God's people in response to Christ, who himself came as one who serves (*diakonon*, Luke 22:27). This is not a passive role; the deacon is an advocate in Christ's name. The deacon stands in solidarity alongside the marginalized as a voice for justice, serving as an "internal watchdog,"[12] seeking the transformation of unjust structures within

---

[3] Susanne Watson Epting, "Common Vows and Common Mission," *Anglican Theological Review* 92, no. 1 (Winter 2010): 76.
[4] Association for Episcopal Deacons, "Former Presiding Bishop Katharine Jefferts Schori Joins AED's Board," (June 2023), https://www.episcopaldeacons.org/uploads/2/6/7/3/26739998/kjs-joinboard.pdf?utm_source=newsletter&utm_medium=email&utm_campaign=bishop_katharine_jefferts_schori_joins_aed_s_board&utm_term=2023-07-10.
[5] Kevin J. McGrane, "The Deacon as Wise Fool: A Pastoral Persona for the Diaconate," *Anglican Theological Review* 100, no. 4 (Fall 2018): 782–83.
[6] Craig L. Nessan, "A Lutheran Theology for *Diakonia* in North American Contexts," in *International Handbook on Ecumenical Diakonia*, ed. Ampony et al. (Oxford: Regnum Books International, 2021), 279–88 (282).
[7] Benjamin L. Hartley, "Deacons as Emissary-Servants: A Liturgical Theology," *Quarterly Review* 19, no. 4 (Winter 1999): 372.
[8] Margaret Ann Crain, *Advancing the Mission: The Order of Deacon in The United Methodist Church* (Nashville: Wesley's Foundery, 2021), 132.
[9] John Chryssavgis, *Remembering and Reclaiming Diakonia: The Diaconate Yesterday and Today* (Brookline, MA: Holy Cross Orthodox Press, 2009), 106–16.
[10] The Episcopal Church and The United Methodist Church, *A Gift to the World: Co-Laborers for the Healing of Brokenness*, 2018, § 6, https://www.unitedmethodistbishops.org/files/websites/www/pdfs/a_gift_to_the_world.pdf.
[11] *Proposal for Exchangeability of the Diaconate: The Episcopal Church and the Evangelical Lutheran Church in America*, unpublished document of the Lutheran Episcopal Coordinating Committee, 11 January 2023.
[12] Thomas E. Breidenthal, "Exodus from Privilege: Reflections on the Diaconate in Acts," *Anglican Theological Review* 95, no. 2 (Spring 2013): 285.

church and world. This role of advocacy is ultimately the call to all of God's people, the *diakonia* of all believers. The deacon's call is to equip, challenge, and lead all the baptized to deepen their commitment to Christ by responding to the needs of God's people in the world.

Recognition and Exchangeability of Deacons

The significance of the 2000 ELCA–Episcopal ecumenical agreement *Called to Common Mission* is that it is the first time that an historic episcopate church in the United States and a church not in the historic episcopate reconciled their ordained ministries, made them exchangeable, and moved into the full communion relationship.[13] In this agreement, Episcopalians and Lutherans affirmed the authenticity and exchangeability of each other's bishops and priests/pastors. This ecumenical breakthrough on ordained ministries came in mutual recognition that "historic episcopate" and "apostolic succession" are not synonymous. Rather, apostolic succession means continuity in faithful ministry, which is indicated by the historic episcopate in the Anglican tradition. *The Niagara Report* of 1987 asserted that the historic episcopate is one way, but not the only way, for a church to demonstrate its apostolic succession, and the report identified other ways by which a church might demonstrate its faithfulness.[14] In the full communion agreement, The Episcopal Church recognized the full validity of the ELCA's non-historic episcopate bishops in the past, while the ELCA pledged to bring its episcopacy into the historic episcopate for the future. All active ELCA bishops are now in the historic episcopate.

When *Called to Common Mission* was inaugurated, there was no option for diaconal exchangeability because the Lutherans had no ordained diaconate. But the reconciliation of the episcopate paved the way for the mutual recognition of deacons when the ELCA adopted an ordained diaconate in 2019. In the subsequent 2023 *Proposal for Exchangeability of the Diaconate*, TEC and ELCA mutually recognize each other's order of deacons as authentic, acknowledge that each other's deacons may be interchangeable in counterpart ministries and joint ministry settings, and renew their commitment to undertake "continuing exploration, renewal, and reform" of the diaconate.[15] The approval

---

[13] Evangelical Lutheran Church in America and The Episcopal Church, *Called to Common Mission: A Relationship of Full Communion Between the Evangelical Lutheran Church in America and Episcopal Church*, 2000, https://download.elca.org/ELCA%20Resource%20Repository/Called_To_Common_Mission.pdf

[14] Anglican–Lutheran International Continuation Committee, *The Niagara Report* (London: Church House Publishing, 1988), § III, https://www.anglicancommunion.org/media/102175/the_niagara_report.pdf.

[15] *Proposal for Exchangeability of the Diaconate.* The Lutheran Episcopal Coordinating Committee, which oversees the implementation of the full communion agreement, appointed a Diaconate Implementation Team in 2021 to draft a proposal as an interpretation of the full communion agreement. The author of this essay chaired that

process for this proposed diaconal exchangeability was still in progress in 2023.[16] For TEC and the ELCA, this diaconal recognition and exchangeability will complete the mutual recognition of the three orders of ministry.

Emerging Convergence on the Diaconate

The commentary that accompanies the 2023 Lutheran–Episcopal *Proposal for Exchangeability of the Diaconate* makes bold claims for the consensus that has been achieved on the diaconate. Those claims are congruent with the dimensions of diaconal ministry defined in the 1996 foundational Anglican–Lutheran *Hanover Report*: worship (*leitourgia*), witness (*martyria*), and service (*diakonia*).[17] This congruence demonstrates continuity and consistency over nearly three decades of national and international dialogue on the diaconate, now coming to culmination.

Regarding worship (*leitourgia*), the *Proposal* roots diaconal theology in the sacrament of baptism and asserts that deacons should be grounded within a worshipping community, with a role in liturgical leadership. Diaconal ordination includes laying on of hands by a bishop, an invocation of the Holy Spirit, and the giving of a deacon stole as a symbol of the office. In terms of witness (*martyria*), deacons equip the *diakonia* of all believers and call the church into the world and the world into the church. As to service (*diakonia*), the *Proposal* indicates that deacons focus on mission and ministry as "participants in and means for God's mission of hope, healing, and reconciliation in God's beloved world."[18]

These claims are bold for the ELCA, whose understanding of diaconal ministry was realigned and redesigned as of 2019. They are also bold for an ecumenical dialogue (ELCA–TEC) that has not yet achieved exchangeability of the diaconate. This visionary, aspirational view of an ecumenical convergence on the diaconate expresses the ways in which the Spirit is calling both churches to see and claim a future together. These points serve as an ecumenical roadmap

---

implementation team. The resulting *Proposal* was presented to the Coordinating Committee on 11 January 2023.

[16] For the ELCA, it was sufficient for the ELCA's Conference of Bishops to review the *Proposal* and to recommend that the Church Council receive it as the method of adoption, which the Council did on 20 April 2023. Note that the term *received* in this context means "ecumenical reception," that is, approval. In TEC, "the Executive Council joyfully urges the full and timely implementation of this Proposal to affirm the moving of the Holy Spirit within, and between, our Churches." The Executive Council and the Domestic and Foreign Missionary Society of the Protestant Episcopal Church in the United States of America, "MB 004 To receive the Proposal for Exchangeability of Deacons in TEC and the ELCA," unpublished document, 15 June 2023. Approval depends on a vote at the Episcopal Church's General Convention in June 2024. The ELCA then plans to revise its Constitution and Bylaws to support the exchangeability of the diaconate.

[17] Anglican–Lutheran International Commission, *The Hanover Report: The Diaconate as Ecumenical Opportunity* (London: Anglican Communion Publications, 1996), ¶52, https://www.anglicancommunion.org/media/102181/the_hanover_report.pdf.

[18] *Proposal for Exchangeability of the Diaconate.*

for living more deeply into common mission, reflecting God's call for a transformed diaconal church catholic. Might this TEC–ELCA *Proposal for Exchangeability of the Diaconate* inspire new approaches for recognition, collaboration, and exchangeability of deacons across North America?

Precedent for Further Diaconal Recognition

The Episcopal–Lutheran *Proposal*'s approach to diaconal recognition and exchangeability offers a precedent for other ecumenical relationships, especially the full communion agreement between the ELCA and The United Methodist Church (UMC).

The UMC revised its theology of ordained ministry in 1996, establishing two "full and equal orders" of deacons and elders. These orders are distinct. Elders are ordained to Word, Service, Sacrament, and Order; deacons are ordained to Word, Service, Compassion, and Justice. The United Methodist order of deacon is congruent with Episcopal vocational deacons and the ELCA's new order of deacons. The UMC and ELCA, however, took different approaches with their prior orders of lay diaconal ministers. The UMC retained an order of laity in diaconal service: deaconesses and home missioners are professionally trained laypersons consecrated and commissioned by a bishop to a lifetime ministry of love, justice, and service.[19] Furthermore, in 1996, the UMC grandparented its lay diaconal ministers, inviting those in good standing to choose whether to continue in the lay order of diaconal service or apply to be ordained into the order of deacons. By contrast, in 2016 the ELCA acknowledged the *diakonia* of its prior rosters of associates in ministry, diaconal ministers, and deaconesses by receiving them into the new roster of deacons without any supplemental liturgical rite.

The ELCA and the UMC have been in full communion since 2009; however, the agreement, *Confessing Our Faith Together*, does not include diaconal exchangeability because the ELCA did not have ordained deacons until 2019.[20] TEC and the UMC's pending proposed full communion agreement, *A Gift to the World*, affirms "the mutual interchangeability of deacons."[21] Now that the TEC–ELCA full communion agreement may be extended to include diaconal exchangeability, it should be a natural extension to close the loop and establish ELCA–UMC diaconal exchangeability based on this TEC–ELCA model.

---

[19] *The Book of Discipline of The United Methodist Church 2016* (Nashville: United Methodist Publishing House, 2016), ¶¶1913–1914.

[20] Evangelical Lutheran Church in America and The United Methodist Church, *Confessing Our Faith Together: A Proposal for Full Communion Between the Evangelical Lutheran Church in America and The United Methodist Church*, 2008, https://download.elca.org/ELCA%20Resource%20Repository/Confessing_Our_Faith_Together.pdf.

[21] TEC–UMC, *A Gift to the World*, § 6.

Contrasts and Remaining Distinctives

While there is a growing convergence on what deacons *are* in TEC, the ELCA, and the UMC, these three traditions do not hold identical definitions of what deacons *do* and where they locate their ministries. Ecumenical convergence does not necessitate agreement on every detail of lived experience. Deacons in ecumenical calls will have the opportunity to demonstrate how denominational distinctives can encourage deacons and their parishes to mutual clarity and intentionality, enhancing each church's understanding of *diakonia*.

Forms of the Diaconate

The ELCA and the UMC have only one form of diaconate. Episcopalians have both transitional and vocational deacons. Since TEC practices sequential ordination, most Episcopal deacons are transitional deacons who will later be ordained to the priesthood. The revival of the vocational diaconate is a more recent development in TEC. The *Proposal* states: "TEC may continue the practice of ordination to the transitional diaconate prior to ordination to the priesthood, whereas the ELCA may continue its practice of direct ordination of pastors into the office of Word and Sacrament."[22] The exchangeability of the *Proposal* pertains primarily to Episcopal vocational deacons with Lutheran deacons. United Methodists discontinued sequential ordination from diaconate to elder in 1996 when the permanent diaconate was established. This change made the UMC diaconate "a distinctive call and a distinctive order."[23]

Relation of Diaconal Ministry to Baptism

In Lutheran theology, ministry derives from baptism: all the baptized are called into a diaconate of all believers, with some of the baptized ordained to specific forms of Word and Service (deacons) or Word and Sacrament (pastors).[24] This is a continuum theology of ministry, emphasizing the sacrament of baptism as the foundational call to love God and serve neighbor. The ELCA's recognition of the diaconal nature of its former lay rosters is consistent with this continuum approach.[25] The ELCA Constitution defines what deacons do: "exemplifying the life of Christ-like service to all persons and creation: nurturing, healing, leading, advocating dignity and justice, and equipping the whole people of God for their life of witness and service within and beyond the congregation for the sake of God's mission in the world."[26]

---

[22] *Proposal for Exchangeability of the Diaconate.*
[23] Crain, *Advancing the Mission*, 99.
[24] See Craig L. Nessan, "The Diaconate of All Believers: Theology, Formation, Practice," *Religions* 14, no. 6, 741 (2023), https://doi.org/10.3390/rel14060741.
[25] Frederick C. Bauerschmidt points out that the Vatican II decree *Ad gentes* understands "[diaconal] ordination as an affirmation of the gift already given." Frederick C. Bauerschmidt, "The Deacon and Sacramental Character," in *The Diaconate in Ecumenical Perspective: Ecclesiology, Liturgy and Practice*, ed. D. Michael Jackson (Durham, UK: Sacristy, 2019), 27.
[26] *Evangelical Lutheran Church in America Constitution* (2019), ¶7.51, https://download.elca.org/ELCA%20Resource%20Repository/Constitutions_Bylaws_

Episcopalians consider ordained ministry to be rooted in baptism while also understanding ordination as an ontological change, a change in one's identity from laity to ordained. The gift in TEC's practice of twofold ordination is that every Episcopal priest and bishop has had their primary vocational identity as a deacon for a period of their ministry. The concept of the diaconate of all believers is gradually becoming more widely accepted in this tradition.[27] The liturgy for ordination of a deacon defines what an Episcopal deacon is to do: "to study the Holy Scriptures ... to make Christ and his redemptive love known by [one's] word and example ... to interpret to the Church the needs, concerns, and hopes of the world ... to assist the bishop and priests in public worship and in the ministration of God's Word and Sacraments..."[28]

The UMC also bases all ministry on the call from baptism: "Deacons fulfill servant ministry in the world and lead the Church in relating the gathered life of Christians to their ministries in the world, interrelating worship in the gathered community with service to God in the world."[29] UMC elders and deacons are complementary and equal. Both are considered essential to the church's mission.[30]

Ordination Rites

Because of its commitment to the historic episcopate as essential to the church, The Episcopal Church's ordination of deacons invariably includes the laying on of hands by a bishop. All ELCA deacons since 2019 are ordained with a new liturgical rite of *Ordination to the Ministry of Word and Service*, in which the synodical bishop presides and lays hands on the head of the candidate.[31] The ELCA received its three prior rosters into the order of ordained deacons based on their consecration or commissioning, and while many of these prior liturgies included an episcopal laying on of hands, some did not. After the 2019 Churchwide Assembly decision, the ELCA created an optional *Rite of Affirmation for Ministers of Word and Service* for those deacons who desired it, though this rite does not include the laying on of hands by a bishop.[32] TEC is

---

and_Continuing_Resolutions_of_the_ELCA.pdf?_ga=2.268559985.1409207301.16890 90585-430729072.1640533808.

[27] Susanne Watson Epting, *Unexpected Consequences: The Diaconate Renewed* (New York: Morehouse, 2015), 126–28.

[28] The Episcopal Church, *The Book of Common Prayer* (New York: Church Hymnal Corp., 1979), 543.

[29] *The Book of Discipline of The United Methodist Church 2016*, ¶328.

[30] See chapter by Crain in this volume.

[31] Evangelical Lutheran Church in America, *Ordination to the Ministry of Word and Service*, 2019, https://download.elca.org/ELCA%20Resource%20Repository/Ordination_Ministers_W ord_Service-pdf.pdf.

[32] Evangelical Lutheran Church in America, *Rite of Affirmation for Ministers of Word and Service*, 2019, https://download.elca.org/ELCA%20Resource%20Repository/Affirmation_Ministers_ Word_Service-pdf.pdf?_ga=2.17909114.2125558543.1645124764- 1108845059.1642190836.

now invited to recognize the ELCA's current deacons, regardless of prior rite, based upon the ELCA's commitment that all diaconal ordinations henceforth will include the laying on of hands by a bishop.

Two historical precedents encourage TEC's recognition of the validity of the ELCA's reception of these prior rosters into the diaconate: one internal and one ecumenical. The internal historical precedent is the reception of consecrated Anglican and Episcopal deaconesses into the order of deacons without any additional liturgical rite, by action of the 1968 Lambeth Conference and 1970 TEC General Convention.[33] The ecumenical precedent is the reconciliation of the differing confirmation practices between the ELCA and TEC, also grounded in the full communion relationship. In TEC, the rite of confirmation requires the laying on of hands by a bishop, whereas confirmation in the ELCA is by the local pastor. TEC recognized the validity of ELCA confirmations by General Convention action in 2003, clarifying that Lutherans joining an Episcopal parish are to be received based on their baptism and profession of faith at their prior confirmation, not confirmed again.[34] The UMC also does not require a bishop for confirmation; the ordained elder confirms.

Roles in the Eucharistic Liturgy

The role of the deacon in the eucharistic liturgy differs between the churches. In the Episcopal eucharistic liturgy, the deacon (or priest, if no deacon is present) bids the prayers, sets the table, reads the Gospel, and speaks the dismissal. In the ELCA eucharistic liturgy, there is no specified liturgical role for the deacon; rather, a lay assisting minister or deacon bids the prayers, sets the table, and speaks the dismissal. The preacher reads the Gospel. UMC deacons assist the elders in administering the sacrament and may even preside at the celebration of the sacrament when "contextually appropriate and duly authorized."[35] When UMC deacons assist with the sacrament, they embody the way the sacrament sends the baptized forth into the world to respond to the needs of the people.[36]

Educational Preparation

Episcopalians, Lutherans, and Methodists have differing requirements for diaconal competencies and education. For the ELCA, these requirements are defined by the church's *Candidacy Manual*, which sets the educational norm for deacons as a seminary master's degree or equivalency based on prior experience

---

[33] *The Lambeth Conference 1968: Resolutions and Reports* (London: SPCK, 1968), 39, 105–106; The Episcopal Church, *Journal of the General Convention of the Protestant Episcopal Church in the United States of America: Otherwise Known as the Episcopal Church, Held in Houston, Texas, from October Eleventh to Twenty-Second, Inclusive, in the Year of Our Lord 1970, with Constitution and Canons* (New York, 1970), 249, 270–71, 769–70.

[34] Amended Canon § 1.7.1c. See The Episcopal Church Office of Ecumenical and Interfaith Relations, *Guidelines for Reception and Confirmation for Persons Joining The Episcopal Church*, revised January 2005, https://edwm.org/wp-content/uploads/2018/08/confirmation.pdf.

[35] *The Book of Discipline of The United Methodist Church 2016*, ¶328.

[36] Crain, *Advancing the Mission*, 122, 124.

or education.[37] The UMC also requires a graduate master's degree. There is no specified educational requirement for Episcopal deacons, and diaconal formation is often through diocesan training programmes. TEC's canons define competencies required for deacons, and each diocese may establish its own additional requirements. Under full communion, deacon candidates will be enriched by drawing upon each church's programmes for diaconal studies for educational preparation, certification, and spiritual formation. Experienced deacons will have a wider range of options for continuing education, programmes, retreats, spiritual direction, and formation opportunities.

Expanding Mission and Ministry

Diaconal exchangeability across denominational lines encourages churches to think expansively about opportunities for deacons in joint and shared ministries, missions, justice work, evangelism, disaster relief, social ministry organizations, and leadership to church and society. Deacons will be able to serve calls to joint parishes and campus ministries. An ELCA deacon might serve in an Episcopal parish or a United Methodist seminary. There are shared call possibilities in church agencies at every level, such as shared judicatory (diocesan, synodical, conference) staff positions. Joint calls are also possible in the churches' coordinated advocacy efforts at the national and state levels. For example, the UMC Building adjacent to the US Capitol in Washington DC is a central convening place for coordinated ecumenical work in advocacy, social action, justice, and dialogue.

The ELCA allows diaconal calls based on employment both within and outside of the church. Almost all Episcopal vocational deacons have calls within the church, while many are also employed outside the church. United Methodist deacons serve in a variety of church or secular employment venues, such as "doctors, lawyers, teachers, counsellors, professors, chaplains, journalists, social workers, community organizers, administrators, musicians, therapists, nurses, artists, yoga instructors, missionaries, and more."[38] Exchangeability of deacons will broaden call possibilities beyond the boundaries of the churches.

The norms for deacon compensation differ as well. The ELCA requires deacons' calls to be paid, though not all calls are funded by the church. The stipend comes from the employing agency, whether congregation, institution, or outside agency. Episcopal deacons traditionally have been uncompensated. While they are eligible for pension arrangements, they must have paid employment to be active in the pension plan. Thus, those who need salary and benefits are often unable to pursue a diaconal call until retirement, or they must work at a secular job while serving, resulting in a class and age differential.[39] In

---

[37] Evangelical Lutheran Church in America, *Candidacy Manual*, revised October 2019, § 2.3.3, https://download.elca.org/ELCA%20Resource%20Repository/CandidacyManualOctober2019.pdf.

[38] Crain, *Advancing the Mission*, 125.

[39] See chapter by Mills-Curran in this volume.

the UMC, deacons are normally compensated. However, they must locate jobs themselves, which can be difficult to find. The question of whether the UMC should take "economic responsibility" for the diaconal order is identified by Margaret Ann Crain as one of three key issues for the UMC diaconate.[40]

Greater flexibility in call sources and in funding through ecumenical call opportunities would have a twofold benefit. First, it would expand options for individual deacons in terms of call placements and provide stipend options related to their call for those who are not economically privileged. Secondly, it would expand options for parishes and agencies of the churches, providing a wider candidate pool of potential deacons to call and offering a wider range of deacon specialties and experience from which to draw.

Conclusion

A transformed and transforming view of the diaconate has the potential to change and energize the ecumenical church in its worship, witness, service, and life in the community of the church and the world. Deacons broaden the *oikumene* of the church catholic as "heralds of unity in faith."[41] The churches' mutual recognition of the validity of each other's diaconate and their endorsement of the exchangeability of diaconal service will enrich each respective church body's *diakonia* and advance their common mission.

Ecumenical convergence will offer creative new opportunities for diaconal formation and ministry. With God's help, it will expand the church's vision of what a deacon is and what a deacon can do in the church and the world. In Christ's name, an ecumenical diaconate will engage the powers of this world on behalf of those who are oppressed. And by the inspiration of the Holy Spirit, it will energize, encourage, and animate the diaconate of all the baptized people of God.

Works Cited

Anglican–Lutheran International Commission. *The Hanover Report: The Diaconate as Ecumenical Opportunity*. London: Anglican Communion Publications, 1996.
https://www.anglicancommunion.org/media/102181/the_hanover_report.pdf.

Anglican–Lutheran International Continuation Committee. *The Niagara Report*. London: Church House Publishing, 1988.
https://www.anglicancommunion.org/media/102175/the_niagara_report.pdf.

Association for Episcopal Deacons. "Former Presiding Bishop Katharine Jefferts Schori Joins AED's Board." June 2023.
https://www.episcopaldeacons.org/uploads/2/6/7/3/26739998/kjs-joinboard.pdf?utm_source=newsletter&utm_medium=email&utm_campaign=bishop_katharine_jefferts_schori_joins_aed_s_board&utm_term=2023-07-10.

---

[40] Crain, *Advancing the Mission*, 149.
[41] Chryssavgis, *Remembering and Reclaiming Diakonia*, 94.

Bauerschmidt, Frederick C. "The Deacon and Sacramental Character." In *The Diaconate in Ecumenical Perspective: Ecclesiology, Liturgy and Practice*, edited by D. Michael Jackson, 24–32. Durham, UK: Sacristy, 2019.

The Book of Discipline of The United Methodist Church 2016. Nashville: United Methodist Publishing House, 2016.

Breidenthal, Thomas E. "Exodus from Privilege: Reflections on the Diaconate in Acts." *Anglican Theological Review* 95, no. 2 (Spring 2013): 275–92.

Chryssavgis, John. *Remembering and Reclaiming Diakonia: The Diaconate Yesterday and Today*. Brookline, MA: Holy Cross Orthodox Press, 2009.

Crain, Margaret Ann. *Advancing the Mission: The Order of Deacon in The United Methodist Church*. Nashville: Wesley's Foundery Books, 2021.

The Episcopal Church. *The Book of Common Prayer*. New York: Church Hymnal Corp., 1979.

———. *Journal of the General Convention of the Protestant Episcopal Church in the United States of America: Otherwise Known as the Episcopal Church, Held in Houston, Texas, from October Eleventh to Twenty-Second, Inclusive, in the Year of Our Lord 1970, with Constitution and Canons*. New York, 1970.

The Episcopal Church and The United Methodist Church. *A Gift to the World: Co-Laborers for the Healing of Brokenness*, 2018. https://www.unitedmethodistbishops.org/files/websites/www/pdfs/a_gift_to_ the_world.pdf.

The Episcopal Church Office of Ecumenical and Interfaith Relations. *Guidelines for Reception and Confirmation for Persons Joining The Episcopal Church*. Revised January 2005. https://edwm.org/wp-content/uploads/2018/08/confirmation.pdf.

Epting, Susanne Watson. "Common Vows and Common Mission." *Anglican Theological Review* 92, no. 1 (Winter 2010): 71–87.

———. *Unexpected Consequences: The Diaconate Renewed*. New York: Morehouse, 2015.

Evangelical Lutheran Church in America. *Candidacy Manual*. Revised October 2019. https://download.elca.org/ELCA%20Resource%20Repository/CandidacyManualOctober2019.pdf.

———. *Constitution*. 2019. https://download.elca.org/ELCA%20Resource%20Repository/Constitutions_Bylaws_and_Continuing_Resolutions_of_the_ELCA.pdf?_ga=2.268559985.1409207301.1689090585-430729072.1640533808.

———. *Ordination to the Ministry of Word and Service*. 2019. https://download.elca.org/ELCA%20Resource%20Repository/Ordination_Ministers_Word_Service-pdf.pdf.

———. *Rite of Affirmation for Ministers of Word and Service*. 2019. https://download.elca.org/ELCA%20Resource%20Repository/Affirmation_Ministers_Word_Service-pdf.pdf?_ga=2.17909114.2125558543.1645124764-1108845059.1642190836.

Evangelical Lutheran Church in America and The Episcopal Church. *Called to Common Mission: A Relationship of Full Communion Between the Evangelical Lutheran Church in America and Episcopal Church*. 2000. https://download.elca.org/ELCA%20Resource%20Repository/Called_To_Common_Mission.pdf.

Evangelical Lutheran Church in America and The United Methodist Church. *Confessing Our Faith Together: A Proposal for Full Communion Between the Evangelical Lutheran Church in America and The United Methodist Church*. 2008. https://download.elca.org/ELCA%20Resource%20Repository/Confessing_Our_Faith_Together.pdf.

The Executive Council and the Domestic and Foreign Missionary Society of the Protestant Episcopal Church in the United States of America. "MB 004 To receive the Proposal for Exchangeability of Deacons in TEC and the ELCA." Unpublished document. 15 June 2023.

Hartley, Benjamin L. "Deacons as Emissary-Servants: A Liturgical Theology." *Quarterly Review* 19, no. 4 (Winter 1999): 372–86.

The Lambeth Conference 1968: Resolutions and Reports. London: SPCK, 1968.

McGrane, Kevin J. "The Deacon as Wise Fool: A Pastoral Persona for the Diaconate." *Anglican Theological Review* 100, no. 4 (Fall 2018): 777–83.

Nessan, Craig L. "The Diaconate of All Believers: Theology, Formation, Practice." *Religions* 14, no. 6 (2023). https://doi.org/10.3390/rel14060741.

———. "A Lutheran Theology for *Diakonia* in North American Contexts." In *International Handbook on Ecumenical Diakonia*, edited by Godwin Ampony et al., 279–88. Oxford: Regnum Books International, 2021.

Proposal for Exchangeability of the Diaconate: The Episcopal Church and the Evangelical Lutheran Church in America. Unpublished document of the Lutheran Episcopal Coordinating Committee. 11 January 2023.

World Council of Churches. *Baptism, Eucharist, and Ministry*. Faith and Order Paper No. 111. Geneva: World Council of Churches, 1982. https://www.oikoumene.org/sites/default/files/Document/FO1982_111_en.pdf.

World Council of Churches and ACT Alliance. *Called to Transformation: Ecumenical Diakonia*. Geneva: WCC Publications, 2022. https://www.oikoumene.org/sites/default/files/2023-02/Called%20to%20Transformation%20Ecumenical%20Diakonia_webMedRes.pdf.

Chapter 4

The Problem and Promise of the Diaconate

Benjamin L. Hartley

Fifteen years ago, Anglican theologian and ecumenist Paul Avis introduced an issue of the journal *Ecclesiology* by stating that "the diaconate is at the same time the most problematic and the most promising of all the ministries of the Church."[1] As someone who has written occasionally about the diaconate for the past twenty-five years, I believe that remains the case today.[2] The purpose of this chapter is to provide some textured elaboration of the problem and to propose a heuristic for working with it. In doing so, I also discuss the promise of the diaconate for imagining ministry in North America and conclude with implications for diaconal studies in the future.

Contested Meanings of Diakonia

The 2022 World Council of Churches (WCC) document, *Called to Transformation*, is the most recent global ecumenical statement about *diakonia*, and it is a noteworthy contribution for several reasons. Not least among those reasons is that it acknowledges the conceptual problem of *diakonia* in a forthright manner. That alone makes this an important text. In the introductory chapter, the authors state that the concept of *diakonia* "is disputed," unevenly used by some denominations but not by others, and sometimes seen as too "churchy" by organizations seeking to appeal to more secular contexts.[3] At one level, the document alludes to the problem of linguistic unfamiliarity. *Diakonie* in German generally conveys the idea of Christian social service. Scandinavian languages, French, Spanish, and Italian have similar terms with like meaning. North

---

[1] Paul Avis, "Editorial: Wrestling with the Diaconate," *Ecclesiology* 5 (2009): 3.
[2] Benjamin L. Hartley and Paul E. Van Buren, *The Deacon: Ministry Through Words of Faith and Acts of Love* (Nashville: General Board of Higher Education and Ministry, The United Methodist Church, 1999); Benjamin L. Hartley, "Deacons as Emissary-Servants: A Liturgical Theology," *Quarterly Review* 19, no. 4 (1999): 372–86; Benjamin L. Hartley, *An Empirical Look at the Ecumenical Diaconate in the United States*, Monograph Series No. 16 (Providence, RI: North American Association for the Diaconate, 2003); Benjamin L. Hartley, "Connected and Sent Out: Implications of New Biblical Research for the United Methodist Diaconate," *Quarterly Review* 24, no. 4 (2004): 367–80. To mark the twenty-fifth anniversary of the United Methodist diaconate in 2021, I wrote three blog posts which may be accessed here: https://missionandmethodism.net/2021/06/02/umc-deacons-at-25-rethinking-deacons-education/.
[3] World Council of Churches and ACT Alliance, *Called to Transformation: Ecumenical Diakonia* (Geneva: WCC Publications, 2022), 15.

American English speakers, however, mostly do not share this European framing of *diakonia* as Christian social service, although the adjective *diaconal* is utilized in this way in some denominations. Churches and seminaries in North America tend to use the language of *mission, ministry,* or *social justice* to convey what Europeans more easily describe as diaconal work through some linguistic variant of *diakonia*.

On a deeper level, the authors acknowledge a theological problem for the concept of *diakonia* that emerged from the robust linguistic work of John N. Collins. In the thirty years since the publication of his landmark text, *Diakonia: Re-Interpreting the Ancient Sources*, Collins has written over thirty articles and three books, all stemming from his earlier linguistic research.[4] Scholarly assessments of Collins's findings over the past three decades have overwhelmingly supported his conclusions. To my knowledge, *Called to Transformation* is the first WCC document to grapple seriously with the implications of Collins's research, even if it did not do so in a sustained manner. Collins's biblical research on the *diakon-* words (appearing about one hundred times in the New Testament) demonstrates that these terms convey a sense of go-between or emissarial relationship to responsible ecclesial authority rather than the character of lowly or humble service, which was the dominant view of *diakonia* during the rise of the diaconal movements in Europe, the United States, and elsewhere in the nineteenth century. Equating diaconal identity with social work remains prevalent today. I discuss this contrast in definitions of *diakonia* more extensively below.

The challenge for Christians today – and especially deacons – is how best to make sense of this research by Collins, which calls into question shared assumptions about the meaning of *diakonia* as lowly or humble service. *Called to Transformation* notes somewhat confusingly: "Reflecting on the essential relevance of biblical meaning of *diakonia* as the most ancient and binding heritage on Christian social service rooted in Biblical tradition, does not minimize the importance of other language traditions."[5] In fact, I argue that as "the most ancient and binding heritage," the meaning of *diakonia* in the Bible *does minimize* – at least to some extent – other interpretations of the term. Other language traditions based their conception of *diakonia* on biblical definitions that Collins's research has found to be erroneous, and thus they deserve to be minimized – at least for Christians who prioritize Scripture in theological reflection.

That said, it is also true that words change meaning over time and that Christian communities have grappled with this fact for millennia; other language traditions concerning the meaning of *diakonia* thus ought not be dismissed. According to Collins, early deacons may not have been seen first as persons engaged in what we might characterize as Christian social service, but in

---

[4] John N. Collins, *Diakonia: Re-Interpreting the Ancient Sources* (New York: Oxford University Press, 1990). For a comprehensive bibliography of Collins's work, see John N. Collins, *Diakonia Studies: Critical Issues in Ministry* (New York: Oxford University Press, 2014), 265–68.
[5] WCC and ACT Alliance, *Called to Transformation*, 43.

subsequent centuries deacons came to be understood in that way, such that the earlier meaning of the *diakon-* words faded and their identity became more exclusively associated with the nature of their work (social service) rather than the nature of their relationship with ecclesial authority as a go-between or emissary.

It is also important to acknowledge, as do the writers of *Called to Transformation*, that there is ample evidence in the New Testament of Jesus modelling a way of ministry that is selfless, gentle, and humble, even if that was not a constitutive part of the field of meaning of *diakonia* and its cognates, as Collins argued. The famous hymn in Philippians of Jesus not considering "equality with God something to be grasped" (Phil 2:6, NRSVUE), Jesus pointing to a child as an example of discipleship (Matt 18:3), and Jesus' own foot-washing actions in the upper room (John 13:1–17) are three obvious instances of how Christians are called to go about ministry. The ancient etymology of a single family of words is not sufficient grounding – although it is important – for theological reflection on ministry today.

The value of Collins's linguistic work with *diakonia* can be better understood by comparing it to etymological insights gained from another ancient biblical term that has likewise lost some of its earlier meaning. One of the more dramatic examples of a shift in meaning of a biblical term from the ancient world to today is in the use of the Greek term *kyrios*, which is translated as "Lord" in modern English Bibles. Modern ears hear the assertion "Jesus is Lord" (Rom 10:9, NRSVUE) in a strikingly different way than first-century Greek and Hebrew speakers. Today, we identify this assertion as one of several titles for Jesus that Christian communities routinely utilize. But for first-century Hebrew speakers accustomed to speaking of Jesus as Messiah, the use of this Greek term for Lord, *kyrios*, because of its association with pagan cult divinities, must have been challenging to accept. Greek-speaking Christians, however, needed this term to make a connection in their own hearts and minds to the Christian concept of the divine, even though it was originally associated with pagan thought patterns and practice. Hebrew-speaking followers of Jesus who were part of the Greek-speaking Jewish Jesus community doubtless would have helped them gradually to see that Jesus was not just one of many deities in a pagan pantheon of gods and that the use of *kyrios* did not suggest that.

When considering the term *diakonia*, I believe Christians have a similar – albeit less dramatic and weighty – challenge. Most Christians in North America, if they know the word *diakonia* at all in church contexts, will make a connection to *diakonia* that is like that found in European languages where it is equated with the idea of Christian social service. That is the inherited cultural association Europeans and some North Americans have for the term, much like first-century Greek-speaking Christians had with *kyrios* as a term associated with a pagan pantheon of deities.[6] *Called to Transformation*, Collins, and other biblical scholars are introducing a corrective to an inherited cultural assumption that

---

[6] This and similar necessary translation challenges for the Christian church are discussed in Andrew F. Walls, *The Missionary Movement in Christian History: Studies in the Transmission of Faith* (Maryknoll, NY: Orbis, 1996), 34.

diakonia should be equated with Christian social service, suggesting that the concept of go-between or emissarial relationship should receive more attention instead. Just like early Greek-speaking Christians' experience in understanding *kyrios*, we also have other biblical examples of what ministry looked like for Jesus and the early disciples, such that we are not dependent on a single word but rather many examples of biblical storytelling and church teaching about ministry.

When teaching prospective deacons about their calling, I do not assume, as the writers of *Called to Transformation* suggested, that our previous ideas about the diaconate or *diakonia* are "complementary" with newer insights from biblical scholarship.[7] In my view, even thirty years after the publication of Collins's research, a corrective is still required. I believe we should encourage one another to hold these ideas together and gradually to seek a kind of synthesis that may minimize *but should not dismiss* linguistic traditions that equate *diakonia* with social service.

Conceptually, I propose a dynamic heuristic model for thinking about deacons and their vocations that may be visualized as an ellipse, which – for the geometrically uninitiated – is defined as an elongated circle with two gravitational centers. The gravitational centers are the "social service" and the "emissarial" foci of meaning for *diakonia*. In Figure 4.1, I depict the "emissarial" identity as having a larger gravitational center. I believe this is helpful to counter the misinterpretation of the biblical meaning of *diakonia* and to promote critical inquiry into the inherited cultural assumptions about *diakonia* that most Christians today have from nineteenth-century diaconal expressions. Discourse about *diakonia* could be seen as constituting the various orbital paths one could take in lesser or greater relationship with the two gravitational centers. I believe this is how a great deal of the conversation about *diakonia* unfolds today and is even exhibited in *Called to Transformation*. While this document acknowledges the importance of Collins's research, it mostly emphasizes the now-traditional understanding of *diakonia* as lowly, humble, social service. Both understandings are "in play" in the document, but these differing conceptions of *diakonia* are not always explicitly highlighted by the authors. I next explore in greater detail the nature of this "elliptical reasoning" for what it might contribute to our understanding of the diaconate.

---

[7] WCC and ACT Alliance, *Called to Transformation*, 43.

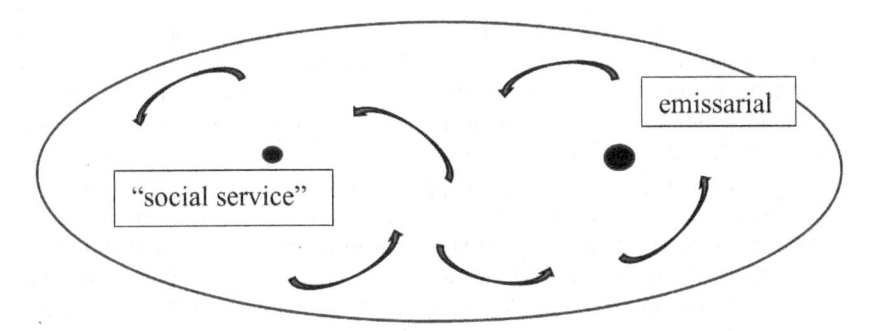

Figure 4.1: Gravitational Centers of Meaning for Diakonia

Diakonia as Social Service

The genesis for understanding *diakonia* as social service mostly comes from interpreting the choosing of the seven in Acts 6 and the tendency of deacons (not known as such in Acts 6) to be associated by the fourth century – at least sometimes – with the imagery of the basin and towel.[8] The understanding of a deacon's vocation to be focused on humble, loving service found expression in Luther's and Calvin's ecclesiology as well.[9] In the nineteenth century, the association between deacons and social welfare work was strengthened further by the work of Theodor Fliedner and Johann Wichern in their work among the poor, which Wichern famously called the church's "Inner Mission."

A one-to-one correspondence developed between deacons' work and loving, humble service such that biblical terms for ministry (*diakonia*, *diakonos*, and so on) similarly took on a strong social service meaning in German and other European languages. Collins identified the 1923 doctoral dissertation by Wilhelm Brandt entitled *Diakonie in das Neue Testament* as the academic source that equated *diakonia* with lowly Christian service in academic circles.[10] During World War II, the diaconal movement in Germany largely acquiesced to the demands of the Nazi Party; diaconal workers were, by definition, humble servants after all. Friedrich von Bodelschwingh (1877–1946) was a noteworthy exception to this in his work to save the aged and mentally ill from being classified as *lebensunwertes Leben* (lives unworthy of life), and he was killed by the Hitler regime.[11] (My own great-grandmother, Marie Stümpfig, who was severely mentally ill during the war, was so classified and killed.)

---

[8] R. Hugh Connolly, *Didascalia Apostolorum: The Syriac Version Translated and Accompanied by the Verona Latin Fragments* (Oxford: Clarendon, 1969), 148–50.

[9] Jeannine E. Olson, *One Ministry Many Roles: Deacons and Deaconesses Through the Centuries* (St. Louis: Concordia, 1992), 99–118.

[10] Collins, *Diakonia*, 6.

[11] Theodor Strohm, *Diakonie im 'Dritten Reich'* (Heidelberg: Heidelberger Verlaganstalt, 1990); Kjell Nordstokke, "The Study of Diakonia as an Academic Discipline," in *Diakonia as Christian Social Practice: An Introduction*, ed. Dietrich et al. (Eugene, OR: Wipf & Stock, 2014).

In the 1980s, a generally subservient understanding of *diakonia* in northern European languages began to be modified somewhat around the concept of "prophetic diakonia" with an effort to infuse a stronger ecclesial dimension into the understanding and practice of *diakonia*.[12] Jürgen Moltmann was one prominent theologian who engaged in theological reflection around the concept of *diakonia* in this period, seeking to apply insights from liberation theology.[13]

Prominent centers of study around *diakonia*, mostly understood as social service, have been established in several European countries. The Institute for the Study of Christian Social Service at the University of Heidelberg is perhaps the most long-standing and influential of these institutes.[14] Some of these institutes have master's-level degree programmes, which acquaint students with European traditions concerning *diakonia*.[15] It is important to ask, in the North American context, whether this language would be helpful and for whom.

Diakonia as Emissarial Activity or Go-Between

The renegotiating of the concept of *diakonia* to be more liberative and prophetic in the 1980s from Moltmann's scholarship was further supported by Collins's groundbreaking linguistic study of 1990. The differences between the older understanding of *diakon-* words and the newer interpretation may be succinctly expressed by comparing the definitions of the term in Bauer's Greek–English Lexicon in the second edition with the third edition, which draws directly from Collins's work.[16] (See Figure 4.2.)

---

[12] Klaus Poser, *Diakonia 2000: Called to be Neighbours, Official Report, WCC World Consultation Inter-Church Aid, Refugee and World Service, Larnaca, 1986* (Geneva: WCC Publications, 1986).

[13] Jürgen Moltmann, *Diakonie im Horizont des Reiches Gottes* (Neukirchen-Vluyn: Neukirchener, 1984).

[14] Das Diakoniewissenschaftliche Institut, Universität Heidelberg, https://www.dwi.uni-heidelberg.de/institut/.

[15] For example, VID Specialized University in Oslo, Norway, https://www.vid.no/en/. See chapters by Dyrstad and Leis-Peters in this volume.

[16] Figure 4.2 is a much-abbreviated and slightly edited depiction of an extensive comparison in two editions of a Greek–English lexicon, which also contains definitions of other *diakon-* cognates such as *diakonia* and *diakonos*. For serious examination of these definitions, consult: Walter Bauer, *A Greek–English Lexicon of the New Testament and Other Early Christian Literature* (Chicago: University of Chicago Press, 1979), 184; Frederick W. Danker, ed., *A Greek–English Lexicon of the New Testament and Other Early Christian Literature*, 3rd ed. (Chicago: University of Chicago Press, 2000), 229. See also Paula Gooder, "Diakonia in the New Testament: A Dialogue with John N. Collins," *Ecclesiology* 3, no. 1 (2006): 46–47.

Comparison of Definitions of *Diakoneo* in the New Testament Bauer's Greek–English Lexicon	
second edition (1979)	third edition (2000)
1) Wait on someone at table.	1) To function as an intermediary, act as a go-between/agent, be at one's service with intermediary function either expressed or implied.
2) Serve generally, of services of any kind.	2) To perform obligations, without focus on intermediary function.
3) Care for, take care of.	3) To meet an immediate need, help.
4) Help, support someone.	4) To carry out official duties, minister. Rendering of specific assistance, aid, support (Acts 6:1); send someone something for support (Acts 11:29).
5) Of the ecclesiastical office serve as deacon.	5) Acts 6:2 poses a special problem: care for, take care of … "look after tables" can be understood of serving food at tables … but it is improbable that some widows would be deprived of food at a communal meal. The term diakonia (verse 1) more probably refers to administrative responsibility, one of whose aspects is concern for widows without specifying the kind of assistance that is allotted.

Figure 4.2: Comparison of Definitions of Diakoneo in the New Testament

Three insights are most critical in this shift of *diakon-* word definitions in the New Testament.[17] First, there has been a significant change in understanding these terms for ministry, such that their field of meaning is increasingly focused on intermediary or emissarial relationships of persons and less on the caring, ethical nature of the acts performed, such as in taking care of or helping someone. It is the relationship with and to the church that is critical to recover here, *not* the officious status that may be associated with terms such as emissary or ambassador.[18] Ministry is something that is given to someone by the church;

---

[17] I have only included the verb *diakoneo* in Figure 4.2, but similar contrasts are evident in related terms *diakonos* and *diakonia*.
[18] John N. Collins, *Deacons and the Church: Making Connections Between Old and New* (Harrisburg, PA: Morehouse, 2002).

thus, calling something "my ministry" is, strictly speaking, an oxymoron.[19] Ministry is something that the church may give to an individual (whether lay or ordained) as a public expression of the church's mission in the world. Something could be designated a ministry through an informal public approval or through a service of ordination; the point is that the work is in some way accountable to the church. Such an emphasis on accountability is something that I see evident in the crafting of *Called to Transformation*. The document defines *diakonia* as "the responsible service of the gospel by deeds and by words performed by Christians in response to the needs of people."[20] I interpret the use of the term "responsible" as a way of accentuating some form of accountability to the church for the service that is done.

Second, as already suggested, the revised definition of *diakon-* terms introduces a greater focus on the missionary meaning of the term, such that *diakonos* (minister) is more closely related to *apostolos* (messenger) than our previous understanding of *diakon-* terms have tended to permit, with its focus on lowly, humble service.[21] Some have argued that the *diakon-* terms still maintain a sense of menial service in some New Testament passages. However, even when menial service is emphasized as part of a minister's vocation, it is still very much related to the minister's emissarial relationship to an authority – and ultimately to Christ.[22] At a personal level, a more apostolic understanding of a minister's vocation may guard against an unhealthy victim complex, whereby one perceives oneself as a burned-out servant of the people more than a sent emissary of God. I believe that the old understanding of *diakonia* and the attendant "servant leader" language is especially vulnerable to such a distortion of ministry – especially if it is left ambiguous whose servant one is.[23] Instead, what is emphasized in the revised understanding of *diakonia* – and, of course, elsewhere in the New Testament – is that one can be radically free to perform menial and self-sacrificial missionary service precisely because of the "high calling" and close emissarial relationship and friendship one can have as a *diakonos* or minister of Jesus.

In a similar way, the definition of *diakonia* as humble, lowly service has contributed to wider problematic ecclesial self-understandings. The missionary impulse of the reign of God does not consist in a timid humility of letting the world set the agenda, as the World Council of Churches proclaimed in Uppsala, Sweden in 1968.[24] In this appeal, the WCC was motivated in part by a well-

---

[19] Paul Avis, *A Ministry Shaped by Mission* (London: T & T Clark, 2005), 46.
[20] WCC and ACT Alliance, *Called to Transformation*, 16.
[21] Carl E. Braaten, *The Apostolic Imperative: Nature and Aim of the Church's Mission and Ministry* (Minneapolis: Augsburg Fortress, 1985); Walter Schmithals, *The Office of Apostle in the Early Church* (Nashville: Abingdon, 1969).
[22] Gooder, "Diakonia in the New Testament," 46.
[23] Avery Dulles, *Models of the Church*, expanded edition (New York: Doubleday, 1987); Mitch McCrimmon, "Why Servant Leadership is a Bad Idea," 16 August 2010, http://www.management-issues.com/opinion/6015/why-servant-leadership-is-a-bad-idea/. See chapter by Yip in this volume.
[24] *The Uppsala Report 1968: Official Report of the Fourth Assembly of the World Council of Churches, Uppsala, July 4–20 1968* (Geneva: WCC, 1968), 39.

intentioned desire to correct the abuses of ecclesiastical hubris. The diaconate was seen as a vehicle to accomplish this in the church.[25] Indeed, ecclesiastical hubris must be rejected always and everywhere, but in doing so one must not be dismissive of the church.[26] The embrace of a revised definition for *diakon-* terms, while of course not refuting true Christian humility, may help the diaconate (and the church as a whole) embrace the radical missionary values of God's reign, whereby the whole church brings the whole Christ to the whole world.[27] Deacons, deaconesses, and missionaries cross boundaries with and for the Gospel; they do not follow an ambiguous or secular "world" that calls the shots for its lowly servants.[28]

A third insight that may be garnered from this new definition of *diakon-* terms is best framed in a negative way: Ministry is not synonymous with activities of Christian discipleship. There has been a rather widespread ecumenical tendency since the 1950s to expand the meaning of ministry to the service of all baptized believers.[29] This tendency resulted in nearly everything being identified as a ministry with little left to be considered a matter of Christian discipleship. Loving one's neighbor, caring for the poor, and proclaiming the Gospel of Jesus Christ are activities all Christians ought to do as a matter of their discipleship and are not necessarily ministries – *although they could be*. As Avis argued, "all baptized believers are *potential* ministers" even if not all Christians are, by virtue of their baptism, ministers.[30] As leaders accountable to the church, missionaries and others are called to encourage and support the serious discipleship of others, whether their activities are recognized by the church (and therefore ministry) or not.[31]

Finally, I believe the new interpretive direction elucidated by Collins is rich with missiological opportunity, and it is here where I find the diaconate to have

---

[25] Margret Morche, *Zur Erneuerung des Ständigen Diakonats: Ein Beitrag zur Geschichte unter besonderer Berücksichtigung der Arbeit des Internationalen Diakonatszentrums in seiner Verbindung zum Deutschen Caritasverband* (Freiburg im Breisgau: Lambertus, 1996).

[26] Robert Hannaford, "The Representative and Relational Nature of Ministry and the Renewal of the Diaconate," in *The Ministry of the Deacon 2: Ecclesiological Explorations*, ed. Borgegård et al. (Uppsala: Nordic Ecumenical Council, 2000).

[27] Of course, in a very important sense it is not the church that brings Christ to places and people where he is totally absent. Nor is it the case that the church is equated with God's reign. The church participates in God's mission through Christ and in the power of the Holy Spirit. Yet Christians affirm that the church is also far from being merely incidental in accomplishing God's mission in the world.

[28] The apostle Paul's description of himself and others as servants or slaves (*doulos*) of Christ (for example, Phil 1:1) highlights an honorific element alongside the menial in a similar way to the revised definition of *diakon-* terms.

[29] John N. Collins, "Ordained and Other Ministries: Making a Difference," *Ecclesiology* 3, no. 1 (2006): 11–32.

[30] Avis, *A Ministry Shaped by Mission*, 52, emphasis added.

[31] Admittedly, denominations differ on this point. Some traditions stress that all the baptized are ministers. Others are more likely to follow Avis's idea here, describing the baptized as *potential* ministers.

the most promise. Collins's paraphrased interpretation of the choosing of the seven in Acts 6 expresses this most poignantly.

> The Greek-speaking members of the community complained against those who spoke Aramaic that their housebound widows were being overlooked in the great preaching (*diakonia*) that was going on day by day in the environs of the Temple. So the Twelve summoned the whole complement of the disciples and said: "We cannot possibly break off our public proclamation before the huge crowds in the Temple to carry out a ministry (*diakonein*) in the households of these Greek-speaking widows. Brothers, you will have to choose seven men from your own ethnic group who are fully respected, empowered by the Spirit, and equipped for the task. We will then appoint them to the role that needs to be filled. That will mean that the Twelve can get on with attending to worship in the Temple and to our apostolic ministry (*diakonia*) of proclaiming the Word there."[32]

The promise of the diaconate that this story most stirs in my imagination is the way countless bilingual and bicultural Christians are today working in a manner like that of "the seven" in this story. The Gospel of Jesus Christ is good news precisely for the way that it always and everywhere must make room for people who have been relegated to the margins due to linguistic, economic, or other social factors. The go-between, emissarial relationship authority given to the seven is important. What the seven did after the events of Acts 6 illustrates the diversity of ministries that are needed today. Stephen became a preacher to the religiously powerful of his day. Philip became an evangelist to a eunuch from another continent on a dusty road. We do not know what the other five did, but I like to imagine that their work was equally creative and prophetic.

Conclusion

Our current understanding and practice of *diakonia* – understood both as religiously motivated social service and as a Greek term in the New Testament for ministry as go-between or emissarial activity – does not seem to be moving very quickly toward an easy resolution. People who speak about *diakonia* seem to be at different places on our ellipse, trying to make sense of one another's orbital paths as best they can. Whether this ambiguity will soon be resolved is impossible to predict. Until then, it is important for deacons, presbyters, and students preparing for these and other vocations at least to be aware that there is ambiguity here so that conversations about *diakonia*, institutional partnerships, and ecumenical relationships might be initiated or strengthened and not side-tracked by misunderstanding.

Persons committed to the diaconate need to grow in their understanding of diaconal studies as it develops throughout the world, especially regarding how biblical and patristic studies are shedding light on this topic. Diaconal education has tended to focus on practical ministry endeavors over theory or careful linguistic study of biblical texts. As we look forward to more serious engagement in North America with the field of diaconal studies, it will be important to have

---

[32] Collins, *Deacons and the Church*, 58.

more members of the diaconate engage in robust biblical scholarship about the biblical meaning of *diakonia* and how key texts have been interpreted over the centuries. It would be a tragically ironic thing indeed for ministry to be stymied because of confusion over *diakonia*.

Works Cited

Avis, Paul. *A Ministry Shaped by Mission*. London: T & T Clark, 2005.

———. "Editorial: Wrestling with the Diaconate." *Ecclesiology* 5 (2009): 3.

Bauer, Walter. *A Greek–English Lexicon of the New Testament and Other Early Christian Literature*. Chicago: University of Chicago Press, 1979.

Braaten, Carl E. *The Apostolic Imperative: Nature and Aim of the Church's Mission and Ministry*. Minneapolis: Augsburg Fortress, 1985.

Collins, John N. *Deacons and the Church: Making Connections Between Old and New*. Harrisburg, PA: Morehouse, 2002.

———. *Diakonia: Re-Interpreting the Ancient Sources*. New York: Oxford University Press, 1990.

———. *Diakonia Studies: Critical Issues in Ministry*. New York: Oxford University Press, 2014.

———. "Ordained and Other Ministries: Making a Difference." *Ecclesiology* 3, no. 1 (2006): 11–32.

Connolly, R. Hugh. *Didascalia Apostolorum: The Syriac Version Translated and Accompanied by the Verona Latin Fragments*. Oxford: Clarendon, 1969.

Danker, Frederick William, ed. *A Greek–English Lexicon of the New Testament and Other Early Christian Literature*. 3rd ed. Chicago: University of Chicago Press, 2000.

Dulles, Avery. *Models of the Church*. Expanded edition. New York: Doubleday, 1987.

Gooder, Paula. "Diakonia in the New Testament: A Dialogue with John N. Collins." *Ecclesiology* 3, no. 1 (2006): 46–47.

Hannaford, Robert. "The Representative and Relational Nature of Ministry and the Renewal of the Diaconate." In *The Ministry of the Deacon 2: Ecclesiological Explorations*, edited by Gunnel Borgegård, Olav Fanuelsen, and Christine Hall, 239–79. Uppsala: Nordic Ecumenical Council, 2000.

Hartley, Benjamin L. "Connected and Sent Out: Implications of New Biblical Research for the United Methodist Diaconate." *Quarterly Review* 24, no. 4 (2004): 367–80.

———. "Deacons as Emissary-Servants: A Liturgical Theology." *Quarterly Review* 19, no. 4 (1999): 372–86.

———. *An Empirical Look at the Ecumenical Diaconate in the United States*. Monograph Series No. 16. Providence, RI: North American Association for the Diaconate, 2003.

———. "UMC Deacons at 25: Rethinking Deacons' Education." Mission and Methodism, 2 June 2021. https://missionandmethodism.net/2021/06/02/umc-deacons-at-25-rethinking-deacons-education/.

Hartley, Benjamin L. and Paul E. Van Buren. *The Deacon: Ministry Through Words of Faith and Acts of Love*. Nashville: General Board of Higher Education and Ministry, The United Methodist Church, 1999.

The Institute for the Study of Christian Social Service. https://www.dwi.uni-heidelberg.de/institut/.

McCrimmon, Mitch. "Why Servant Leadership is a Bad Idea." 16 August 2010. http://www.management-issues.com/opinion/6015/why-servant-leadership-is-a-bad-idea/.

Moltmann, Jürgen. *Diakonie im Horizont des Reiches Gottes*. Neukirchen-Vluyn: Neukirchener, 1984.

Morche, Margret. *Zur Erneuerung des Ständigen Diakonats: Ein Beitrag zur Geschichte unter besonderer Berücksichtigung der Arbeit des Internationalen Diakonatszentrums in seiner Verbindung zum Deutschen Caritasverband*. Freiburg im Breisgau: Lambertus, 1996.

Nordstokke, Kjell. "The Study of Diakonia as an Academic Discipline." In *Diakonia as Christian Social Practice: An Introduction*, edited by Stephanie Dietrich, Knud Jørgensen, Kari Karsrud Korslien and Kjell Nordstokke, 46–61. Eugene, OR: Wipf & Stock, 2014.

Olson, Jeannine E. *One Ministry Many Roles: Deacons and Deaconesses Through the Centuries*. St. Louis: Concordia, 1992.

Poser, Klaus. *Diakonia 2000: Called to be Neighbours, Official Report, WCC World Consultation Inter-Church Aid, Refugee and World Service, Larnaca, 1986*. Geneva: WCC Publications, 1986.

Schmithals, Walter. *The Office of Apostle in the Early Church*. Nashville: Abingdon, 1969.

Strohm, Theodor. *Diakonie im "Dritten Reich"*. Heidelberg: Heidelberger Verlaganstalt, 1990.

The Uppsala Report 1968: Official Report of the Fourth Assembly of the World Council of Churches, Uppsala, July 4–20, 1968. Geneva: WCC, 1968.

Walls, Andrew F. *The Missionary Movement in Christian History: Studies in the Transmission of Faith*. Maryknoll, NY: Orbis, 1996.

World Council of Churches and ACT Alliance. *Called to Transformation: Ecumenical Diakonia*. Geneva: WCC Publications, 2022. https://www.oikoumene.org/resources/publications/ecumenical-diakonia.

Chapter 5

Strengthening *Diakonia* for a Thriving Church

Margaret Ann Crain

The work of *diakonia* has been part of the mission of Christianity since the time of Jesus. Jesus, of course, was enacting values already well established by Jewish tradition and sacred texts. He and his disciples fed hungry people, healed sick people, and openly challenged the oppressive Roman Empire. The passage in Acts 6:1–6, does not use the title *deacon*, but shows the fledgling Christian community tending to the widows, both Hellenist and Hebrew, making sure that resources of food were justly distributed. The author of Acts uses words with the *daikon-* root to describe the "distribution of food to needy widows" and "the activity of serving this food at tables" as well as "the prime responsibility of the Twelve in 'the ministry' of preaching the word."[1] Since then, leaders of *diakonia* have taken a variety of forms and titles: diaconal minister, deaconess, and deacon. Ecumenical discussions about diaconal ministry since World War II have revolved primarily around the centrality of the diaconal mission and the leaders needed for it. Should the leaders of diaconal ministries be lay or ordained? Should they be subordinate to bishop or presbyter, and where should their ministry be focused? What is their proper place in the liturgy?

This chapter argues that the ministry of the diaconate is central to the mission of the Christian church and that ordaining diaconal leaders clarifies the mission. In my tradition, The United Methodist Church (UMC), both deacons and presbyters (called elders in Methodist denominations) are ordained to Word and Service, representing complementary features of these aspects of mission. Elders have responsibility for liturgical leadership to inspire the laity to join with God in God's work in the world. Deacons lead the church's effort to bring love and justice to all creation through equipping and leading laity. Elders and deacons meet at the altar, incarnationally representing two aspects of the mission of the church: to proclaim and teach the Gospel and to join with God in bringing the kingdom of God to fulfilment. The present ordering of ministry in the UMC serves as a case study. While current forms of the diaconate are theoretically well conceived, this chapter describes some of the unresolved issues hindering its full potential.

Theological Conceptualization

In the late nineteenth century, the deaconess movement was growing and clamoring for a place in Christianity. A robust deaconess movement evolved in

---

[1] John N. Collins, *Deacons and the Church: Making Connections Between Old and New* (Harrisburg, PA: Morehouse, 2002), 50.

Germany and in North America. For instance, The Methodist Episcopal Church formally approved the office of deaconess in 1888. This was a lay office for women, and its mission was primarily located in urban settlement houses. During the twentieth century, *diakon-* offices evolved in two steps in the UMC: (1) through the consecrated office of diaconal minister begun in 1976 and (2) through the order of ordained deacon established in 1996. The 1996 General Conference instituted two orders of ordained ministry, envisioned as equal partners with separate identities. The elder would continue its traditional pastoral or presbyter role. The second order, the deacon, would lead the church in *diakonia*. The theology was based on the baptismal call to the Way of Jesus. The Christian Way is for all, not just the ordained, and the Way of Jesus seeks to bring God's beloved community to all creation.

The creation of an ordained deacon (permanent, not transitional) was the result of the evolution of three theological foci: ministry, mission, and ordination. First, as late as 1964 the Methodist Church maintained that *ministry* was a term limited to the work of ordained elders. That restrictive meaning was explicit in the denomination's book of law. Just four years later, the General Conference officially adopted the understanding that baptism initiates a call to ministry derived from the ministry of Jesus. All baptized Christians are to love God and neighbor. By 1972, the church stated that "All Christians are called to ministry."[2] This broadened the understanding of ministry significantly and located it in both church and world. In addition, it reflected a Christology emphasizing the healing, reconciling, and feeding ministries of Jesus. All Christians are called to these ministries.

The second theological shift occurred in this church's understanding of its mission. The church's mission had been focused primarily on salvation and conversion of those who did not know Jesus. In practical terms, the emphasis was to build up the church. For several decades after World War II, that task was executed successfully. Sunday Schools, mission projects, colleges and universities, the church as institution, and church attendance were growing. With a broader understanding of ministry, the denominational mission statement grew more expansive. By 2016 it read, "to make disciples of Jesus Christ for the transformation of the world by proclaiming the good news of God's grace and by exemplifying Jesus' command to love God and neighbor, thus seeking the fulfillment of God's reign and realm in the world."[3] With these understandings of mission, ministry, and ordination, diaconal ministry emerges as a necessary part of the church, prompting questions such as: Why does the church exist? What is its purpose?

The purpose of the church is to form people who love God and love neighbor and who participate with God in bringing God's realm into this world.[4] In other

---

[2] *The Book of Discipline of The United Methodist Church 1972* (Nashville: United Methodist Publishing House, 1972), ¶301.

[3] *The Book of Discipline of The United Methodist Church 2016* (Nashville: United Methodist Publishing House, 2016), ¶121.

[4] Neighbor must be understood to include the whole created order. See chapter by Moore in this volume.

words, the mission is to incarnate the prayer, "Thy kingdom come, Thy will be done on earth, as it is in heaven." The transformation is toward a just society. A recent United Methodist document states that deacons enable "the church to engage the world with a heart of compassion and a prophetic longing for God's justice to prevail."[5] This grand vision echoes the expressed mission of this church to seek the transformation of the world. The UMC understands that its mission does not stop at the doors of the church. *Diakonia* is essential to this mission and central to being the church. What kind of leaders does the church need for this broader transformative mission? Answering this question required revisiting the UMC's understanding of ordination.

For centuries, ordination was reserved for the priestly work of sacrament, liturgy, and interpretation of the Word. The shorthand ordination questions in Methodism still reflect that understanding; a person discerning a call to ordination is asked, Are you called to preach? Are you called to sacramental ministry? If the answers are yes, the person is directed to the office of elder. While pastoral leaders for the church remain critically important in the formation of disciples today, other ordained leaders are needed for the work of transforming the world.

The Order of Ordained Deacon

The reconsideration of mission resulted in two actions related to ordination by the 1996 General Conference. The first was to discontinue the traditional Anglican two-step ordination practiced in most expressions of Methodism, with first ordination as a transitional deacon and final ordination as elder. In practice, the transitional deacon gave lip service to the work of *diakonia* but was more an apprenticeship for "full ordination" as elder. After years of debate, the United Methodist General Conference of 1996 approved two distinct, equal, and complementary ordained orders. Neither was subservient to the other. Nor were they intended to push laity into a subservient role. "The ministry of all Christians is complementary. No ministry is subservient to another. All United Methodists are summoned and sent by Christ to live and work together..."[6] The outcome was an order of deacons called to ministries of Word, Compassion, and Justice. The ministry of deacons focuses on equipping and leading laity into their role as transformative disciples. Deacons go between church and world, bringing the good news of the Gospel to the world and the concerns of the world back to the church. The transitional deacon was eliminated; the order of elder was defined by ministry of Word, Sacrament, and Order. Both orders are ordained to service. These definitions of orders of ordained ministry in the UMC continue to the present.

---

[5] Commission on the General Conference, The United Methodist Church, "Advance Daily Christian Advocate, Volume 2, Section 2, Reports and Proposed Legislation" (Nashville: United Methodist Publishing House, 2020), 1013, https://s3.amazonaws.com/Website_Properties/general-conference/2020/documents/ADCA-English-Vol-2-Sec-2.pdf.

[6] *The Book of Discipline of The United Methodist Church 2016*, ¶131.

Living into this new ordering of ministry was controversial. Many mourned the loss of the transitional deacon. Others saw ordination as reserved for those who preach and preside at the liturgy. More than a quarter century has passed. Deacons have been called, trained, tested, and ordained. Some have retired. The order of deacons is firmly established. The emphasis on deacons leading the people of God into their ministries in the world remains vital. Some deacons work primarily in the church or its agencies. They help prepare the people for their work in the world. Deacons are employed in the church as educators, musicians, retreat leaders, yoga instructors, pastoral visitors, preachers, artists, missionaries, administrators, counsellors, web designers, and many other roles that help the church equip its members for their ministries. Other deacons are primarily in the world, bringing compassion and justice into the contexts where they are sent. Deacons serve as doctors, nurses, lawyers, teachers, counsellors, chaplains, professors, therapists, coaches, artists, journalists, social workers, spiritual directors, and many other roles where they bring the values of compassion and justice to the world. Those whose work is in the secular world are also tasked with bringing the needs of the world back to the church so that it may respond. The breadth of vocations to which persons have been called as deacons continues to expand. There appears to be no limit to the places where deacons may join in the *missio Dei* on behalf of the church.

Boards of Ministry and bishops have all expanded their definition of the work of deacons. Deacons are engaged in so many kinds of ministry. Yet, candidates for deacon are still asked, Why do you need to be ordained to do this? Of course, one does not need to be ordained to be a teacher or nurse or spiritual director! But God calls people to these forms of ministry, and it is qualitatively different to answer that call as an ordained agent of Jesus Christ and his church. In addition, persons practicing these ministries are expected to bring the needs of the world back to the church, so that it may respond with compassion and help to bring justice to the places where injustices persist. Deacons symbolize the needs of the world as they assist elders in the liturgy and participate in offering the sacraments. The church needs deacons leading the people of God in ministries that embody the reality of the Gospel!

During the COVID-19 pandemic, congregations learned the hard way that their mission simply cannot remain in their buildings! As someone said during the pandemic, "The church is not closed. The church has temporarily left the building!" Much of the busy work that kept programmes going and buildings operating suddenly shut down. And the needs of people everywhere became powerfully apparent. Who better to lead us in responding to these needs than our deacons! The UMC declares, "The people of God, who are the church made visible in the world, must convince the world of the reality of the gospel, or leave it unconvinced."[7] The pandemic provided an opportunity to enact the Gospel by feeding people who had lost their jobs, teaching children whose schools were closed, housing unhoused persons in the empty church buildings, and reaching out to lonely shut-ins with phone calls and visits on the lawn. Deacons in our city helped the people be the church and organize these ministries.

---

[7] *The Book of Discipline of The United Methodist Church 2016*, ¶130.

In Nashville, Tennessee, two congregations came together and created a mission church called The Commons, a ministry for some of this city's most vulnerable people. They built a village of tiny houses in which vulnerable persons who had been unhoused could find safe shelter as they received medical treatment. They are cooperating with nonprofits to grow gardens, care for pets, feed people, and offer recovery groups. This is an inspiring implementation of the vision of the church's mission. Surely this project can convince the world of the reality of the Gospel. Four deacons and one pastor are leading The Commons. Missional imagination brought this to fruition.

The missional imagination of the elder, deacon, and lay leaders in the small suburban church that I attend tripled the space allocated to the food pantry and acquired refrigerators and freezers so that much more fresh food could be given to hungry neighbors who were suddenly unemployed. In addition, rooms were remodeled to accommodate transitional housing for unhoused persons as they prepared to qualify for permanent housing. Our deacon kept us informed about the needs that were multiplying all around us. Indeed, as the words of the song proclaim, "I am the church. You are the church. We are the church together. All of God's people, all around the world. Yes, we're the church together."[8] Together we found the resources to accomplish these projects.

Unresolved Issues Preventing the Full Potential of *Diakonia*

Ordaining deacons brings *diakonia* to the center of the mission of the church. This shift is a powerful sign of commitment to the task of bringing God's will to fruition. Our diaconal leaders are called, equipped, and set apart for this mission. However, the promise of the ordained deacon has not been fully realized in The United Methodist Church. In my observation, it has not been fully realized in any of the larger Christian denominations. What are some of the unresolved issues preventing its full realization?

First, diaconal leaders in every expression of the church lack critical mass; there are too few of us. The theory is that a group needs to represent about 20 percent of the whole to rise to a critical mass within a large body or institution. Without critical mass, a group can be ignored or invisible. Without critical mass, a group's work will not maintain itself. In many denominations, very few have been called and ordained as deacons. They are not visible. Many congregations have never seen or experienced the leadership of a deacon. There is simply not enough energy in the body to generate more deacons and more ministry.

While many United Methodist lay persons are doing creative work toward justice, few have seriously considered that God might be calling them to be ordained for this work. There is a qualitative difference in compassionately running a food bank to feed families and doing the same work as a deacon of the church, who not only feeds families but offers pastoral care and makes plain the unjust systems that leave families without enough food to eat. How wonderful it

---

[8] Richard K. Avery and Donald S. Marsh, "We Are the Church," in *The United Methodist Hymnal*, no. 558 (Nashville: United Methodist Publishing House, 1989).

would be if we had at least one ordained deacon in every congregation doing the work of compassion and justice in the community and also leading the congregation in its work of compassion and justice! The world could indeed be transformed! Many Western Protestant churches are large institutions. Diaconal leaders are not at a critical mass in any of them. We need more diaconal leaders to reach that mass. More deacons will generate more deacons.[9]

The second barrier to the full potential of diaconal ministries is a misunderstanding of the terms *deacon* and *diaconal* and their connection to service. The root of the word deacon is the Greek *diakonia*. Most English translations of the Bible use *servant* or *service* to translate *diakonia* from the Greek. Particularly in the United States of America, with our miserable legacy of the enslavement of peoples, the term servant is entwined with the connotation of slave. *Service* implies lack of agency, one who is "lesser than" or at the whim of the more powerful. Combining this legacy with the word *deacon* can result in a lack of empowerment. In practice, too many diaconals (deacons, deaconesses, diaconal ministers, and others) are convinced that to serve is to allow others to direct their ministry. We get confused about who we serve. We do not serve the senior pastor. We serve Christ. Theologically, *service* is the right word, but it comes with a lot of baggage and misunderstanding. It constantly requires interpretation. Furthermore, the Church is not willing to support diaconal leaders financially, limiting the freedom of the deacon to "engage the world with a heart of compassion and a prophetic longing for God's justice to prevail."[10] Prophetic justice work stirs up the systems that people are accustomed to and resistance follows. Sometimes this means that a United Methodist deacon becomes unemployed. Economic instability is the unfortunate result.

Recent scholarship provides guidance for interpreting *diakonia*. John N. Collins's extensive linguistic research revealed that "when ancient Greeks used these [*daikon-*] words they were never trying to express a notion of loving and caring service."[11] Thus, the document *Called to Transformation* states: "In ancient Greek, *diakonia* rather means an assignment, or a task, as messenger or go-between."[12] Deacons are agents of the community of the church, offering leadership in the congregation and in the wider community as an incarnated extension of the liturgy. The Eucharist bids us to "Pour out your Holy Spirit on us gathered here, and on these gifts of bread and wine ... By your Spirit make us one with Christ, one with each other, and one in ministry to all the world."[13] When the diaconal worker is present at the eucharistic table, they represent or

---

[9] The Roman Catholic Church has larger numbers of deacons in some areas, such as the archdiocese of Chicago, but their primary responsibility is liturgical. In addition, only men may be ordained as Roman Catholic deacons. Their wives complete the same training but are not allowed to be ordained.

[10] Commission on the General Conference, "Advance Daily Christian Advocate, Volume 2, Section 2," 1013.

[11] Collins, *Deacons and the Church*, 13.

[12] World Council of Churches and ACT Alliance, *Called to Transformation: Ecumenical Diakonia* (Geneva: WCC Publications, 2022), 44.

[13] *The United Methodist Hymnal* (Nashville: United Methodist Publishing House, 1989), 10.

incarnate that ministry to all the world. They go between church and world, seeking to confront the oppressive powers and transform the world through compassion and justice.

Third, residual patriarchal systems continue to limit the power of *diakonia*. Since diaconal ministries are overwhelmingly female (except in the Roman Catholic Church, where only men may qualify as deacons), the office tends to be seen as subordinate or inferior.[14] I saw patriarchy repeatedly expressed as pressure on young men who were gifted, prepared, and called to diaconal ministry. When they presented themselves as candidates for deacon, they were pushed to consider becoming an elder instead. "Don't you really want to be an elder? You have great gifts for ministry." The unsaid implication was, you are too smart or too skilled or too promising to waste your gifts in the (inferior) order of deacon. The opposite happened to young women who offered themselves as candidates for ordination as elder and who were often asked if they had considered the order of deacon. The unsaid implication was that women would be more comfortable in the service side of leadership. Both biases are rooted in that residual patriarchal assumption that men should lead the church in the role of elder. In addition, candidates for deacon are often challenged about why they need to be ordained to lead ministries of compassion and justice. That, too, relates to the patriarchal practices of ordaining men to preside over sacraments: limiting ordination to sacramental presidency downplays the importance of all the other aspects of a call to elder. Patriarchal values are expressed financially too. Deacons are paid less than elders and are too often seen as expendable. When a congregation faces financial stress, it is the deacon position that is eliminated first.

Patriarchal values made diaconal ministry particularly attractive to white, middle-class women in the mainstream Protestant churches of North America. White women who were economically able were attracted to diaconal offices, where they could use their gifts and talents to make a difference. US culture in the 1950s promoted an ideal of women as homemakers and men as financial supporters. This was only practical for some families, but it was a powerful ideal. Women became more and more restive, prompted by the women's liberation movement and feminist theologies. They sought ways to use their intellect, skills, and energies outside the home. The church was available, and they were called and equipped. In some communions, women were willing to serve in non-stipendiary positions because they could afford it. In the UMC, many of the early consecrated diaconal ministers (a lay office instituted in 1978) were women who were willing to work in the church part time and for small salaries. A supportive spouse usually made that arrangement workable. To meet requirements for consecration, they took graduate-level seminary courses, eager to learn but willing to serve with little sense of their own authority. Those same women

---

[14] Approximately 85 percent of deacons in the UMC are female.

learned, gained confidence, claimed agency in their ministries, and eventually became some of the strongest advocates for an ordained diaconate.[15]

In most expressions of Protestant Christianity (and in the Roman Catholic Church), candidates for the diaconate are educated in diocesan programmes, separate from those who are preparing for the priestly role. The United Methodist Church went against the prevailing practice. Deacon candidates are educated alongside those preparing to be ordained as elders in our graduate schools. The norm is for both deacons and elders to earn a theological master's degree to qualify for ordination. Because people seeking ordination are studying together in a graduate programme, they learn to appreciate the distinct calls to both elder and deacon and are better prepared to complement one another in leading the church. Slowly but surely, patriarchy is losing its grip.

A fourth barrier limiting *diakonia* in the white-majority mainline denominations is systemic racism and the dominance of white culture. Systemic racism permeates our identification of persons who are called to ordination and to which order. Anecdotal evidence indicates that the vetting processes are making it very difficult for persons of color to be approved for ordination in the UMC. Nevertheless, God calls diverse people to the work of compassion and justice, and their ministry settings are very diverse. But the order of deacons in the UMC is predominantly white. This should not be surprising. Why would persons of color choose a second layer of marginalization for themselves? Persons of color might not choose an order that is misunderstood and oppressed within the church. Supporting deacons of color who have insights and truths to share must become a priority as denominations continue to address the systemic racism that infects them.

A fifth barrier for a strong diaconate is lack of missional imagination and financial commitment. The church lacks the willingness to really take on ministries of justice. In the United States, we have this great devotion to the notion of the separation of church and state. For many people this means that the church should never do anything "political." Thus, churches turn a blind eye to many injustices. During the pandemic, when the horrific news of the murder of George Floyd surfaced, our pastor, our deacon, and others in the congregation spoke out to affirm the #BlackLivesMatter movement. Within days, two adult Sunday School classes walked out *en masse* and moved their membership to a church down the road. It was "too political," they said; and "the church should not be political." But justice is part of the political landscape, and the law of the land often needs to be evaluated to make it more just.

Too often we settle for ministries of compassion and avoid the hard work of addressing injustice. We do not confront the white supremacy that dominates much of evangelical and mainline Protestantism. We give food to those who are hungry but do nothing about the systems that do not support a living wage for workers. Meanwhile, the Earth is heating up. The church is allocating little of its resources to combat climate change or to draw attention to eco-justice. Every

---

[15] The effort to accept an ordained permanent diaconate in the UMC took twenty years. Ordained deacons are defined as distinct, complementary, and equal to ordained elders, combating the sexist, oppressive practices that beset the lay office of diaconal minister.

congregation could call a deacon to lead in these issues, both for the congregation's practices and for the community in which it resides. The problems created by global warming, such as the increase of extreme weather events, are experienced far more by those who are unhoused or those who labor outdoors. In times of excessive heat, people of means may travel to the mountains or remain in their air-conditioned spaces. What is the church doing to address this injustice? Deacons need to be deployed to lead us in this work, and this will require a commitment of resources.

The Promise of *Diakonia*

When the schools that train clergy for the congregations in North America include *diakonia* as part of the curriculum, some of the barriers to full realization of the promise of diaconal ministry will begin to recede. Since 1996, deacons and elders have been educated side by side in the graduate schools approved by the UMC. The educational requirements are similar. Students experiencing a call to deacon learn alongside students experiencing a call to elder. They learn to honor the differences and to appreciate the contributions each one can make to the flourishing of the church. I long for that parity and appreciation to be part of other communions. All clergy will benefit from diaconal studies, as that is a major portion of the mission of the church.

The promise of *diakonia* will remain unrealized without a commitment of resources. Jerome Del Pino, a former denominational executive, told me: "I wish that every conference could claim that they've got deacons who are assigned to city councils or state legislatures. Deacons should be appointed to be in the public square and in the centers of power where the questions of justice are addressed."[16] Meanwhile, the UMC is consumed with disunity and survival. I believe that this preoccupation must cease. Instead, we must listen for God's nudges and invitations to join in the *missio Dei*. The church will thrive or collapse, but it will have pleased God.

Revitalization of the church calls for strengthening the diaconate, the clergy order focused on equipping and leading all the baptized in their ministry in the world. If the church exists to help us love God and love neighbor, we need both elders and deacons as ordained leaders. We need leaders who are more focused on helping us to know and love God and other leaders who are more focused on helping us to know and love all our neighbors, including the whole of creation. All clergy need theological education so that they can discern the right ways for those things to happen. We need to ordain both deacons and elders for that ministry, and neither is more important than the other. In fact, without both missional emphases, the church is incomplete.

---

[16] Personal conversation, 14 February 2021.

Works Cited

Avery, Richard K., and Donald S. Marsh. "We Are the Church." In *The United Methodist Hymnal*, no. 558. Nashville: United Methodist Publishing House, 1989.

The Book of Discipline of The United Methodist Church 1972. Nashville: United Methodist Publishing House, 1972.

The Book of Discipline of The United Methodist Church 2016. Nashville: United Methodist Publishing House, 2016.

Collins, John N. *Deacons and the Church: Making Connections Between Old and New*. Harrisburg, PA: Morehouse, 2002.

Commission on the General Conference, The United Methodist Church. "Advance Daily Christian Advocate, Volume 2, Section 2, Reports and Proposed Legislation." Nashville: United Methodist Publishing House, 2020. https://s3.amazonaws.com/Website_Properties/general-conference/2020/documents/ADCA-English-Vol-2-Sec-2.pdf.

The United Methodist Hymnal. Nashville: United Methodist Publishing House, 1989.

World Council of Churches and ACT Alliance. *Called to Transformation: Ecumenical Diakonia*. Geneva: WCC Publications, 2022. https://www.oikoumene.org/resources/publications/ecumenical-diakonia.

PART 2

Liberating Diaconal Praxis

Chapter 6

Christian Diaconal Practice Through the Lens of Human Dignity

Ignatius Swart

Valuable conceptual insight can be found in the intentional shift in contemporary diaconal studies "away from traditions of conceptualizing *diakonia* as humble service" and as "paternalistic charity" to a mode of relating that fundamentally respects those in perceived need of help as human beings and subjects in their own right.[1] This paradigm shift is intentional in its aim of leading diaconal practice to a new mode of relating to those human beings at the center of its calling: people in perceived need of help or assistance of whom the most poignant group could be considered people living in contexts of endemic poverty.

To consider this "relational element" in diaconal studies, I first pay concrete attention to the ways in which the human dignity of people living in poverty is being violated. From a more pertinent diaconal studies interest, I then proceed to draw from the scholarly work of Hendrik Pieterse, a South African practical theologian specializing in the field of Christian homiletics, and Susanne Johnson, a practical theologian from the United States specializing in the field of Christian education.[2] These two authors offer fruitful grounds for comparative reflection on the relational element in diaconal practice directed toward the poor, albeit from different contexts and conceptual orientations. I argue that their respective conceptualizations can both be upheld as exemplars toward the new paradigm of *diakonia*. My ultimate argument, however, is that Johnson's conceptualization provides a more credible effort to sustain the progressive relational element important for respecting and supporting human dignity. This leads me, in conclusion, to present such emphasis on human dignity as foundational toward

---

[1] See, for example, Stephanie Dietrich, Kari Karsrud Korslien, Kjell Nordstokke, and Knud Jørgensen, "Introduction: Diakonia as Christian Social Practice," in *Diaconia as Christian Social Practice: An Introduction*, ed. Dietrich et al. (Oxford: Regnum Books International, 2014), 2; Stephanie Dietrich, "Reflections on Core Aspects of Diaconal Theory," in *Diakonia as Christian Social Practice*, 13–26; Ignatius Swart, "The Transformative Power of Diakonia: Theological Reflections from South Africa," in *International Handbook on Ecumenical Diakonia*, ed. Ampony et al. (Oxford: Regnum Books International, 2021), 62.

[2] For details of this analysis, see Ignatius Swart, "Relating to the Poor: Conceptualizations of Christian Diaconal Practice Considered Through the Lens of Human Dignity," *Diaconia* 7, no. 1 (2016): 3–26.

diaconal studies' faithful realization of a paradigm not only rendering a primary agency role to the marginalized and poor as actors of *diakonia* but also prioritizing the life-worlds of the rich and powerful as new objects of transformation.

Violations of Human Dignity

In presenting my understanding of human dignity, I move away from abstract conceptions of human dignity in order to devote more attention to its "violations" – what it means for human beings all over the world to be degraded, humiliated, and dehumanized because of the lives of permanent poverty to which they are subjected.[3]

I begin with Peter Schaber's focus on absolute poverty. His point of departure is the "inherent dignity" of every human person, which in turn he closely relates to "the claim to self-respect" that all persons rightly have. He states: "The dignity of a person relates to the claim to be acknowledged as a being [who] is allowed to live his or her life according to his or her own ideas – in other words, to live a life with self-respect."[4] Consequently, poverty fundamentally deprives humans from such self-respect, as it makes them dependent on others for their survival. This leads to the realization that the violation caused by poverty can be overcome only when people living in poverty have options and when their survival "is not entirely at the mercy of others."[5]

Schaber further presupposes that when people have options, they will not only have access to the necessary material goods but also possess the abilities or capabilities to realize their options through "a right to basic education," for example. For Schaber, however, this does not mean that the principle of human interdependence is undermined as an indispensable part of "the *conditio humana*." Instead, his concern lies with the essential degrading element at stake:

---

[3] I am very much indebted to ideas advanced some years ago in a Swiss-initiated interdisciplinary and international scholarly initiative conducted under the rubric "Humiliation, Degradation, Dehumanization: Human Dignity Violated." Against this backdrop, I find it particularly valuable to draw on two chapters from the ensuing volume that engage very pertinently with the problem of poverty, respectively from the perspective of its absolute and relative manifestations. In both cases, they have helped me, in accordance with the essential aim of the volume, to attend to violations of human dignity. See Peter Schaber, "Absolute Poverty: Human Dignity, Self-Respect, and Dependency," in *Humiliation, Degradation, Dehumanization: Human Dignity Violated*, ed. Kaufmann et al. (Dordrecht: Springer, 2011), 151–58; Julia Müller and Christian Neuhäuser, "Relative Poverty: On a Social Dimension of Human Dignity," in *Humiliation, Degradation*, ed. Kaufmann et al., 159–72. Here, I provide a very brief synopsis of the ideas emanating from the respective chapter discussions. For a more elaborate discussion of the two chapters, see Swart, "Relating to the Poor," 5–10. For introductory orientations in this regard, see Manfred Nowak, "Foreword," in *Humiliation, Degradation*, ed. Kaufmann et al., v–vi; Paulus Kaufmann, Hannes Kuch, Christian Neuhäuser, and Elaine Webster, "Human Dignity Violated: A Negative Approach – Introduction," in *Humiliation, Degradation*, ed. Kaufmann et al., 1–5.

[4] Schaber, "Absolute Poverty," 153.

[5] Schaber, 155–56.

"the lack of reasonable options ... regardless of whether or not it is self-induced."[6]

While shifting their focus to the problem of relative poverty, the point of departure for Julia Müller and Christian Neuhäuser is otherwise remarkably similar to that of Schaber, inasmuch as the notion of self-respect likewise becomes central to their own understanding. They state: "We want to argue that relative poverty is a kind of violation of human dignity, because it is humiliating and destructive to the agent's self-respect."[7] Müller and Neuhäuser argue that relative poverty represents "a genuine moral problem of its own." Although conditions of relative poverty may be perceived to be less degrading, as people may have access to particular basic goods, the point is that relatively poor people have reason to experience themselves as "second-class citizens" who have much less and not the same access to goods and opportunities as their more well-off fellow-citizens. In a qualitative sense, relatively poor people, in comparison to their more well-off compatriots, have "very limited or no healthcare at all," experience a very different standard of health care, are allowed "very different and fewer education opportunities," and must live in segregated residential areas because anything else is simply unaffordable to them.[8]

I argue that engaging with the notion of human dignity and its violations along the above lines could more sharply focus the merits and deficiencies of the relational element of diaconal practice when viewed through the works of Hendrik Pieterse and Susanne Johnson. My discussion therefore aims to consider the modes of relating to people living in contexts of endemic poverty and the extent to which each respective mode consciously addresses the violations of human dignity experienced by the beneficiaries (that is, poor people living in contexts of endemic poverty) as a result of diaconal actions, practices, and outreach.

Pieterse's "Homiletic Theory for Praxis"

Hendrik Pieterse develops a "homiletic theory for praxis" to assist preachers to communicate the Gospel message effectively in the South African situation of poverty; that is, a communication that will promote diaconal practices of social change in South Africa's many poor communities.[9] Essential to this undertaking are two theological concepts, "a preferential option for the poor" and "pastoral closeness," whereby Christian preachers listen very closely to the stories of poor people and their views of life, God, the church, government, and other people.[10]

---

[6] Schaber, 156–57.
[7] Müller and Neuhäuser, "Relative Poverty," 161.
[8] Müller and Neuhäuser, 168–69.
[9] For an extensive citation of Pieterse's work, see Swart, "Relating to the Poor," 11–16.
[10] See Hendrik J.C. Pieterse, "Communicative Rationality and Hermeneutical Insights for Preaching in a Context of Poverty," *Dutch Reformed Theological Journal* 43, no. 3/4 (2002): 555–62; Hendrik J.C. Pieterse, *Preaching in a Context of Poverty* (Pretoria: Unisa, 2004); Hendrik J.C. Pieterse, "Prophetic Preaching in the Contemporary Context of South Africa," *In die Skriflig/In Luce Verbi* 47, no. 1 (2013): 1–6.

When both concepts have been adopted, Christian preachers will necessarily engage in a mode of preaching known in the tradition of South African liberation theology as "prophetic preaching." Through their sermons, Christian preachers will now inspire the faithful – and in particular the faithful poor – with a new message of hope based on God's liberating word in the biblical text. At the same time, they will, as an integral part of their message, confront head on the situation of poverty and abuses of power in society.[11]

In Pieterse's theory, a direct causal relationship has to be drawn between the act of prophetic preaching as inspired by a preferential option for the poor and the newly found activation of a "diaconal, diaconally oriented church."[12] He postulates that prophetic preaching ought to become the cultivating source for a church that is fundamentally diaconally oriented, by taking on a mode of relating to the poor that not only resembles that of its preachers but also distinguishes itself through a new "partnership relationship" between "congregations for the poor" and "congregations of the poor."[13] In this relationship, congregations *of* the poor provide the direction in terms of the courses of action to be taken for their members' liberation from poverty. In the new partnership relationship, it is the congregations *of* the poor who not only lead the congregations *for* the poor in listening to the poor but also "determine the needs, think of projects, and then receive support as they proceed to help themselves."[14] In real-life contexts, this mode of interaction, best captured by the concept of "diaconal community development," leads to the socio-economic empowerment of the poor.[15]

In Pieterse's final thinking, however, his rather radical ideas about prophetic preaching and the diaconal practice emanating from such preaching become ultimately absorbed into his argument about "community development projects" as the most concrete expression of such a practice. Based on a grounded theory analysis of sermons by preachers from the Dutch Reformed Church and Uniting Reformed Church (all using Matt 25:31–46 as sermon text), he found it fitting to distinguish between two categories of diaconal projects among the poor: "congregational projects of charity" and "congregational projects of empowerment" (Figure 6.1). Pieterse remained appreciative of both types of projects as contributing meaningfully to addressing South Africa's poverty problems and presenting signs of a renewed South African church in the twenty-first century making a social difference.

---

[11] Pieterse, "Communicative Rationality," 557; Pieterse, *Preaching*, 88–90; Pieterse, "Prophetic Preaching," 4–6.
[12] Hendrik J.C. Pieterse, "The Human Face of God for the Poor," *Practical Theology in South Africa* 16, no. 1 (2001): 95; Pieterse, *Preaching*, 111.
[13] Pieterse, "The Human Face of God," 95–97; Pieterse, "Communicative Rationality," 558–59; Pieterse, *Preaching*, 111–13.
[14] Pieterse, "The Human Face of God," 99; Pieterse, *Preaching*, 115–16; see also Pieterse, "Communicative Rationality," 559.
[15] Pieterse, "The Human Face of God," 99–102; Pieterse, "Communicative Rationality," 559–61; Pieterse, *Preaching*, 116–20; Pieterse, "Prophetic Preaching," 5–6.

Main category I: Projects of charity

Subcategory I A: Food provision
Example (from 8*): Congregations provide food for jobless people waiting in the streets for piece jobs.
Property: Food provision for jobless people waiting to be employed.

Subcategory I B: Clothes provision
Example (from 2*): Congregations provide clothes for families in need.
Property: Clothes provision for families.

Main category II: Projects of empowerment

Subcategory II A: Relationships with the poor
Example (from 4*): Congregations provide food for jobless people waiting in the streets for jobs.
Property: Food provision for jobless people waiting to be employed.

Subcategory II B: Financial support
Example (from 3*): Congregations provide financial support for poor inhabitants of old age homes.
Property: Financial support for people in old age homes.

Subcategory II C: Medical support
Example (from 2*): Congregations provide help in preparation of medicine at state clinics.
Property: Medical support at state clinics.

Subcategory II D: Educational support
Example (from 2*): Congregations provide money and food for poor learners in nursery, primary, and high schools.
Property: Educational support for nursery, primary, and high schools.

Subcategory II E: Building support
Example (from 3*): Congregations provide helpers for the building of houses and start a vegetable garden to care for orphans.
Property: Building support in housing for orphans.

Subcategory II F: Self-help support
Example (from 6*): Congregations provide skills training for leadership and entrepreneurship for poor people, plus seed money to start own businesses.
Property: Training and seed money to start own businesses.

* Indicates total number of examples listed under each subcategory by Pieterse.

Figure 6.1: Pieterse's Classification of Congregational Projects Among the Poor Based on Sermon Analyses[16]

---

[16] Pieterse, "A Grounded Theory Approach," 5–6. For a selected sample of publications on Pieterse's research that led to his classification of the two categories of diaconal projects, see Hendrik J.C. Pieterse, "A Grounded Theory Approach to the Analysis of Sermons on Poverty: Congregational Projects as Social Capital," *Verbum et Ecclesia* 33, no. 1 (2012): 1–7, http://dx.doi.org/10.4102/ve.v33i1.689; Hendrik J.C. Pieterse, "An

Johnson's Theme of Remembering the Poor

An essential feature of Susanne Johnson's work is the way she takes up the universal theological theme of "remembering the poor" (based on Gal 2:10) to (re)think critically Christian social practice in a world largely dominated by economic globalization and neo-liberal market capitalism. This critical, political-economic perspective compels her to deliver a stringent critique of how North American mainline, middle-class Christians and their congregations have themselves become culturally compromised by the culture of consumerism and corporate capitalism.[17] There is, she argues, a direct correlation between their compromised position and what such Christians understand as the only paradigm for social service and outreach: a "servanthood model" that "mirrors mainline, middle-class piety" and favors projects that address one or more immediate, emergency need of persons or families for food, clothing, or shelter.[18]

Johnson's critical ideas find even greater depth in the way she incorporates the issue of power as part of her argument. In the Christian servanthood model, she comments, the position of "power" remains firmly within the middle-class "serving the needy."[19] This manifests in the way that everything said, done, thought, and conceived is "from the point of view of the one who serves, never from the point of view of the one being served."[20] No attempt is made "to see the reality of the poor from the perspective of the poor" and to act accordingly.[21] Service remains defined as what "middle- or upper-class Christians, unilaterally give or do to and do for" the other. As such, it is a mode of relating that comprises a "one-way street in which the agency of 'the other' disappears into thin air," as if "the ones receiving Christian service have no moral agency, no power, no creativity of their own – only 'need.'"[22] By implication, the mode of diaconal practice at play not only displays no sensitivity for the violated human dignity of those it claims to serve but even sustains that violation.

It follows that Johnson's further argument may be read as a plea or challenge to contemporary diaconal scholarship and practice to exert itself toward the development of diaconal ministry in a "new paradigm," one that will address the

---

Emerging Grounded Theory for Preaching on Poverty in South Africa with Matthew 15:31–46 as Sermon Text," *Acta Theologica* 33, no. 1 (2013): 175–95; Hendrik J.C. Pieterse, "Theoretical Strengthening of the Concept of Appealing in Analysed Sermons on Matthew 25:31-46 in the Context of Poverty in South Africa," *In die Skriflig/In Luce Verbi* 47, no. 1 (2013): 1–8.

[17] Susanne Johnson, "Remembering the Poor: Transforming Christian Practice," in *Redemptive Transformation in Practical Theology: Essays in Honor of James E. Loder*, ed. Dana R. Wright and John D. Kuentzel (Grand Rapids: Eerdmans, 2004), 192–99.

[18] Susanne Johnson, "Women, Children, Poverty, and the Church: A Faith-Based Community Revitalization Approach to Addressing Poverty," in *Poverty, Suffering and HIV-AIDS: International Practical Theological Perspectives*, ed. Pamela D. Couture and Bonnie J. Miller-McLemore (Cardiff: Cardiff Academic, 2003), 160; Johnson, "Remembering the Poor," 199–201.

[19] Johnson, "Remembering the Poor," 208.

[20] Johnson, 211.

[21] Johnson, 201.

[22] Johnson, 211.

deficiencies of the service delivery paradigm and lead to a practice that will "remember the poor" in a radically different way.[23]

For Johnson, the new paradigm ought to start with a vision for alternative thinking and practice that will inspire a "new economic orientation" toward radical inclusion and social justice in opposition to the institutionalized inequalities and rule of the rich as upheld and deepened by the workings of economic globalization. As a logical consequence, Johnson's new orientation also clearly prioritizes a mode of practice that will reverse the one-way movement from the middle-class and the rich in the servanthood model. At the heart of this reversal, she envisions the formation of a new "partnership relationship" between Christians – poor and non-poor, working class and middle class – working together to resist the institutionalized inequalities of economic globalization and *de facto* rule by the rich.[24]

The idea that primacy of voice be given to the poor and their perspective on reality in the new partnership relationship is indeed the starting point of everything else: where power relations are starting to be addressed; where "in small supportive grassroots groups" people begin to "pour out their pain, anger and suffering"; and where the stories emanating from such outpouring "become the basis for collective critique of ideology" and a starting point for interrogating the wider systemic context.[25]

For Johnson, the "local, distressed neighborhoods" of the poor constitute the context in which these dynamics need to take place.[26] This leads her to introduce the concept of "community revitalization" and its three dimensions of "community organizing," "community building," and "community development" as the most concrete, strategic ways in which the new partnership relationship will unfold. The emphasis rests on the initiation of processes of "revitalization," "redevelopment," and "reinvestment" in poor communities, prompted by the residents' identification of their available assets and the resources they need.[27]

Not least, Johnson appreciates the mediating, community-organizing role that churches and other faith-based structures can play in such processes of community revitalization.[28] She points to their contributing role in creating "a new culture of conversation" that will enable working-class families in particular to "have more effective voice and visibility" in their communities and neighborhoods. She also envisions a pertinent role for churches and other faith-based structures in establishing the necessary connections between "people and institutions across neighborhood lines, from all geographic and economic sectors of a city, town, or village."[29] She postulates that these faith-based roles could

---

[23] Johnson, "Women," 160; Johnson, "Remembering the Poor," 213.
[24] Johnson, "Remembering the Poor," 213–14.
[25] Johnson, "Remembering the Poor," 214; see also Johnson, "Women, Children, Poverty, and the Church," 164–66.
[26] Johnson, "Women," 162; Johnson, "Remembering the Poor," 215.
[27] Johnson, "Women," 160–66; Johnson, "Remembering the Poor," 215.
[28] Johnson, "Women," 160–66.
[29] Johnson, 163.

become the foundation for broad-based redevelopment and reinvestment in a plethora of programmes, practices, and initiatives (Figure 6.2).

Community organizing
- multi-sector partnerships
- engaging local authorities to invest in services making it safer for children – police patrol, paved streets, speed bumps, garbage pick-ups, street lights, strategic location of parks, libraries, schools
- school reform in poor performance schools
- after-school programmes
- living wage job campaigns
- job creation and skills training programmes
- health care and medical insurance programmes
- utility reform
- crime prevention
- creation of affordable housing
- health and environmental justice
- removal of toxic waste sites
- "soft mortgage" loans
- school and neighborhood safety for children
- improved voter participation
- on-the-job mentoring in skills and attitudes to participate in public life
- creation of public venues for people's direct voice (in view of basic and public services)
- development of human and social capital for community leadership

Community building
- building relationships of mutual trust and accountability
- identifying and tapping into under-utilized individual and collective assets
- cleaning up garbage-strewn lots
- building community gardens
- neighborhood crime watches
- sponsoring block parties for children and youth

Community development
- affordable housing
- commercial retail stores
- small businesses
- job counselling and training
- quality childcare
- job creation

Figure 6.2: Johnson's Examples of Faith-Based Community Revitalization[30]

---

[30] Johnson, 162–66.

Human Dignity and Diaconal Practice

The conceptualizations of Hendrik Pieterse and Susanne Johnson do indeed offer fruitful grounds for comparative reflection on the emerging paradigm shift in diaconal thinking, a shift that appears to be very intentional in directing Christian diaconal practice to a new mode of relating to the people at the center of its calling. Furthermore, putting the violations of human dignity at the center reveals the respective merits of the two conceptualizations.

Pieterse brings a unique (and necessary) "homiletic theory for praxis" to the field of diaconal studies, and Johnson an equally unique (and necessary) critical political economic perspective. Both further aspire to advance a relational element aligning with the emerging paradigm shift in diaconal thinking. Both also envision far-reaching new partnerships between the poor and non-poor leading to a fundamentally different orientation and outlook for a diaconal church. While distinctions remain – between poor and non-poor Christians and between congregations *of* the poor and congregations *for* the poor – there is nevertheless a deliberative common effort to rethink the new partnership relationship along the lines of pastoral closeness, a new mode of genuine listening and rendering voice and agency to the poor and congregations *of* the poor.

My argument up to this point suggests that much can be gained by viewing the merits of both conceptualizations as serving the emerging new paradigm of *diakonia*. Yet, having said this, I also feel compelled to depart from my appreciation of Pieterse. I remain rather puzzled by the seeming discrepancy between the radical and challenging inclination in the homiletic dimension of his conceptualization, on the one hand, and his ultimate emphasis on congregational "projects of charity" and "empowerment" as the most practical outcome of the prophetic mode of preaching and relating that he prioritizes, on the other. Effectively, this discrepancy constitutes a prevailing weakness in diaconal studies and practical theological scholarship to convert progressive theological ideas into more sophisticated conceptualizations of actual diaconal practice.[31] Whether categorized under the denominator of "projects of charity" or "projects of empowerment," it becomes very difficult indeed to see them as anything else but acts of "mercy" or "comfortable compassion"[32] – a one-way movement of congregations *for* the poor providing handouts and support – that could hardly contribute toward developing a sense of enhanced human dignity on the part of its beneficiaries.

Thus, I find Johnson's conceptualization a more credible effort to sustain the progressive relational element that she so strongly advocates. In contrast to Pieterse, she not only persists in her opposition to the idea of projects directed toward poor people but also proceeds to advance the appealing idea that poor and non-poor (or middle-class) Christians could find new common ground and vision in the multi-dimensional strategic paradigm of community revitalization.

---

[31] Swart, "Relating to the Poor," 25.
[32] Charles Elliot, *Comfortable Compassion? Poverty, Power and the Church* (London: Hodder and Stoughton, 1987).

My appreciation precludes neither giving more substance to Johnson's strategic and practical proposals nor recognizing their limitations, both in terms of addressing the systemic problem of global neo-liberal capitalism and being rather exclusively confined to the practice of "neighborly love" between Christians. Nevertheless, the evoked image of poor and non-poor Christians working as equal partners for revitalization, redevelopment, and reinvestment in poor communities through an array of programmes and practices is inspirational and hopeful. Considered through the lens of human dignity, this conceptualization projects an image of new-found human success that does not forsake the principle of human interdependence. Yet, at the same time, it also grants people and whole communities, degraded by conditions of poverty, ample opportunity to enhance their independence from others, take on agency roles in their own right in accordance with their own choices and ideas, and gain an increasing sense of enhanced (first-class) citizenship equal to that of their non-poor counterparts.

Conclusion

My essential endeavor in this chapter was to make a conceptual contribution to what is emerging within the worldwide Christian ecumenical movement as a faithful and deliberate aspiration toward a new paradigm of diaconal practice, one that wants to take far more seriously than before the human dignity of poor people. Against this backdrop, I have drawn on an understanding of human dignity as well as two more developed conceptualizations of Christian diaconal practice that offer important vistas for the road toward the new paradigm. However, my comparative reflection also advanced a line of argumentation that does not remain uncritical toward the selected conceptualizations. Consequently, it is the merits but also shortcomings that I identified through a lens of human dignity that provide fruitful grounds for an ongoing diaconal studies research agenda striving to make further conceptual progress into the new paradigm.

In view of making the envisaged further progress, this chapter has steered the diaconal discussion decisively toward one of the most hopeful and faith-inspiring theological themes in the contemporary ecumenical conversation on Christian *diakonia*. Advanced under the heading "The *Diakonia* of the Marginalized People," the emphasis in this ecumenical conversation, in line with my own, lies with the assertive reimagination of *diakonia* from the vantage point of the marginalized and poor. In this assertion, the marginalized and poor are in their own right affirmed as recipients of God's power to become leading agents of God's mission and a transformative *diakonia* realizing its alternative vision of the world.[33] As such, it is a theological assertion that proclaims the Christian church to constitute the first site of transformation by turning onto its head the entrenched view of the marginalized and poor as recipients or objects of the

---

[33] See Carlos E. Ham, "Colombo: Theological Perspectives on *Diakonia* in the Twenty-First Century," *The Ecumenical Review* 64, no. 3 (2012): 383–92; Swart, "The Transformative Power of Diakonia," 65–66; World Council of Churches, *Called to Transformative Action: Ecumenical Diakonia* (Geneva: WCC, 2018), 26–30.

churches' diakonia.[34] However, it is an assertion that I want to contend also needs to take the idea of equal partnership between poor and non-poor Christians a step further to consider an even more radical theological idea. This is the still underdeveloped theme in the ecumenical conversation on *diakonia* that the rich, the non-poor, and not least the believers belonging to the church *for* the poor need to become the new objects of *diakonia*. In this redirection, the command to both the church *for* the poor and church *of* the poor is to exert themselves toward nothing less than a conscientization of the traditional agents of *diakonia*, leading them to the profound social-theological insight that the imperative of renewal, conversion, and change should be directed as much to the life-worlds of the economically and politically rich and powerful.[35] This should be regarded as a paramount task for a diaconal research agenda striving to make decisive progress toward the emerging new paradigm.

Works Cited

Dietrich, Stephanie, Kari Karsrud Korslien, Kjell Norstokke, and Knud Jørgensen. "Introduction: Diakonia as Christian Social Practice." In *Diakonia as Christian Social Practice: An Introduction*, edited by Stephanie Dietrich, Knud Jørgensen, Kari Karsrud Korslien, and Kjell Nordstokke, 1–9. Oxford: Regnum Books International, 2014.

Dietrich, Stephanie. "Reflections on Core Aspects of Diaconal Theory." In *Diakonia as Christian Social Practice: An Introduction*, edited by Stephanie Dietrich, et al., 13–26. Oxford: Regnum Books International, 2014.

Elliot, Charles. *Comfortable Compassion? Poverty, Power and the Church*. London: Hodder and Stoughton, 1987.

Ham, Carlos E. "Colombo: Theological Perspectives on *Diakonia* in the Twenty-First Century." *The Ecumenical Review* 64, no. 3 (2012): 383–92.

Johnson, Susanne. "Women, Children, Poverty, and the Church: A Faith-Based Community Revitalization Approach to Addressing Poverty." In *Poverty, Suffering and HIV-AIDS: International Practical Theological Perspectives*, edited by Pamela D. Couture and Bonnie J. Miller-McLemore, 155–68. Cardiff: Cardiff Academic, 2003.

———. "Remembering the Poor: Transforming Christian Practice." In *Redemptive Transformation in Practical Theology: Essays in Honor of James E. Loder*, edited by Dana R. Wright and John D. Kuentzel, 192–99. Grand Rapids: Eerdmans, 2004.

Kaufmann, Paulus, Hannes Kuch, Christian Neuhäuser, and Elaine Webster, eds. *Humiliation, Degradation, Dehumanization: Human Dignity Violated*. Dordrecht: Springer, 2011.

---

[34] Ham, "Colombo," 384.
[35] Elliot, *Comfortable Compassion?* 118, 173–74; Ignatius Swart, "Meeting the Challenge of Poverty and Exclusion? The Emerging Field of Development Research in South African Practical Theology," *International Journal of Practical Theology* 12, no. 1 (2008): 133–36, https://doi.org/10.1515/IJPT.2008.6.

———. "Human Dignity Violated: A Negative Approach – Introduction." In *Humiliation, Degradation, Dehumanization: Human Dignity Violated*, edited by Paulus Kaufmann et al., 1–5. Dordrecht: Springer, 2011.

Müller, Julia and Christian Neuhäuser. "Relative Poverty: On a Social Dimension of Human Dignity." In *Humiliation, Degradation, Dehumanization: Human Dignity Violated*, edited by Paulus Kaufmann et al., 159–72. Dordrecht: Springer, 2011.

Nowak, Manfred. "Foreword." In *Humiliation, Degradation, Dehumanization: Human Dignity Violated*, edited by Paulus Kaufmann et al., v–vi. Dordrecht: Springer, 2011.

Pieterse, Hendrik J.C. "The Human Face of God for the Poor." *Practical Theology in South Africa* 16, no. 1 (2001): 75–104.

———. "Communicative Rationality and Hermeneutical Insights for Preaching in a Context of Poverty." *Dutch Reformed Theological Journal* 43, no. 3/4 (2002): 555–62. https://hdl.handle.net/10520/EJC83792.

———. *Preaching in a Context of Poverty*. Pretoria: Unisa, 2004.

———. "A Grounded Theory Approach to the Analysis of Sermons on Poverty: Congregational Projects as Social Capital." *Verbum et Ecclesia* 33, no. 1 (2012): 1–7. http://dx.doi.org/10.4102/ve.v33i1.689.

———. "Prophetic Preaching in the Contemporary Context of South Africa." *In die Skriflig/In Luce Verbi* 47, no. 1 (2013): 1–6. http://dx.doi.org/10.4102/ids.v47i1.114.

———. "An Emerging Grounded Theory for Preaching on Poverty in South Africa with Matthew 15:31-46 as Sermon Text." *Acta Theologica* 33, no. 1 (2013): 175–95.

———. "Theoretical Strengthening of the Concept of Appealing in Analysed Sermons on Matthew 25:31-46 in the Context of Poverty in South Africa." *In die Skriflig/In Luce Verbi* 47, no. 1 (2013): 1–8. http://dx.doi.org/10.4102/ids.v47i1.692.

Schaber, Peter. "Absolute Poverty: Human Dignity, Self-Respect, and Dependency." In *Humiliation, Degradation, Dehumanization: Human Dignity Violated*, edited by Paulus Kaufmann et al., 151–58. Dordrecht: Springer, 2011.

Swart, Ignatius. "Meeting the Challenge of Poverty and Exclusion? The Emerging Field of Development Research in South African Practical Theology." *International Journal of Practical Theology* 12, no. 1 (2008): 104–49. https://doi.org/10.1515/IJPT.2008.6.

———. "Relating to the Poor: Conceptualizations of Christian Diaconal Practice Considered Through the Lens of Human Dignity." *Diaconia: Journal of Christian Social Practice* 7, no. 1 (2016): 3–26. https://doi.org/10.13109/diac.2016.7.1.3.

———. "The Transformative Power of Diakonia: Theological Reflections from South Africa." In *International Handbook on Ecumenical Diakonia*, edited by Godwin Ampony, Martin Büscher, Beate Hofmann, Félicité Ngnintedem, Dennis Solon, and Dietrich Werner, 62–67. Oxford: Regnum Books International, 2021.

World Council of Churches. *Called to Transformative Action: Ecumenical Diakonia*. Geneva: WCC, 2018.

Chapter 7

Liberating *Diakonia* in a Brazilian Perspective

Dionata Rodrigues de Oliveira

Brazil is among the most unequal countries in Latin America and is known as the country of inequalities.[1] Social inequality is the result of years of exploitation and poverty that has worsened over time.[2] A great deal of wealth is in the hands of a few, while little wealth is shared among many. Like other colonized countries, Brazil is in some sense "trapped" in history, as it continues to experience exploitation from which Brazilians are not yet free. They are consequently subjugated to hierarchical and enslaving structures, the result of a colonization process by which Brazil provides labor, raw materials, and resources for the development of its colonizers.[3] *Diakonia* – service in faith through the love of Jesus, with the aims of supporting and dignifying human life – needs to be the church's response.[4]

As an integral part of the church's mission in Brazil, *diakonia* has three basic elements: mediation/reconciliation, empowerment, and transformation.[5] These elements of diaconal method focus on planning, implementation, and outcomes. Through the process, diaconal actors are empowered and equipped to follow in solidarity with people. This methodology is fundamental to the church's mission in the world and in the Latin American context.[6] In my work as a theological advisor for education and *diakonia* in the Sínodo Nordeste Gaúcho of the

---

[1] Régis Bonelli and Lauro Ramos, "Income Distribution in Brazil: Evaluation of the Long-term Tendencies and Changes in Inequality Since Mid-1970s," *Brazilian Journal of Political Economy* 13, no. 2 (April–June 1993), https://doi.org/10.1590/0101-31571993-0728. I would like to extend my sincere gratitude to Lori Mills-Curran for her valuable contribution to the translation and revision of my chapter. Her diligent support and expert insights significantly enhanced the quality of the work. I deeply appreciate the time and effort she devoted, which were instrumental to the success of this project.
[2] Francisco Mesquita de Oliveira, "Social Inequality: A Trajectory of Insistence in Brazil," *Contribuciones a las Ciencias Sociales* 16, no. 7 (2023): 6756, https://doi.org/10.55905/revconv.16n.7-151.
[3] Giselle Avila Leal de Meirelles, "Productive Restructuring of Capital, Impoverishment and Social Inequality in Latin America," *Serviço Social em Revista* 18, no. 2 (January/June 2016): 55, https://doi.org/10.5433/1679-4842.2016v18n2p52.
[4] Rodolfo Gaede Neto, *A Diaconia de Jesus: Contribuição para a Fundamentação Teológica da Diaconia na América Latina* (São Leopoldo: Sinodal, 2001), 49.
[5] Kjell Nordstokke, ed., *Diakonia in Context: Transformation, Reconciliation, Empowerment: An LWF Contribution to the Understanding and Practice of Diakonia* (Geneva: Lutheran World Federation, 2009), 43.
[6] Nordstokke, 43.

Evangelical Church of the Lutheran Confession in Brazil, I recognize the need to follow this methodology to achieve the expected goal of transformation.[7]

This chapter presents a structured dialogue based on the praxis of liberation theology, proposing that theory and practice occur simultaneously and be monitored continually in the work of *diakonia*. I first offer a brief account of spontaneous solidarity arising from the first Lutheran communities in Brazil. Next, I provide definitions and examples of their practices, such as diaconal methodology, transformation, and empowerment. These guide us throughout the chapter toward a diaconal methodology that leads to mediation/reconciliation, transformation, and empowerment.

Diakonia Among the First Lutheran Communities in Brazil

Lutheranism arrived in Brazil in 1824 and diaconal care took place effectively, because the immigrants needed to take care of each other. Midwives and nurses were completely necessary in the new context. This is how Lutherans practiced *diakonia* in Brazil. The first task of the immigrants was to understand their new context and figure out how to live in this new country. The question that guided immigrants was: How can we live and be a church in this new context?[8]

Coming from Germany and other Lutheran countries, many who immigrated to Brazil fled a context of war, hunger, or poverty.[9] During their passage by ship, these immigrants undertook a true pilgrimage, enduring poor sanitary conditions and lacking even minimally nutritious food and access to many basic human needs. When they arrived in Brazil, the immigrants received a land grant from the colonial government but no resources to work the land. Generally, they were merely pointed in the direction they should go. They were expected to open access over precarious roads and clear land in dense forests.[10] Faced with all the difficulties of adapting to the new context, they discovered solidarity.

Over the years, as reflection on this subject received greater theological analysis, the practice of spontaneous solidarity came to be called *diakonia*.[11] This concern for wellbeing, initially based on solidarity and the faith that immigrants brought with them, manifested itself in catechisms, hymnals, and the Bible, generating local communities with strong diaconal characteristics. Meeting specific needs, they acted concretely to transform contexts of suffering into

---

[7] The Sínodo Nordeste Gaúcho is one of eighteen divisions of the Evangelical Church of the Lutheran Confession in Brazil.
[8] Marlon Ronald Fluck, "500 Anos de Evangelização na América Latina," *Boletim Teológico* 6, no. 19 (December 1992): 43–64, http://www.repci.co/repositorio/handle/123456789/546.
[9] Hans-Jürgen Prien, *Formação da Igreja Evangélica no Brasil: Das Comunidades Teuto-Evangélicas de Imigrantes Até a Igreja Evangélica de Confissão Luterana no Brasil* (Petrópolis-São Leopoldo: Vozes Editora Sinodal, 2001), 25.
[10] Prien, 25.
[11] Gisela Beulke, "A História do Ministério Diaconal na IECLB," *Estudos Teológicos* 47, no.1 (2007): 144–65, http://periodicos.est.edu.br/index.php/estudos_teologicos/article/view/470/425.

contexts marked by strength and resilience for the continuation of social and religious life.[12]

Diaconal Methodology

The church is not church without *diakonia*. In the early days of Lutheranism in Brazil, spontaneous *diakonia* by the church was enough for its full growth and development in the country. Yet, throughout the years, improvements to Lutheran *diakonia* had to be addressed. Through intentional action and reflection, the church needed to develop and articulate a diaconal methodology.

If we want precise and lasting diaconal action in the church and society, we must prioritize the use of methodology and planning. According to Gisela Beulke, the word "methodology" means "the path to be used to achieve a certain end or objective."[13] Methodology is significant because planning opens the horizon and deepens the scope of the path to be taken through evaluation, discussion, and action. This is the practical path of praxis: "*reflection* and *action* directed at the structures to be transformed."[14] According to Luiz Stephanou, "Planning is possible and necessary" and does not require specific doctoral knowledge or advanced research.[15] Preparation and dedication are necessary, as is the case with everything in life. For diaconal practice, the question of being intentional about methodology continues to be all important. "n essential task is to identify working methods that favor processes of participation and empowerment, and that affirm the basic values of diaconal work."[16] Although there is no single form of diaconal methodology, research, action, and *diakonia* meet, methodologically speaking, through reflection on the life of Jesus.

Diaconal methodology must be founded in biblical theology with the model of Christ as a guiding element. "[I]f we say that our service is based on serving Jesus, we can base our way on his way of acting."[17] Genuine *diakonia* means keeping our attention fixed on what Jesus says to blind Bartimaeus: "What do you want me to do for you?" (Mark 10:51, NIV). Jesus himself found it necessary to reflect before acting. Action must be rooted in context. Reading the context means asking about needs and listening to personal pain and suffering. Thus, drawing a comparison between our approach and the life and actions of Jesus, Beulke characterizes the steps of diaconal methodology as a spiral, displacing and propelling us to different places: Jesus actively engaged with people, observing and understanding their real circumstances (Matt 9:35); he empathized with their pain, listened to their concerns, and provided a space for them to

---

[12] Prien, *Formação da Igreja Evangélica no Brasil*, 50.
[13] Beulke, "A História do Ministério Diaconal na IECLB," 14.
[14] Paulo Freire, *Pedagogy of the Oppressed*, 30th anniv. ed., trans. Myra Bergman Ramos (New York: Continuum, 2000[1970]), 126, original emphasis.
[15] Luís Stephanou, "Planejar é Possível e Necessário," in *Planejando as Ações Diaconais da Comunidade: E Como Que se Faz Isso?* ed. Hildegart Hertel (Porto Alegre: IECLB-Departamento de Diaconia, 2001), 32.
[16] Nordstokke, *Diakonia in Context*, 59.
[17] Nordstokke, 83.

express themselves; he spent time in the company of people, fostering dialogue and reflection to help them gain insights into their situations (Luke 24:13); in his interactions, he utilized elements from nature, involving those who sought him in their own healing and liberation processes (John 9:1); and to facilitate the acceptance and reintegration of lepers into society, he instructed them to present themselves to the priests (Luke 17:14).[18]

Diaconal action cannot be effective when it is uninformed by the expectations and viewpoint of the individual who has the needs. It cannot consist of doing things for someone without listening to what the other person expects. In this way, *diakonia* is not a spontaneous action but must be planned.

Diaconal methodology remains little explored within the church. It is characteristic of *diakonia*, at least among Brazilian Lutherans, to be concerned about the doing, not the recording of or reflecting upon this knowledge. "There are still faith congregations in the Brazilian context where there is no clarity between reflection and action, and that is why it is necessary to consider diaconal methodology as a prerequisite for joint learning among the parties involved in a diaconal action."[19] There is always pressure to do *diakonia* but little demand that it be reflected upon. Another structural reason for the lack of reflection on *diakonia* is that *diakonia* in the Brazilian Lutheran Church is often exercised primarily by women, who have been authorized to work, but not necessarily to speak, by the male leaders of the church. Reflection on diaconal methodology would give voice to those who perform the work, demanding that oppressive, sexist, hierarchical structures enter into deeper dialogue with women workers. This is not always welcomed by those who benefit from patriarchy. We need to talk about diaconal methodology to give voice to those involved in diaconal practice who suffer from being undervalued and overlooked.

Two examples of diaconal action by my diaconal groups in the Sínodo Nordeste Gaúcho illustrate the importance of diaconal methodology. The first example demonstrates the poor outcomes to be expected when the methodological praxis just outlined is not well integrated into diaconal action. In a slum in a major city, there was a family living in extreme poverty, with no access to basic resources, clean water, or minimally usable toilets. One of the groups decided to support this family by building a bathroom for them. However, the family was not consulted about it, even though they accepted the construction. Upon returning to check on the family's situation, we realized that the issue required education to prepare them to use the bathroom correctly, as they had never had one at home before. This breakdown in communication and planning by all parties did not result in effective transformation of their suffering, and health problems persisted.

By contrast, a methodically planned action, which involved not only the group but also the synod and the national church, took place during the COVID-19 pandemic. In 2020 and 2021, due to the federal government's long-time neglect of the country's needs, all kinds of challenges were revealed. More than half the

---

[18] Beulke, "A História do Ministério Diaconal na IECLB," 14.
[19] Angela Lenke, "Metodologia Diaconal," (master's thesis, Escola Superior de Teologia, São Leopoldo, Brazil, 2006), 20.

Brazilian population experienced food and health insecurity. Reflection on theory and practice enabled the identification of urgent issues and possible resources. With the public health care system so weak, and the shortages of vaccines, medications, and even food so extreme, faith communities engaged these needs through increased *diakonia* across denominational lines. Synods and parishes were involved in this activity. Good praxis involved these methodological steps: a preliminary action, reflecting on an action, and evaluating its results from different perspectives to improve practice.

Certain actions emerged as priorities for *diakonia* in this context. Top priorities of care for elderly people included making protective masks and lab coats to control contagion and gathering food, cleaning supplies, and hygiene products. Volunteer work unfolded, including reflection to evaluate and change ineffective practices that were ill-adapted to the local context. For example, an effort to secure a donation of coats was discontinued because the time invested was not worth the minimal benefit obtained. All these actions were only possible because of theological-diaconal praxis, which looked at the context, reflected on what needed to be transformed, raised up resources and volunteers, and made donated materials available. Practically speaking, national coordination of *diakonia*, together with the inclusion of the Brazilian Lutheran Church, motivated and made financial and personnel resources available. These examples demonstrate how liberative diaconal methodology met the challenge within a specific Brazilian perspective.

Diaconal actions methodologically structured with focus and objectivity can change any context. They can make people protagonists of their own struggles and achievements, thus allowing them agency and autonomy. A very important source for Latin American theology is liberation theology, originating with the thoughts and writings of Gustavo Gutiérrez. This new way to live theology was authorized by the Roman Catholic bishops' conference in 1968 at Medellín, Colombia, with epistemological developments in the 1990s, leading to work with specific target audiences and not only with poverty as the central issue. Thus, there has been a reinforcement of concerns and issues related to the indigenous population, gender violence, LGBTQIA+ phobia, and other contextual demands in Latin America. For liberation theology, discussing diaconal methodology means asking questions, being willing to listen, and collaboratively implementing the planning with all those involved in the process of problem recognition and resolution. It is not about doing *for* but doing *with*.[20]

Features of *Diakonia*

The importance of diaconal methodology cannot be overstated. It serves as the bridge between theory and practice, enabling the planning, execution,

---

[20] It is important in this regard to name the contribution of Clodovis Boff, whose work addressed the development of method in liberation theology and helped liberation theology adapt to the Brazilian reality. Clodovis Boff, *Theology and Praxis: Epistemological Foundations* (Maryknoll, NY: Orbis, 1987).

evaluation, and improvement of diaconal actions. According to the Lutheran World Federation, "transformation, reconciliation and empowerment" are "three dimensions of mission" that "permeate all mission endeavors."[21] This methodology ensures that actions are well informed, context-specific, and grounded in dialogue and collaboration with those involved. For the Brazilian context, transformation, mediation/reconciliation, and empowerment reflect the essential features of diaconal work.

Transformation

Transformation is at the heart of *diakonia*. Without a focus on transformation, diaconal actions fall short of their potential. If a so-called diaconal practice does not involve transformation as its central objective, one should question it as a genuine act of *diakonia*.

Rooting *diakonia* in transformation addresses on a practical level one of the most relevant aspects of diaconal epistemology. Kjell Nordstokke stated the core value:

> Transformation presupposes change. In this process of altering, changing, transforming, it is very important not to act without reflection. That's why anyone who works on transformation needs theoretical clarity, existential passion. Theoretical clarity is knowing what to transform, how to transform, and why to transform. Existential passion is political will, it is determination, it is conviction. Both strengths are motivated by the love of God. The love that God has for human beings and for all creation that groans and screams. Can we ask what to transform? Yes, it is necessary to transform structures when they serve as generators of death.[22]

Here we affirm what we stated at the beginning: knowing what to transform is the beginning of diaconal planning.

Transformation must have a guaranteed place in planning for diaconal action. Transformation "is a continuous process of rejection of that which dehumanizes and desecrates life and adherence to that which reaffirms the sanctity of life and gifts in everyone and promotes peace and justice in society."[23] To understand the importance of the transformative dimension, we can view it theologically: "Transformation engages and changes all who are a part of it. In that manner, transformational diakonia helps to overcome so-called helpers' syndromes, practices and relations that separate 'we' from 'they.'"[24] Transformation is thus fundamental for those who practice *diakonia*. If they do not aim for transformation, they need to review their parameters, concepts, methodologies, and practices. Just as the event of the cross itself was transformative, Jesus' action and ministry – diaconal and transformative in essence – has already turned death into life, not only for Jesus himself but for all those who crossed his path.

---

[21] Lutheran World Federation, *Mission in Context: Transformation, Reconciliation, Empowerment: An LWF Contribution to the Understanding and Practice of Mission* (Geneva: Lutheran World Federation, 2004), 32; Nordstokke, *Diakonia in Context*, 43.
[22] Translation by Dionata Rodrigues de Oliveira. Kjell Nordstokke, "*Diaconia: Fé em Ação*," 3rd ed. (São Leopoldo, RS: Sinodal, 1998), 83.
[23] LWF, *Mission in Context*, 32–33.
[24] Nordstokke, *Diakonia in Context*, 43–44.

One example of transformation from my own experience comes from a diaconal group I worked with a few years ago. The congregation had no contact with people experiencing homelessness in the city of Campinas in the state of São Paulo. Therefore, a diaconal group was initiated within the congregation. This group, after analyzing the issues in the area, decided to explore various avenues and settled on reaching out to individuals without homes. Subsequently, the group volunteered at a homeless shelter where the municipal social services were already involved. This allowed them to get to know the people they were assisting.

They decided to engage in conversations with these individuals to understand their needs and problems as well as to comprehend how they wished to be helped. Initially, if they had been thinking from their own experiences, they might have concluded that these persons needed to leave the streets, find employment, stop drinking or using drugs, and live a socially acceptable life. However, upon listening to the homeless population, they discovered that they truly wanted to escape their situation, but to do so they needed assistance with their addiction issues, alcoholism, identification documents, and a place they could register as their residence before finding employment. Therefore, the group shifted the focus toward providing shelter and disease prevention. Along with this, they offered spiritual support, providing an opportunity for participation in Sunday worship where individuals were even welcomed at the communion table.

Holistic transformation took place in this context. Homeless individuals found acceptance and care in the church, and some managed to move forward in their lives with this support. I witnessed a transformation within the Lutheran congregation as well, as they opened their doors to the unknown and shared communion with them. They assisted their own Bartimaeus to heal, and not only was he healed, but the people of the congregation were also healed. They were healed of their prejudices as they welcomed the blind man and allowed him to come to Jesus.

Mediation/Reconciliation

Mediation/reconciliation and transformation go hand in hand when it comes to thinking about *diakonia*. Mediation is the process led by a person or group which provides the necessary measures for those who are in a difficult situation to overcome it. An example might be the process of securing food for a family whose providers are unemployed or ill. Helping to get a job is also mediation, as is helping to get health treatment. In contrast, transformation is the goal of diaconal action. Every action must have an objective to be achieved, because we do not aim to maintain the individualistic, charity model of donating food, clothing, or other necessities of life. Mediation is also called for by the LWF as a form of reconciliation, the way the church provides resources and contributes wellbeing to a society in profound crisis.

Diakonia can be considered as mediation between two dimensions of the same reality. Exploring a new methodological direction, Dierk Starnitzke searched biblically and historically for the place where *diakonia* operates in different times, societies, and places:

The church represents the inner side: the gathering of the local community, in which this miracle of Christ's resurrection and ever-new presence is believed, shared, celebrated, and sometimes even experienced. At the same time, *diakonia* deals with the external relations of the church, and a merely socio-charitable understanding of *diakonia* is expanded by a new fundamental aspect: ultimately, diaconal work is an expression of the promise and gives faith that, in this external relationship with outsiders, where one would never imagine it, they find Christ.[25]

Because we have not yet understood Starnitzke's claims about the place of *diakonia* and its importance, diaconal methodology, although the subject of some relevant research, remains little explored within academia.

Starnitzke proposes the redefinition of *diakonia* from its historical depiction as humble and kind charity. While *diakonia* does have a service dimension, it is primarily a theological and social action that mediates tension and opens dialogue between church and society in different contexts. *Diakonia* is responsible for bringing to light existing problems in the church and world. To this end, it involves elements of civil society in the search to eliminate suffering. It brings the identity of Christ into constant dialogue with other areas of knowledge, such as psychology, social work, nursing, and pedagogy. *Diakonia* enters places – the dirty corners and strange alleys – that often would not even be considered church.

Empowerment

Empowerment is another vital aspect of *diakonia*. It recognizes the uniqueness of each person, autonomy over one's own decisions, and the affirmation of each one's intrinsic abilities and gifts. Empowerment is related to the biblical understanding of creation: every human being is created in the likeness of God, with abilities and skills, regardless of their apparent social condition. And each person is unique, with their own story and autonomy over their decisions, created by God to care for the vast garden that is the Earth, as the creation narrative describes, with humanity appointed its stewards. Jesus himself empowers people, freeing them from burdens and enabling them to follow their paths. Empowerment is not about control but rather provides support to effect change and development.

Regarding empowerment, I cite an example by one of my diaconal groups. We know that *diakonia* deals with extreme situations. One such situation presented itself to the group: a couple who could not sustain their marriage due to many conflicts. Aware of this, the diaconal group, along with the congregation's deacon, attempted to salvage the marriage, but this was no longer possible. Therefore, the couple needed assistance in getting a divorce. However, they were unable to maintain two households and start from scratch, as their life as a couple already had very few resources. They needed empowerment to set up a new home in a different location. This was enabled through donations from the group, as well as dialogue about what a new life would be like for them as divorced persons on their own. Sharing collectively, the group empowered the

---

[25] Translation by Lori Mills-Curran. Dierk Starnitzke, *Diaconia*: *Fundamentação Bíblica – Concretizações Éticas* (São Leopoldo: Sinodal, 2013), 59.

former couple to move forward in their lives with greater confidence. They came to realize that, in the Lutheran congregation, they did not receive a message that insisted on saving their marriage at any cost. As they were empowered, they could openly express their suffering, receive care, and discover support to continue their lives in peace, free from the burden of maintaining marriage for the sake of appearances.

Real transformation requires focusing on the person to be empowered. Otherwise, we fail theologically by violating a foundational understanding of the Christian church as demonstrated at Pentecost. The promise of Pentecost involved receiving power: "you will receive power when the Holy Spirit has come upon you, and you will be my witnesses" (Acts 1:8, NRSVUE). The transformation involved all the people who, at the Pentecost event, witnessed the descent of the Holy Spirit that moved them toward the fulfilment of the mission of Jesus Christ: to wash the feet and care for people just as he did (John 13:1–17). The missionary expansion following Pentecost and the travel to reach new places occurred through transformative action by Jesus Christ. Jesus empowered people through his acts of mediation and reconciliation, indicating that they should follow their paths without the burdens that had previously weighed them down. Jesus empowered people for their Gospel work, indicating that they should follow him, and he would make them "fishers of people" (Mark 1:17, NRSVUE).

Diakonia, creation, and Pentecost are essentially interrelated. The church is convinced that God continues to empower people, not only the apostles and those who assumed leadership, but especially those who rarely, if ever, are given the opportunity to speak. This conviction should determine diaconal action, its methodology, and scale of priorities.[26] The empowerment process requires the same reflection Jesus demonstrated. Jesus empowered Bartimaeus through *diakonia* and he became active in his own story. Jesus called out and asked those who tried to silence him to encourage Bartimaeus to come to him. Moreover, Jesus asked, "What do you want me to do for you?" At this very moment, Bartimaeus could speak for himself, expressing his desires, his life, and his concerns in the simple phrase, "Rabbi, I want to see" (Mark 10:51, NIV). Jesus empowered Bartimaeus by calling him, motivating others to make room, and listening to what he had to say. For Bartimaeus, seeing meant autonomy, being able to defend himself from violence, navigate uneven terrain, and work to secure his livelihood. All empowerment provides spaces where people can be active in their own healing or in the challenges they face, by listening to what they have to say.

The way empowerment is developed directly affects the result to be achieved. When empowered by other people, they remain under their own command and have directed autonomy. When one is empowered and protagonist of the process, tools are developed so that a situation can change significantly within the expected transformation project. Thus, empowerment is not control but rather

---

[26] Nordstokke, *Diakonia in Context*, 43.

support for change.[27] Empowerment provides people, contexts, families, and communities with the support they need to continue to develop fully, making people moral agents, subjects of their own history.

Final Considerations

The *diakonia* of the Evangelical Church of the Lutheran Confession in Brazil is deeply rooted in a history of immigration, stemming from a context of suffering and exploitation, leading to a context marked by inequalities. *Diakonia* is a powerful tool for addressing these social inequalities, exploitation, and poverty. It is grounded in a rich history of solidarity and faith, guided by diaconal methodology characterized by mediation/reconciliation, transformation, and empowerment. These elements ensure that *diakonia* remains a dynamic force for positive change in the lives of individuals and the broader society.

Works Cited

Beulke, Gisela. "A História do Ministério Diaconal na IECLB." *Estudos Teológicos* 47, no.1 (2007): 144–65. http://periodicos.est.edu.br/index.php/estudos_teologicos/article/view/470/425.

Boff, Clodovis. *Theology and Praxis: Epistemological Foundations*. Maryknoll, NY: Orbis, 1987.

Bonelli, Régis, and Lauro Ramos. "Income Distribution in Brazil: Evaluation of the Long-term Tendencies and Changes in Inequality Since Mid-1970s," *Brazilian Journal of Political Economy* 13, no. 2 (April–June 1993). https://doi.org/10.1590/0101-31571993-0728.

Fluck, Marlon Ronald. "500 Anos De Evangelização Na América Latina." *Boletim Teológico* 6, no. 19 (December 1992): 43–64. http://www.repci.co/repositorio/handle/123456789/546.

Freire, Paulo. *Pedagogy of the Oppressed*, 30th anniv. ed. Translated by Myra Bergman Ramos. New York: Continuum, 2000 (1970).

Lenke, Angela. "Metodologia Diaconal." Master's thesis, Escola Superior de Teologia, São Leopoldo, Brazil, 2006.

Lutheran World Federation. *Mission in Context: Transformation, Reconciliation, Empowerment: An LWF Contribution to the Understanding and Practice of Mission*. Geneva: Lutheran World Federation, 2004. https://www.lutheranworld.org/sites/default/files/DMD-Mission-in-Context-EN-low.pdf.

Meirelles, Giselle Avila Leal de. "Productive Restructuring of Capital, Impoverishment and Social Inequality in Latin America." *Serviço Social em Revista* 18, no. 2 (January/June 2016): 52–72. https://doi.org/10.5433/1679-4842.2016v18n2p52.

---

[27] Angelique J.W.M. van Zeeland, "Solidarity Economy, Diakonia and Transformational Development: Dialogues in Construction," *Anais do Congresso Internacional da Faculdades EST* 2 (2014): 1150.

Neto, Rodolfo Gaede. *A Diaconia de Jesus. Contribuição para a Fundamentação Teológica da Diaconia na América Latina*. São Leopoldo: Sinodal, 2001.

Nordstokke, Kjell. *Diaconia: Fé em Ação*, 3rd ed. São Leopoldo, RS: Sinodal, 1998.

———. "Diaconia." In *Teologia Pratica no Contexto da América Latina*, edited by Christoph Schneider-Harpprecht, 268–90. São Leopoldo: Sinodal, 1998.

———, ed. *Diakonia in Context: Transformation, Reconciliation, Empowerment: An LWF Contribution to the Understanding and Practice of Diakonia*. Geneva: Lutheran World Federation, 2009. https://www.lutheranworld.org/sites/default/files/DMD-Diakonia-EN-low.pdf.

Oliveira, Francisco Mesquita de. "Social Inequality: A Trajectory of Insistence in Brazil." *Contribuciones a las Ciencias Sociales* 16, no. 7 (2023): 6750–66. https://doi.org/10.55905/revconv.16n.7-151.

Prien, Hans-Jürgen. *Formação da Igreja Evangélica no Brasil: Das Comunidades Teuto-Evangélicas de Imigrantes Até a Igreja Evangélica de Confissão Luterana no Brasil*. Petrópolis-São Leopoldo: Vozes Editora Sinodal, 2001.

Starnitzke, Dierk. *Diaconia: Fundamentação Bíblica – Concretizações Éticas*. São Leopoldo: Sinodal, 2013.

Stephanou, Luís. "Planejar é Possível e Necessário." In *Planejando as Ações Diaconais da Comunidade: E Como Que se Faz Isso?* edited by Hildegart Hertel, 32–40. Porto Alegre: IECLB-Departamento De Diaconia, 2001.

Zeeland, Angelique J.W.M. van. "Solidarity Economy, Diakonia and Transformational Development: Dialogues in Construction." *Anais do Congresso Internacional da Faculdades EST* 2 (2014): 1145–60.

Chapter 8

A Theology of *Diakonia* at the Margins

Norma Cook Everist

Meeting Christ the servant at the open tomb, we go forth to all places in the world, serving on behalf of the church. Rooted in a theology of the cross and resurrection, we are called to *diakonia* among those in need, particularly the marginalized. We are part of a diverse, historic, and global diaconal community. The church dares to notice, not to pass by, to grow in skills of caring and working for justice with and among marginalized people, and to learn from them.

Ministers of Word and Service are called to be servants in interpreting and meeting needs within the church and in diverse cultures and to empower the ministry of the baptized. Diaconal studies is extremely important. Diaconal ministers need a solid theological education because discerning how to serve is challenging.

We need to be grounded in Scripture. We need to be able to discern the needs of the world and to theologize in that context so that the Gospel relates clearly to that situation. In every age, the diaconate needs to claim its calling and to help the church claim its calling to speak, serve, and act in the world.[1]

Jesus uses the word *diakonia* (*diakonos*) about himself: "I am among you as one who serves" (Luke 22:27, NRSVUE). "The Son of Man came not to be served but to serve" (Matt 20:28, NRSVUE). In his death on the cross Christ endured the consequence of his own diaconal ministry. The church is the body of Christ (Rom 12; 1 Cor 12; Eph 4). When we consider people as one body, rather than as a hierarchy, leaders become partners. In the resurrection of Jesus, in a world dancing with death, death no longer has dominion. The Gospels show us Jesus' powerful servanthood.

A common symbol of diaconal ministry is the towel and basin: feet washing. This does not represent subservience but rather caring service. Jesus washed the feet of his disciples, not to relinquish his authority but as an expression of serving them. Tired feet need cleansing. There are many ways to "wash" feet. We feed the hungry, support those who are tired, provide housing and advocacy, and so much more. Diaconal ministers are sustained by prayer; therefore, this chapter concludes with the Diaconal Litany of the Lutheran Diaconal Association.

---

[1] DIAKONIA World Federation is an international and ecumenical community to support diaconal ministers in living out their ministries with vision and hope, and to remind the church of God's call to service, justice, compassion, and peace. Among the communities and associations in over thirty-five countries there are three regions: DIAKONIA of the Americas and the Caribbean (DOTAC); Diakonia Asia Pacific (DAP); and Diakonia Region Africa–Europe. (DRAE).

An Ecclesiology of a Diaconal Church

Being diaconal ministers and a diaconal church means recognizing that the world is filled with suffering, some of which will never go away. We see and experience deception and betrayal. So did Christ. People are alienated from one another. Many feel their lives are meaningless; people are rejected and persecuted. There is inequity and violence. A diaconal church is not a place to escape but rather a place to explore such problems and to face them.

Christians need to be in the world to be the church.[2] This is our ecclesiology. Yes, people are leaving the church. We need young people, not to save the church but to make a difference in the world. Young people are looking for that.

A resurrection theology means ministry that is going beyond pity and is not mired in guilt. Marginalized people do not need people's guilt but inclusion, support, and opportunity. It means freedom to get into good trouble for the sake of the Gospel. What is good trouble? Certainly not giving in to violence and inequities, nor being overwhelmed by the problems. It means claiming the power of Jesus Christ to be active. It means advocacy and, yes, risk, even getting into trouble through our activism. Good trouble.[3]

A diaconal church needs *diakonia* studies and theological education, which may take a variety of forms. At Wartburg Theological Seminary in Dubuque, Iowa, where I taught for thirty-eight years, we have three degrees, one of which is a Master's in Diaconal Ministry. Students who are becoming pastors and deacons study together to grow in collaborative partnership. Throughout the curriculum, there is an emphasis for all students on diaconal, servant leadership and for equipping the baptized for ministry in the world. An action/reflection methodology prepares students for a lifetime of learning.

Diakonia is not an appendage to the Gospel. *Diakonia* is neither merely the *carrier* of the Gospel, nor offered just so people will be *ready to hear* the Gospel. *Diakonia* is Gospel action.

The ecclesiology of a diaconal church is to be ecumenical. I was a participant in the Anglican–Lutheran International Consultation and Commission which met in Kent, England 24–30 April 1995, and 5–11 October 1995, in Hanover, Germany. It published "The Diaconate as Ecumenical Opportunity," the Hanover Report. We concluded that faithful diaconal ministry has been done and is being carried out in a variety of circumstances. The theological basis is in the resurrection of Jesus Christ. The goal is peace with justice. The means is compassion for the marginalized.[4]

---

[2] I am currently a member of Trinity Lutheran Church, a large, growing church with the motto of "A servant church in the heart of Mason City" (Iowa, USA). This congregation is a diaconal community.

[3] John Lewis, a civil rights activist and US representative for Georgia who devoted his life to racial justice and equality, often used the phrase, "Get into trouble. Good trouble."

[4] Anglican–Lutheran International Commission, "The Diaconate as Ecumenical Opportunity: The Hanover Report of the Anglican–Lutheran International Commission" (London: Anglican Communion Publications, 1996), 5–10, https://www.anglicancommunion.org/media/102181/the_hanover_report.pdf.

Marginalization and *Diakonia*

Throughout the centuries, the church has been tempted to turn away from people in situations it cannot bear to watch and reluctant to claim its diaconal calling. There is something at stake in forgetting – disregarding – those who are marginalized and keeping the marginalized marginalized. The church has often marginalized diaconal ministers, those who serve on behalf of marginalized people. We are called to remember and to act! Deacons do that.[5]

Marginalization manifests itself in racism, sexism, ageism, classism, ableism, and more. So-called wealthy nations marginalize nations with fewer resources: "Forget them." Meanwhile, rich nations that ignore poorer nations choose to be ignorant, refusing to learn from the disregarded.

Diaconal ministers have often been marginalized by the church because the people served were seen as of less worth. People who are unhoused are named "homeless." Differently abled people were named invalids: "in-valid." People with disabilities are part of many families. Their families also are often marginalized. Each human is of great worth. Each needs respect and honor.

For a dozen years we lived in inner cities, thought of as neighborhoods of no worth. Our streets were not cleaned. We had no police protection. People who lived there were considered dirty and dangerous. Those with power could justify gentrification. Just get rid of "them." Go away! But where? Disappear! Replace them by building homes for the wealthy ("worthy") people through redevelopment. Diaconal ministry means serving amid marginalized people, creating caring, diverse communities.

Minorities are often marginalized. Their culture, looks, and language seem different, so they are considered outside the norm. Should they be? What is normal? To say we "welcome the stranger" assumes the other is "strange." However, we are no doubt also strange to them. The goal is, by God's grace, to create trustworthy places to be "different together."[6]

Marginalized people are not always in the minority. In fact, when a particular ethnic or racial group grows numerically, they seem to be the most threatening to the majority. This is magnified by white supremacy. Once again, we see disenfranchisement. Discrimination intensifies. The intent is to keep "those" people from voting. Through ever-new forms of discrimination, people are not only relegated to the margins but pushed behind the margins, permanently excluded.

The token stage has often been the most dangerous. Those in the majority, those with power, think, "They are gaining on us." Their fear is the assumption "they" might take over. When our church body, the Evangelical Lutheran Church in America, was founded in 1988 with three Lutheran church bodies coming together, it set representational principles. Literally overnight, women and laity

---

[5] "For diaconal ministers, there is the added burden of some people not trusting, or understanding, the very office of diaconal ministry." Norma Cook Everist and Craig L. Nessan, *Transforming Leadership: New Vision for a Church in Mission* (Minneapolis: Fortress, 2008), 11.

[6] An important phrase from "The Diaconal Litany," printed at the end of this chapter.

and people of color and those whose language was other than English were on committees, at conferences, and could vote. The room finally seemed normal, and not so dangerous. More equal numbers of lay and clergy, both men and women, looked like the world looked. *Diakonia* meant everyone's gifts were used in service.

Diakonia is in essence caring about becoming an inclusive community. We engage in *diakonia* with people who are marginalized. I live with a disability. I am not my disability. As my disability became more acute, I was embarrassed that I would have to sit when leading worship. Eventually I realized that the whole community would not only embrace me with my disability but was becoming an inclusive, caring community for people with all kinds of disabilities. This formed students to serve. One time, I, who had difficulty in walking, and the assisting minister, who was legally blind, were leading worship together. I could see the steps for her from the altar to the table and she helped me walk down them. Students would tell me years later that experiencing an inclusive community shaped them and formed them.

A Trinitarian View of Marginalization

All are created by God and joined in Christ Jesus. The Spirit moves among us. The Creator God has made and loves the Earth and all of its people. Do we truly believe that?

People who are marginalized are not "the problem." Being excluded is the problem. We all participate in systemic sin, the reality that we have corporate responsibility for sinful actions that hurt people. Jesus experienced marginalization: from his birth, unhoused, to rejection and death; his diaconal ministry included everyone, especially those with disabilities.

Theologian Letty Russell often said that Jesus did not say to the blind person, "You can walk," nor to the person who could not walk, "You can see." Christ met people in the midst of their lives and asked, "What do you want me to do for you?" Jesus cared both about people and about the societal problems related to human need in the worlds in which they lived.[7]

By the power of the Spirit, we can be responsive to the pain of the world and love with boldness. For example, for people with certain physical disabilities, it is difficult in worship to hear "Please stand." That excludes. Hearing "Please stand in body or in spirit" includes. We stand for each other, those who can and those who cannot. People often want me to "get over it," afraid they will catch my disability. Marginalization continues. However, for years in seminary chapel, whoever was next to me sat with me as the worshipping community stood. This "tradition" just developed (no vote was ever taken) by people noticing, not ignoring. This is *diakonia*. This is solidarity. *Koinonia* is a partner with *diakonia*.

---

[7] See Letty M. Russell, *Human Liberation in a Feminist Perspective: A Theology* (Philadelphia: Westminster, 1974), 28, 53, 157.

Laos in Diaconal Ministry

Laos means people. People sometimes say of themselves, "I'm *only* a layperson." But that misses the gifts of all the people and limits the diaconal work of the church in the world. We need to think of the *diakonia* of all believers.[8]

Everyone in the body of Christ has a ministry in daily life. Those who are theologically educated (deacons, deaconesses, diaconal ministers) alongside of their own distinct positions are called to be leaders in equipping the *laos* for their ministries in daily life. Not everything we do is ministry, but everything we do in each arena of our daily lives has the potential for becoming ministry.

Ministry begins in baptism. People enter "the ministry" through baptism. The ministry of the baptized is sacramental and communal. Baptized people go forth from the worshipping assembly to serve in the public world. This includes standing with the poor, powerless, and marginalized by committing oneself to their needs.

We need to be able to name the human predicaments – complex, personal, communal, and systemic – in the arenas of daily life. We are transformed by grace in those places, in the languages of daily life, the "vernacular."[9] The *laos* are experiencing the human predicament and serving people who suffer. The actions of the baptized are Gospel good news.

"Deacons represent, serve, lead, and equip the whole people of God in service to God's world. Deacons come from, accompany, stand by, and are for the whole ministry of the baptized. In this way, deacons uniquely incarnate the church's call to *diakonia* and inspire renewed action."[10]

A Ministry of Justice and Reconciliation

Imagine the future: We need to be spokespersons for the Gospel, for justice, and for global peace, particularly in places where people are fascinated by guns and terrorize one another. We pursue peace, show hospitality, and engage in ministries of prophetic *diakonia*. We are called to ministries of reconciliation. *Diakonia* is relational. Mercy is not a piety of pity. *Diakonia* is rooted in the mercy of God.

There are many manifestations of *diakonia*. "Deacons are ordained to word, service, justice, and compassion and are called to be a bridge between the church

---

[8] Everist and Nessan, *Transforming Leadership*, 200–203. Various terms are used for this radical reformation concept: "The Priesthood of all Believers"; "Ministry of the Baptized"; "*Laos* in Ministry"; "The Ministry of the Whole People of God"; "the diaconate of all believers"; and "Ministry in Daily Life."
[9] Norma Cook Everist, *Seventy Images of Grace in the Epistles …: That Make All the Difference in Daily Life* (Eugene, OR: Cascade, 2015), xvi.
[10] Statement from the ELCA Deacons Ecumenical Engagement Affinity Group presented at the Diakonia of the Americas and the Caribbean conference, Minneapolis, MN, August 2023.

and the world."[11] Some diaconal ministers are in salaried positions, some non-salaried. Some are called by a congregation or judicatory. Others are salaried by other institutions when working in chaplaincy, criminal justice, or social work. There are diaconal ministers within prisons. We have diaconal ministry lawyers and medical workers. Our identity is not in our role but in Christ; therefore, we are freed to take any one of a variety of roles for servanthood.[12]

Justice and reconciliation call for immediate and long-term action. Caring people give first aid when a person has been cut or burned or needs immediate shelter. Surely, also, diaconal ministers establish long-term housing, social service agencies, and holistic medical facilities. They work so that everyone has a home. They work on the climate crisis. We need to go deeper. What are the reasons why there are so many unhoused people? Why are there so many refugees? Why do some people live in poverty? It must be "their fault!" These issues deserve study, theological discussion, and continued commitment. Deep, sustainable *diakonia* leads the church to be engaged in long-term societal change and justice.

Christians Freed from Subservience for Powerful Servanthood

We are called to be faithful to Christ. He "came not to be served but to serve and to give his life a ransom for many" (Mark 10:45, NRSVUE). Those with hierarchical power often seem threatened by powerful servants. Why? With trust in Christ, we do not need to be threatened by another person's power. Historically, diaconal ministers, in particular deaconesses, were often required to be subservient to those in power.

In the Spirit's economy, power is unlimited. Your having more power does not mean I have less, and I having more power does not mean you have less. In Christ we are called to a future of partnership and collaboration. Then ministry is multiplied. Can you imagine that?

Luther wrote in his *Treatise on Christian Liberty*: "The Christian individual is a completely free lord of all, subject to none. The Christian individual is a completely dutiful servant of all, subject to all."[13] This was one of the core

---

[11] Statement of the United Methodist Deacons and Diaconal Ministers presented at the Diakonia of the Americas and the Caribbean conference, Minneapolis, MN, August 2023.

[12] The history of the modern diaconate from 1836 to today has had three phases: 1) training in motherhouses, service within or connected to the institutions of church bodies; for example, hospitals, congregational service; 2) diaconal communities moving out into the world; for example, being called by church bodies and often "employed" by other agencies; for example, social service, criminal justice, mental health; and 3) now today emphasizing service as advocacy, prophetic voice, social justice, inclusive love, a diaconal church.

[13] Originally published in 1520, "A Treatise on Christian Liberty" is one of Martin Luther's most well-known and enduring writings. Martin Luther, *The Freedom of a Christian, 1520, The Annotated Luther Study Edition*, ed. Timothy J. Wengert (Minneapolis: Fortress, 2016), 488. The German Reformer examines Christian ethics and how justification by faith alone impacts the liberty of believers.

convictions of Martin Luther. He believed that, being liberated by God's grace, we are set free from being lorded over. We are free to serve others. Luther believed that serving the neighbor through diaconal work is everyone's vocation. For this, we need ongoing diaconal studies to enliven the future of *diakonia*.

The Diaconal Litany

The Lutheran Diaconal Association, of which I am a member, was founded in 1919. Various types of service evolved. Members of this community make a lifelong commitment of faith and service. They are accountable to one another through mutual discernment of call. As a multi-Lutheran diaconate, this Association is comprised of one diaconate with two communities, the Lutheran Deaconess Conference for women and the Community of Lutheran Deacons for men.

The Diaconal Litany was written in 1959. Over the decades, our diaconate has prayed this continuously, every Monday evening, whether together or individually, wherever we are. This remarkable continuity binds us together.

THE DIACONAL LITANY

O God, our caring creator:
Make us bold to trust you as beloved children.

Christ Jesus, our Redeemer and friend, who for joy became our servant:
Lead us to joyful service among those in any need or trouble.

Holy Spirit, giver of life to the Church:
Nourish our life on the breath of God.

Holy, blessed Trinity, author of the mystery of our salvation:
Unite our hearts to praise your name.

Gracious God, who created all humanity in your image:
Make us grateful for the companionship of other people, receiving them as gifts of your grace;
Shape us into companions for all who yearn for community;
And satisfy with your own gracious gifts those of us who work in isolated places.

Jesus, suffering servant and praying priest:
Empower us to spread the peace you bring through your life, death, and resurrection;
By steadfast endurance, without envy or resentment, to demonstrate your victory;
By persistent and faithful prayer to carry our neighbor into your grace-filled presence.

Jesus, friend of sinners, companion of the outcast, advocate for justice:
> **Open our eyes to see you in our neighbors who suffer injustice.**

Holy Spirit, purifier of sinners, making us sharers in the holiness of God:
> **Bestow on us the mind of Christ, that we neither think more highly of ourselves than we ought to think**
> **nor diminish ourselves in self-deprecation, calling common what you have called clean.**

Holy Spirit, fire of God, coming down from heaven, moving among us, and filling the Church:
> **Warm our hearts to love God, our neighbor, and all creation with our whole being.**

Holy Spirit, guide into all truth:
> **Endow us with patience to discern your wisdom;**
> **Teach us to speak the truth in a spirit of love;**
> **Free us from fear so that we can learn from each other; And give us your grace to be different together.**

Merciful Creator, compassionate Son, consoling Spirit:
Remember in mercy those who are sick and dying,
> **The suffering and persecuted, fearful and distraught, bored and despairing.**
> **By your goodness grant relief to all in need**
> **and strengthen them to trust you.**

Son of Righteousness:
> **Take the side of all who are oppressed;**
> **Protect the vulnerable, especially the young and the old; Restore all that is broken; Reconcile creation; And turn all hearts to receive your righteous judgement.**

Source and end of our salvation:
> **Draw to yourself those who deny you;**
> **Arouse those who have become dull toward you;**
> **Enlighten those who have closed their eyes to you; Strengthen those who trust you;**
> **Guide those who seek you.**

I believe that God has made me and all creation:
> **Teach me, O my maker, to look upon my person and my abilities as your gifts,**
> **So that I may trust your care for me,**
> **So that I may be delivered from jealousy and envy,**

So that I may see you hidden in my neighbor and there serve you with gladness.

I believe that Jesus Christ is my savior:
By your cross, loving Redeemer, crucify in me all evil desires and unbelief;
By your unspotted righteousness, clothe me in your own self that I may be delivered to God forever;
By your glorious resurrection from the dead, raise me to live with you eternally.

I believe in the Holy Spirit, giver, and sustainer of life:
Raise me up anew, creator Spirit, by confidence in your daily and rich forgiveness of my sins;
Bind me in unity of love with the saints in your community;
Awaken me to the presence of your saints in unexpected places;
Quicken in me the lively anticipation of my resurrection from the dead.
God of grace, who reveals yourself in creation,
and who inspired the holy scriptures to be written for our learning:
Speak to us, we are listening; strengthen us in our need.

God of grace, who joined us to the death and resurrection of your son in our baptism:
Make our whole lives a living from and returning to that holy font.
God of grace, who, nourishing us on the body and blood of Christ, create us into a new community:
Make us to be indeed the body of Christ and a vehicle of love and joy in this world,
until we offer the full and perfect praise forever. Amen.[14]

Works Cited

Anglican–Lutheran International Commission. "The Diaconate as Ecumenical Opportunity: The Hanover Report of the Anglican–Lutheran International Commission." London: Anglican Communion Publications, 1996. https://www.anglicancommunion.org/media/102181/the_hanover_report.pdf.

Everist, Norma Cook. *Seventy Images of Grace in the Epistles …: That Make All the Difference in Daily Life*. Eugene, OR: Cascade, 2015.

Everist, Norma Cook and Craig L. Nessan. *Transforming Leadership: New Vision for a Church in Mission*. Minneapolis: Fortress, 2008.

Luther, Martin. *The Freedom of a Christian, 1520, The Annotated Luther Study Edition*. Edited by Timothy J. Wengert. Minneapolis: Fortress, 2016.

---

[14] Written in 1959, Revised in 1997, 2012, and 2022, Lutheran Diaconal Association. All rights reserved. This may be duplicated for use if origin is noted. 1304 Laporte Avenue, Valparaiso, Indiana 46383, United States of America.

Lutheran Diaconal Association. "The Diaconal Litany." Rev. 2022. Valparaiso, Indiana.

Russell, Letty M. *Human Liberation in a Feminist Perspective: A Theology*. Philadelphia: Westminster, 1974.

Chapter 9

The Work of *Diakonia* Toward *Koinonia* Among LGBTQIA+ Persons and the Church

Leo Yates Jr.

The spirit of *diakonia* connects individuals and communities with Christ's ministries. The Spirit also inspires deacons, deaconesses, diaconal ministers, and other ministers to reconcile, heal, affirm, seek justice, empower, support, equip, educate, advocate, and provide care and encouragement to persons who identify as lesbian, gay, bisexual, transgender, queer, intersex, asexual, and other silent letters (LGBTQIA+) and who have also been outcast and marginalized. These examples of *diakonia* were modelled by Christ the servant in his ministry and are gifts to the diaconate for leading and supporting the church. As diaconal pathways of compassion and justice, these activities can support LGBTQIA+ persons deprived of *koinonia* and bridge them to grace and wholeness. In this chapter, I discuss the role of deacons in supporting relationships among LGBTQIA+ persons, thereby restoring *koinonia* (communion or fellowship) more fully within their faith communities.

Koinonia

Koinonia enables the church to experience deeper discipleship and the Lord's presence. God's love draws us to love (1 John 4:19), manifested in diverse and plentiful ways. Jesus encouraged his followers to love one another as he loved us (John 13:34). According to Martin Luther King Jr., "Love is the greatest force in the universe. It is the heartbeat of the moral cosmos."[1] These quotes reflect the *koinonia* that churches can experience.

The Hebrew Scriptures require us to love and treat strangers as equals (Lev 19:34). The early church also valued persons living in harmony and the centrality of fellowship as a community of faith. Paul appealed to the church in Corinth not to have divisions over theology and leadership and called for unity (1 Cor 1:10). Paul emphasized how the body consists of many members and that one member should not say to another that they are less valued or are not needed. When living and practicing their faith together, the faith community that experiences *koinonia* – a spiritual communion – exemplifies what the body of Christ should look like.

Grace draws us to *koinonia*. When the Christian fellowship gathers and connects, the church thrives and grows as a part of the body of Christ. What a

---

[1] Alicia Lee, "Martin Luther King Jr. Explains the Meaning of Love in Rare Handwritten Note," *CNN*, 9 Feb 2020, https://www.cnn.com/2020/02/09/us/martin-luther-king-jr-handwritten-note-for-sale-trnd.

gift *koinonia* is for individuals, families, and the wider community! Love that shares everything in common (Acts 2:44) cannot help but spill over into our communities, drawing in more people. The fellowship flourishes with "glad and sincere hearts" (Acts 2:46, NIV), inviting us as church not only to praise God for one another but also to invite more people into our fellowship (Acts 2:47). Today's church has reclaimed *koinonia* as a model of loving community, including interrelationships among its members.

At the heart of *koinonia*, Christ extends a hand of welcome and invitation to all who seek him, even before we realize it. Takesure Mahohoma of the University of South Africa describes *koinonia* as a relationship where trust, friendship, and confidence are the basis, giving *koinonia* rich meaning as community and interdependence.[2] In Wesleyan theology, grace is better experienced in fellowship and *koinonia*. *Koinonia* moves beyond inclusion to a place of belonging.

Deacons

As a deacon in full connection with The United Methodist Church, like many of my co-laborers in Christ, I create pathways to and from the church, inviting others to engage and participate in our ministries and congregations. In the early church, deacons not only served their bishop for the Gospel's sake but also prepared and led the people in the church's mission and ministries. Deacons are fundamentally called to compassion and justice.[3] Within the Wesleyan tradition, social holiness integrates our love for God with our neighbor.[4] The social holiness aspect of a deacon's work comes in many forms, whether pastoral care, hospitality, faith development within the church, or mission and service.[5] Deacons often work with persons on the margins to foster connections with the church, create pathways to services, and offer support on behalf of the church.

While the modern deacon may not be set apart to serve their bishops, deacons still are called to serve in ministry on behalf of their bishops, thus extending the bishop's authority through various servant ministries in the church's community. Characteristically, many deacons share servanthood on the front lines of ministry, leading the church by supporting the laity in fulfilling their diaconal ministries, some within the bounds of the church and others outside the church.

Bridging and connecting persons, groups, and communities with the church (and vice versa) is at the heart of a deacon's ministry. Whether through social justice, pastoral care, or other involvements, deacons serve unique functions to unite the church and community. Jesus marked the character of apostolic ministry as *diakonia* (John 13:1–15). The apostles continued Jesus' vision for

---

[2] Takesure Mahohoma, "Difficult Texts: *Koinonia*, Acts 2:42," *Theology* 120, no. 5 (Sept–Oct 2017): 364, https://doi.org/10.1177/0040571X17710202.
[3] Margaret Ann Crain, *The United Methodist Deacon: Ordained to Word, Service, Compassion, and Justice* (Nashville: Abingdon, 2016), 15.
[4] Crain, 17.
[5] Crain, 21–27.

the church by setting apart deacons through the laying on of hands and authorizing their ministry to serve the poor and marginalized (Acts 6).

Throughout church history, deacons have fed the poor, visited the sick in hospitals and prisons, taken responsibility for charity work, shared love, and assisted bishops in administrative work, including supervising clergy and leading churches in their diaconal ministries. Deacons either worked side by side with priests and bishops or were tasked with supporting their ministries for the betterment of the church. Deacons were often the first to see the needs of the community. Learning about the needs of those who have been neglected, ignored, or treated with hostility by the wider community and society, deacons have always been the bridge, ministering and supporting these persons and communities.

LGBTQIA+ Inclusion

It is no surprise that persons who identify as LGBTQIA+ have been historically marginalized by the church because of rigid views based on Scripture. Many have been ostracized by families, communities, and faith communities. It is tragic that many have been excommunicated and have endured homophobia and transphobia through the teachings of heteronormativity and binary beliefs, among other societal biases toward LGBTQIA+ persons.

The modern church has not been kind to and has often excluded persons identifying as LGBTQIA+ within their faith communities. Apart from cis-hetero identities, the word queer is sometimes used as an umbrella term, a catch-all, to include all non-conforming sexual and gender identities. Most churches are made up primarily of heterosexual and cisgender persons, and the various sexual and gender identities may be unfamiliar to them. This is partly due to heterosexual "straight" privilege, which often isolates persons from the realities of those different from them. It is also due to one-sided teachings about homosexuality that are debated and typically support heteronormative understandings of the Bible.[6]

There are many other verses in both the Hebrew Scriptures and the New Testament that focus on persons and communities living in harmony. Consider, for example, "I am fearfully and wonderfully made; your works are wonderful" (Psalm 139:14, NIV). These passages emphasize being at peace with one another and providing hospitality – like welcoming the stranger – for the sake of supporting faith communities through *koinonia*. Only focusing on a few references, such as the "clobber passages," as opposed to the wider biblical text, mistakenly perpetuates prejudices from the pulpit – and reinforces homophobia, biphobia, sexism, and transphobia.[7] These verses exclude rather than include

---

[6] Robert K. Gnuse, "Seven Gay Texts: Biblical Passages Used to Condemn Homosexuality," *Biblical Theology Bulletin* 45, no. 2 (May 2015), 68, https://doi.org/10.1177/0146107915577097.

[7] Seven passages typically include Genesis 9:20–27 (Noah and Ham), Genesis 19:1–11 (Sodom and Gomorrah), Leviticus 18:22, 20:13 (Levitical laws), 1 Corinthians 6:9–10

people. Naturally, these prejudices impede the work of *koinonia* for which the church strives.

In his life and ministry, Jesus never spoke against or condemned LGBTQIA+ persons. The account of Jesus speaking about eunuchs – some being "born that way" and some "for the sake of the kingdom of heaven" (Matt 19:12, NIV) – indicates both the existence of non-binary persons and Jesus' early acknowledgement of gender diversity. Some scholars see eunuchs as intersex or as persons who identify as transgender, while other scholars see this eunuch passage as Jesus' message of inclusivity toward those who were marginalized.[8]

Jesus did not show disapproval toward the centurion (either in Luke or Matthew) over his relationship with his male servant when he asked for the servant to be healed; moreover, Jesus was more impressed with the centurion's faith – as a non-Jew at that – than expressing concern over his sexual relationship with his servant. The nuance in Luke 7:2 indicates that he highly valued the servant, whereas Matthew 8:5–13 indicates the servant experienced some form of tormenting paralysis. *The Queer Bible Commentary* states that the centurion cared deeply for his "boy."[9]

These same-gender relationships were common knowledge among some Roman soldiers, as Caesar needed soldiers regardless of their sexual orientation.[10] To teach or preach only one view or interpretation of sexual and gender differences (such as the clobber passages) and not to share the different cultural contexts can and will perpetuate homophobia, sexism, and transphobia.

The sense that too much emphasis has been placed on a person's sexual and gender identity has contributed to marginalization of queer persons and their families within churches. Individuals, families, groups, and congregations who have been victimized over their sexual and gender identities have written about their church-related traumas.

The Work of *Diakonia* Within the Church

Deacons lead congregations in their servant ministries and care both for those within the church and those in the community. The deacon, together with other church staff, supports individuals and groups within the church, ministering to them about the importance of supporting persons who may be marginalized or disadvantaged by society.

Deacons, not by their own doing but with the spirit of *diakonia*, are called to support and lead the church to capture and sustain *koinonia*, assisting the clergy and laity to live out their discipleship and diaconal ministries. Deacons are uniquely positioned to speak to the church's deprivation of *koinonia*, pointing out compassion and justice concerns. Consider the advocacy concerns brought

---

and 1 Timothy 1:10 (forbidding sexual immorality), and Romans 1:26–27 (condemning same-sex relations).

[8] Thomas Bohache, "Matthew," *The Queer Bible Commentary* (Norwich, UK: SCM, 2015), 511.
[9] Bohache, 512.
[10] Bohache, 512.

to the apostles in Acts 6 that provided the church with a diaconate model. This diaconate model shows us how seven persons were selected to support and bridge cultural differences between the Hellenistic Jews and Judeo-Christians on behalf of the apostles.

The servant ministry in Acts 6 was focused on food distribution and bringing the Word of God among the Hellenistic Jews, who likely perceived they were neglected and quite possibly discriminated against due to their non-Jewish upbringing. However, the spirit of *diakonia* supported the ministry of the seven persons selected and empowered them to preach, spiritually gifted them for the work, and supported their Christ-like compassion on behalf of the apostles. This diaconate model of *koinonia* also applies to LGBTQIA+ inclusion.

When restoring *koinonia* within the congregation, deacons may lead and support the inclusion and empowerment of LGBTQIA+ persons within their church. This takes shape in a variety of ways.

Potlucks and Meals

For faith communities with more than a few LGBTQIA+ members and their allies, hosting potluck meals once a month is a common activity to support *koinonia*. Hosting a potluck at the church or in one of the homes in the community, the deacon may wish to co-organize with a church member, offering support and possibly a prayer during the meal. Some may share their past experiences with the deacon, and some may have some initial mistrust. While the deacon may or may not be the one to organize the gathering, the deacon's attendance shows support and solidarity with this part of the queer community.

The same consideration might be made for parents of LGBTQIA+ youth and young adults who gather to support and learn about their shared experiences. Due to the parents' own church experience, it is not uncommon for families to leave churches due to their child or children coming out as LGBTQIA+. The deacon can be a gift to these parents, some of whom go through their own coming out experience as the parent of a child who self-identifies as LGBTQIA+.

Weddings

Ordained deacons are permitted to officiate weddings. This affords deacons the opportunity to officiate at weddings for LGBTQIA+ couples and show to the queer community that the church is affirming. The act of hospitality that weddings offer can be a gateway for persons to return to the church, supporting the restoration of *koinonia*. Certainly, the wedding liturgy should be adapted to the couple.

Deacons who officiate weddings may also provide pre-marriage counselling. Considering that pre-marriage counselling materials often focus on heterosexual couples, the nuances that LGBTQIA+ couples experience should be discussed, such as monogamy versus an open relationship, being closeted to some family members, different orientations (such as pansexual and transgender), name changes, continuing friendships with exes, and having children – including the legal restrictions they may face in some states. Deacons must be aware of their own internal biases so as not to impose their negative values.

Small Groups

Deacons may wish to organize or lead small groups specifically for persons who identify as LGBTQIA+. Small groups that bring together LGBTQIA+ persons for study provide a natural way to deepen relationships, encourage fellowship, and support the group's faith journey. Whether studying queer history, queer theology, or biblical texts, the small group gathering is the heart of the activity; the deacon seeks to foster the spiritual experience of the group's *koinonia*.

Policies and Statements

Deacons are advocates. For churches committed to the inclusion of LGBTQIA+ persons, the deacon's leadership and involvement may involve supporting the church's policies and statements that reinforce LGBTQIA+ inclusion. Saying that "all are welcome" is not enough, as this statement does not specifically speak to LGBTQIA+ persons. Historically and up to the present, they have been the exception to this declaration of welcome. Current policies and statements should be reviewed, and new policies and statements should meet the church's commitment to LGBTQIA+ inclusion.

Gender-Neutral Bathrooms

Having at least one gender-neutral bathroom provides equal access to transgender and non-binary persons. By learning about this need and the reasons behind it, the deacon can better advocate and educate church leadership and the church board about the need to have gender-neutral bathrooms in the church. Sam Killermann's *A Guide to Gender* provides a thorough explanation of this topic, giving reasons for and against restroom equity.[11]

Diversity, Equity, and Inclusion Training

Deacons who lead or organize diversity, equity, and inclusion training among the church leadership – including ministry leaders who represent the church through its ministries and programmes – can reduce discrimination among minority groups. The training can and should include information regarding sexuality, gender identities, and inclusion, as well as (queer) persons with disabilities. Including training in church membership classes orients parishioners to expectations at the church. *A Guide to Gender* is also a helpful resource to cover gender identity-related information.

LGBTQIA+ Leadership

Deacons often encourage and foster servant ministries among the congregation. In this capacity, deacons can encourage LGBTQIA+ persons to assume leadership roles. Seeing LGBTQIA+ persons in leadership roles helps normalize their involvement in the church's life, while affirming their gifts for ministry. Supporting LGBTQIA+ leaders furthers the work of *koinonia* by recognizing their place in the body of Christ.

---

[11] Sam Killerman, *A Guide to Gender: The Social Justice Advocate's Handbook*, 2nd ed. (Austin, TX: Impetus, 2017), 165.

Queer BIPOC

In her book, *Our Lives Matter: A Womanist Queer Theology*, Pamela Lightsey pointed out that queer Black, indigenous, and persons of color (BIPOC) have different experiences than white persons.[12] The added layers of racial and ethnic prejudice should not be ignored, including the bias they may experience within the Black church.[13] Queer people and queer BIPOC often mistrust conservative, white, evangelical preachers and theologians. Notably, Lightsey educates readers that, for Black queers, the term gay is closely identified with white males and the politics of the 1970s gay rights movement, which did not include the struggles of Black gay men.[14] Deacons are encouraged to learn more about each group's unique struggles to support the church's welcome and affirmation of them.

Queer Persons with Disabilities

When looking at the intersectionality of queer persons, every person has a different identity, such as those with a disability. Aware and informed deacons are indispensable as allies to queer persons with disabilities. Queer persons with disabilities face additional discriminations, further preventing their inclusion and hampering the church's *koinonia*.[15] Advocacy by deacons and other ministry leaders can support accessibility. Full inclusion can help reduce or eliminate ableism.[16] Deacons might consider taking on the role of an accessibility coordinator as a part of their church responsibility or simply supervise a volunteer in this role. Conducting a periodic accessibility audit helps identify barriers with the hope of removing them. Empowering queer persons with disabilities in the life of the church helps to transform the mindset of ministry leaders from ministering to them to ministering with them.

Queer Children and Youth

Some deacons actively engage in Christian education. Children and youth who come out (self-identify) early will likely need the deacon's pastoral support. Ministry programme leaders, whether in Sunday School, children's choirs, youth groups, or the like, should be oriented toward the inclusion of LGBTQIA+ persons and ensure there is no bullying, including cyberbullying. LGBTQIA+ youth are more at risk for mental health problems and suicide than others in their age range. Deacons can share information and resources with other ministry leaders. The Trevor Project, for example, is a nationwide organization with a hotline and text messaging that supports youth contemplating suicide and experiencing a crisis.[17]

---

[12] Pamela R. Lightsey, *Our Lives Matter: A Womanist Queer Theology* (Eugene, OR: Pickwick, 2015).
[13] Lightsey, *Our Lives Matter*, 5.
[14] Lightsey, 33.
[15] Leo Yates Jr., *Deaf Ministries: Ministry Models for Expanding the Kingdom of God*, 4th ed. (North Charleston, SC: KDP, 2021), 249.
[16] Yates, 251.
[17] The Trevor Project, www.thetrevorproject.org.

Deacons can lead conversations with church leadership about navigating children and youth who come out to them. Being non-judgmental and offering empathetic listening are important, but much more is needed to support them. Ministry leaders working with children and youth need to learn about gender and sexuality, not only to educate others but also to inform themselves.

Resources from the Reconciling Ministries Network, a non-profit organization affiliated with The United Methodist Church, offers a Youth Leader Toolkit to educate ministry leaders about serving and working with LGBTQIA+ youth.[18] Whether working in Christian education or a different church role, deacons can learn to orient ministry leaders and volunteers about gender and sexuality. The "Guide to Being an Ally to Transgender and Nonbinary Young People" by The Trevor Project is another resource.[19] Vacation Bible School materials by the Reconciling Ministries Network are another useful resource that deacons and ministry leaders can consider.

Pastoral Care

Deacons responsible for pastoral care to their congregation will also need to care for LGBTQIA+ persons. Pastoral care may be specific to LGBTQIA+ persons coming out, offering education about the stages of coming out, suggesting community and national resources, and being supportive. The deacon must be comfortable with sexuality and gender issues, not so much to become the expert but to enable active listening. Persons who come out later in life after already establishing a heteronormative family have an added layer of complication, as some family and friends will likely need to adjust to their new sexual or gender identity. Being authentic and self-accepting in pastoral care can provide healing for the individual. Pastoral care is also vital for persons facing stressful life events, such as grieving, mental health and addiction challenges, or relationship problems.

The LGBTQIA+ person's journey is also a spiritual journey, with parallels to the Hebrews who left Egypt.[20] They, too, were afraid to leave Egypt, yet they did leave and then wandered in the desert before arriving at the Promised Land. Yahweh journeyed with the Israelites and now journeys with persons coming out who are settling into their new lives.

Community of Care

In *Ministry Among God's Queer Folk: LGBTQ Pastoral Care*, Bernard Schlager and David Kundtz recommend that faith communities become a "community of care."[21] This includes being welcoming, having LGBTQIA+ church leaders,

---

[18] Reconciling Ministries Network, "Resource Toolkit for LGBTQ+ Christian Teens," https://rmnetwork.org/resource-full-library/.
[19] The Trevor Project, "Guide to Being an Ally to Transgender and Nonbinary Young People," https://www.thetrevorproject.org/resources/guide/a-guide-to-being-an-ally-to-transgender-and-nonbinary-youth/.
[20] Darryl W. Stephens et al., *Out of Exodus: A Journey of Open and Affirming Ministry* (Eugene, OR: Cascade, 2018), 2.
[21] Bernard Schlager and David Kundtz, *Ministry Among God's Queer Folk: LGBTQ Pastoral Care*, 2nd ed. (Eugene, OR: Wipf and Stock, 2019), 154.

Diaconal Studies

creating alliances with queer-related organizations, using LGBTQIA+-inclusive language in bulletins and on the church website, and being known as an ally. Deacons leading these efforts will make friends for life, and the spirit of *diakonia* will be spread among the church and the community when the church is experienced as a community of care.

The Work of *Diakonia* Within the Community

Deacons often work in the community as they do within the church. This is their gift to the church. In doing so, deacons who serve and work with the queer community offer a ministry of presence and support. The deacon's relationship with the queer community can unite, heal, and express love.[22]

Social Justice

Deacons whose primary responsibility focuses on social justice can bring attention to a single issue or multiple social justice issues when they work in the church and community. Anti-discrimination is an important feature of social justice work, often focusing on improving equality for LGBTQIA+ persons. The National Center for Transgender Equality and the Human Rights Campaign promote social justice issues.[23] Deacons who lead or partner with church ministry groups and community organizers should become familiar with these and other issues specific to their community.

Awareness and education are part of the work of social justice, as deacons whose focus is social justice will testify. Deacons can organize small group discussions, offer book studies, promote panel discussions, and invite guest speakers to inform the faith community. By celebrating and sponsoring LGBTQIA+ observances, the church shows support to the queer community. For instance, deacons can organize HIV/AIDS awareness services in December.

Pride Parade and Events

Attending events and gatherings within the church's community shows solidarity with the queer community. For many LGBTQIA+ persons with religious trauma or bad experiences with the church, supporting queer community events fosters reconciliation. Deacons and other ministry leaders who show up and actively support these events, such as a Pride parade, are showing their solidarity. Whether marching in the parade or offering hospitality, such as cups of lemonade to marchers, deacons can bridge relationships between the queer community and the church. Since bars and clubs are often gathering places for the queer community, lending support to or even attending their community events puts deacons in a position to be visible and present.

---

[22] Schlager and Kundtz, *Ministry Among God's Queer Folk*, 154.
[23] The National Center for Transgender Equality, https://transequality.org/; Human Rights Campaign, "Our Work," https://www.hrc.org/our-work.

Queer Seniors and Older Adults

Deacons can be an asset to queer seniors and older adults by being sensitive to their needs. Deacons can partner with a national organization, SAGE: Advocacy & Services for LGBTQ+ Elders, to support queer seniors and older adults in their community. If there is a SAGE group in the community, the deacon can attend and support their programmes and learn about the specific concerns and disparities experienced by queer seniors and older adults. The SAGE website offers resources specific to LGBTQIA+ ageing persons, such as caregiving, health care, housing, and finances.[24] Sharing the needs of the world with the church is a part of the deacon's responsibility.

Becoming a Welcoming and Affirming Congregation

Some denominations have specialty ministries that support welcoming and affirming churches. The Reconciling Ministries Network, associated with The United Methodist Church, is an advocacy group that supports such efforts by providing resources, videos, and consultation. Queer caucuses and LGBTQIA+ advocacy groups organized by denominations are listed on the GayChurch.org website.[25] Deacons can learn about the advocacy groups specific to their denomination and partner with them. It is common for churches to go through a discernment process before making a commitment to become welcoming and affirming. These advocacy groups and caucuses provide general information and guidance. The deacon can serve as the liaison for these groups and help bridge conversations.

Conclusion

Koinonia is better experienced by the church when queer persons and their families are seen as equals and provisions are made to support their presence and participation within the body.[26] Advocating for and educating about the importance of *koinonia* encourages deacons to show faith communities how the church can be a place of welcome and hospitality for our queer siblings in Christ. Healing the harm and rebuilding trust are crucial to this work. For the sake of expanding sexual and gender diversity, the church can re-examine its practices and policies to achieve better *koinonia* – the love of Christ within our communities. Amen.

---

[24] SAGE: Advocacy & Services for LGBTQ+ Elders, "Your Rights & Resources," https://www.sageusa.org/your-rights-resources/.
[25] GALIP Foundation, "Affirming Denominations," www.gaychurch.org/affirming-denominations/.
[26] Brooke N. Petersen, *Religious Trauma: Queer Stories in Estrangement and Return* (New York: Lexington, 2022), 2.

Works Cited

Bohache, Thomas. "Matthew." *The Queer Bible Commentary*. Norwich, UK: SCM Press, 2015.

Crain, Margaret Ann. *The United Methodist Deacon: Ordained to Word, Service, Compassion, and Justice*. Nashville: Abingdon, 2016.

GALIP Foundation. "Affirming Denominations." www.gaychurch.org/affirming-denominations/.

Gnuse, R.K. "Seven Gay Texts: Biblical Passages Used to Condemn Homosexuality." *Biblical Theology Bulletin* 45, no. 2 (May 2015): 68–87. https://doi.org/10.1177/0146107915577097.

Human Rights Campaign. "Our Work." www.hrc.org/our-work.

Killerman, Sam. *A Guide to Gender: The Social Justice Advocate's Handbook*. 2nd ed. Austin, TX: Impetus, 2017.

Lee, Alicia. "Martin Luther King Jr. Explains the Meaning of Love in Rare Handwritten Note." *CNN*, 9 Feb 2020. https://www.cnn.com/2020/02/09/us/martin-luther-king-jr-handwritten-note-for-sale-trnd.

Lightsey, Pamela R. *Our Lives Matter: A Womanist Queer Theology*. Eugene, OR: Pickwick, 2015.

Mahohoma, Takesure. "Difficult Texts: *Koinonia*, Acts 2:42." *Theology* 120, no. 5 (September–October 2017): 364–66. https://doi.org/10.1177/0040571X17710202.

The National Center for Transgender Equality. https://transequality.org/.

Petersen, Brooke N. *Religious Trauma: Queer Stories in Estrangement and Return*. New York: Lexington, 2022.

Reconciling Ministries Network. "Resource Toolkit for LGBTQ+ Christian Teens." https://rmnetwork.org/resource-full-library/.

SAGE: Advocacy & Services for LGBTQ+ Elders. "Your Rights & Resources." https://www.sageusa.org/your-rights-resources.

Schlager, Bernard and David Kundtz. *Ministry Among God's Queer Folk: LGBTQ Pastoral Care*. 2nd ed. Eugene, OR: Wipf and Stock, 2019.

Stephens, Darryl W., Michael I. Alleman, Andrea Brown, Ruth A. Daugherty, and Mary Merriman. *Out of Exodus: A Journey of Open and Affirming Ministry*. Eugene, OR: Cascade, 2018.

The Trevor Project. www.the trevorproject.org.

———. "Guide to Being an Ally to Transgender and Nonbinary Young People." https://www.thetrevorproject.org/resources/guide/a-guide-to-being-an-ally-to-transgender-and-nonbinary-youth/.

Yates, Leo. *Deaf Ministries: Ministry Models for Expanding the Kingdom of God*. 4th ed. North Charleston, SC: KDP, 2021.

Chapter 10

De-Subjugating the Servant Image as a Theo-Diaconal Intervention

Man-Hei Yip

⁵ Let the same mind be in you that was in Christ Jesus,
⁶ who, though he existed in the form of God,
did not regard equality with God
as something to be grasped,
⁷ but emptied himself,
taking the form of a slave,
assuming human likeness.
And being found in appearance as a human,
⁸ he humbled himself
and became obedient to the point of death –
even death on a cross.
⁹ Therefore God exalted him even more highly
and gave him the name
that is above every other name,
¹⁰ so that at the name given to Jesus
every knee should bend,
in heaven and on earth and under the earth,
¹¹ and every tongue should confess
that Jesus Christ is Lord,
to the glory of God the Father. (Phil 2:5–11, NRSV)

Philippians 2:5–11 is frequently quoted in *diakonia*-related discourse. *Diakonia* means service, and deacons are servants – that is what we often hear. And that is also what we would accept without a second thought, simply because Christ Jesus "emptied himself, taking the form of a slave" (Phil 2:7, NRSV). No clear distinction between slave and servant has been made; slave seems to qualify the nature of a servant for easy idealization of those who dedicate their time for God's work, in this case, a deacon. While Christ's obedience and humility are embodied in the form of a slave, that form of service – the service of a slave to his master – easily becomes the reference point or role model for how Christians engage in diaconal work. An uncritical use of the slave language, however, causes harm and perpetuates hierarchical relationships, particularly in contexts where communities of people continue to be haunted by the institution of slavery.

This chapter interrogates the concept of servanthood and points out that the romanticization of service overemphasizes the sacrificial language and fails to honor the living memories of those who went through dehumanization, subjugation, and oppression. Furthermore, it obscures the unhealthy master/slave relationship inherited from history. History remembers those who made slaves a symbol not only of success but also as authorized by God. Victims of slavery and those who are suffering from the residual impact of the slave trade – Black, Brown, and Yellow – are unfortunately vanished from the narratives.

De-subjugating the servant image is both urgent and necessary for the reconceptualization of *diakonia* in the age of the new normal, post-COVID-19. This chapter contends that problematizing the concept of servanthood can subvert and destabilize the narrative of Jesus' identity as a submissive and subservient servant in Christian discourse and reconceptualize *service* within a broader framework that considers, respects, and takes heed of people's memory for the task of healing and reconciliation.

Problematizing the Servant Image

Diakonia and other *diakon*-words in Greek have been understood as "humble service" because these services were normally related to menial tasks. In his important work, *Diakonia: Re-Interpreting the Ancient Sources*, John N. Collins re-engaged the concept of *diakonia* and found that most sources, including non-Christian materials in the Hellenic contexts, referred to the *diakon*-word group as "messenger,"[1] "emissary,"[2] or "go-between."[3] Collins made clear that these words did not refer to service of humble origins.[4]

Collins argued that we need to put the word *diakonia* back in its original context. Those who are involved in service are entrusted with an important task or a special mission. Ministries, such as caring for the sick, ministering to the poor, or advocating for justice, are performed by people commissioned to perform those services and tasks. According to Collins, putting *diakonia* back into the larger biblical and theological contexts gives us a bigger picture of how we could relate *diakonia* to the salvific work of God in Jesus Christ.

Analyzing other scholarly work, Collins indicated a shift from Jesus' serving to Jesus' saving.[5] In a diaconal turn, Mark 10:45, for instance, shows how Jesus as a servant of God fulfilled the mission of God the Father. That particular kind of mission could only be fulfilled by Jesus and, by fulfilling that mission, the *diakonia* of Jesus was linked with his salvific work. Collins admitted the difficulty of naming the kind of service the Son of Man referred to, but he never ruled out the relationship between the Son of Man's *diakonia* and his death, even stating: "by the death that the commission to effect the ransom entails for the Son of man."[6] Only the Son of Man could effect this ransom, and the

---

[1] John N. Collins, *Diakonia: Re-Interpreting the Ancient Sources* (New York: Oxford University Press, 1990), 104–5.
[2] Collins, 195–226.
[3] Collins, 77–95.
[4] Collins, 194.
[5] Collins, 46–47.
[6] Collins, 252.

commissioning of Jesus in realizing the mission suggested that his *diakonia* is no small thing but is rather connected with his suffering, death, and salvation.

The biblical and theological concept of *diakonia* that Collins offered is helpful, as it rejected any idea that associates *diakonia* with menial tasks and broadened its meaning by binding it with God's salvation for the world. His proposal, however, largely focuses on "from-above" thinking; that is, God's purpose and plan for humanity, which does not communicate well with the complexity of social realities. In fact, the situation is more complicated when the servant image and the history of slavery become entangled. When servant discourse overemphasizes Jesus' self-sacrifice, obedience, and submission to fulfil salvation for the world, it is hard to speak meaningfully to the poor and oppressed, as many of them are no stranger to the experience of being enslaved in the larger political and socio-economic systems.

In problematizing the servant image, it is necessary to name the danger of mixing the servant image with slave language to expose the contradictions deposited in this language. Jacquelyn Grant pointed out that concepts such as service, servant, and servanthood used in the Christian faith are usually overly romanticized and perhaps even misused and manipulated to support unjust and unequal relationships, especially within the dominantly white Christian community. The notion of servanthood cannot be understood in isolation. Grant linked it to a larger context, the institution of slavery, and criticized, "The masters intended that the slave would understand his/her servanthood status not only to be ordained by God, but to be of God. What followed slavery and replaced it was the institution of domestic service wherein blacks were still perceived to be the servants of white masters."[7]

Romanticizing the Christian notion of servanthood runs the risk of endorsing servitude. Grant's argument further shows how the intertwining of the servant image with the history of slavery creates unnecessary hierarchies between the servants of God and servants/slaves of earthly masters, thus reinforcing the "daily sociopolitical positioning" of the poor and oppressed.[8] Not only does that positioning of people fail to speak against injustice but it also ends up supporting coercive systems and supremacist ideologies. Grant provided a concrete example of how the notion of servanthood has "become a mechanism for perpetuating evil and suffering" by examining the Black mammy and "live-in" traditions.[9] In these traditions, there are consistent and persistent violations of the humanity of Black women – always being ready to serve, doing things around the clock, and being there 24/7. Grant was very specific about the internalization of inferiority in a Black woman servant.[10]

---

[7] Jacquelyn Grant, "Servanthood Revisited: Womanist Explorations of Servanthood Theology," in *Black Faith and Public Talk: Critical Essays on James H. Cone's* Black Theology and Black Power, ed. Dwight N. Hopkins (Waco, TX: Baylor University Press, 2007), 126.
[8] Grant, 127.
[9] Grant, 127.
[10] Grant, 130.

This mechanism confines people to their spaces politically, socially, economically, ideologically, and religiously. Grant unveiled how this notion of servanthood can "demonstrate not only how distasteful the position of servant is, but how oppressive and in fact sinful it is."[11] This servant is neither a servant of God who enjoys higher status in church and society nor someone commissioned to perform special mission, but is rather a Black woman ordained to serve and be subordinate to earthly masters.

When servants are forced to sacrifice their sense of self, dignity, and personhood in fulfilling their role, there is nothing glorious and praiseworthy about this form of sacrificial service. Such sacrificial language, along with remaining obedient and submissive, could not be more emotionally laden. This prompts us to ask: Beyond all the binary relationships and worldviews, who exactly is Christ for? What does it mean to say Jesus, our prototype as God's servant, became *doulos* (a slave) for us when there are communities that are plagued with and continue to suffer from the history of slavery? When being *doulos* (slave) defines the nature of Jesus' *diakonia*, who is this Christ and what is this Christian faith telling us?

In *The Black Christ*, Kelly Brown Douglas argued that there are two Christs – the white Christ and the Black Christ – and the battle between these two Christs can be traced back to the history of slavery.[12] Douglas asked: How could they [Christian slaveholders] espouse Christian justice and freedom while "participating in the bondage of other human beings?"[13]

Engaging *diakonia* in the context of North America, we must ask the following questions: How can we espouse justice and freedom when the daily sociopolitical positioning of persons in society and the church suggests that slaves are not human? How can we talk about service and being a servant when the institution of servanthood negatively impacts the perceived humanity of entire communities of people among the marginalized? Idealizing the servant image without critiquing its connections with the slave language only amplifies the distress and pain of the oppressed. Their voices become hidden and invisible from the historical narratives. How can *diakonia* uncover these lost voices and affirm their personhood?

Diakonia as Remembering

Diakonia should not be understood as service in a romanticized sense, with deacons idealized as self-sacrificial servants for God. De-subjugating the servant image means taking seriously the voices of the oppressed. It involves creating sites of memory to reconstruct the past, giving people agency to resist systemic dehumanization and marginalization. In remembering the people and their past, we remember the way that Jesus remembered us on the cross. Remembering necessitates reconsidering the *diakonia* of Jesus and its relation to his being

---

[11] Grant, 127.
[12] Kelly Brown Douglas, *The Black Christ*, 25th anniv. ed. (Maryknoll, NY: Orbis, 2019), 2–3.
[13] Douglas, 5.

doulos (slave) for us. Instead of relegating Christ to the space polarized by slaveholding Christianity and slave Christianity, I propose that we consider Jesus' salvific work as both an intervention to disrupt (imperial) domination/subjugation and an act of solidarity with the poor and oppressed. This reimagining subverts the narrative of Jesus' identity as submissive and subservient in *diakonia* discourse.

How are sites of memory related to *diakonia*? The intermingling of the servant image with slavery history prioritizes and standardizes the sacrificial language justifying servitude and the oppression of people. Against the normalization of sacrificial language, it is necessary to create an opportunity for storytelling, creating sites of memory. Through re-telling the story, memory of the vanished can be brought alive to confront the constructed and oppressive narratives in history.

Dominant history is constructed to serve the vested interests of a few people and tends to silence the voice of others – those who are deemed losers, unwanted, and unworthy. Honoring people's memory will inevitably challenge discourse about the otherized individuals. Emilie Townes is convinced that "for oppressed or subjugated peoples, memory may serve as a corrective to dominant sociocultural portrayals of history."[14] According to Townes, sites of memory "include archives, museums, cathedrals, palaces, cemeteries, and memorials; concepts and practices such as commemorations, generations, mottos, and all rituals; objects such as inherited property, commemorative monuments, manuals, emblems, basic texts, and symbols."[15] Through sites of memory, people tell their own stories. They reject any theorization or chauvinism that turns them into an object or a form of cultural representation. They refuse to be represented; they speak for themselves. Their voice and their authentic self constitute what a site of memory might look like and ask us not to forget who they are but remember what needs to be remembered.[16]

To remember is a call. Christians are called to remember. As those who remember, we affirm that the poor, oppressed, and marginalized are the subject of their stories, and their agency is not compromised in the process of memory creation and preservation. We remember because of the one who first remembered us on the cross. This call necessitates us to root our remembering in the cross as well as under the foot of it. According to Mary Solberg, the epistemology of the cross provides a "frame of reference" for "adjudicating questions about the conditions, legitimacy, and adequacy of knowers, knowing, and knowledge."[17]

---

[14] Building on the work of Pierre Nora and Werner Sollors regarding memory and the reconstruction of the past, Emilie Townes argued that "memory may become a kind of counterhistory." Emilie M. Townes, *Womanist Ethics and the Cultural Production of Evil* (New York: Palgrave Macmillan, 2006), 15.

[15] Townes, 14.

[16] Townes, 14.

[17] Mary Solberg, "Notes Toward an Epistemology of the Cross," *Currents in Theology and Mission* 24, no.1 (1997): 15.

Considering the sufferings of the world as "a symptom of a power that destroys and kills," Vítor Westhelle contended that the cross is a form of "transgressive knowledge" that asserts we need to be transformed.[18] Westhelle wrote: "a theologian of the cross should constantly transgress the limits of accepted epistemes, either to corroborate the decision to convey that frame of meanings or to criticize it ... the moment when a conventional meaning breaks apart to open new possibilities."[19] The cross requires us to examine what we know and how we know about things. Unlearning prepares us to be awed and enriched by new learnings.

The call to remember invites us to analyze the sacrificial language of Jesus as *doulos* within a larger framework: the imperial context. As Richard Horsley maintained, "It is difficult to understand why the Roman governor, Pontius Pilate, would have bothered to crucify such a figure" when we depoliticize Jesus the Christ.[20] Far from a spiritualized and romanticized fantasy, Jesus exceeded those expectations, transgressing the boundaries by being *doulos* as his way of being human. As *doulos*, Jesus became one among the lowliest in society who endured systemic oppression, humiliation, and dehumanization. Jesus as *doulos* spoke against the Roman rule that capitalized on the master/slave relationship to confine people to their spaces, immobilize them, and silence them.

To remember Jesus' suffering on the cross to the point of death is to remember who Jesus is. Jesus is not a submissive figure, nor was his death purely spiritual salvation so that we are removed from our sins and allowed happily to continue our business as usual. Against the normalization of domination and subjugation, Jesus assumed the role of the *doulos* who challenges unhealthy and hierarchical relationships.

As we think about how relationships can give life, we need to explore an alternative way of understanding the Greek word *doulos*. Anna Mercedes worked on the language of *slave* in the Christ hymn, which reads, "who, though he [Jesus Christ] was in the form of God, did not regard equality with God as something to be exploited, but emptied himself, taking the form of a slave, being born in human likeness. And being found in human form, he humbled himself and became obedient to the point of death – even death on a cross" (Phil 2:6–8, NRSV). Aware that the language of slave could be used as an ideology to promote servitude, objectify and commoditize others, and even justify racism, Mercedes suggested *doula* over *doulos*, because the feminine form of the word could signify "a gesture of generosity ... to foster new life."[21]

On the cross, Christ as the *doula* embodies "a gesture of generosity"[22] amid violence. By being generous, Christ withholds nothing and becomes a no-form:

---

[18] Vítor Westhelle, *The Scandalous God: The Use and Abuse of the Cross* (Minneapolis, MN: Fortress, 2006), 84.
[19] Westhelle, 84.
[20] Richard A. Horsley, *Jesus and Empire: The Kingdom of God and the New World Disorder* (Minneapolis, MN: Fortress, 2003), 8.
[21] Anna Mercedes, "Who are You? Christ and the Imperative of Subjectivity," in *Transformative Lutheran Theologies: Feminist, Womanist, and Mujerista Perspectives*, ed. Mary J. Streufert (Minneapolis, MN: Fortress, 2010), 90.
[22] Mercedes, 90.

"Christ lost even the honor a human *deserves* in that Christ was murdered."[23] Christ as the *doula* provides a diaconal intervention that says no and brings an end to the abusive and humiliating master/slave relationships, pointing to the one who is life-giving and life-sustaining. Meanwhile, by being totally disgraced and disposed, Christ allows himself to be in solidarity both with those who are oppressed and with those who are confused about their identity – not knowing who they truly are and not living as fully human. Christ emptying himself on the cross is more than being submissive; his action exposes the cruelty of oppression. This subversive act fosters new life by affirming the full humanity of stigmatized and dehumanized persons. This is salvation for those who are living and struggling in death-dealing situations.

Furthermore, M. Shawn Copeland described the cross of the crucified Jesus of Nazareth as "an authentic praxis of solidarity."[24] Copeland asserted, "Through a praxis of solidarity, we not only apprehend and are moved by the suffering of the other, we confront and address its oppressive cause and shoulder the other's suffering."[25] Such solidarity reached its climax on the cross. Whenever we turn ourselves to the cross and gather in front of the cross, no matter where we are, the crucified Christ connects and communicates with our bodies through Jesus' solidary love on the cross.

This radical form of love forces us to realize our own creatureliness. We are not immune from suffering. That reckoning opens our hearts and minds to see our limitations and recognize our vulnerabilities in our shared humanity. This kind of solidarity is not based on the premise of sameness, drawing on similarities between different groups to achieve common ground that only reinforces an ideology of homogeneity. The continuation of the homogenous force fails to explore how bias, interest, and motive are entangled in the unequal structures and systems that impact the life of different individuals. For marginalized communities who live with poverty, health inequities, and other social problems, any outbreak or political misstep could be especially brutal.

Refusing to deny, minimize, and homogenize people's experience, we remember the cross. We remember the one who exposes the constraint, contradiction, confusion, and complexity built into the power structures and who persistently establishes communion with all marked bodies, bodies that are unfree and subjugated.

Creating Sites of Memory

What does de-subjugating the servant image say about *diakonia*, and how does it help with its reconceptualization? The de-subjugation of the servant image is facilitated by a form of theological imagination that disassociates itself from unrealistic speculation. The task of theological imagination serves as an

---

[23] Mercedes, 91.
[24] M. Shawn Copeland, *Enfleshing Freedom: Body, Race, and Being* (Minneapolis, MN: Fortress, 2019), 99.
[25] Copeland, 94.

intervention that stops us from making totalizing claims about the particularity of the people. We avoid perpetuating the subjugation of the people through attention to the complexity of realities and sensitivity to the craziness of the world.

De-subjugating the servant image leads us to rethink the *diakonia* of Jesus. If the *diakonia* of Jesus is rooted in Jesus' salvific act, including his participation in suffering, death, and resurrection, Jesus' *diakonia* is never silent about oppression in the face of imperial domination. By taking the form of a slave, the *diakonia* of Jesus challenges the power that causes the suffering and death of the innocent. Such remembering inevitably demands us to let the cross speak: the cross speaks against oppressive powers that promote the homogenization, objectification, and commodification of life. Meanwhile, with Jesus' empathetic solidarity,[26] the cross remembers, comforts, and affirms those who are undergoing exclusion and marginalization.

Diakonia embodies the cross by turning death into life. It gives witness to how the cross disrupts routines that kill. De-subjugating the servant image urges us not to forget and dismiss Jesus' earthly ministry. We cannot talk about Jesus without talking about the ways in which he challenged the "unjust status quo."[27] Christ is never "for the maintenance of an oppressive social-economic system."[28] Christ taking the form of a slave subverts the narrative of the white Christ who "provided the religious justification of the chattel system, eliminated reservations about holding Christians as slaves, and obscured the tensions between Christianity and the cruelty of slavery."[29]

The *diakonia* of Jesus took place in its own time and place yet continues to speak and relate to our current contexts. As it speaks against the use of sacrifice language to deprive certain communities of their humanity and subjugate their bodies for domineering purposes, the *diakonia* of Jesus provides a counter narrative to the history constructed to preserve the supremacy of the privileged by giving agency to the people for resisting systemic oppression and dehumanization. *Diakonia* is thus a call to remember. Deacons are among the cloud of rememberers, not sitting still but participating in the life of others, including the poor and oppressed. *Diakonia* brings all bodies together, regardless of who they are.

By bringing people together for the purpose of remembering, sites of memory are created. These sites of memory are the places where *diakonia* is birthed and incarnated. They uncover the voices of those who have been made to vanish in history, challenge attempts to categorize people, and subvert a rationality that rallies around sectoral interests to protect the interests of only a few. By creating spaces for the people to grieve and rejoice, these sites of memory summon forth a faithful reorientation of human desires and imagination for new practices and ministries that bring healing, reconciliation, and human flourishing. *Diakonia* is

---

[26] Copeland asserted that "solidarity has become a category in Christian theology and, as such, denotes the empathetic incarnation of Christian love." Copeland, 93.
[27] Douglas, *The Black Christ*, 14.
[28] Douglas, 14.
[29] Douglas, 14.

incarnated at the critical juncture of fragmentation among human communities. It expresses itself as a form of solidaristic love, which is experienced with its climax on the cross to re-member bodies that are despised and rejected.

Not only does a reconceptualized understanding of *diakonia* renew and revitalize our identity in Christ, but it also readies us to challenge coercive powers and confront privileges that perpetuate injustice, including attempts to deny the horrific past by erasing the memory of the people and their humanity. Remembering as a theo-diaconal intervention transforms *diakonia* into an embodied form of epistemic and ethical disobedience that unmasks hegemony and inspires a bold new path to social relationships, cultivating a desire for justice and inclusion. This expansive vision of *diakonia* makes possible the diaconate of all believers regardless of race, ethnicity, culture, and language. This vision can reshape the practice of *diakonia* in a world in need of healing and reconciliation.

Conclusion

Diakonia is understood as a theological concept with two aspects: "One is that diakonia is a theological concept that points to the very identity and mission of the church. Another is its practical implication in the sense that diakonia is a call to action, as a response to challenges of human suffering, injustice, and care for creation."[30] *Diakonia* as a "theological concept" reminds us to see once again the need of disconnecting *diakonia* from the sacrificial language that subjugates people and underscores the urgency of conceptualizing it anew in our current contexts.

The reconceptualization of *diakonia* in the age of the new normal remembers how COVID-19, #BlackLivesMatter, and racism and discrimination against Asian Americans and Pacific Islanders have defined our era. The task of theological imagination acts as an intervention to counter sweeping generalizations about the reality of the people and informs diaconal practices that remember and affirm the humanity of the oppressed by addressing equity issues. *Diakonia* re-members all the dehumanized and desacralized bodies, including those who continue to be enslaved in the larger socio-economic and political systems.

Diakonia as remembering allows people to be themselves and speak for themselves. By creating sites of memory, the disposition of theo-diaconal intervention provides hope and inspiration for communities in their ongoing battles against structural and systemic oppression. Out of these oppressive structures and systems, God is present. God cares. God acts. *Diakonia* as remembering testifies that God in Jesus Christ is not silent about oppression but actively participates in the struggle of humanity in our everyday lives. On behalf

---

[30] Kjell Nordstokke, ed., *Diakonia in Context: Transformation, Reconciliation, Empowerment: An LWF Contribution to the Understanding and Practice of Diakonia* (Geneva: Lutheran World Federation, 2009), 8, https://www.lutheranworld.org/sites/default/files/DMD-Diakonia-EN-low.pdf.

of subjugated peoples, God – through the *diakonia* of Jesus – materializes the practice of justice in human relationships.

Diakonia invites us to hold space for unveiling the darkness that destroys and devalues bodies that are different from our own. Such an enlarged vision of *diakonia* attests to the diaconate of all believers regardless of race, ethnicity, culture, and language. This vision can reshape diaconal practice in a world in need of healing and reconciliation.

Works Cited

Collins, John N. *Diakonia: Re-Interpreting the Ancient Sources*. New York: Oxford University Press, 1990.

Copeland, M. Shawn. *Enfleshing Freedom: Body, Race, and Being*. Minneapolis, MN: Fortress, 2019.

Douglas, Kelly Brown. *The Black Christ*, 25th anniv. ed. Maryknoll, NY: Orbis, 2019.

Grant, Jacquelyn. "Servanthood Revisited: Womanist Explorations of Servanthood Theology." In *Black Faith and Public Talk: Critical Essays on James H. Cone's* Black Theology and Black Power, edited by Dwight N.Hopkins, 126–37. Waco Texas: Baylor University Press, 2007.

Horsley, Richard A. *Jesus and Empire: The Kingdom of God and the New World Disorder*. Minneapolis, MN: Fortress, 2003.

Mercedes, Anna. "Who are You? Christ and the Imperative of Subjectivity." In *Transformative Lutheran Theologies: Feminist, Womanist, and Mujerista Perspectives*, edited by Mary J. Streufert, 87–98. Minneapolis, MN: Fortress, 2010.

Nordstokke, Kjell, ed. *Diakonia in Context: Transformation, Reconciliation, Empowerment: An LWF Contribution to the Understanding and Practice of Diakonia*. Geneva: Lutheran World Federation, 2009. https://www.lutheranworld.org/sites/default/files/DMD-Diakonia-EN-low.pdf.

Solberg, Mary. "Notes Toward an Epistemology of the Cross." *Currents in Theology and Mission* 24, no.1 (1997): 14–22.

Townes, Emilie M. *Womanist Ethics and the Cultural Production of Evil*. New York: Palgrave Macmillan, 2006.

Westhelle, Vítor. *The Scandalous God: The Use and Abuse of the Cross*. Minneapolis, MN: Fortress, 2006.

Chapter 11

Developing a Trauma-Informed Diaconal Praxis

Darryl W. Stephens

What has *diakonia* to do with trauma? With advances in trauma studies over the past thirty years, we now know that trauma is one of the most pervasive and widespread causes of broken relationships and estrangement from community. If, as Paul claimed, "God … has given us the ministry [*diakonīan*] of reconciliation" (2 Cor 5:18), reconciliation and repair among individuals and within communities broken by trauma are central to the diaconal vocation of all Christians. This work becomes liberative when compassion is wedded to social analysis and empowerment. As illustrated in recent ecumenical thought, diaconal workers strive to join in solidarity with persons who are suffering, enhancing their moral agency and the flourishing of each member of the community. Thus, the theology and practice of *diakonia* must become trauma informed.

Ecumenical *diakonia* is a specific expression of "the diaconate of all believers."[1] It is the most recent development of modern approaches to *diakonia*, building on a tradition of institutionalized piety and service and, later, a renewed understanding of the church's ministry through liturgy and ordination.[2] Ecumenical *diakonia* is provocative, "calling into being … new ways of seeing, judging and acting."[3] A trauma-informed praxis of *diakonia* aims to see, judge, and act in ways that contribute to human flourishing – for the good of victim-survivors, the human community, and all of creation. Since ecumenical *diakonia* is relational and focused particularly on the needs of the oppressed and marginalized, it requires a community-based, liberative ethic.

Contemporary ecumenical *diakonia* is focused on liberation and empowerment of the poor, suffering, and oppressed. Most North American diaconal actors are not poor, though, and attempts at solidarity are laden with power differentials. How can persons of privilege participate in a liberative praxis? An ethic of bearing witness to victim-survivors of trauma can assist diaconal workers attempting to serve as ambassadors of God's reconciliation in the world.

---

[1] World Council of Churches and ACT Alliance, *Called to Transformation: Ecumenical Diakonia* (Geneva: WCC, 2022), 16.
[2] Kjell Nordstokke, *Liberating Diakonia* (Tondheim: Tapir Akademisk, 2011), 18.
[3] WCC and ACT Alliance, *Called to Transformation*, 15. This trifold schema arises from Latin American liberation theology and is influential in Roman Catholic and ecumenical documents. Carlos E. Ham, "Seeing-Judging-Acting: A Learning Method for Empowerment in Diaconia from a Latin American Perspective," in *International Handbook on Ecumenical Diakonia*, ed. Ampony et al. (Oxford: Regnum Books International, 2021), 631–38; and Nordstokke, *Liberating Diakonia*, 35.

This chapter contributes to the development of diaconal methodology in the context of trauma, exploring points of connection between trauma-informed response and diaconal praxis. Through an interdisciplinary approach, drawing on trauma studies, theology, and ethics, trauma-informed ethics becomes a tool for ecumenical *diakonia*, alongside responsible interfaith encounter (*diapraxis*) and community building (*conviviality*).[4] Where conviviality begins with the question, "How can we live together?" a trauma-informed approach begins with the question, "How can we live together in the aftermath of trauma?" The model presented here provides guidance for diaconal workers bearing witness to individual victim-survivors, equipping both to participate in social change movements for justice, healing, and possible reconciliation.

Trauma and Trauma-Informed Response

Trauma begins with an event that overwhelms one's sense of safety and agency. A person experiences an event as traumatic when their very existence is threatened and autonomic impulses of fight, flight, freeze, or fawn govern their response. However, trauma does not end when the danger has subsided. The effects of trauma reside deep in the body, altering one's physiology.[5] According to the Substance Abuse and Mental Health Services Administration (SAMHSA), trauma is characterized by "lasting effects on the individual's functioning and mental, physical, social, emotional, or spiritual well-being."[6] These effects are most noticeable when a trauma survivor is triggered by external stimuli. During a flashback, the trauma survivor's autonomous systems respond as if the original threat were present. However, such misplaced survival responses are maladaptive and disruptive, further alienating the person from their immediate environment, relationships, community, and even their sense of self. The effects of trauma can be felt throughout a community and through the generations.[7]

Healing from trauma is a lengthy and arduous process requiring community support. According to Judith Herman, trauma traps the survivor in a continual, traumatic moment in which the survivor may feel helpless in the face of existential threat.[8] To aid recovery, the individual trauma survivor can be assisted by a trained therapist and a community of support, including individuals bearing

---

[4] My methodology is inductive, analytical, interdisciplinary, and liberation focused. Thus, my critical reflection on the praxis of *diakonia* finds common cause with Nordstokke's development of "the science of *diakonia*." Nordstokke, *Liberating Diakonia*, 29–37, 60–62.

[5] Bessel A. van der Kolk, *The Body Keeps the Score: Brain, Mind, and Body in the Healing of Trauma* (New York: Penguin, 2014), 21.

[6] SAMHSA, "SAMHSA's Concept of Trauma and Guidance for a Trauma-Informed Approach," HHS Publication No. (SMA) 14-4884 (Rockville, MD: SAMHSA, 2014), 7, https://store.samhsa.gov/product/SAMHSA-s-Concept-of-Trauma-and-Guidance-for-a-Trauma-Informed-Approach/SMA14-4884.

[7] Resmaa Menakem, *My Grandmother's Hands: Racialized Trauma and the Pathways to Mending Our Hearts and Bodies* (Las Vegas: Central Recovery Press, 2017), 45.

[8] Judith Herman, *Trauma and Recovery: The Aftermath of Violence – From Domestic Abuse to Political Terror*, 2nd ed. (New York: Basic, 2015), 47–50.

witness to their humanity and suffering. I interpret four stages of trauma recovery in Herman's work: overcoming relational barriers, such as shame and secrecy; safety, "making intolerable feelings bearable through connection with others"; reconstruction of narrative, including "grieving the past"; and reconnection and restoration to community.[9] These stages provide part of the scaffolding for a trauma-informed response.

Herman's depiction of the helpless victim presents a problem of agency, though. If a trauma victim is considered helpless, what is the victim's role in her own survival and recovery? And how do well-meaning supporters, such as diaconal workers, avoid reinforcing victimhood, both in the lives of individuals and in the ways we characterize them? Traci West, a Black feminist Christian ethicist, brought attention to this problem in her research on sexual violence against Black women. As a corrective to Herman, West developed *resistance ethics* to recognize the inner resources women bring to their own survival.[10] To recognize and empower Black women and others, West coined the term *victim-survivor*, symbolizing the moral agency of those harmed by violence and sexual abuse.[11] While the victim-survivor's moral agency can be enhanced through supportive relationships, her agency must not be supplanted by those desiring to help. Equipped with Herman's feminist approach and West's Black feminist liberationist corrective, we can now turn to the practice of response to trauma.

To promote healing and recovery, communities can become trauma informed. A trauma-informed response assumes that every person with whom we interact is potentially a survivor of trauma and seeks to serve their best interests. People in a trauma-informed setting "realize how widespread trauma is, recognize signs and symptoms, respond by integrating knowledge into practice, and resist doing further harm."[12] Trauma-informed response is not a substitute for the trained expertise of trauma specialists attending to acute needs. Rather, trauma-informed response is a tool for all sectors endeavoring to make their community a safer and more welcoming place, conducive to healing. Becoming trauma informed requires significant study, training, and practice – and, I argue, it is intimately related to diaconal methodology.

---

[9] Herman, *Trauma and Recovery*, v, 3, 276.
[10] Traci C. West, *Wounds of the Spirit: Black Women, Violence, and Resistance Ethics* (New York: New York University Press, 1999), 55. For a development of West's resistance ethics through a trauma-informed lens, see Darryl W. Stephens, "Bearing Witness: A Trauma-Informed Approach to Christian Ethics," *Journal of Feminist Studies in Religion* 39, no. 1 (2023): 155–74, https://doi.org/10.2979/jfs.2023.a893198.
[11] West, *Wounds of the Spirit*, 1, see also 57–67, 152.
[12] SAMHSA, "Spotlight: Building Resilient and Trauma-Informed Communities – Introduction" (2017), https://store.samhsa.gov/product/Spotlight-Building-Resilient-and-Trauma-Informed-Communities-Introduction/SMA17-5014. See also SAMHSA, "SAMHSA's Concept of Trauma," 9.

Methodology for Diaconal Praxis

Care for those who are suffering is rooted in the Levitical edict to love one's neighbor as oneself.[13] Reinforced throughout the Hebrew Scriptures in special protections for widows, orphans, immigrants, and the poor and emphasized throughout Jesus' ministry and teaching, this call to compassion found organizational structure in the early church (Acts 6:1–7). Through the intervening centuries, Christians have provided care for others in myriad ways, including hospitals, schools, and direct assistance to individuals in need. Care and compassion for the suffering became synonymous with *diakonia*, defined in some contexts as Christian-motivated social service. However, *diakonia* is currently undergoing an ecumenical rebirth with a more sophisticated sense of responsibility to respond to oppressive social structures. Contemporary diaconal methodology provides the connective tissue between compassion, social justice, and reconciliation.

Ecumenical diaconal praxis goes well beyond individual acts of mercy. The holistic and prophetic nature of ecumenical *diakonia* is rooted in justice: "We cannot understand or practice *diakonia* apart from justice and peace. Service cannot be separated from prophetic witness or the ministry of reconciliation. Mission must include transformative *diakonia*."[14] Thus, scholars note a paradigm shift toward a more ecclesial, holistic, and prophetic practice of *diakonia*, moving from "humble service" to solidarity with the oppressed.[15] Contemporary *diakonia* is contextual, aims to alleviate suffering, is rights-based, involves an analysis of power structures, and is ultimately action-oriented.[16] This evolving understanding of ecumenical *diakonia* exposes social sin and is committed to social justice, human rights, and enhancing the capabilities and participation of everyone in human community. Thus, the accompaniment of *diakonia* aims to support others in being the subjects of their own liberation.

The question of agency again becomes problematic, though, due to power differentials between victim-survivors and persons attempting to serve victim-survivors. Diaconal workers are in a position of relative privilege when engaging in acts of mercy and working toward reconciliation. Working with the poor through diaconal action is a power-laden endeavor, necessitating keen attention to the ethics of these encounters.[17] For example, the Addis Ababa consultation

---

[13] See, for example, Johannes Eurich, "Ethics of Diaconia: The Relevance of Good Life, Common Good and Global Justice in Diaconia," in *International Handbook on Ecumenical Diakonia*, ed. Ampony et al. (Oxford: Regnum Books International, 2021), 542.

[14] WCC and ACT Alliance, *Called to Transformation*, 33.

[15] Stephanie Dietrich et al., "Introduction: Diakonia as Christian Social Practice," in *Diakonia as Christian Social Practice: An Introduction*, ed. Dietrich et al. (Oxford: Regnum Books International, 2014), 2.

[16] WCC and ACT Alliance, *Called to Transformation*, 16–17, 32.

[17] See, for example, WCC and ACT Alliance, *Called to Transformation*, 113–14; and World Council of Churches, Pontifical Council for Interreligious Dialogue of the Roman Catholic Church, and the World Evangelical Alliance, "Christian Witness in a Multi-Religious World: Recommendations for Conduct" (2011),

on *diakonia* created guidelines for a diaconal code of conduct in 2008.[18] The guidelines name the central obligations and responsibilities of diaconal work: healing and reconciliation, integrity of creation, peace and justice, service, mutual transformation, respect, and accountability, as well as solidarity, participation, and building alliances.

While the diaconal worker overcomes the bystander problem by getting involved, she must be careful not to usurp the agency of the persons she intends to help. An ethic of solidarity is necessary for allies to enhance rather than override the agency of victim-survivors. Privileged actors often prioritize reconciliation over attending to the causes of injustice and suffering. This is an acute problem when white people attempt to address systemic racism, for example.[19] The desire of the privileged to reconcile prematurely is due to differences in perspective and experience with oppression – but reconciliation cannot be separated from justice. Ecumenical diaconal methodology provides tools for the difficult journey from compassion to justice to reconciliation.

The prophetic dimension of ecumenical *diakonia* requires a contextual methodology. For example, *Called to Transformation* employs a contextual lens to Christian social service. This document asserts, "diaconal intervention reflects social reality and seeks in its performance to alleviate human suffering and promote justice, peace and human dignity."[20] As a contextual theology rooted in action, "*diakonia* therefore includes an analysis of the social and political environment."[21] This contextual analysis is essential to the "see–reflect–act" methodology of ecumenical *diakonia* – a process that privileges the perspective of the poor and marginalized, employs a hermeneutics of suspicion about power and privilege, and promotes wide participation and empowerment.[22] Thus, ecumenical *diakonia* is not simply service or loving action; rather, ecumenical *diakonia* necessitates social analysis and an evaluation of power structures.

Ecumenical *diakonia* claims a responsibility to respond to oppressive social structures through solidarity and empowerment. When diaconal actors build alliances, Christians partner with persons of many faiths (or of no faith tradition) to achieve common goals through dialogue and action – diapraxis.[23] Thus, LWF described an example of diapraxis in India as "action together in solidarity that

---

https://www.oikoumene.org/resources/documents/christian-witness-in-a-multi-religious-world.

[18] Kjell Nordstokke, ed., *Diakonia in Context: Transformation, Reconciliation, Empowerment: An LWF Contribution to the Understanding and Practice of Diakonia* (Geneva: Lutheran World Federation, 2009), 91–92.

[19] For analysis and discussion of this problematic tendency among white Christians, see Jennifer Harvey, *Dear White Christians: For Those Still Longing for Racial Reconciliation*, second edition (Grand Rapids, MI: Eerdmans, 2020).

[20] WCC and ACT Alliance, *Called to Transformation*, 16.

[21] WCC and ACT Alliance, 17.

[22] Nordstokke, *Diakonia in Context*, 59–60.

[23] Nordstokke, 88, citing Lissi Rasmussen, "From Diapraxis to Dialogue. Christian–Muslim Relations," in *Dialogue in Action: Essays in Honour of Johannes Aagaard*, ed. Lars Thunberg, Moti Lal Pandit, and Carl V.F. Hansen (New Delhi: Prajna 1988), 282. See also WCC and ACT Alliance, *Called to Transformation*, 84–85.

engages in the promotion of justice, a better quality of life, and the alleviation of human suffering."[24] The practice of dialogue combined with collaborative work toward shared material goals resonates with insights from intercultural missional theology, pragmatic ethics, and critical community research.[25] Ecumenical diaconal action is rights-based and focuses on building citizenship, community, and alliances for the betterment of society.[26]

When contextual sophistication prioritizes the voices and needs of the oppressed, *diakonia* becomes a powerful, liberative praxis rooted in discipleship.[27] *Diakonia* advocates for dignity, love, justice, and solidarity in cooperation with all who hold those values. According to *Called to Transformation*, "Diaconal action thus includes care for creation and commitment to promote human dignity and justice, in solidarity with the poor and excluded, working with all people of good will."[28] Methodologically, ecumenical *diakonia* involves an intentional cycle of action, theory, and reflection, mutually reinforcing and deepening our understanding of ourselves and our actions in light of God's continuing action in the world. *Diakonia* is therefore a political theology in the most profound sense, motivating and theorizing the work of discipleship with a contextual awareness of social structures and a sense of justice to transform and reshape power.

The concept of conviviality provides a vision for this kind of liberative diaconal methodology. Conviviality is a political and economic vision for recentering relationships of trust within cultures overrun by the divisions and individualism created by neo-liberal, globalized market economies. It offers a liberative, relational corrective to the development model of *diakonia*.[29] According to a publication of the Lutheran World Federation, "Conviviality refers to the art and practice of living together" and is based on relationality, respect of difference among persons and communities, and "reciprocal relationships … as a foundation for life together."[30] When combined with

---

[24] Lutheran World Federation, *Mission in Context: Transformation, Reconciliation, Empowerment: An LWF Contribution to the Understanding and Practice of Mission* (Geneva: Lutheran World Federation, 2004), 52.

[25] Respectively, see, for example, my discussion of the work of Hendrik R. Pieterse and Robert Hunt in Darryl W. Stephens, *Reckoning Methodism: Mission and Division in the Public Church* (Eugene, OR: Cascade, forthcoming), chapter 5; Willis Jenkins, *The Future of Ethics: Sustainability, Social Justice, and Religious Creativity* (Washington, DC: Georgetown University Press, 2013), 9, 18; and Tony Addy, "Community Practice and Critical Community Research: Perspectives from Conviviality and the CABLE Approach," *Diaconia* 10, no. 2 (2020): 161–79.

[26] Nordstokke, *Diakonia in Context*, 61–66.

[27] On the connections between liberation theology and diaconal methodology, see Craig L. Nessan, "Liberation Theology and Diaconia: Methods of Learning," in *International Handbook on Ecumenical Diakonia*, ed. Ampony et al. (Oxford: Regnum Books International, 2021), 591–96; and in this volume, chapters by Dollaga, Nessan, and Oliveira.

[28] WCC and ACT Alliance, *Called to Transformation*, 46.

[29] WCC and ACT Alliance, 29–30.

[30] Tony Addy, ed., *Seeking Conviviality: Reforming Community Diakonia in Europe* (Geneva: Lutheran World Federation, 2014), 18.

diaconal commitments, the vision of conviviality helps the church move away from a service provision mentality, in which we provide *for* others, to a more liberative mentality, in which we work *with* others in shared community.[31] According to Tony Addy, conviviality equips the diaconal church to "move ... toward sharing life, based on empathy, reciprocity and presence."[32] These commitments of contemporary ecumenical *diakonia* resonate deeply with trauma-informed ethics.

Bearing Witness Through *Diakonia*

Bearing witness is an ethical model rooted in the recognition of common human dignity and expressed through love, justice, and solidarity for the flourishing of all.[33] This model correlates insights from Herman and SAMHSA in four "perspectival moments," each aligned with a mode of transcendence, moral theme, and practice of social action (Figure 11.1). This trauma-informed model of ethics mirrors diaconal praxis and method and equips relatively privileged diaconal workers to bear witness to victim-survivors of trauma and other persons who may be suffering.

Perspectival Moment	Mode of Transcendence	Moral Theme	Practice of Social Action	Trauma-Informed Response (SAMHSA)	Stage of Trauma Recovery (Judith Herman)
I. Existence	recognition	dignity	grounded being	realize	overcoming relational barriers
II. Present	empathy	love	attentive presence	recognize (identify and name)	safety
III. Past	memory	justice	historical clarity	respond	reconstruction of narrative
IV. Future	imagination	solidarity	meaningful participation	resist	reconnection and restoration

Figure 11.1: Bearing Witness in Four Moments

The model of bearing witness presented in Figure 11.1 is rooted in the universal human experience of spirituality and transcendence. Recognition of each other's shared humanity, as equally created and loved by God, provides an existential grounding for overcoming relational barriers. Empathy, memory, and imagination allow us to transcend ourselves to make meaning in temporal

---

[31] Tony Addy, "Seeking Conviviality: A New Core Concept for the Diaconal Church," in *The Diaconal Church*, ed. Dietrich et al. (Oxford: Regnum Books International, 2019), 168.
[32] Addy, 168.
[33] I first presented this framework and the accompanying figure in Darryl W. Stephens, "Bearing Witness as Social Action: Religious Ethics and Trauma-Informed Response," *Trauma Care* 1, no. 1 (June 2021): 57–58, https://doi.org/10.3390/traumacare1010005. See also Stephens, "Bearing Witness: A Trauma-Informed Approach," 155–74.

dimensions (present, past, and future). In practice, these perspective moments are intermingled and do not occur in an orderly fashion.

Suffering knows no creed. The spatial and temporal perspectival moments and corresponding modes of transcendence are rooted in the human experience as such, even though they may be interpreted differently by various faith traditions.[34] For example, *recognition* is the ability of humanity to see dignity in each person, transcending oneself to realize the widespread occurrence of trauma as part of the common human existence. Three other modes of transcendence – empathy, memory, and imagination – describe how humans connect with each other, God, and all of creation.[35] Thus, this model treats spirituality and transcendence as a point of common connection for all of humanity, to which individuals and communities may bring their own faith commitments. Thus, this model of bearing witness is well-suited to responsible interfaith encounter (diapraxis) and community building (conviviality) as well as the specific commitments of ecumenical *diakonia*.

Diaconal praxis brings a faith-based understanding to the universal moral themes of dignity, love, justice, and solidarity that animate this model of bearing witness. These connections arose organically from my research with United Methodist deaconesses and others in ministry on the margins. Through personal interviews, I heard stories of bearing witness to suffering persons in many contexts, grounded in shared human dignity. United Methodist deaconesses are mandated to alleviate suffering, to eradicate causes of injustice, and to develop full human potential and build global community. Respectively, I interpreted these mandates as love, justice, and solidarity and could see clear evidence of these moral themes in the day-to-day ministries of persons in a variety of ministries, past and present.[36]

Human dignity is the existential ground for rights-based advocacy and the first objective of diaconal work.[37] The concept of dignity, expressed theologically as the image of God, is central to a convivial approach to diaconal praxis.[38] Dignity honors each person as a bearer of rights with their own subjectivity.[39] The importance of grounding ministry in shared human dignity is evident, for example, when pioneering white women insisted on meeting with Black women as equals in the racially segregated Methodist Episcopal Church, South in the

---

[34] Notably, SAMHSA, an agency of the US federal government, identifies spiritual disruption as a characteristic of trauma. SAMHSA, "SAMHSA's Concept of Trauma," 7. On the universality of these themes, see discussion in Stephens, "Bearing Witness as Social Action," 52–55.

[35] On these modes of transcendence in process theology, see Marjorie Hewitt Suchocki, *The Fall to Violence: Original Sin in Relational Theology* (New York: Continuum, 1994), 36.

[36] Several examples offered below are presented in detail in Darryl W. Stephens, *Bearing Witness in the Kin-dom: Living Into the Church's Moral Witness Through Radical Discipleship* (New York: United Methodist Women, 2021).

[37] Nordstokke, *Diakonia in Context*, 91. See also WCC and ACT Alliance, *Called to Transformation*, 42.

[38] Addy, *Seeking Conviviality*, 13, 21–23.

[39] Eurich, "Ethics of Diaconia," 544.

1930s. Acknowledged dignity and equality are also prerequisites to community for LGBTQIA+ persons, many of whom have suffered trauma because of their sexual or gender identity. From a trauma-informed perspective, dignity honors the agency of the victim, recognizing, "Traumatised people are survivors."[40] Thus, upholding the dignity of victim-survivors is preliminary to any diaconal work to overcome relational barriers imposed by trauma.

Upholding human dignity entails recognizing one's own dignity as a diaconal worker. Nothing in this model requires a diaconal worker to bear witness to someone's else's trauma at the expense of their own dignity or wellbeing. God loves and bestows worth on each of us, including those of us in ministry. We should love ourselves as well as our neighbor. Even voluntary "diaconal suffering" has necessary limits.[41] For diaconal workers to be fully present and attentive to bear witness to others, we must attend to our own trauma histories, seek reconciliation in our own lives, and welcome the healing presence of God's grace within ourselves. We are not only wounded healers but also healing healers, persons in the process of healing seeking to accompany others in a process of healing.

Having established a grounding in shared existence, diaconal workers seeking to love their neighbors can exercise empathy in a trauma-informed way through attentive presence. This begins with empathetic listening, the first step in liberative methodology for *diakonia*.[42] According to the Lutheran World Federation, "diaconal" means "to focus on listening to and accompanying the 'marginalized other.'"[43] The Addis Ababa consultation asked for "a culture of listening" in diaconal work.[44] The vision of conviviality also names our listening presence as the first step in developing community.[45] Listening with empathy allows us to transcend ourselves to be fully present with another person, attending to their expressed needs. Empathy means encountering our neighbor on their own terms, as an equal with a distinct identity and experiences from ourselves.[46] For example, empathy can motivate a deaconess to provide food and medication to refugee families waiting to cross the Mexican border into the United States. Empathy can also motivate one to provide water to someone waiting in line for hours to vote or to offer a haven for a woman suffering abuse by her husband. Ministry presence of this kind is essential for diaconal service, and we must be attentive to hear from the person we are serving what their needs are – rather than assume that we already know what is best for them. When trauma-informed, attentive presence creates a sense of safety for victim-survivors and is a profound form of love.

---

[40] Christine Gühne, "Diaconia in Contexts of Traumatisation – An Introduction," in *The Diaconal Church*, ed. Dietrich et al. (Oxford: Regnum Books International, 2019), 454.
[41] Nessan, "Liberation Theology and Diaconia," 593.
[42] Nessan, 594.
[43] Addy, *Seeking Conviviality*, 12.
[44] Nordstokke, *Diakonia in Context*, 71.
[45] Addy, *Seeking Conviviality*, 32.
[46] Addy, 16.

Bearing witness proceeds by seeking historical clarity about issues of justice and oppression, both for the victim-survivor and the one bearing witness to them. Reconstruction of memory is a necessary part of healing and recovery from trauma. At its core, bearing witness is honoring the truth of someone else's story; that is, how they narrate their past. Thus, for traumatized societies, "truth-telling is an essential element of the reconciliation process and trauma healing."[47] Furthermore, the church in mission can facilitate healing through diaconal action that engages in social and political analysis. By interrogating power structures and our own complicity, individually and collectively, we can expose the root causes of suffering and oppression.[48] How are non-white, non-heterosexual, and non-cisgender persons put at risk by laws, policies, and other forms of discrimination? Why are so many immigrants attempting to enter the United States from Mexico? Why are voter lines so long in certain precincts? Why are rates of intimate partner abuse so high? Social analysis leads to historical clarity and is a prerequisite to the work of reconciliation and healing. According to Robert Schreiter, memory work is "acknowledging the truth of what has happened, seeking justice to redress the wrongdoing that has occurred, and creating the social space for a different relationship" to the past and those involved in past harms.[49] Historical reckoning is central to the diaconal methodology see–reflect–act, illuminating why "no diaconal action can be seen in isolation from its societal and political context."[50] The focus on justice as part of the prophetic dimension of ecumenical *diakonia* prepares us for meaningful participation in God's transformation of the world.

The final perspectival moment of bearing witness is to join in solidarity with victim-survivors of trauma, collaboratively imagining a more just future conducive to the flourishing of all creation. From a trauma-informed perspective, this moment emphasizes nurturing connection and restoration among victim-survivors and resisting re-traumatization. Exercising a preferential option for the marginalized, diaconal workers must support the persons they serve to imagine and create their own future. From a diaconal perspective, empowerment and transformation are key features of this diaconal workers' meaningful participation in community with the suffering. What kind of future does this refugee family want for themselves? What kind of voting experience do the citizens in this precinct prefer? What kinds of supports and legal protections do LGBTQIA+ persons in my community say they need? What do my Black neighbors say they need for our community to become actively anti-racist? The work of meaningful participation is illustrated by the Addis Ababa consultation's priority of "local expertise and commitment … open for mutual

---

[47] Nagaju Muke, "Diaconia in Traumatised Societies: Learning from the Rwandan Context," in *The Diaconal Church*, ed. Dietrich et al. (Oxford: Regnum Books International, 2019), 461.

[48] The perspectival moment of reckoning with the past encompasses the middle three elements of the liberative, action-reflection (praxis-oriented) methodology described in Nessan, "Liberation Theology and Diaconia," 593–94.

[49] Robert J. Schreiter, "Reconciliation and Healing as a Paradigm for Mission," *International Review of Mission* 94, no. 372 (Jan 2005), 81.

[50] Nordstokke, *Diakonia in Context*, 62.

empowerment."[51] The agency of those we intend to serve must be supported and enhanced. Diaconal workers are called to be allies, not substitute agents, in the work of reconciliation. To work convivially is to establish relationships of trust, building up community so that those persons most affected by trauma and suffering may find means to flourish through their own initiative.

Conclusion

Sensitivity to past and current trauma is necessary for diaconal work in today's world. This chapter has explored a deep resonance between the methodology and theology of ecumenical *diakonia* and a model of trauma-informed ethics called "bearing witness." A trauma-informed approach to ministry is consistent with the values and commitments of ecumenical *diakonia* and complements existing tools, such as diapraxis and conviviality. A liberative, trauma-informed approach to diaconal praxis helps us answer the question: How can we work with people on the margins without causing harm?

This question pinpoints the need for an ethical and informed approach to diaconal praxis. A liberative, trauma-informed response is a necessary partner to diaconal theology and praxis in today's world, underscoring the problems of moral agency that can arise. Furthermore, diaconal theology provides a point of spiritual connection for secular workers on the front lines of trauma response, providing theological framing for its spiritual and transcendent dimensions.

As diaconal methodology adopts a trauma-informed approach, several issues need continual attention: self-care, power and agency, and the goal of reconciliation. Vicarious trauma is an ever-present risk. As diaconal workers encounter persons with trauma histories and enter spaces fraught with trauma, we must be attentive to our own health and flourishing, at times removing ourselves from the situation to attend to our own care. Diaconal work is unavoidably encumbered by power differentials. As diaconal workers, we must recognize and prioritize the moral agency of those persons and communities we seek to serve, resisting the urge to substitute our own expertise and capabilities for theirs. We must act in solidarity and support; answers and solutions must arise within community; our role is that of an ally not a patron. Finally, we cannot subvert the process of bearing witness. As diaconal workers, we must resist the temptation to seek reconciliation without the necessary work of grounded being, attentive presence, historical clarity, and meaningful participation. Our simple desire for a world without trauma is insufficient. The ministry of reconciliation requires bearing witness with dignity, love, justice, and solidarity.

---

[51] Nordstokke, 71.

Works Cited

Addy, Tony. "Community Practice and Critical Community Research: Perspectives from Conviviality and the CABLE Approach." *Diaconia* 10, no. 2 (2020): 161–79.

———. "Seeking Conviviality: A New Core Concept for the Diaconal Church." In *The Diaconal Church*, edited by Dietrich et al., 158–70. Oxford: Regnum Books International, 2019.

———, ed. *Seeking Conviviality: Reforming Community Diakonia in Europe.* Geneva: Lutheran World Federation, 2014. https://www.interdiac.eu/resources/seeking-conviviality-reforming-community-diakonia-in-europe.

Ampony, Godwin, Martin Büscher, Beate Hofmann, Félicité Ngnintedem, Dennis Solon, and Dietrich Werner, eds. *International Handbook on Ecumenical Diakonia: Contextual Theologies and Practices of Diakonia and Christian Social Services – Resources for Study and Intercultural Learning.* Oxford: Regnum Books International, 2021.

Dietrich, Stephanie, Knud Jørgensen, Kari Karsrud Korslein, and Kjell Nordstokke, eds. *The Diaconal Church.* Oxford: Regnum Books International, 2019.

———. "Introduction: Diakonia as Christian Social Practice." In *Diakonia as Christian Social Practice*, edited by Dietrich et al., 1–9. Oxford: Regnum Books International, 2014.

———, eds. *Diakonia as Christian Social Practice: An Introduction.* Oxford: Regnum Books International, 2014.

Eurich, Johannes. "Ethics of Diaconia: The Relevance of Good Life, Common Good and Global Justice in Diaconia." In *International Handbook on Ecumenical Diakonia*, edited by Ampony et al., 542–47. Oxford: Regnum Books International, 2021.

Gühne, Christine. "Diaconia in Contexts of Traumatisation – An Introduction." In *The Diaconal Church*, edited by Dietrich et al., 452–55. Oxford: Regnum Books International, 2019.

Ham, Carlos E. "Seeing-Judging-Acting: A Learning Method for Empowerment in Diaconia from a Latin American Perspective." In *International Handbook on Ecumenical Diakonia*, edited by Ampony et al., 631–38. Oxford: Regnum Books International, 2021.

Harvey, Jennifer. *Dear White Christians: For Those Still Longing for Racial Reconciliation*, second edition. Grand Rapids, MI: Eerdmans, 2020.

Herman, Judith. *Trauma and Recovery: The Aftermath of Violence – From Domestic Abuse to Political Terror.* 2nd ed. New York: Basic, 2015.

Jenkins, Willis. *The Future of Ethics: Sustainability, Social Justice, and Religious Creativity.* Washington, DC: Georgetown University Press, 2013.

Lutheran World Federation. *Mission in Context: Transformation, Reconciliation, Empowerment: An LWF Contribution to the Understanding and Practice of Mission.* Geneva: Lutheran World Federation, 2004.

https://www.lutheranworld.org/sites/default/files/DMD-Mission-in-Context-EN-low.pdf.

Menakem, Resmaa. *My Grandmother's Hands: Racialized Trauma and the Pathways to Mending Our Hearts and Bodies*. Las Vegas: Central Recovery Press, 2017.

Muke, Nagaju. "Diaconia in Traumatised Societies: Learning from the Rwandan Context." In *The Diaconal Church*, edited by Dietrich et al., 456–67. Oxford: Regnum Books International, 2019.

Nessan, Craig L. "Liberation Theology and Diaconia: Methods of Learning." In *International Handbook on Ecumenical Diakonia*, edited by Ampony et al., 591–96. Oxford: Regnum Books International, 2021.

Nordstokke, Kjell, ed. *Diakonia in Context: Transformation, Reconciliation, Empowerment: An LWF Contribution to the Understanding and Practice of Diakonia*. Geneva: Lutheran World Federation, 2009. https://www.lutheranworld.org/sites/default/files/DMD-Diakonia-EN-low.pdf.

———. *Liberating Diakonia*. Tondheim: Tapir Akademisk, 2011.

Schreiter, Robert J. "Reconciliation and Healing as a Paradigm for Mission." *International Review of Mission* 94, no. 372 (January 2005): 74–83.

Stephens, Darryl W. "Bearing Witness as Social Action: Religious Ethics and Trauma-Informed Response." *Trauma Care* 1, no. 1 (June 2021): 49–63. https://doi.org/10.3390/traumacare1010005.

———. "Bearing Witness: A Trauma-Informed Approach to Christian Ethics." *Journal of Feminist Studies in Religion* 39, no. 1 (2023): 155–74. https://doi.org/10.2979/jfs.2023.a893198.

———. *Bearing Witness in the Kin-dom: Living Into the Church's Moral Witness Through Radical Discipleship*. New York: United Methodist Women, 2021.

———. *Reckoning Methodism: Mission and Division in the Public Church*. Eugene, OR: Cascade, 2024.

Substance Abuse and Mental Health Services Administration (SAMHSA). "SAMHSA's Concept of Trauma and Guidance for a Trauma-Informed Approach." HHS Publication No. (SMA) 14-4884 (Rockville, MD: SAMHSA, 2014). https://store.samhsa.gov/product/SAMHSA-s-Concept-of-Trauma-and-Guidance-for-a-Trauma-Informed-Approach/SMA14-4884.

———. "Spotlight: Building Resilient and Trauma-Informed Communities – Introduction." 2017. https://store.samhsa.gov/product/Spotlight-Building-Resilient-and-Trauma-Informed-Communities-Introduction/SMA17-5014.

Suchocki, Marjorie Hewitt. *The Fall to Violence: Original Sin in Relational Theology*. New York: Continuum, 1994.

Van der Kolk, Bessel A. *The Body Keeps the Score: Brain, Mind, and Body in the Healing of Trauma*. New York: Penguin, 2014.

West, Traci C. *Wounds of the Spirit: Black Women, Violence, and Resistance Ethics*. New York: New York University Press, 1999.

World Council of Churches, Pontifical Council for Interreligious Dialogue of the Roman Catholic Church, and the World Evangelical Alliance. *Christian*

Witness in a Multi-Religious World: Recommendations for Conduct. 2011. https://www.oikoumene.org/resources/documents/christian-witness-in-a-multi-religious-world.

World Council of Churches and ACT Alliance. *Called to Transformation: Ecumenical Diakonia.* Geneva: WCC Publications, 2022. https://www.oikoumene.org/resources/publications/ecumenical-diakonia.

PART 3

Diaconal Leadership and Spirituality

Chapter 12

The Diaconal Spirituality of Activism in the Philippines

Norma P. Dollaga

There is a line of thinking that social justice ministries, or activism, dilute the teachings of the church. Truth be told, this misrepresentation is painful to many members of the body of Christ. It provides fertile ground for bigotry, misjudgment, and biases to flourish. It clouds one's ability to share love and grace with the diverse worshipping people of God. Diverse people and ideas must be welcomed and embraced. The people's diversity and the varied gifts that come with them make the church of God more vibrant, beautiful, and colorful.

Activism is a political stance that aims to change the world. We witness this kind of prophetic engagement in the Magnificat when Mary sang: "[God] has brought down the powerful from their thrones and lifted up the lowly; he has filled the hungry with good things and sent the rich away empty" (Luke 1:52–54, NRSVUE). We witness activism when Jesus retorted to the rich young man, "if you wish to be perfect, go, sell your possessions, and give the money to the poor, and you will have treasure in heaven; then come, follow me" (Matt 19:21, NRSVUE). The transformation of individuals from self-absorbed persons into selfless and thoughtful persons serving others is not always appreciated and celebrated.

People often unwittingly rant that social and political engagements divide the church, leading only to cynicism and disbelief among churchgoers. However, what divides the church is not activism but rather the incapacity of some of the unforgiving faithful to love one another sincerely and who reject the participation of some people in nourishing the gifts of service to others. What divides the church is the refusal to welcome to the fold the poor, deprived, and oppressed who seek justice and a fair share in the promised abundant life for all in Jesus Christ – not only in the hereafter but in the here and now. Prophetic engagement does not take faith away from us but rather leads us to seek the things that fulfil our hearts. It leads us back to Jesus and his selfless service to others and away from empty piety and servility to oppressive, greedy, and materialistic systems.

In the Philippines, diaconal ministry enfleshed in social activism draws attention to injustice, oppression, and exploitation. We see unconstrained violence in bureaucratic corruption, centuries of feudal bondage, and an economic system that denies workers a living wage. At the heart of *diakonia* reside difficult questions about the life and ministries of the church. What is the role of the church in holding government accountable? How does the church address human rights abuses and extra-judicial killings? When thousands of poor were killed in the name of the war on drugs, did we question the policy? How should the church respond to the COVID-19 pandemic? How does the church respond to joblessness, hunger, and poverty? How does the church minister to migrant workers? How do we pursue climate justice?

In this chapter, I connect diaconal ministry to the observance of five hundred years of Christianity in the Philippines and its relevance during times of economic turmoil and tyranny. I celebrate the lives of four United Methodist deaconesses. Rev. Glofie Baluntong, defender of human rights, served as a deaconess for twenty-four years before being ordained to serve in ministry with the poor. Rev. Marie Sol Villalon, minister of compassion and justice, first served as a deaconess and later as clergy; she is deeply engaged in ministry with migrants. Deaconess Rubylin Litao, advocate with the poor, seeks justice for the victims of the war on drugs by the former president of the Philippines. These three deaconesses, still living, are my co-workers in humanitarian ministries of justice, peace, human rights, and women's empowerment. A fourth, Deaconess Filomena Asuncion, was martyred for embracing revolutionary spirituality while opposing an unjust regime. They are all graduates of Harris Memorial College, a school for deaconesses established in 1903. Their stories, which I have recorded through personal conversations – together with my own story – provide testimony of relevant, risk-taking diaconal response, manifesting the meaning of church in such a time as this.

Rev. Glofie Baluntong, Defender of Human Rights

> "Good day, Rev. Baluntong. Are you referring another case on human rights violation?" asked her lawyer.
>
> "No, attorney. I am not referring another person. This time, I will be your client. I have been charged with attempted murder."

On 18 August 2021, Baluntong faced a trumped-up charge of attempted "murder," which purportedly occurred on 25 March 2021, at three in the afternoon. On that date and at that time, she was officiating a funeral service for a church member. With the help of individuals and a show of solidarity from the ecumenical community, we raised the necessary bail, amounting to 120,000 pesos (USD 2,145). A year later, she received a subpoena requiring her to answer another criminal case, this time for an alleged violation of the Anti-Terrorism Act of 2020. The complaint was dismissed by the Office of Provincial Prosecutor due to insufficient evidence, without prejudice to re-filing if ever evidence so warrants.

In the Philippines, many human rights defenders, national liberation movement activists, trade unionists, environmentalists, and other activists are harassed by state agents and considered enemies of the state. They are red-tagged and imprisoned; worst of all, they become victims of extra-judicial killings. Church people are not spared. They are subjected to harassment and malicious judgements intended to discourage them from working with the poor or to accompany them on redemptive journeys of dignity and liberation. Baluntong is one of them.

Her favorite verse, "to do justice and to love kindness and to walk humbly with your God" (Micah 6:8, NRSVUE), guides and helps her endure the harassment and persecution. She draws inspiration from the masses of poor people as they struggle and persevere to experience a community where everyone lives life in its fullness. She believes that if her faith is compatible with the hope and struggle of the masses, then she can contribute something to the collective salvation of the people.

In her most trying moment, Baluntong summarized her understanding of the diaconal ministries of the church:
1. Diaconal ministries are vital in church life, especially in its teaching ministry. They can help nourish faith that expresses justice in everyday life.
2. Diaconal ministries can go beyond the church premises, wherever needs arise. The skills and talents of a deaconess can help empower communities for the improvement of their situation.
3. Diaconal ministry is not a job that stops after office hours. Being a deaconess, like other forms of diaconal work, is a lifetime commitment and vocation, in which time, resources, talents, and life itself contribute to the continuing struggle for the realization of God's reign here on Earth.

Baluntong receives inspiration from church people who manifest the meaning of diaconal ministries and who are ready to give their lives for the sake of others. She gives her highest recognition for their unwavering commitment.

Rev. Marie Sol Villalon, Minister of Compassion and Justice with Migrants

There is no stand-alone story. One story is woven to the fiber of other stories until it becomes the sum of our collective story. Villalon's awareness of social justice issues came during her first five years as a deaconess and student: "When I became a member of Student Christian Movement, I learned about the plight of indigenous Mangyans and peasants in Mindoro Island."

The Philippines is one of the global exporters of labor. Families survive by working abroad. Rampant joblessness and wages lower than the standard of living force adult family members to work abroad – some through legal means, others through illegal recruitment and deception. It is estimated that ten million Filipinos, about a tenth of the population, work abroad.[1] It is not uncommon for Filipinos working in strange lands to suffer discrimination, hardship, and exploitation.

Under these circumstances, Villalon initiated a programme of migrant ministries born out of passion and compassion coupled with advocacy for good government, accountability, and justice. She views diaconal ministry as a relevant, contextual, and engaging work of the church.

> The work of a deaconess must be service to people in need. Church work, serving members of the church, is also part of her work but it should go beyond church membership because suffering and poverty are found in communities, in basic poor sectors of society, among the rural and urban poor, including indigenous peoples,

---

[1] Aurora Almendral, "Heroes of the Philippines," *National Geographic* (December 2018): 138–49.

among struggling peasants and farm workers, among contractual workers who are not receiving minimum wage, [and] among abused, exploited, trafficked persons and migrant workers/seafarers.

She is the programme manager for anti-human trafficking and migrant ministry in the Manila Episcopal Area, Philippine Central Conference of The United Methodist Church. She works with the families of overseas workers, especially when their loved ones abroad are under physical hardship, emotional anguish, and suffering from abuse and exploitation by employers.

Villalon recounted:

> With a number of ten million Filipinos working overseas because of massive unemployment in the Philippines, most of whom are forced to migrate to find better jobs in foreign lands, it is very important that a programme of services for those who experience abuse and exploitation of different types is offered by the church in partnership with other organizations with the same direction and ministry. Serving and giving hope to trafficked persons and oppressed migrants, both land-based and sea-based, are expressions of diaconal work.

She serves around the clock. Sometimes she receives calls for pastoral assistance in the middle of the night, for example, to accompany a bereaving family whose loved ones were arriving at the airport in caskets. Since she has no transportation of her own, she rushes to the families by public transportation, such as it is. She offers prayers, pastoral support, and paralegal services to families, including negotiating with government agencies so that the families may receive assistance. She serves as a liaison for them with government agencies and requests for repatriation.

Once, she facilitated the escape of trafficked women abroad. Using her mobile phone, she instructed the women to make a mental map of the apartment in which they were staying in relation to the street outside and to an evangelical church nearby. By that time, she had already made connections and arrangements with the church. The women pretended to be throwing out garbage, but inside the bags lay hidden important items, including passports and other identification, clothes, and some food. Synchronizing the actions of the trafficked women with the church women ready to welcome them, she successfully carried out the plan of escape. Others arranged for their flight back home. She then coordinated with the families to welcome them.

For Villalon, diaconal ministry takes the form of activist engagement to demand systemic change. She is not afraid to effect change through the agencies and establishments of power, because she has stories to tell. The lived experiences of distressed migrant workers are the very source of her energy and power to fight. Her commitment to the work led her to a deeper resolve to fight for justice and stand with the poor, who are forced to go abroad and suffer multi-layered oppressions. She works with Migrante, an organization of families and overseas workers who are victims themselves. They find their strength in serving other victims by assisting them in documenting cases, advocating for their rights, and demanding social change. She is like the widow in the parable of Jesus who would not stop until justice was done (Luke 18:1–8). Her work is both an act of compassion and solidarity and a demand for justice. For Villalon, activist work is prophetic work.

Deaconess Rubylin Litao, Advocate Standing with the Poor Against Duterte

The sham war on drugs of the former president, Rodrigo Duterte, has caused the deaths of thousands of poor people. Poverty has become a fertile ground for the sale of drugs though so-called addicts and small-time runners as well as among non-addicts. Poor families and their kin, who have seen their loved ones killed in the most brutal ways, find it hard to get justice. They face bureaucratic intricacies and extensive legal procedures. Grinding poverty grips their daily survival. They struggle to survive as vendors, vegetable peddlers, messengers, sales barkers, and scavengers who compete with stray dogs and cats for mounds of garbage that can be salvaged or sold in order to eat, hoping to earn at least one hundred pesos (USD 1.79) a day to feed themselves and their families. Theirs is not an option to be poor; theirs is a bequeathed predicament, a conspiracy of injustice and violence.[2]

The killing of the poor is unacceptable. As church people, we felt the urgency to act, respond, and resist. To be quiet is to be an accomplice. Rise Up for Life and for Rights was co-initiated by the Ecumenical Center for Development and the Promotion of People's Response in collaboration with other church-related institutions and organizations. It is a network including advocates of human rights and the families of the victims of the war on drugs. Litao, whose Episcopal assignment is at the Ecumenical Center for Development, is the Rise Up Coordinator.

Litao's decision to accept this risky assignment to question the war on drugs was borne out of compassion and her strong adherence to a human rights framework for addressing the problem of addiction.

> As a deaconess, my exposure to the ecumenical community became the venue of my engagement and participation in justice ministry. Through forums, community visits, and [direct] exposure, I learned the situation and struggles of workers, peasants, urban poor, indigenous peoples, women, and youth. These learnings and experiences opened me to get involved with their situation, struggles, and demands. I allowed myself to be part of the advocates of human rights, justice, and peace. Thus, red letter dates became part of my monthly activities. I became visible to different mobilisations called by the different sectors.[3]

For Litao, ministry with the poor is a diaconal practice.

> At present, I am part of the team doing advocacy and service ministries with urban poor communities, particularly with the families of drug war victims. I see the work of a deaconess in extending words/prayers of comfort to the mothers who lost their

---

[2] Norma P. Dollaga, "Not a Solution to the Drug Problem," *Philippine Daily Inquirer*, 29 August 2017, https://opinion.inquirer.net/106693/not-solution-drug-problem. See also, Norma Dollaga, "Doing Human Rights in the Philippines as a Church Amid Shrinking Democracy," *United Methodist Insight*, 26 January 2022, https://um-insight.net/in-the-world/advocating-justice/doing-human-rights-in-the-philippines-as-a-church-amid-shrin/.

[3] "War on Drugs: Activist Complains That 'Duterte Tells Lies' to Filipinos," *PIME Asia News*, 21 June 2019, https://www.asianews.it/news-en/War-on-drugs:-Activist-complains-that-Duterte-tells-lies"-to-Filipinos-47350.html.

sons, to a widow who lost her husband – their loved ones were killed because of the government's war on drugs. I see the work of a deaconess in inviting the mothers and young people to join and participate in the human rights education seminar. I see the work of a deaconess in encouraging the families to be part of the public actions as an opportunity to express their call for justice.

Under her leadership, the work of *Rise Up* went as far as to challenge the national and international agencies. Some victims' cases were communicated to the International Criminal Court.

Litao, along with a team, dared set foot in lonely, crowded, and poor communities where she did not know the people. She came back to the office full of stories of how their loved ones were killed. Although they actually happened, she could not believe how brutal the murders were. She considers the stories shared by the families as lamentation to highest heaven. Three commitments summarize her reflection:

> One, the deaconess [diaconal] ministry can contribute something in making our country a better place – not only for us but for many generations to come. Second, diaconal ministry is relevant as long as it relates to the issues of the people struggling for a better and friendlier tomorrow. Third, diaconal ministry can facilitate a relevant education process, which will create a condition that will eventually move the learners/participants to be involved in specific concerns or issues, until the victims themselves become human rights advocates.

Diaconal ministry gave her a meaningful perspective on the work and ministries of the church.

Deaconess Filomena Asuncion, Martyr for Revolutionary Spirituality

Filomena Asuncion's death will not be in vain. She left us with a poem:

> How, I, wish too, wish to speak
> Of the roses' fragrance
> Listen to the fluttering wings of butterflies
> As they lift from flower to flower
> Sing the gifts whispered by rain
> Search for the rainbow
> In every dewdrop of a pure morning
> But I cannot.
>
> Someday
> I will praise the roses
> Search for the rainbow
> Whisper to the wind of hope
> Yes, Why not
> When truth has finally reigned.

Her name is inscribed on the wall of Bantayog ng mga Bayani. This Monument of Heroes is a museum, monument, and research center that honors the works, sacrifices, and heroism of activists, freedom-loving people, and mass movement leaders under the martial law of Ferdinand Marcos Sr., former president. When Marcos imposed martial law in 1972, progressive organizations were considered subversive; members went underground to avoid reprisal. The revolutionary movement grew under this repressive rule, while the most impoverished and exploited found no sigh of relief from Marcos's tyrannical rule and corruption. The revolutionary option for national liberation became a sacred response, even among the church people. Filomena Asuncion, a deaconess, was one of them. She became a martyr.

Would diaconal ministry entail a revolutionary option under circumstances where resistance becomes a correct line of struggle against an unjust state? From the tales told by her batchmates, Filomena (or Lumen) was a very quiet and modest student. She loved music. In fact, she sang well and played guitar with gusto. She did not like the activism of her classmates and criticized those who demonstrated in the streets. For her, the most important work of church people was to improve the church.

When she graduated from Harris in 1976, she was assigned to a church whose members were mostly poor farmers. During her fourth year, martial law was imposed in the entire country. Day after day, she realized the poor situation of the farmers and the legitimacy of their struggle for land and justice. She became involved in the ecumenical movement, which found meaning and dynamic engagement by siding with the oppressed and exploited people.

A Roman Catholic religious sister, with whom I had a sacred conversation before she passed to embrace Eternal Life, told a story about Lumen:

> Norma, we were very young and full of optimism. We were very sure of our vision, and our dreams made our daily work exciting. We were very committed. Lumen became more deeply involved. President Marcos used all his power to shrink the democratic space, and all those who would oppose him suffered persecution.

Under Marcos, the economy worsened. Farmers suffered, hunger was everywhere, and repression against dissent grew.[4] The revolutionary movement gained strength against the state, which promoted and espoused feudalism, foreign subserviency (imperialism), and bureaucratic capitalism.

Many church people took the side of the struggling masses. As repression intensified, some joined the revolution. It was a difficult option. We can only acknowledge that, at the crossroads of one's faith journey, one can take the path of a narrow, muddy, hilly road to engage in people-oriented land (agrarian) reform and health and education services, and build a government that would address the poverty and other century-old problems of the Filipino people.

According to this religious sister, Lumen did not find it contradictory for a person of faith to join the revolution. No one forced her to join. She shared these remembrances with me:

> She was more courageous than I was. My commitment has its own depth. I guess hers was deeper. It was a lovely day. There was a little rain softly touching our faces. Her direction turned towards the countryside. My direction was towards the city to continue the mission that I was capable of performing. She was my sister and friend. I am glad that I met you, Norma, a Methodist deaconess. Somehow you reconnected me to Lumen.

---

[4] Norma P. Dollaga, "The Collapse of a Regime," *World Mission*, February 2022, https://worldmissionmagazine.com/archives/february-2022/collapse-regime.

In a context like the Philippines, it should not surprise us when church people like Lumen, with a deep understanding of diaconal ministry, opt to join a revolution.

I think Lumen underwent her own faith introspection. Her practical steps led her to the people, the *anawim* of Yaweh, who cry and lament – not because they are romantically broken hearted but because the bondage of poverty and hunger are gripping them. To side with the poor, taking the path of revolution, is not an option rendered by the privileged but comes through a commitment, like the prophets of old.

Personal Testimony

In my own journey, I have realized that activism is no stranger to diaconal work. Diaconal ministry is attuned to the rhythm of movements of people seeking meaningful change, liberation, and the redemption of humanity. Collective activism is a spirit-filled movement. It adds life to a dying hope. It keeps believing in a cause that truly counts. It keeps on moving despite the persecution and cynicism promoted by the agents of institutions comfortable with the status quo. It is ever faithful and unbending amid tests and challenging situations.

> We cannot GIVE up HOPE
> The HOPE that springs from the well of people's suffering and struggle
> The HOPE that is ready to take the risk of denouncing neutrality
> The HOPE that is willing to carry on the IMPOSSIBLE DREAM of the People
> While the standard of this world says, "you fool, the situation is irreversible, and beyond change."
> HOPE IS believing that philosophies and theologies are great, but the thing is how to change the world until everyone can sit under the fig tree and rest.
> Because on that day, there is no more exploitation.

The spirituality of diaconal work begins with the collective affirmation: "Until Oppression Exists No More!"

My deaconess journey molded me to live an activist's life – full of life, ever meaningful each day – because each day is a day to look forward to the fulfilment of the promise of life. This spirit-filled activism invites me into soulful sensitivity and awareness of poverty, hunger, lack of access to social services, massive corruption, the moral bankruptcy of the ruling system, political repression, and environmental degradation – social concerns that this world and humanity face. Our faith mandates us to struggle and defend life and human dignity as co-nurturers of our human destiny!

This life's invitation to a deaconess ministry has encouraged me to embrace the gift of life and its endowed beauty and to reclaim the tradition of resistance against all acts of terrorism against our life and liberty, dignity, and rights. Through this work, I reclaim and affirm the spirituality of struggle and hope in the name of our ancestors who lived a life of compassion for the needy and passion for justice.

In the name of contemporary heroes and martyrs who unlearned the ways of compromise to the standards of the worldly worship of silver and gold for the sake of generations to come and for those who would bear the fruits of struggle – faith, hope, and love – I offer this poetic prayer:

> I get older each year
> Born many times over
> Lived and died and lived
> In thousands' cries and tears
> In the silent and strong protests
> In people's clenched fists, and open hands
> In the smiles and prophetic wisdom of children
> In the daring power of youth
> In the wisdom of the sages
>
> Born many times over
> From great lessons learned
> From the imprisoned because of their belief, yet free in mind and hearts
> From the landless peasants whose dignity cannot be bought by silver and gold
> From the migrants living in strange lands who choose to survive, fight, and live for their loved ones
> From the intellectuals and artists who decide with humility whom they should serve
> From those whose hearts, minds, bodies and souls are offered only for the sake of others
>
> Born many times over
> From the welcoming camaraderie of friends
> Offering their homes, hearts, and their understanding
> Giving their blessings and generosity
> Sharing their spontaneity, humor, and laughter
> Making me a part of their journey, allowing me to hear their stories.
>
> Born many times over
> In the hopes and dreams of a better life for all
> In the faith that unseen vision
> Will dawn on us
> And even if it may not be mine to behold the prophesy fulfilled
> Still will I have no regrets that I dreamt with the believers
>
> Without people's movement, this would not be possible.
> Lead me through, I pray.

Conclusion

Prophetic social engagement as an expression of diaconal ministry challenges us to rise from the dead values that kill and desecrate human beings created in the image of God. A dynamic church is a rising church, one that has come out of the emptiness due to lack of compassion, individualism, and selfish indulgences. We must humbly learn the ways of self-criticism and willingly subject ourselves to remolding our character to values compatible with the kingdom of God in heaven and on Earth. A church that believes in the resurrection of the body is a church driven by LOVE in action for others. "No one has greater love than this, to lay down one's life for one's friends" (John 15:13, NRSVUE).

The diaconal work and ministries of Rev. Glofie Baluntong, Rev. Marie Sol Villalon, Deaconess Rubylin Litao, and Deaconess Filomena Asuncion are lived testimonies of the spirituality of activism. These deaconesses are unapologetic in their commitment to the people. They do not consider their work as unique or extra-special. For them, the lived articulation of their lives and mission define the innate power of diaconal work. It must not surprise the church if other women take their path of daring and risky mission. The suffering of the poor, the vulnerable, and victims of injustice are far greater than we imagine.

Works Cited

Almendral, Aurora. "Heroes of the Philippines." *National Geographic* (December 2018): 138–49.

Dollaga, Norma P. "The Collapse of a Regime." *World Mission*, February 2022. https://worldmissionmagazine.com/archives/february-2022/collapse-regime.

———. "Doing Human Rights in the Philippines as a Church Amid Shrinking Democracy." *United Methodist Insight*, 26 January 2022. https://um-insight.net/in-the-world/advocating-justice/doing-human-rights-in-the-philippines-as-a-church-amid-shrin/.

———. "Not a Solution to the Drug Problem." *Philippine Daily Inquirer*, 29 August 2017. https://opinion.inquirer.net/106693/not-solution-drug-problem.

"War on Drugs: Activist Complains That 'Duterte Tells Lies' to Filipinos." *PIME Asia News*, 21 June 2019. https://www.asianews.it/news-en/War-on-drugs:-Activist-complains-that-Duterte-tells-lies"-to-Filipinos-47350.html.

Chapter 13

Women Shaping Diaconal Theology in The Episcopal Church

Valerie Bailey

The theology of the diaconate continues evolving, especially along the axis of service and addressing needs on behalf of the church. However, the theology of the diaconate was challenged in the early 1970s as canon law in The Episcopal Church (US) changed to allow for women to become ordained as deacons in holy orders and equal to male deacons. Women had been deaconesses and set apart as lay ministers under an 1889 canon. However, the 1970 Deacons' Canon raised new questions about how holy orders and ordination impact diaconal theology for churches in which deacons are ordained clergy. Diaconal theology may focus on service, but how is this complicated when deacons became part of the hierarchy?

This question is addressed by examining this liminal period between 1970 and 1974. Despite their correspondence and participation in the National Conference of Deaconesses, there were still two distinct groups of women deacons: those set apart under the 1889 canon and those ordained under the 1970 Deacons' Canon. They viewed the diaconate in very different ways. Furthermore, in 1974, after years of lobbying, resistance, and frustration, eleven women deacons, known as the Philadelphia Eleven, were irregularly ordained by three bishops, two years before the General Convention authorized the ordination of women.[1] The priestly ordinations of these deacons were accepted (regularized) by the church in 1976 when the General Convention changed the canons to allow women to become priests and bishops. On the eve of women's ordination to the priesthood, the theology of the diaconate was pivoting around priesthood, not servanthood.

This chapter contends that conversations about diaconal ministry were interrupted in 1974, when the first women were ordained to the priesthood. Before the canon change, diaconal ministry (deaconesses and male deacons) in The Episcopal Church focused on service to marginalized persons on behalf of the church. Afterwards, diaconal theology began to address issues of gender equality and the relationship between ordination, holy orders, and servant leadership. Reviewing this liminal space and how the two groups of women interacted during this period deepens our understanding of the relationship

---

[1] Don S. Armentrout, "The Philadelphia Eleven," in *An Episcopal Dictionary of the Church: A User-Friendly Reference for Episcopalians*, ed. Don S. Armentrout and Robert Boak Slocum (New York: Church Publishing, 2000), 400. The women ordained as priests were Merrill Bittner, Alla Bozarth-Campbell, Alison Cheek, Emily Hewitt, Carter Heyward, Suzanne Hiatt, Marie Moorefield, Jeanette Piccard, Betty Schiess, Katrina Swanson, and Nancy Wittig.

between the transitional deacon and the permanent deacon. It also contributes to the general conversation about the theology of the diaconal experience, including the ministry of the transitional deacon. The confusion in this period over questions of hierarchical power and service still lingers within The Episcopal Church's understanding of the diaconate.

The 1970 Deacons' Canon

According to canon law in The Episcopal Church, all priests must first be ordained as deacons before becoming priests. While some men were ordained as permanent deacons, the diaconate for men who were going to become priests was more of a transition to priesthood than a focus on diaconal ministry. In most cases, these men served more as priests in training than deacons. The "transitional diaconate" became complicated after the 1970 Deacons' Canon, which allowed women to become deacons in holy orders – ordained clergy and equal to male deacons. The lay order of deaconess was absorbed into the 1970 Deacons' Canon. Both lay deaconesses and newly ordained female deacons were considered clergy in holy orders, equal to male deacons. The question arose: If female and male deacons were equals, and male deacons could become priests, did this mean that women could also become priests?

The 1970 Deacons' Canon was adopted during the second wave of the women's movement in the United States, when women were challenging institutional sexism and the exclusion of women in jobs viewed as being for men only.[2] The efforts to open priesthood to women were part of how Episcopalians were challenging the exclusion of women from the church's hierarchy. Many of the women ordained under the 1970 Deacons' Canon were hoping that their diaconate would become a transition to the priesthood.[3] Women priesthood advocates continued lobbying church leaders for access to priesthood. Church leaders listened to their concerns but made no changes to church policy about ordaining women to the priesthood.[4] Church leaders opposed to women priests were prone to interpret the 1970 Deacons' Canon as a permanent diaconate without priesthood for women.

In the late 1960s, women and male allies lobbied The Episcopal Church's leadership to change its canon law to allow women to become deacons, priests, and bishops. Suzanne Hiatt, one of the Philadelphia Eleven, led these lobbying efforts in presenting a resolution to allow women to become ordained as priests.[5] Hiatt referred to the 1970 Deacons' Canon as "a booby prize."[6] In the hierarchy of holy orders, the priesthood and the episcopate are higher than the diaconate.

---

[2] Hiatt connects the organizing efforts for women priesthood with the women's movement. Suzanne Hiatt, *The Spirit of the Lord Is Upon Me: The Writings of Suzanne Hiatt*, ed. Carter Heyward and Janine Lehane (New York: Seabury, 2014), 7.
[3] Heather Huyck, "Indelible Change: Woman Priests in the Episcopal Church," *Historical Magazine of the Protestant Episcopal Church* 51, no. 4 (1982): 387.
[4] Huyck, "Indelible Change," 388.
[5] Hiatt, *The Spirit of the Lord Is Upon Me*, 9.
[6] Hiatt, 153.

Hiatt viewed the adoption of the 1970 Deacons' Canon as setting women up for ordination only as permanent deacons.

In the context of failed woman-priesthood legislation, Pauli Murray, civil rights lawyer and the first Black woman Episcopal Church priest, made the 1970 Deacons' Canon sound like the license to a lesser order. In her autobiography, Murray wrote:

> The General Convention of 1970 bypassed our report, but it did move one step forward by removing language that limited the lowest level of the ordained ministry, the diaconate, to males, thereby opening the way for women to enter ordained clergy. I was so disappointed over a half-measure intended to keep women in a subordinate category that I stopped going to church. Like many other women on the periphery of organized religion, I began to question the authority of a traditional faith which continued to treat half of its membership as less than fully human. My rejection of the church left me floundering in a wilderness of doubt.[7]

Murray eventually recovered from her spiritual crisis, returned to church, entered the ordination process, and became a priest. Jeannette Piccard (one of the Philadelphia Eleven) also was hoping for priesthood after her ordination to the diaconate under the 1970 Deacons' Canon. Piccard said she was led to believe that the church was in the process of changing the status of the deaconess to perpetual deacon, equal to male perpetual deacons.[8] The writings of women ordained under the 1970 Deacons' Canon acknowledged confusion about the interpretation of the new canon, but many women deacons ordained after 1971 were hopeful that eventually canon law would change and women would be able to become priests.

Meanwhile, the 1970 Deacons' Canon was celebrated by deaconesses pleased with new possibilities for their dwindling order. They hoped that the new canon would bring clarity to a diaconal theology of ministry, new possibilities for pension benefits, and access to holy orders: ecclesiastical authority and apostolic connection embodied in the roles of bishops, priests, and deacons.[9] They hoped this canon would revitalize the diaconate in The Episcopal Church. However, women priesthood advocates, who at first despised the 1970 Deacons' Canon, later viewed the new canon as a means of becoming priests. As a result, for the newer women deacons, theological clarity about the diaconate was less concerned with service and servant leadership and more concerned with gaining access to the church hierarchy. To that end, many of the newer deacons viewed

---

[7] Pauli Murray, *Song in a Weary Throat: Memoir of an American Pilgrimage* (New York: Liveright, 2018), 547–48.

[8] Sheryl K. Hill, "'Until I Have Won': Vestiges of Coverture and the Invisibility of Women in the Twentieth Century: A Biography of Jeannette Ridlon Piccard" (PhD Thesis, Ohio University, 2009), 296.

[9] Rima Lunin Schultz, "'To Realize the Joy of Dedication and Vocation in the Grace Conferred in Our Order': Deaconesses in Twentieth Century Chicago," *Anglican and Episcopal History* 73, no. 3 (2004): 335–36.

the diaconate as a transition to the priesthood and access to the priesthood as a justice issue.[10]

The National Conference of Deaconesses and its director, Frances Zielinski, invited the new women deacons to their deaconess meetings and rostered these new deacons along with women set apart under the 1889 Deaconess Canon.[11] Several of the Philadelphia Eleven were rostered as part of the deaconess conference while they continued to lobby for women priesthood. During that same period, the older deaconesses were concerned with pension benefits, while the younger women deacons were concerned with becoming priests. As the national deaconess conference retained the name deaconess, women priesthood advocates were holding meetings with bishops and arranging protests.[12] To better understand the differences between the two groups of women deacons, we must be familiar with the history of the deaconess movement in The Episcopal Church.

Brief History of the Deaconess Movement

The first women recognized as deaconesses in The Episcopal Church were set apart in 1856 by William Whittingham, Bishop of Maryland.[13] The bishop's efforts to set apart deaconesses were well received by other church leaders. Others also began setting apart women as deaconesses, but the definition of a deaconess role was not entered into the canons until 1889. Between 1856 and 1889, Episcopal Church leaders discussed several models of women's ministries and diaconate.

Deaconess theology and methodology were significantly influenced by Theodor Fliedner (1800–1864) of Kaiserswerth, Germany, John Saul Howson (1816–1885), Dean of Chester Cathedral, England, and William A. Muhlenberg (1796–1877) of the Dioceses of Pennsylvania and New York. Fliedner founded the first deaconess training center in 1836.[14] By 1856, he defined *Diakonie* as more than just "helping"; it was more like an office of servant love (*ein Amt der*

---

[10] For example, Carter Heyward's theology focused on the role of priesthood, with little to no reflection on the diaconate. Carter Heyward, *A Priest Forever* (New York: Harper & Row, 1976), 34–36.

[11] Jean Felix Piccard, Jeannette Ridlon Piccard, and Don Piccard, "Deaconess Newsletter 10, November 1971" (Manuscript Division, Library of Congress, Washington, DC, 1 November 1971), Part II: Subject File: Jeannette Piccard, Deacons and Deaconess, 1971–1977, Box II: 44, Folder 4, Piccard Family Papers, circa 1470–1983, https://hdl.loc.gov/loc.mss/eadmss.ms998008.

[12] Jean Felix Piccard, Jeannette Ridlon Piccard, and Don Piccard, "Piccard Family Papers, circa 1470–1983" (Manuscript Division, Library of Congress, Washington DC, 1 November 1971), Numerous Files, Piccard Family Papers, circa 1470–1983, https://hdl.loc.gov/loc.mss/eadmss.ms998008; Hiatt, *The Spirit of the Lord Is Upon Me*, 9.

[13] See chapter by Noyes in this volume.

[14] Adolph Spaeth, "Phebe the Deaconess," in *The Lutheran Church Review*, ed. Henry Eyster Jacobs and Theodore Emanuel Schmauk, vol. 4 (Philadelphia: Philadelphia Alumni Association of the Evangelical Lutheran Theological Seminary, 1885), 219.

dienenden Lieben).[15] Howson described deaconess work as "servant love" and espoused a theology of women's subordination to validate the deaconess role as one of service and not church leadership. Howson translated *diakonia* as helper, which he equated with the Greek word for help. He saw the call to servant love and helping work related to women's nature as established by Eve, who was made to be Adam's helper (Gen 2:18). To that end, Howson taught that whenever helping work is done, the woman is in her place.[16] Muhlenberg, along with Anne Ayres, formed the Sisterhood of the Church of the Holy Communion in the United States in 1845.[17] Muhlenberg insisted that the Episcopal sisterhoods were not an attempt to copy what was being done by Elizabeth Ann Seton's Sisters of Charity or any Roman Catholic order, but more like the emerging deaconess model.[18]

Church leaders debated and discussed women's networks throughout the mid-nineteenth century. After years of discussion in General Convention, church leaders adopted a vague resolution, which led to the formation of the Woman's Auxiliary to the Board of Missions in 1871. This group became a collective of small women's mission networks that raised money for church missions.[19] The conversation about deaconesses and sisterhoods continued, and with the support of the Woman's Auxiliary, church leaders adopted the Deaconess Canon in 1889.[20] The canon defined deaconesses as lay women without holy orders. Mary S. Donovan described the development of the deaconess profession in The Episcopal Church as "a curious blend of tradition and nineteenth-century sentimentality."[21] Compensation was precarious and rarely, if ever, included a pension.[22]

---

[15] John N. Collins, *Diakonia Studies: Critical Issues in Ministry* (Oxford: Oxford University Press, 2014), 11, citing Theodor Fliedner, "Gutachten die Diakonie und den Diakonat Betreffend" (1856) in *Diakonie Pragmatisch: Der Kaiserswerther Verband und Theodor Fliedner*, eds N. Friedrich, C.R. Muller, and M. Wolff (Neukirchen-Vluyn: Neukirchener, 2007), 34.
[16] Collins, *Diakonia Studies*, 10; John Saul Howson, *Deaconesses in the Church of England* (New York: E.P. Dutton & Company, 1880), 15.
[17] Robert W. Prichard, *A History of the Episcopal Church*, 3rd ed. (New York: Morehouse, 2014), 194.
[18] The nineteenth-century Episcopal Church was divided along party lines: low church evangelicals preferred deaconesses, and high church Anglo-Catholics supported religious orders like sisterhoods. Anne Ayres, *The Life and Work of William Augustus Muhlenberg* (New York: Harper & Brothers, 1880), 222–23.
[19] Mary S. Donovan, *A Different Call: Women's Ministries in the Episcopal Church, 1850–1920* (Wilton, CT: Morehouse-Barlow, 1986), 66.
[20] *Journal of the Proceedings of the Bishops, Clergy, and Laity of the Protestant Episcopal Church in the United States of America Assembled in a General Convention 1889* (Austin, TX: The Archives of the Episcopal Church, 2022), 134–35, https://www.episcopalarchives.org/sites/default/files/publications/1889_GC_Journal.pdf
[21] Donovan, *A Different Call*, 89.
[22] The desire for compensation and holy orders had been discussed by deaconesses since the early 1920s. Schultz, "Deaconesses in Twentieth Century Chicago," 335–36.

Despite the lack of holy orders, deaconesses in the early twentieth century viewed their role in continuity with deacons from the early church: a vocational identity from the pastoral model of Jesus Christ through a relationship with the church via their bishop. Rima Schultz wrote, "they acted as if they were deacons and in their own minds and hearts, they accepted their calling and felt that they had been ordained to the diaconate."[23] In a report from the 1897 Lambeth Conference, church leaders acknowledged that deaconesses were valuable to the church.[24] The 1919 General Convention said deaconesses were not clergy (in holy orders).[25] However, the 1920 Lambeth Conference declared that deaconesses were in holy orders.[26] While the Pietists, evangelicals, and non-conforming church leaders were opposed to all things Catholic, leaders within the Church of England were open to ordaining deaconesses in holy orders after the 1920 Lambeth Conference supported Apostolic Approval for the female diaconate.[27]

While some leaders in the Church of England were open to women in holy orders, women began to lose ground in the United States. During the 1925 General Convention, a resolution that considered accepting lay women as readers passed the House of Deputies but was rejected by the House of Bishops.[28] The 1930 Lambeth Conference also took a step backwards and declared that deaconesses were not in holy orders through a resolution that affirmed the ministry of deaconesses and lay women church leaders.[29] The number of women set apart for the office of deaconess began to decline in 1922: the 1930 Living Church listed 222 active deaconesses; by 1950 the number dropped to 164; by 1960, there were 86 active and retired deaconesses.[30] Traditional deaconess

---

[23] Schultz, 335–36.

[24] *The Lambeth Conference Resolutions Archive from 1897* (London: Anglican Communion Office, 2005), https://www.anglicancommunion.org/media/127725/1897.pdf.

[25] *Journal of the General Convention of the Protestant Episcopal Church in the United States of America 1919* (Austin, TX: The Archives of the Episcopal Church, 2022), https://www.episcopalarchives.org/sites/default/files/publications/1919_GC_Journal.pdf.

[26] *The Lambeth Conference Resolutions Archive from 1920* (London: Anglican Communion Office, 2005), https://www.anglicancommunion.org/media/127731/1920.pdf.

[27] Robert W. Prichard, *A History of the Episcopal Church*, rev. ed. (New York: Morehouse, 1999), 216.

[28] *Journal of the General Convention of the Protestant Episcopal Church in the United States of America 1925* (Austin, TX: The Archives of the Episcopal Church, 2022), https://www.episcopalarchives.org/sites/default/files/publications/1925_GC_Journal.pdf.

[29] *The Lambeth Conference Resolutions Archive from 1930* (London: Anglican Communion Office, 2005), http://www.anglicancommunion.org/media/127734/1930.pdf.

[30] Schultz, "Deaconesses in Twentieth Century Chicago," 335–36. Schultz reviewed archives (1917–1970) from the Central House of Deaconesses, a deaconess training school and the "motherhouse" of the Episcopal deaconess movement. There have never been more than 250 deaconesses at the same time. According to combined archives, by 1961 there were only eighty-one deaconesses left, and only thirty were under the age of sixty-five.

positions declined with the increase of secular nurses and social workers; many of the small congregations once served by deaconesses were closed. The increased use of the automobile also led to the consolidation of smaller rural and urban parishes, decreasing the deaconesses' domestic ministry field.[31]

Theology on the Eve of the 1970 Deacons' Canon

The Lambeth Conference of 1968 marked a major turning point for the diaconate. Before 1968, diaconal theology was defined in the negative – either not ordained or not a woman or not Catholic. Lambeth 1968 recommended that the diaconate combine service of others with liturgical functions and proposed opening a permanent diaconate to men and women either in secular occupations or full-time church work, and to men selected for the priesthood.[32] This resolution also recommended that the ordinals be revised to remove the reference to the diaconate as an inferior office and continued to uphold the *diakonia* element in the ministry of priests and bishops.

This was a major theological shift. Lambeth 1968 revisited the liturgical and historical roots of *diakonia* and began to define the diaconate in terms of ministry and service. The adoption of the 1970 Deacons' Canon reinvigorated discussions about diaconal identity. Thus, diaconal theology at the time of the adoption of the 1970 Deacons' Canon was informed by an ecumenical, comprehensive discussion rooted in history, the liturgical movement, and ministry as servant leadership.

This conversation continued to unfold, but the focus shifted to the diaconate as a transition to priesthood during the liminal period between the 1970 Deacons' Canon and the 1974 irregular ordination of the Philadelphia Eleven. Schultz described this period as ironic: the "dying order" of deaconesses managed to challenge the male hierarchy under which their order had been placed in a subordinate role and became the means to open the door to the ordination of women.[33] While deaconesses may have opened the door for priesthood, the 1970 Deacons' Canon had few rewards for them. Pensions were still not easily secured and conversations about diaconal theology were secondary to the conversations about women priesthood. Nevertheless, the deaconesses were now in holy orders.

Correspondence Between Zielinski and Piccard

Much of the theology of this liminal period may be gleaned from the correspondence between the women deacons ordained after 1971 and the deaconesses. The oldest deacon among the Philadelphia Eleven, Jeannette

---

[31] Prichard, *A History of the Episcopal Church*, 306.
[32] *The Lambeth Conference Resolutions Archive from 1968* (London: Anglican Communion Office, 2005), Resolution 32:1968, https://www.anglicancommunion.org/media/127743/1968.pdf.
[33] Schultz, "Deaconesses in Twentieth Century Chicago," 335–36.

Piccard, along with six men and Suzanne Hiatt, was ordained a deacon on 19 June 1971 in Philadelphia using a trial liturgy. Based on her correspondence with Frances Zielinski, Piccard was concerned that her ordination to the diaconate in 1971 under the new 1970 Deacons' Canon was as a "perpetual deacon." The Perpetual Deacons' Canon was renewed on the same day that the 1970 General Convention adopted a canon admitting deaconesses to holy orders and allowing women to be ordained to the diaconate.[34]

In a letter to Zielinski, Piccard expressed concern that the term deaconess was still being used by the deaconesses ordained under the 1889 canon. Piccard wrote in a letter to Zielinski:

> I understand that the Bishop of Chicago insists on calling The Rev. Zielinski, "Deaconess." If I were in his diocese and he insisted on calling me deaconess, I should tell him that since he is the Bishop, he can call me what he likes ... It really doesn't matter so long as he and everyone else recognized that there is no difference between my duties, privileges, and obligations and those of any other deacon. The danger in the use of the title deaconess is that the functions of a deaconess have been clearly defined in the church for over a hundred years and these functions are those of a lay woman, not a member of the clergy. The change in status should be recognized by proper title.[35]

Two theologies of holy orders emerge in Zielinski's and Piccard's correspondence. Piccard viewed the 1970 Deacons' Canon as releasing holy orders from a patriarchal system, while Zielinski viewed the 1970 Deacons' Canon as an opportunity to finetune her theology of the diaconate. For example, Zielinski argued in a letter to Piccard that deaconesses were always in holy orders, even if deaconesses had been considered a lay order. For Zielinski, the 1970 Deacons' Canon made holy orders clearer than the 1889 Deaconess Canon, and she cited the 1920 Lambeth reports in defending deaconesses as being in holy orders. While a 1930 Lambeth discussion and report rejected deaconesses as being in holy orders, Zielinski seems to have rejected this rejection: "In our judgement the ordination of a deaconess confers on her Holy Orders. In ordination she receives the character of a deaconess in the Church of God, and therefore the status of women ordained to the diaconate has the permanence of Holy Orders."[36]

---

[34] *Journal of the General Convention of the Protestant Episcopal Church in the United States of America otherwise known as The Episcopal Church 1970* (Austin, TX: The Archives of the Episcopal Church, 2022), 170, 243, 249, https://www.episcopalarchives.org/sites/default/files/publications/1970_GC_Journal.pdf.

[35] Jean Felix Piccard, Jeannette Ridlon Piccard, and Don Piccard, "Letter, January 16, 1971 from Jeannette Piccard to Frances Zielinski, Questioning Her Use of the Title Deaconess" (Manuscript Division, Library of Congress, Washington, DC, 16 January 1971), Part II: Subject File, Jeannette Piccard, Deacons and Deaconesses 1971–1977, Box II:42, Folder 4: Piccard Family Papers, circa 1470–1983, https://hdl.loc.gov/loc.mss/eadmss.ms998008.

[36] Jean Felix Piccard, Jeannette Ridlon Piccard, and Don Piccard, "Letter, September 30, 1971 from Frances Zielinski to Jeannette Piccard, Defending Holy Orders for Deaconesses," in Part II: Subject File, Jeannette Piccard, Deacons and Deaconesses 1971–1977, Box II:42, Folder 4, Piccard Family Papers, circa 1470–1983 MSS36145

It is hard to tell what Zielinski's and Piccard's relationship may have been. Zielinski was a powerful supporter of the diaconate; records show that she was on committees and meetings where women priesthood resolutions were being discussed. Did she support women in the priesthood and the diaconate? Or did she have the foresight to be involved in all deliberations about women in holy orders, seeing that any resolution about women's ordination had the potential of helping the deaconesses reach their goals for holy orders and pensions? Zielinski, Piccard, and Murray also attended the April 1970 Graymoor Conference where women priesthood advocates planned strategies to lobby for a women priesthood resolution.[37]

In September 1973, Edith Booth discussed a survey of women deacons that found many of the newer women deacons ordained under the 1970 Deacons' Canon were not interested in being part of the National Conference of Women Deaconesses. Booth quoted remarks from Hiatt: "the new deacons are not a homogenous group, not even with each other. They have different lifestyles (some are married) and different ministries. They are not called to the diaconate only, they are just 'passing through.'"[38] Booth said the new deacons were afraid that joining the National Conference of Women Deacons meant that they did not want to go on to the priesthood.[39] Three years after the first women priesthood resolution failed in 1970, and one month after this survey, the second women priesthood resolution failed at the October 1973 General Convention.

At a meeting of self-supporting clergy in December 1973, months before the July 1974 irregular ordination, Zielinski's hope for a more expansive conversation about the diaconate was interrupted by the new women deacons' desire to become priests. By 1977, the self-supporting clergy organization was in the process of finishing its ministry and closing. This organization credited input from both Roman Catholic ministry partners and Zielinski of the National Center for the Diaconate (formerly Central House for Deaconesses) in Evanston, Illinois, with helping the church develop "a newfound understanding of the identity and functions of the deacon (most of whom are self-supporting in both communions)."[40] Eleven women deacons were irregularly ordained to the priesthood in July 1974. During the same year, the Women Deaconesses

---

(Manuscript Division, Library of Congress, Washington, DC: Library of Congress, n.d.), https://hdl.loc.gov/loc.mss/eadmss.ms998008.

[37] Prichard, *A History of the Episcopal Church*, 256.

[38] Jean Felix Piccard, Jeannette Ridlon Piccard, and Don Piccard, "Report of Our Corporate Communion and Triennial Dinner, September 28, 1973, in the National Conference of Women Deacons," in Part II: Subject File: Jeannette Piccard, Deacons and Deaconess, 1971–1977, Box II:44, Folder 4, Piccard Family Papers, circa 1470–1983 MSS36145 (Manuscript Division, Library of Congress, Washington, DC: Library of Congress, n.d.), https://hdl.loc.gov/loc.mss/eadmss.ms998008.

[39] "National Ordination Group Disbands," *Episcopal News Service: The Archives of the Episcopal Church*, 15 February 1977, https://episcopalarchives.org/cgi-bin/ENS/ENSpress_release.pl?pr_number=77044.

[40] "Self-Supporting Clergy Conference Held," *Diocesan Press Service: The Archives of the Episcopal Church*, 21 December 1973, https://episcopalarchives.org/cgi-bin/ENS/ENSpress_release.pl?pr_number=73282.

Association changed its name to the National Center for the Diaconate, dropping the name deaconess and serving both men and women deacons.

Conclusion

What was happening in 1973 when the deaconess organization was becoming discouraged over their efforts to incorporate the women deacons ordained under the 1970 Deacons' Canon? Did the challenges related to integrating the women ordained under the 1970 Deacons' Canon contribute to Zielinski's new efforts to change the name of the deaconess conference to the National Center for the Diaconate? Discussing the self-supporting clergy organization, Zielinski described the theology of the diaconate: "The deacon has a ministry of liturgy, a ministry of the Word, and a ministry of Service. It is the latter from which the diaconate takes its peculiar identity, and which separates it from being just a 'mini-priesthood.'"[41] Is it possible that Zielinski helped direct diaconal theology in the late twentieth and early twentieth-first century toward a ministry of liturgy, word, and service?

Zielinski may have been unable to shift diaconal theology back toward service during that liminal period. However, she seems to have accepted that the diaconate was more than just service and embraced the expansion of the diaconate to include liturgical and teaching ministries. This expansion of diaconal identity happened without the support of the women deacons initially ordained under the 1970 Deacons' Canon, and it is still evolving today.

Perhaps Zielinski learned from her experience with the early women deacons that to shape the theology of the diaconate, the focus needed to return to the ministry of service, as well as to the ministry of liturgy and the ministry of the word. Could a theology be infused into the orders of priest and bishop that is based on the theology of the diaconate? Does ordination to priesthood mean the person is no longer a deacon? Currently, the transitional diaconate remains unclarified – those ordained as priests become deacons briefly, but their ministry appears to be more shaped by the priesthood than the diaconate. But is it possible to turn a holy order into a transitional space?

What are other ways that diaconal theology could evolve, especially with the experiences of women deacons? Zielinski did not want the diaconate to become a pass-through order or a mere transition between laity and priesthood. Zielinski wanted to set the new diaconate in a direction that had continuity with its call to service mandated in the Book of Acts. What would happen to the theology of the priesthood and the episcopacy if it embraced the theology of servant leadership in the diaconate instead of ignoring the holy order of deacon? Perhaps in the future another liminal time and space will allow reflection on this question.

---

[41] "National Ordination Group Disbands."

Works Cited

Armentrout, Don S. "The Philadelphia Eleven." In *An Episcopal Dictionary of the Church: A User-Friendly Reference for Episcopalians*, edited by Don S. Armentrout and Robert Boak Slocum, 400. New York: Church Publishing, 2000.

Ayres, Anne. *The Life and Work of William Augustus Muhlenberg*. New York: Harper & Brothers, 1880.

Collins, John N. *Diakonia Studies: Critical Issues in Ministry*. Oxford: Oxford University Press, 2014.

Donovan, Mary S. *A Different Call: Women's Ministries in the Episcopal Church, 1850–1920*. Wilton, CT: Morehouse-Barlow, 1986.

Heyward, Carter. *A Priest Forever*. New York: Harper & Row, 1976.

Hiatt, Suzanne. *The Spirit of the Lord Is Upon Me: The Writings of Suzanne Hiatt*. Edited by Carter Heyward and Janine Lehane. New York: Seabury, 2014.

Hill, Sheryl K. "'Until I Have Won': Vestiges of Coverture and the Invisibility of Women in the Twentieth Century: A Biography of Jeannette Ridlon Piccard." PhD thesis, Ohio University, 2009.

Howson, John Saul. *Deaconesses in the Church of England*. New York: E.P. Dutton & Company, 1880.

Huyck, Heather. "Indelible Change: Woman Priests in the Episcopal Church." *Historical Magazine of the Protestant Episcopal Church* 51, no. 4 (1982): 385–98.

Journal of the General Convention of the Protestant Episcopal Church in the United States of America 1919. Austin, TX: The Archives of The Episcopal Church, 2022. https://www.episcopalarchives.org/sites/default/files/publications/1919_GC_Journal.pdf.

Journal of the General Convention of the Protestant Episcopal Church in the United States of America 1925. Austin, TX: The Archives of the Episcopal Church, 2022. https://www.episcopalarchives.org/sites/default/files/publications/1925_GC_Journal.pdf.

Journal of the General Convention of the Protestant Episcopal Church in the United States of America otherwise known as The Episcopal Church 1970. Austin, TX: The Archives of the Episcopal Church, 2022. https://www.episcopalarchives.org/sites/default/files/publications/1970_GC_Journal.pdf.

Journal of the Proceedings of the Bishops, Clergy, and Laity of the Protestant Episcopal Church in the United States of America Assembled in a General Convention 1889. Austin, TX: The Archives of the Episcopal Church, 2022. https://www.episcopalarchives.org/sites/default/files/publications/1889_GC_Journal.pdf.

The Lambeth Conference Resolutions Archive from 1897. London: Anglican Communion Office, 2005. https://www.anglicancommunion.org/media/127725/1897.pdf.

The Lambeth Conference Resolutions Archive from 1920. London: Anglican Communion Office, 2005. https://www.anglicancommunion.org/media/127731/1920.pdf.

The Lambeth Conference Resolutions Archive from 1930. London: Anglican Communion Office, 2005. http://www.anglicancommunion.org/media/127734/1930.pdf.

The Lambeth Conference Resolutions Archive from 1968. London: Anglican Communion Office, 2005. https://www.anglicancommunion.org/media/127743/1968.pdf.

Martimort, A.G. *Deaconesses: An Historical Study*. San Francisco: Ignatius, 1986.

Murray, Pauli. *Song in a Weary Throat: Memoir of an American Pilgrimage*. New York: Liveright, 2018.

"National Ordination Group Disbands." *Episcopal News Service: The Archives of the Episcopal Church*, 15 February 1977. https://episcopalarchives.org/cgi-bin/ENS/ENSpress_release.pl?pr_number=77044.

Piccard, Jean Felix, Jeannette Ridlon Piccard, and Don Piccard. "Deaconess Newsletter 10, November 1971." Manuscript Division, Library of Congress, Washington, DC, 1 November 1971. Part II: Subject File: Jeannette Piccard, Deacons and Deaconess, 1971–1977, Box II:44, Folder 4. Piccard Family Papers, circa 1470–1983. https://hdl.loc.gov/loc.mss/eadmss.ms998008.

———. "Letter, January 16, 1971 from Jeannette Piccard to Frances Zielinski, Questioning Her Use of the Title Deaconess." Manuscript Division, Library of Congress, Washington, DC, 16 January 1971. Part II: Subject File, Jeannette Piccard, Deacons and Deaconesses 1971–1977, Box II:42, Folder 4: Piccard Family Papers, circa 1470–1983. https://hdl.loc.gov/loc.mss/eadmss.ms998008.

———. "Letter, September 30, 1971 from Frances Zielinski to Jeannette Piccard, Defending Holy Orders for Deaconesses." In Part II: Subject File, Jeannette Piccard, Deacons and Deaconesses 1971–1977, Box II:42, Folder 4, Piccard Family Papers, circa 1470–1983 MSS36145. Manuscript Division, Library of Congress, Washington, DC: Library of Congress, n.d. https://hdl.loc.gov/loc.mss/eadmss.ms998008.

———. "Piccard Family Papers, circa 1470–1983." Manuscript Division, Library of Congress, Washington, DC, 1 November 1971. Piccard Family Papers, circa 1470–1983. https://hdl.loc.gov/loc.mss/eadmss.ms998008.

———. "Report of Our Corporate Communion and Triennial Dinner, September 28, 1973, in the National Conference of Women Deacons." In Part II: Subject File: Jeannette Piccard, Deacons and Deaconess, 1971–1977, Box II:44, Folder 4, Piccard Family Papers, circa 1470–1983 MSS36145. Manuscript Division, Library of Congress, Washington, DC: Library of Congress, n.d. https://hdl.loc.gov/loc.mss/eadmss.ms998008.

Prichard, Robert W. *A History of the Episcopal Church*. Rev. ed. New York: Morehouse, 1999.

———. *A History of the Episcopal Church*. 3rd ed. New York: Morehouse, 2014.

Schultz, Rima Lunin. "'To Realize the Joy of Dedication and Vocation in the Grace Conferred in Our Order': Deaconesses in Twentieth Century Chicago." *Anglican and Episcopal History* 73, no. 3 (2004): 335–36.

"Self-Supporting Clergy Conference Held." *Diocesan Press Service: The Archives of the Episcopal Church*, 21 December 1973. https://episcopalarchives.org/cgi-bin/ENS/ENSpress_release.pl?pr_number=73282.

Spaeth, Adolph. "Phebe the Deaconess." In *The Lutheran Church Review*, edited by Henry Eyster Jacobs and Theodore Emanuel Schmauk, vol. 4. Philadelphia: Philadelphia Alumni Association of the Evangelical Lutheran Theological Seminary, 1885.

Chapter 14

Reclaiming the Lessons and Legacies of the Earliest Episcopal Deaconess

Daphne B. Noyes

A twenty-first-century person with an interest in *diakonia* might be forgiven for assuming that the lives and ministries of nineteenth-century deaconesses are irrelevant – that a now-obsolete Christian ministry of women in The Episcopal Church has earned its place on the ash heap of history. Admittedly, that view colored my own thinking until I encountered Adeline Blanchard Tyler (1805–1875) and her companions, the four women who together became the first deaconesses in The Episcopal Church in 1856. Their easy dismissal can be attributed to the paucity of histories of the deaconess movement, the eventual extinction of their order, and the prevalence of incorrect information. This chapter begins to set the record straight by highlighting some of the extraordinary events, situations, and people that played a role in those early days, and by presenting these first deaconesses as mentors who, like Abel, by faith still speak, even though they are dead (Heb 11:4, NRSV).

Initially, my fascination with Tyler was based on the seductive allure of exceptionalism. First deaconess in The Episcopal Church. First to found a Deaconess House. First nurse to care for Union soldiers in the Civil War. First Lady Superintendent of the Children's Hospital in Boston. First, first, first! What I failed to observe at first but learned over time was the importance of community in sustaining Tyler's ministry.[1]

The crucial role of community for those engaged in a life of diaconal service is now recognized in the canons of The Episcopal Church: "Deacons canonically resident in each Diocese constitute a Community of Deacons, which shall meet from time to time."[2] No such canons existed in Tyler's day.[3] The first deaconesses carved out new territory for Episcopal women who sought to address societal needs from a Christian locus, while supported by like-minded

---

[1] This research was supported in part by grants from the Episcopal Women's History Project and the Historical Society of the Episcopal Church. For an audio and visual presentation, see Daphne B. Noyes, "Adeline Blanchard Tyler: The First Episcopal Deaconess," 47 min. video, 7 May 2023, https://www.youtube.com/watch?v=L_JyvKDMQuU.

[2] "Of the Life and Work of Deacons," in *Constitution and Canons, Together with the Rules of Order* (The Episcopal Church, Adopted and Revised in General Conventions, 1785–2022), Title III, Canon 7, Section 2.

[3] The office of deaconess was not formally accepted by the General Convention of the Episcopal Church until 1889. See chapter by Bailey in this volume.

colleagues. The need for community sprang organically from their lives and work together.

In the Beginning

The ministries of the first deaconesses were based in parishes, but the scope of their service soon expanded to reach well beyond parochial boundaries. Their work encompassed nursing, social work, advocacy, teaching, fundraising, counselling, and material and spiritual support, the latter with equal emphasis on sacrament and word. The advent of the deaconess movement opened the possibility of a consecrated life for Episcopal women. Over time, this would challenge the norm of women's exclusion from holy orders.

While the order of deaconesses was by definition gendered, the men who played a critical role in its restoration in The Episcopal Church deserve acknowledgement. They came from the highest echelons of the Episcopal hierarchy, from common clerical positions and from religious orders. They came from medicine, law, and the fourth estate. They were tradesmen, merchants, and philanthropists. Regardless of their social or ecclesiastical standing, they were adamant about the entwined needs of the church and the world for deaconesses. The rector of Grace Church in New York City trumpeted: "The revival of that office is indispensable to the fullest and most efficient development of the Church's working powers, and for want of it … 'The Church has long remained *maimed in one of her hands.*"[4] One can almost hear his fist thumping on the pulpit.

Equally important were the deaconesses' collaborations with other faithful women who were unable or unwilling to join their ranks due to personal considerations or family responsibilities, but who nonetheless desired to effect social change. These allies used their skills, relationships, and resources to organize benefits, write books and articles, provide essential supplies in the face of wartime shortages, and offer lasting friendship.

"[P]ious women desirous of having a set share in the work of the Church," deaconesses challenged institutional and cultural barriers not by breaking them down but by redefining their borders.[5] There is no indication that they sought to enter – some might say usurp – the ministries of men; rather, they set out to claim for their own a primacy of place side by side with the ill and infirm, the forlorn and forgotten, the destitute and desperate. In the same way, deacons today may aspire to reach through barriers – institutional, cultural, even clerical – that limit or confine their roles, to find their places among those most in need, where they can honor and emulate the one who "came not to be served, but to serve" (Matt 20:28, NRSV).

---

[4] Henry C. Potter, *Sisterhoods and Deaconesses at Home and Abroad* (New York: E.P. Dutton & Company, 1873), 14, italics in the original.

[5] William Rollinson Whittingham to Potter, 3 November 1863, in William Francis Brand, *Life of William Rollinson Whittingham, Fourth Bishop of Maryland*, vol. 2 (New York: E. & J.B. Young & Co., 1883), 110.

The four women who became the first Episcopal deaconesses had been immersed in diaconal ministries in Boston and Baltimore well before they received the threefold charge from William Rollinson Whittingham, Bishop of Maryland: to be "servants of the Lord Jesus ... servants of the sick and poor and needy of every class, for Jesus' sake ... servants to one another."[6] Who were the members of this newborn community? Tyler, fifty, and her friend, Caroline Elizabeth Guild, twenty-nine, were both freshly arrived from Boston. In Baltimore they joined Eveline Black, thirty-one, and Catherine Minard, nineteen, who for nearly a year had resided in the rectory of St. Andrew's Church with Horace Stringfellow, his wife, Mary, and their three children, sharing in the young minister's dream of "alleviating the destitution both temporal and spiritual ... [by] returning to the church the primitive order of Deaconesses." The young women "gave their entire time to ... ministering to the poor" and, with Stringfellow's wife, organized a thriving charity school. Most poignantly, before the Infirmary had even opened, Black and Minard cared for the youngest Stringfellow, Louis, barely a year old when he died in April 1856. The grief-stricken father reported, "that little one was probably the first patient the Ladies had."[7]

The Infirmary was formally opened on 21 September 1856, the Feast of St. Matthew. As the eldest and most experienced, Tyler was appointed its head. Now living together under the same roof, the four women sought out those beyond the parish walls, presciently living out the words that more than a century later would be used in the ordination of a deacon: "Your life and teaching are to show Christ's people that in serving the helpless they are serving Christ himself."[8] Not yet formally admitted to the office of deaconess, they were nonetheless committed to bringing hope and comfort, material and spiritual support, to their neighbors in need.

At that time, The Episcopal Church lacked an authorized ritual for setting apart deaconesses, nor was there any financial support other than that which each woman might bring with her or that was supplied by the collection plate or private donations. Despite his passionate inspiration drawn from visits to the infirmaries of English and French sisterhoods, Stringfellow became overtaxed by parochial and family concerns and could not persevere; he resigned abruptly forty days after the Infirmary opened and left Baltimore. Undaunted, the women continued to distribute "flour, meal, wood, meat &c" to the sick and destitute not

---

[6] Whittingham manuscript for the setting apart of deaconesses, n.d., Episcopal Diocese of Maryland (EDOM) Archives. See also *Kaiserswerth Deaconesses, Including a History of the Institution, the Ordination Service and Questions for Self-Examination by A Lady*, First American Edition (Baltimore: Joseph Robinson, 1857), 45, EDOM Archives.

[7] Horace Stringfellow to Whittingham, 31 January 1857, EDOM Archives.

[8] *The Book of Common Prayer and Administration of the Sacraments and Other Rites and Ceremonies of the Church, Together with the Psalter or Psalms of David, According to the Use of The Episcopal Church* (1979), 543.

resident in the Infirmary and to care for those who occupied its twenty beds.[9] Not yet officially deaconesses, Tyler and her companions immediately wrote to Whittingham requesting his "Pastoral Supervision and Visitorial Care," which he quickly granted.[10] The bishop recorded in his journal: "Visited the Infirmary ... and formally accepted the Rule of it as offered to me by the Associate Sisters in their Instrument, to that effect, dated November 3rd." Thus, they were received by the bishop as deaconesses, serving under his authority.[11]

Pain and Privilege

Born in Billerica, Massachusetts, and raised in the Congregational Church, Tyler was prepared for her vocation as a deaconess by her life circumstances. A teenager when her father died, she completed her schooling and promptly entered one of the few professions considered suitable for a young woman: she became a teacher. In her early twenties she married John Tyler, a widower more than twice her age, and moved to Boston. Within a year she was thrust into the role of nurse when he suffered an attack of rheumatoid arthritis, leaving him partially disabled for the rest of his life. Despite this infirmity, he continued to work as a successful merchant and auctioneer. His death shortly after their twenty-fifth wedding anniversary left her a widow with adequate resources, a passion for Christian charity, and "a sorrow, only softened by the belief in a future life" – a sorrow that joined other, earlier bereavements.[12] After Tyler's elder brother, rector of St. Anne's Episcopal Church in Annapolis, died unexpectedly, her niece observed: "[S]he began to feel the importance of caring for her soul, she was naturally inclined to seek the Church which he had so loved."[13] Tyler set about with a grief-goaded energy – seeking, serving, ministering to the women, men, and children who were in greatest need, without regard to race, class, or age. This same passion, so often with similar roots in loss or brokenness, frequently appears as a common denominator in the ministries of today's deacons: chaplains in hospitals or prisons, nurses or other medical professionals, social service workers, community organizers, advocates, and counsellors.

The necessity of being self-supporting is a condition that continues to apply to vocational Episcopal deacons, nearly all of whom serve in a non-stipendiary capacity. This situation restricts the possibility of entrance into the diaconate for people whose energies first must go toward earning a living, often while raising a family. The need for a frugal lifestyle, personal wealth, or paid secular

---

[9] *The Church Infirmary of the Diocese of Maryland – St. Andrew's Infirmary*. [An Article from *The Monitor* of 13 February 1857]. (Baltimore: Joseph Robinson, n.d. [1857?]), 16, EDOM Archives.
[10] Whittingham to Beloved Sisters in Christ: Mrs. Tyler, Miss Black, Miss Guild, Miss Minard, 4 November 1856, EDOM Archives.
[11] Whittingham journal entry, 8 November 1856, 203-4, EDOM Archives.
[12] From an unpublished memoir of Tyler by her sister, Catherine Blanchard Gilman, with her niece, Elizabeth Blanchard Randall; edited by Orlando Hutton (hereinafter cited as Gilman-Randall manuscript), EDOM Archives.
[13] Gilman-Randall manuscript.

employment severely limits the pool of possible deacons, especially factoring in the costs of formation.[14]

After becoming widowed, released from the day-to-day care of her husband and financially independent, Tyler continued the charitable work she had started during her marriage, now with sharply focused dedication and more time to offer. She had previously collaborated with like-minded people from Trinity Church, Boston, in founding Trinity Hall for the education of poor children, the City Mission Chapel and Home for the Destitute, and the Seaman's Aid Chapel, and in organizing St. Stephen's Chapel. One cleric involved in these efforts remarked: "Nothing could deter her from undertaking any service to the poor, the sick and the destitute of any class and description."[15]

In 1846 she began to attend the Church of the Advent, "recently organized to secure the ministrations of the Protestant Episcopal Church to the poor & needy in a manner free from unnecessary expense and all ungracious circumstances."[16] This meant that it was a "free church"; there was no pew rent, as was usual in other churches in Boston and elsewhere. There was instead a striking emphasis on identifying and responding to the needs of the surrounding community. Tyler became a member of its newly established Parish Guild, whose male membership voted to admit women just a year after its founding.[17] Horatio Southgate, the parish's second rector, proudly declared that the decision to include women "has led to a result which has proved one of the greatest blessings … our work among the Poor is a perfect system, accomplishing, at least, three times as much as formerly, and accomplishing it incomparably better."[18]

By the second year of the Guild's operation, Southgate reported "We have about 50 children in the School, all that our present room will accommodate; and of these, 10 are the children of colored [sic] Parishioners."[19] In addition to a practical education and catechetical instruction, children were provided with clothing and shoes. The Guild served adults as well, providing access to apothecaries, doctors, lawyers, and nurses, as well as spiritual support, religious education, and training in sewing and other skills. Tyler's roles in the Parish Guild – both Matron of the School and Superintendent of the Home for Widows and Aged Couples – led to her being known as the "Lady Abbess."[20]

Tyler's reputation spread throughout the high church realm through which she moved so comfortably and ultimately led her to be called to Baltimore by

---

[14] See chapter by Mills-Curran in this volume.

[15] John Lee Watson, in Gilman-Randall manuscript.

[16] *Records of the Wardens and Vestry of the Parish of the Advent*, 13 November 1844, Church of the Advent Archives, Boston.

[17] *Canons and Prayers of the Holy Guild of the Parish of the Advent, Boston, Mass.*, adopted 1853, rev. 1855 (Boston: John M. Hewes, 1857), 3.

[18] Horatio Southgate, "Sermon Preached on the Second Anniversary of the Holy Guild of the Church of the Advent" (Boston: J. Howe, 1855), 13–14, Horatio Southgate Papers, Manuscripts and Archives, Yale University Library.

[19] Southgate, "Sermon Preached on the Second Anniversary," 13n.

[20] Gilman-Randall manuscript.

Stringfellow. He later recalled: "From all that I could learn of her character I became satisfied that she was eminently suited to the work."[21]

Sacred Purposes, Solemn Responsibilities

Tyler's gifts for ministry now had a larger field, and she tackled her expanded role in Baltimore with intensity.

> [S]he was called to devote her every capacity and energy to relieve the sorrows of her fellow creatures ... Her whole Christian character, in a word, was the outgrowth of convictions that deepened and ripened in her experience and undertaken labours to which she devoted herself with singular fidelity and entire trust in her Lord.[22]

Within two years, the success of St. Andrew's Infirmary, the profound needs of the city's poorest residents, and the efficiency of consolidating philanthropic resources led to the merger of the Infirmary with Baltimore's Church Home. Housed in a former medical college, the new Church Home and Infirmary was supported by the Episcopalians of Baltimore and the State of Maryland with staffing by the deaconesses. Despite her initial misgivings about the wisdom of housing severely ill patients under the same roof as the elderly and infirm, Tyler rose to the occasion, tending to the residents' temporal and spiritual needs. She created and furnished a chapel, established a custom of daily morning prayer, and donated a baptismal font of her own design and communion silver to ensure the sacraments were offered by the assigned chaplains. In their absence, she would read the lessons.

Under Tyler's supervision, the deaconesses' work and their numbers expanded far beyond the parochial and neighborhood scope of St. Andrew's Infirmary; they now cared for people from near and far, of all ages, races, and backgrounds. As Chief Deaconess, Tyler received letter after letter imploring care for all sorts and conditions of men, women, and children: a boy from New Jersey, "an entire stranger, taken sick upon the street"; a "bright and pretty" ten-year-old girl from Washington, DC, whose uncle offered her to be indentured to the institution; a man described as "one of Christ's poor, who has nothing but a diseased constitution ... entirely dependent on charity"; "a lady of unblemished Christian character and of highly respectable connection and position in society"; a "worthy Church of England woman with two little children"; a member of the Greek Church who "expresses a great desire to go to the Lord's table"; and a destitute woman from Virginia, abandoned by her husband, together with her young daughter, who would soon become an orphan.[23]

By 1860 the Church Home had nearly one hundred residents, including six deaconesses and five probationers, some from as far away as Canada, England,

---

[21] Stringfellow to Whittingham, 1857.
[22] Gilman-Randall manuscript.
[23] Adeline B. Tyler Letter Book, 1857–1860, in Adeline B. Tyler, Papers, 1856–1861, EDOM Archives.

Ireland, Holland, and Germany.[24] Yet despite her devotion to the institution and its mission, Tyler was no longer among them. In response to her insistent desire to enlarge the ranks of deaconesses, she left the Church Home to establish a Deaconess House in Baltimore, "where those desirous of giving themselves to a life of religious devotion in works of Charity and Mercy, may find a careful training, a sick one care and nursing, and a weary one find a quiet rest from toil."[25]

In April 1861, days after the attack on Fort Sumter, Union soldiers from Massachusetts were assaulted by a violent mob when their regiment was passing through Baltimore en route to Washington. Seeking to aid the men from her home state, Tyler negotiated the release of the two most severely wounded from the police station where they were being held. She had them transported to the Deaconess House where they spent a month recovering. This earned Tyler a formal commendation from the Massachusetts State Legislature praising her "kind, humane and christian [*sic*] services" and led to her being honored as the first nurse to care for Union soldiers in the Civil War.[26] She was next called to serve at a military hospital in Baltimore but was forced to leave after her even-handed treatment of both Confederate and Union soldiers led to accusations of being a "rebel sympathizer."[27] Tyler subsequently directed the nursing staff of military hospitals in Chester, Pennsylvania, and Annapolis, Maryland, recruiting women from Maine and Massachusetts to serve alongside her. They shared the daily responsibility of caring for as many as a thousand men suffering from battle wounds, homesickness, recent amputations, malnutrition, starvation, pneumonia, typhoid, and even smallpox. Union or Confederate, regardless of race or rank, all received compassionate care.

Like the deacons of the twenty-first century, Tyler and her companions again and again were forced unflinchingly to confront two central questions: Who is my neighbor? How do I shape my ministry in response to the world around me?

The divisions and debates of the Civil War brought them face to face with strongly held opinions within and outside the deaconess community, requiring them to navigate increasingly volatile relationships and to balance faithfully their own consciences with their call to Christian service. The atmosphere was highly charged:

---

[24] Bill and Martha Reamy, compilers, *1860 Census of Baltimore City, Volume Two, 3rd and 4th Wards* (Westminster, MD: Family Line, 1989), 80.

[25] Tyler to Richard Clarence Hall, 11 February 1860, in Tyler Letter Book, in Adeline B. Tyler, Papers, 1856–1861, EDOM Archives.

[26] Quincealea Brunk, "Caring without Politics: Lessons from the First Nurses of the North and South," *Nursing History Review* 2, no. 1 (January 1994): 120, DOI: 10.1891/1062-8061.2.1.119; "Resolve Rendering the Thanks of the General Court of Massachusetts to Adeline Tyler, of Baltimore, in the State of Maryland," 1862 *Massachusetts* Resolves, 49, https://archive.org/details/actsresolvespass1862mass/page/224/mode/2up.

[27] Robert Atkinson in Catherine Blanchard Gilman, unpublished manuscript, MS 1450, H. Furlong Baldwin Library, Maryland Center for History and Culture, Baltimore.

In Baltimore the rending of hearts and homes was without parallel. In every house, in every family, in every Church, members lined themselves under their respective banners. Father against son, brother against brother, pastor against people ... Mrs. Tyler's strong personality and deep conviction in the righteousness of the Northern cause was known to the whole body of her co-laborers. Many of these were southern women of equally strong prejudices, who finding irksome conditions in store for them, applied ... to be released from their obligations as Deaconesses.[28]

Minard was one of these who applied to be released. She left the deaconess community to found the Sisterhood of the Good Shepherd, "a parochial institution ... with no claim to recognition outside of the parochial limits of its rector."[29]

Tyler responded to the national strife and turmoil by writing to women she hoped might be called to the life of a deaconess, acknowledging both the challenges and the rewards of diaconal ministry: "the only advantage we have at this time [is] the spiritual benefits derived by enduring the hardships of our calling by humble faith casting our bread upon the waters assured that we shall find it after many days."[30] The years of relentless labor during the Civil War placed her in the midst of immense suffering on a massive scale. At the same time, she experienced personal bereavement at the deaths of her sister's husband and her beloved seven-year-old step-grandson, while struggling with her own declining health. Beset by pervasive loneliness, at Thanksgiving she recalled "the former times, when in the midst of peace and plenty we gathered around the festive board with dear ones whose earthly pilgrimage has ended and with it music that made life sweet to us."[31] On the advice of her physicians, in 1864 she left the war-torn country and departed for Europe for rest and recovery, not to return until after the war's end.

The Midnight Mission

Somewhat restored by her time abroad, Tyler next served at the Midnight Mission for the Rescue of Fallen Women, an Episcopal charity established in 1867 in Brooklyn, New York. As head of the Ladies' Committee, Tyler was reunited with Guild and Black, who served on the staff as Lady in Charge, as did Tyler for a time.

In a descriptive pamphlet, the Mission's gentlemen managers called the work "a peculiar and delicate one."[32] Their *modus operandi* encapsulates the norms of Victorian society:

---

[28] Gilman-Randall manuscript.
[29] Whittingham to Potter, in Brand, *Life of Whittingham*, vol. 2, 111. The Sisters left Baltimore for Missouri, Minard's home state, in 1872. Minard died in Kentucky in 1917.
[30] Tyler to My dear Xian [Christian] friend. Recruitment letter, n.d. (c. 1860 or 1861), EDOM Archives.
[31] Tyler to My dear Sister, 29 November 1863, in Catherine Blanchard Gilman, unpublished manuscript, MS 1450, H. Furlong Baldwin Library, Maryland Center for History and Culture.
[32] Midnight Mission pamphlet. n.d. (c. 1868), 1, EDOM Archives.

Christian men go out upon the streets two evenings in the week with cards of invitation and religious tracts, trying, by kind words and urgent appeals to conscience to persuade these poor despised ones to forsake their evil ways, and to come with us to our Mission rooms, where a kind reception awaits them, where Christian ladies lovingly welcome them, listen patiently and sympathisingly to the story of their wrongs and their confessions of guilt; offer them simple refreshments for the body; counsel them in their various difficulties, and draw them to that Saviour who never turns a deaf ear to the penitent.[33]

The singing of hymns bookended the evening's programme, which included a brief address and prayer. The Mission's location seemed to be ideal for Tyler. She had friends and relatives nearby, and the cities where other relatives and friends resided – Baltimore and Annapolis to the south and Boston to the north – could be reached by a short journey. In the reunion of Tyler, Black, and Guild, the shared ministry of the deaconesses survived, even in the absence of a formally recognized community.

"My Own Heart Work"

Tyler's little community was once again scattered in 1869. Black, in ill health, resigned from her position at the Mission; Guild left to travel in Europe.[34] But God had one more "first" in store for Tyler: she was recruited by a prominent Boston physician to be the first Lady Superintendent of the new hospital for children being established in that city. She told the head of the Mission she felt "urged by a higher claim" to take the position.[35] In Boston, the disconnection from her fellow deaconesses was made bearable by the proximity of family members in the area, enduring friendships with members of the Church of the Advent, and attendance at the Church of the Messiah, a free church located near the hospital. Just as she had at St. Andrew's Infirmary and the Church Home and Infirmary, Tyler created an oratory in the new hospital, again ensuring both spiritual and physical care for the young patients and the staff. Under her superintendency, the Children's Hospital outgrew its first location within a year and moved to larger quarters nearby.

Years of arduous labor and advancing age took a severe toll on Tyler's body and spirit. In late February 1872, she confided to her sister, "I am intending to resign my Supervision soon ... It is very trying to my feelings to give up this my own heart work."[36] Later, informing Whittingham of her resignation, she wrote, "I was obliged to make judgement take precedence of my affections & yield the heart's love for the better conduct of our growing institution. Feeling my ability

---

[33] Midnight Mission pamphlet, 2–3.
[34] Black died in Baltimore at the Church Home and Infirmary in 1875. Guild died in Boston in 1880.
[35] Tyler to Wolcott Richards, 26 April 1869, MC 1, Box 1, Folder 19, Boston Children's Hospital Archives.
[36] Tyler to My dear Sister, Second Wednesday in Lent [22 February], 1872, MC1, Box 1, Folder 59, Boston Children's Hospital Archives.

weakening & that any time the institution was libel [*sic*] to be left without a head, in justice to it, I give it up."[37]

She first made certain that the hospitalized children, whom she affectionately called her "little family," would continue to be well cared for in body and spirit. She arranged for members of the Sisters of Saint Margaret, an Anglican nursing order, to come from England and assume charge of the hospital. Her painful leave-taking inspired reflection on how her faith had supported her:

> This separating from a work so dear to my heart & for which I have given so many prayers & labors of love rends my inmost soul & I sometimes think it will be too much for my strength. By God's help I hope to be sustained; He has led me by ways I knew not & can still keep me under His wing.[38]

Faithful unto Death

Tyler did not live to see the peak of the deaconess movement in The Episcopal Church. But by the time of her death in January 1875, the movement had grown to include deaconesses in the dioceses of Alabama (1864) and Long Island (1872).[39] In 1889, the General Convention of The Episcopal Church finally adopted a canon recognizing the order of deaconess.[40] Over time their numbers grew to hundreds, who served in the United States and across the world, challenging the church to live into *diakonia* by modelling lives of consecrated service and whose ministries, like Tyler's, belong in the historical narrative of diaconal studies.

In 1970, when women were allowed entry into the Sacred Order of Deacons for the first time in The Episcopal Church, the order of deaconess was abolished. As a result, all deaconesses were declared to be deacons, a change that many deaconesses met with resistance. Their reason for holding steadfast to the order to which they were called is made clear by the concluding Collect from the Ordinal then in use, which describes the diaconate as an "inferior Office," praying that deacons "may be found worthy to be called unto the higher Ministries in thy Church."[41] For deaconesses, there could be no higher ministry than theirs.

---

[37] Tyler to Whittingham, Tuesday next before Easter [26 March], 1872, MC 1, Box 1, Folder 63, Boston Children's Hospital Archives.
[38] Tyler to My dear Sister, Easter Monday [1 April] 1872, MC 1, Box 1, Folder 65, Boston Children's Hospital Archives.
[39] Potter, *Sisterhoods and Deaconesses*, 180, 255.
[40] "Of Deaconesses," Committee on Canons, Report No. 23. *Journal of the Proceedings of the Bishops, Clergy, and Laity of the Protestant Episcopal Church in the United States of America Assembled in a General Convention 1889*, 108–9.
[41] "The Form and Manner of Making Deacons," *The Book of Common Prayer* (1928), 534.

Works Cited

The Book of Common Prayer and the Administration of the Sacraments and other Rites and Ceremonies of the Church According to the Use of the Protestant Episcopal Church in the United States of America Together with the Psalter or Psalms of David. New York: The Church Pension Fund, 1929.

The Book of Common Prayer and the Administration of the Sacraments and Other Rites and Ceremonies of the Church Together with the Psalms of David According to the Use of the Episcopal Church. New York: The Church Hymnal Corporation, 1979.

Brand, William Francis. *Life of William Rollinson Whittingham, Fourth Bishop of Maryland*, Volume 2. New York: E. & J.B. Young & Co., 1883.

Brunk, Quincealea. "Caring without Politics: Lessons from the First Nurses of the North and South." *Nursing History Review* 2, No. 1 (January 1994): 119–36. DOI: 10.1891/1062-8061.2.1.119.

Canons and Prayers of the Holy Guild of the Parish of the Advent. Adopted, 1853. Revised, 1855. Boston: J.M. Hewes, 1857.

The Church Infirmary of the Diocese of Maryland – St. Andrew's Infirmary. [An Article from *The Monitor* of 13 February 1857.] Baltimore: Joseph Robinson, n.d. Episcopal Diocese of Maryland Archives.

Constitution and Canons, Together with the Rules of Order, For the Governance of the Episcopal Church in the United States of America, Otherwise known as The Episcopal Church, Adopted and Revised in General Conventions, 1785–2022.
https://extranet.generalconvention.org/staff/files/download/238.

Gilman, Catherine Blanchard, with Elizabeth Blanchard Randall; Orlando Hutton, editor. Unpublished manuscript, n.d. Episcopal Diocese of Maryland Archives, Baltimore.

———. Unpublished manuscript, MS 1450, H. Furlong Baldwin Library, Maryland Center for History and Culture, Baltimore.

Journal of the Proceedings of the Bishops, Clergy, and Laity of the Protestant Episcopal Church in the United States of America Assembled in a General Convention 1889.
https://www.episcopalarchives.org/sites/default/files/publications/1889_GC_Journal.pdf.

Kaiserswerth Deaconesses, Including a History of the Institution, the Ordination Service and Questions for Self-Examination by A Lady. Baltimore: Joseph Robinson, 1857. Episcopal Diocese of Maryland Archives, Baltimore.

Noyes, Daphne B. "Adeline Blanchard Tyler: The First Episcopal Deaconess." 47 min. video. 7 May 2023.
https://www.youtube.com/watch?v=L_JyvKDMQuU.

Potter, Henry C. *Sisterhoods and Deaconesses at Home and Abroad.* New York: E.P. Dutton & Company, 1873.

Reamy, Bill and Martha, compilers. *1860 Census of Baltimore City, Volume Two, 3rd and 4th Wards.* Westminster, MD: Family Line, 1989.
https://msa.maryland.gov/bca/files/1860_census_ward_3_and_4.pdf.

Records of the Wardens and Vestry of the Parish of the Advent, November 8, 1844 through July 12, 1929. Church of the Advent Archives, Boston.

"Resolve Rendering the Thanks of the General Court of Massachusetts to Adeline Tyler, of Baltimore, in the State of Maryland." 1862 *Massachusetts Resolves*, 49.
https://archive.org/details/actsresolvespass1862mass/page/224/mode/2up.

Southgate, Horatio. "Sermon Preached on the Second Anniversary of the Holy Guild of the Church of the Advent," The First Sunday of Advent [3 December], 1854. Boston: J. Howe, 1855. Horatio Southgate Papers. MS 77, Box 15: A Collection of Letters and Other Memorabilia ... Collected by Kenneth Walter Cameron. Manuscripts and Archives, Yale University Library.

Stringfellow, Horace to William Rollinson Whittingham, 31 January 1857. Episcopal Diocese of Maryland Archives, Baltimore.

Tyler, Adeline Blanchard. Papers, 1856–1861. Episcopal Diocese of Maryland Archives, Baltimore.

———. Papers, 1869–1873. MC 1. Boston Children's Hospital Archives, Boston.

Whittingham, William Rollinson. Papers. Episcopal Diocese of Maryland Archives.

Chapter 15

Imagining the Future of *Diakonia*

Jessica Bickford

The last one hundred years has been the most rapidly changing era in history. From technology and medical advances to cultural and social constructs, today's world is very different from that of previous generations. If we take time to think about it, our minds quickly become overwhelmed. When change occurs (either chosen or imposed), it can feel as if we are Alice falling down the rabbit hole to Wonderland. Things can appear as they did before, but what was up is now down, and what made sense no longer does. For some, change is exciting. The possibilities are endless, and the space to be creative or think out of the box is liberating. For others, change invokes anxiety when asked to try something new or conceptualize a different way.

Many churches are uncertain about change. Growing up, I was told that the motto for the Anglican Church was: "We've never done it that way before!" Throughout the centuries the church has been consistent in its branding and rituals. This organizational culture, supported by national political leadership, has permitted churches a regimented and dominant role within Western society. Although the church played its role within its societal context, in the late 1990s the Anglican Church of Canada begin to recognize an exponential decrease in membership, attendance, and level of community involvement by its parishes. Many attributed these changes to different social constructs, such as people having to work or children playing sports on Sundays. As time has passed, church membership numbers have continued to decrease, and the church has not been able to adjust.

In a presentation to the Council of General Synod for the Anglican Church of Canada, Neil Elliot outlined the statistical trends of the Anglican Church of Canada from 1961 to 2017. He analyzed five areas of diocesan data: the number of clergy, the number of other church employees, church membership, attendance, and pastoral offices performed (baptisms, confirmations, marriages, and funerals). From 1961 to 2001, there was a 50 percent rate of decline across all categories. Furthermore, there was another 50 percent decline from 2001 to 2017. In other words, it took half the amount of time for the same amount of decline. Elliot concluded that, if this trend continues, the Anglican Church in Canada will run out of members by 2040.[1] With the changing makeup of North American society and the decrease in parochial numbers, it would be fair to assume that the church finds itself in its own version of Wonderland and with an

---

[1] Tali Folkins, "Gone by 2040?" *Anglican Journal*, 6 January 2020, https://anglicanjournal.com/gone-by-2040/.

identity crisis. As the church discerns its role and place, opportunities emerge for new forms of leadership and organizational structure.

This chapter explores: 1) how the diaconate and its continued study can be utilized as a model for ministry within the current societal context, 2) power structures and how to convert a hierarchal approach to a diaconal model of ministry, and 3) a process of evaluation to enable organic transitions. It is important to highlight that this chapter is written from a white colonial perspective. Within the Canadian context, descendants of white colonial settlers are in the process of reconciling relationships with the indigenous communities as well as communities of color. These ethnic expressions of faith and church communities are vast and unique. One cannot presume that the representation of church within this chapter speaks for these communities and their understandings of church.

The Role of the Church

It is time for the church to become radical, not necessarily in the sense of new and innovative, but in the sense of returning to its roots. In other words, the church must get back to the roots of Jesus Christ's message and ministry. Circumstances must be created that return the church to the beginning of the Christian story, peeling away religious infrastructure and personal expectations. To determine the role of the church at this juncture, diaconal studies is imperative. By discerning the church's role through a diaconal lens, a foundation of service and social justice can be laid.

The New Testament not only describes the life of Jesus Christ; it also serves as an oral training manual for the first disciples. Matthew 22:37–39 provides a mission statement for ministry: "'Love the Lord your God with all your heart and with all your soul and with all your mind.' This is the first and greatest commandment. And the second is like it: 'Love your neighbor as yourself'" (NIV). We are first called to love God. If we love God, then we must love like God: unconditionally. Historically the church has used its position to create criteria for people to work toward becoming worthy of God's love. These standards have led the church to being viewed as judgmental and hypocritical, because the actions of its leaders have not complied with the standards they have established. By focusing on love (heart, mind, and soul), we fully connect ourselves to the source of love, which is God. The second part of this Bible passage highlights the need for service: to love others as we love ourselves.

Jesus' approach to ministry was twofold. The first step was to show love; the second step was to provide service. Whenever Jesus encountered a "sinner," he always showed love, a respect that others in the community withheld. He then provided a service, supporting sinners where he found them. Through these actions, Jesus exemplified a message of love and service. Another instance of service can be seen in the passage describing the Last Supper. Traditionally, service is taught as putting the needs of others before our own, even to the extreme of sacrificing ourselves. This is not a true act of service. This type of thinking has led to many incidents of abuse within the church. During the Last Supper, Jesus' act of washing Peter's feet was not about lessening ourselves but about being available to each other in those places of vulnerability (John 13:1–17). By sharing love, revealing our authentic selves, and being in a place of vulnerability, we foster a space of grace, evoking God's presence.

A diaconal model focuses the mission of the church on love and service. Continued study of the diaconate builds in a level of accountability so the church can maintain this new standard of values. These priorities have additional ramifications for the church's organizational structure if we are bold enough to imagine them.

The Church in Wonderland

Returning to the metaphor of Alice in Wonderland, I explore the current situation of the Anglican Church in Canada and its ecclesiastical infrastructure. I have always found the story of Alice in Wonderland a source of support in my ministry.[2] Alice is a girl who spots a white rabbit who can talk. She follows this creature down a rabbit hole where she finds a world that is both strange and beautiful. When first ordained, I identified many of the characters in the stories with those I encountered in my ministry. I imagined the church's infrastructure using the following characters and representations:

- The Queen of Hearts represents authority figures.
- The White Rabbit represents administrators.
- The Deck of Cards represents parochial leadership.
- The Garden of Flowers represents churches.
- The Mad Hatter's Tea Party represents the diaconate.

These images gave me a guiding framework for navigating the infrastructure of the church, a structure that I thought I knew as a longtime member but encountered anew as an ordained deacon.

The Queen of Hearts as Authority Figure

The Queen of Hearts is a figure of authority. This includes, but is not limited to, primates, archbishops, and bishops. Those in these positions are the primary representatives of the institution within a given territory. They are responsible for the church's response to current events, societal norms, ethical decisions, spiritual expression, and development. They are also responsible for holding the church accountable and measuring success.

The current priority involves the sustainability of churches in the face of declining church statistics. This priority has created a survival mentality among churches. While a survival mentality may be seen as simply holding congregations accountable, it places grassroots workers in a precarious place of fear. When working from a place of fear, those working to achieve the milestones set by those in authority can be paralyzed by one wrong move – and it is "off with your head." Instead of dreaming of what can be done next, the grassroots vision is limited to internal matters.

---

[2] Lewis Carroll, *Alice in Wonderland* (Auckland, New Zealand: The Floating Press, [1865] 2008).

The White Rabbit as Administrator

If the Queen of Hearts sets the standards for success in each area, the White Rabbit symbolizes all those in administrative positions, such as vicar generals, executive archdeacons, and territorial archdeacons. Parishes are assured that the episcopacy and diocesan offices are there to support parish leadership. While this is true, the mandates are to ensure that the parishes are fulfilling the obligations set forth by the Queen of Hearts (authority figures). It is not my intention to over-generalize and imply that authority figures and administrators are indifferent to the needs of the grassroots. But when a parish is struggling financially, often there is minimal collaboration to connect parishes to resources that would help support current ministries and missions. The focus is on how the bills will be paid. This disconnect contributes to the environment of fear that the grassroots may be experiencing.

The Deck of Cards as Parochial Leadership

This misalignment between the hierarchy and the grassroots catches church leadership between the standards of success and the needs of the congregations they serve. This dynamic can be symbolized by the character of the Deck of Cards. In the story, the Deck of Cards has been ordered to paint the roses red, but when the Queen arrives, the cards are in trouble because she has changed her mind and wants the roses to remain white. Church leaders (especially priests) tend to be in the same predicament. How do they strike a balance between meeting the standards set by authority figures and empowering the communities they serve?

One support that parishes receive is through diocesan programmes. Although these programmes are cloaked with the intention of support, there is a hidden expectation that these programmes will spark interest and increase parish membership. For some parishes this may be the result, but for the majority, these (what I like to call) "cookie cutter" programmes perpetuate the same models, thinking, and Christian branding, leaving little room for the Holy Spirit.

The Garden of Flowers as Churches

Continuing our journey through Wonderland, we come to the Garden of Flowers. In the story, the Garden was unsure what kind of flower Alice was. In the end, the flowers think Alice is a weed and push her out of the garden. Like a garden, churches represent different forms and expressions of spiritual communities. The roots run deep; change is not easy. Like the flowers responding to Alice, how does the church respond to newcomers? Are churches like roses – beautiful to look at, but if you get too close, you might get pricked? Or are they a shy violet, watching as the newcomer approaches but not getting involved too quickly? Churches are close-knit communities, and they have their greatest impact at the grassroots level. Churches can feel insecure about opening themselves to new people, making it difficult for newcomers to enter the garden.

The Mad Hatter's Tea Party as the Diaconate

The final stop on this tour of Wonderland is the Mad Hatter's Tea Party. I have always thought that the diaconate best represents this gathering. For the most part, deacons, like the Mad Hatter and the March Hare, are seen as those who are outside the box, doing their own thing away from everyone else.

In the Canadian context, the role of the diaconate is broad. Although congregations are happy to support the ministry of a deacon, there is still a lack of information around the role of the deacon, the diaconate, and *diakonia*. This gap has resulted in the diaconate (of some regions) being a more symbolic role and that reveals inconsistencies in how this ministry is empowered. Another variable affecting this dynamic is the hierarchical structure within the ordained ministries. Deacons and priests are coequal orders. Unfortunately, due to the current hierarchal structure, the ministry of the deacon can be greatly affected by changes in parish leadership or interpersonal conflict. Through continued study, mechanisms must be implemented to preserve the role, function, and ministry of the deacon. It is imperative that the diaconate and the presbyter find a synergy for maximum success.

All in all, the Mad Hatter's Tea Party represents what the church could look like when implementing a diaconal model of ministry: everyone is welcome to have tea, everyone can make the tea, no one has a designated seat, and no one group is in charge of the tea. The tea party is because they are.

Imaginatively Transforming the Church

Wonderland is not an exhaustive model of church organizational culture, but it provides a framework for the Canadian context. The challenge now is to discover how to implement a diaconal model of ministry of love and service in this infrastructure. To do this, we must change two main factors: decision making and priorities. First, we must examine how we communicate and make decisions to hear all voices, concerns, perspectives, and needs. We must transform the traditional hierarchical model of ministry and implement a consensus-based model. Second, we need to balance the need for sustainability with diaconal values: reaching the marginalized; hospitality; reconciliation and making amends; authentic partnerships with other community groups; and providing space for spiritual exploration and expression. To become better stewards of our resources and church business, we must look beyond the needs of the church. We next explore the impact of a diaconal model of ministry on the rest of Wonderland.

The Queen of Hearts

- Reconfigure the hierarchal structure by implementing a consensus model of leadership based on the needs of the grassroots. Instead of "my way," this approach changes to "our way." Deconstruct the culture of competition between parishes while promoting regional collaborations.
- Provide a space of healing for victims of the institutional church, working on reconciliation for its mistreatment of ethnic and cultural groups.
- Reconstruct religious traditions to emphasize cultural expressions of faith and prioritize personal spiritual development instead of expecting conformity.

- Establish measures of success that prioritize spiritual and communal health.
- Transition from sustainability to stewardship of resources.
- Support grassroots from positions of strength (where are the gifts?) to determine action plans and connect them with gifts and talents necessary to complete their objectives.
- Include training at seminary level for community development.
- Implement evaluation for human resources that include: self-evaluation, evaluation from the parish, and evaluation of goals and objectives set at the regional level.

The White Rabbit

- Shift from supporting the Episcopal vision to being an advocate for the vision of the grassroots.
- Ensure that a consensus model is being maintained at all levels of administration as well as the grassroots and that all voices are being heard.
- Connect ministries with resources (both fiscal and human) to support efforts, including outside sources of funding (grants, bursaries, and so on).
- Organize training and resources on how to connect to community resources.

The Deck of Cards

- Continue a consensus model in parochial decision making.
- Implement mechanisms so that the ministry of the deacon will not be disrupted by changes in parish leadership.
- Provide space and opportunities for forms of leadership in addition to parochial.
- Provide a place to explore faith and spirituality in the church versus a franchise model of Christian branding.
- Cultivate a deeper understanding of spiritual practices and traditions.
- Nurture an approach that encourages questioning versus leadership that conforms to one ideology or theology.

The Garden of Flowers

- Become a space where seekers and members can explore, share, and grow in the love of God.
- Prioritize the diakonia of the people, enabling parishioners and seekers to become active in their spiritual journeys and callings.
- Eliminate the proprietor mentality within church culture, welcoming all persons to participate and to learn from leadership.
- Create a database of parishioners' community involvement, connections, and interests.
- Commit to involvement on community tables and committees.
- Implement regular forms of short- and long-term planning and evaluation.

Evaluation as a Roadmap

Although these are tangible elements that we can currently implement, we must continue to make room for the Holy Spirit to lead. Historically, the church has limited the role of the Spirit. In doing so, we have again run the risk of ossifying the church at every level into an institutional model of ministry. One strategy to prevent ossification is to implement forms of evaluation.

Often the process of evaluation is seen as time consuming and is therefore skipped. By engaging in an evaluation process, we provide ourselves with a roadmap for the journey in the wilderness. It allows us to see where we have been and where we need to go. Although I describe evaluation at the congregational level, this process can be used at all levels of the church's organizational structure. At the congregational level, churches typically engage in a discernment process when they complete a congregational profile for new leadership. At the same time, when a church engages in an evaluation process, we are more familiar with those that give us quantitative data that tells us whether something is working or not. Within a diaconal model of ministry, I combine evaluation and discernment. In doing so, we not only determine what is working but also open ourselves to hear where the Spirit is leading us.

To do this, I envision a four-step process. In the first step, we ask, "Where are we coming from?" Here we list all the projects we have been working on. In the second step, we ask, "Where are we now?" Here we list quantifiable data from an evaluation of each programme area: number of participants, participant satisfaction, etc. In the third step, we rate each project or ministry on a scale of 1 to 5 (1 being the lowest and 5 being the highest), based on how well we believe the programme is working. In the final step, we determine what we need to continue, support, improve, or discontinue this area of ministry. It is okay to stop an area of ministry and not see this as a failure but simply as a change. This method gives us space to change directions as well as the ability to notice seeds growing where we did not intend them.

Churches at every level (from grassroots to national offices) are used to doing ministry in a certain way. We are so used to doing things the way we always have that it can be difficult to see or hear the new directions to which the Holy Spirit may be calling us. Along with initiatives and programmes, we can apply this process to discern the direction of a ministry at all levels of the church. To do so we must apply this process to all areas of ministry. I find the Eight Components of a Comprehensive Ministry with Young People identified by the United States Conference of Catholic Bishops helpful.[3] Although these components are intended to express the Roman Catholic Church's relationship with youth, these categories encompass the priorities needed to examine current efforts through the diaconal model. I offer the following questions for each component:

1. Advocacy: How do we reach, understand, and support the marginalized?

---

[3] United States Conference of Catholic Bishops, "Principles of Youth Ministry," n.d., https://www.usccb.org/topics/youth-and-young-adult-ministries/principles-youth-ministry.

2. Catechesis/Christian Formation: What teachings do we share with seekers and believers alike? How do we provide opportunities for spiritual exploration of the teachings of Jesus as well as other religious and cultural practices or traditions?
3. Community Life: How healthy is our spiritual community? How are we hospitable and welcoming, making sure that members and seekers have a place? How do we work with the local community?
4. Evangelisation: How do we promote and model God's message of love and service, as well as the opportunities and collaborations we provide?
5. Justice and Service: How do we reach out to, understand, and support the marginalized? What are the needs of the community? What are we doing to be involved in our communities? How do we use our power to hold other leaders accountable?
6. Leadership Development: How are we nurturing the diakonia of the people and helping individuals discern their callings? Where do we provide leadership within the church community? How do we hold leaders accountable?
7. Pastoral Care: How do we care for one another and those outside the walls of the church?
8. Prayer and Worship: How do we provide opportunities for seekers to connect and spend time with God?

A diaconal model provides a bridge between the church and the world. By evaluating ministries through these definitions and the process outlined, we ensure that the church continues to have one foot inside the church and one foot in the world, while listening for where the Spirit is calling us to go.

Conclusion

There are many reasons we can blame for the current state of the church. The church is not a victim and bears much of the responsibility for these circumstances. To improve any situation, we must first admit that there is a problem. The Holy Spirit is calling the church into a new way of being. By returning to the foundational message and ministry of Jesus Christ, we can learn to root ourselves in love and service. With this foundation, we can enable a diaconal model of ministry. This model provides an infrastructure that is inclusive and reconciles a relationship between the church and the world. As we continue to study the diaconate, we implement a mechanism of accountability to ensure that this new model provides opportunities for growth and openness to hearing God.

This will take some faith. We are assured, however, that if we follow God's call, the Spirit will provide for our needs: "But if God so clothes the grass of the field, which is alive today and tomorrow is thrown into the oven, will he not much more clothe you – you of little faith? Therefore do not worry, saying, 'What will we eat?' or 'What will we drink?' or 'What will we wear?'" (Matt 6:30–31, NIV). We must have faith and go into the wilderness. Although we are on a new path, we are not without guides. If we are to have a diaconal focus, we must empower the diaconate to take the lead. Through its leadership, the diaconate can provide connections to tools and resources within the congregation, as well as be a barometer for advocacy, community needs, and social justice to ensure that we stay on this path. By fostering the continued study of the diaconate, we create a mechanism of accountability.

Change and growth are not easy. As we journey through growing pains in this new configuration, we will experience moments when we feel that our goals are impossible. We must remember that we are not doing this on our own but by the power of the Holy Spirit: "Glory to God, whose power at work in us is able to do infinitely more than we can ask or imagine."[4] In the story of Alice in Wonderland, she too felt that things were impossible. The best advice comes from the Mad Hatter, who responded to Alice, "Only if you believe it is."[5]

Works Cited

Burton, Tim, dir. *Alice in Wonderland.* Walt Disney Pictures, 2010.
Folkins, Tali. "Gone by 2040?" *Anglican Journal*, 6 January 2020. https://anglicanjournal.com/gone-by-2040/.
Book of Alternative Services of the Anglican Church of Canada. Toronto: Anglican Book Center, 1985.
Carroll, Lewis. *Alice in Wonderland.* Auckland, New Zealand: The Floating Press (1865) 2008.
United States Conference of Catholic Bishops. "Principles of Youth Ministry." n.d. https://www.usccb.org/topics/youth-and-young-adult-ministries/principles-youth-ministry.

---

[4] *Book of Alternative Services of the Anglican Church of Canada* (Toronto: Anglican Book Center, 1985), 214.
[5] *Alice in Wonderland,* directed by Tim Burton (Walt Disney Pictures, 2010).

Chapter 16

Reclaiming Spirituality in Diaconal Work in Germany

Johannes Eurich

Since the beginning of the world's first welfare state at the end of the nineteenth century in the German Empire, there has been a close relationship between state politics and the diaconal work of the churches. This partnership between the German welfare state and diaconal agencies has been strengthened and enlarged over time. Up to 90 percent of diaconal social services are now financed through the state. The secular welfare state is interested in this partnership because it is based on the same ethical principles, like human dignity, justice, solidarity, and fairness, even though the argumentation for these principles in the welfare state is derived from various traditions, including Christianity, humanism, and other sources. Yet, diaconal organizations are engaged in a critical cooperation with state agencies. Relying on firsthand insights from their practical work, they take part in legislative procedures to promote social justice and human dignity from a Christian perspective. Thus, today's diaconal work in Germany is based on two pillars: the biblical tradition and a welfare state partnership.

This twofold outlook has created unique opportunities as well as challenges. How can *diakonia* act as a partner of the welfare state without losing its Christian traditions and independence? As early as the nineteenth century, the partnership of *diakonia* (at that time called "Inner Mission") emphasized a strong faith foundation. This challenge deepened with the professionalization of social and health services in the twentieth century. Professional codes rather than neighbor love characterized the forefront of service delivery. Against this background, diaconal organizations have taken on various ways of reclaiming faith and spirituality for their work. I address this challenge in three steps. First, I reflect on different understandings of spirituality. Second, I discuss the relation of Christian spirituality to helping action per se. Third, I explore how spirituality can be implemented in the rendering of diaconal services and discuss the implications of this research for the development of diaconal studies.

Different Understandings of Spirituality in *Diakonia*

It is not without reason that there are many intentional efforts today to cultivate or recover Christian spirituality in diaconal institutions.[1] On the one hand, there is a need for spiritual reflection, especially in times of crisis, which at the same

---

[1] See Joachim Reber, *Christlich-spirituelle Unternehmenskultur* (Stuttgart: Kohlhammer, 2013).

time serves as potential access points for diaconal action.² Unemployment, the death of family members, or illnesses can decisively change our concepts of life and require new reflection, leading to a new orientation. One can assume that different forms of spirituality are practiced in the individual contexts of diaconal commitment. On the other hand, the increasing view of diaconal work as a profession and a science requires a factual orientation, in which the spiritual dimensions of helping activities recede and must again be opened up.³ Is there something like a common center?

Lutheran spirituality is determined by the *Spiritus Sanctus*, which breaks into the reality of human beings. In a Lutheran perspective, this happens through Word and Sacrament as a means of grace (Augsburg Confession, Article 5). In the Word, which creates faith, God makes Christ present. The soul then does not need other sources of affirmation. Accordingly, Augsburg Confession, Article 6 calls for a new obedience, not a new spirituality. This already shows that the Lutheran understanding of faith is not about spirituality per se but about faith and love. Thus, Luther described Christians not as the pious but those created from faith and love. He wrote, "On the Freedom of a Christian":

> From all this follows the conclusion that a Christian man does not live in himself, but in Christ and in his neighbor; in Christ by faith, in his neighbor by love. Through faith he goes above himself into God, from God he goes below himself again through love and yet always remains in God and divine love.⁴

With this definition, it becomes clear that spirituality in a Lutheran perspective consists in rooting one's existence through faith in Christ and in living out faith by the love of one's neighbor. From this center of faith, forms of spiritual life and spiritual experiences can be taken up.

This definition of spirituality is significant for diaconal action, insofar as the exercise of faith in love is given a high priority, not only in a Lutheran perspective but generally in Christianity.⁵ According to Paul's dictum, "Whoever loves has fulfilled the requirement of God's law" (Rom 13:8, translation by the author), offering practical help can have a spiritual dimension: in fulfilling God's will, communion with God is experienced with the Holy Spirit as the source of strength for the helper (Rom 8:26). In this traditional understanding, spirituality is understood as an expression of faith in God, determined in content by faith and filled by the Holy Spirit. Thus, there are classical forms of this spirituality in diaconal work that relate helping to the Christian faith and thereby enable an opening for the work of the *Spiritus Sanctus*. These include devotions, church services, the celebration of the Lord's Supper, pastoral care, home (or prayer)

---

[2] Brian Steensland, Xiaoyun Wang, and Lauren Chism Schmidt, "Spirituality: What Does it Mean and to Whom?" *Journal for the Scientific Study for Religion* 57, no. 3 (2018): 450–72, https://doi.org/10.1111/jssr.12534.

[3] Cornelia Coenen-Marx, "Dem Geist Gottes Raum geben. Spiritualität als diakonische praxis pietatis," in *Spiritualität in der Diakonie*, ed. Beate Hofmann and Michael Schibilsky (Stuttgart: Kohlhammer, 2001), 52.

[4] Martin Luther, "Von der Freiheit eines Christenmenschen [On the Freedom of a Christian]," *Weimarer Ausgabe* 7/38, 20–38.

[5] In this chapter, Lutheran spirituality is not being contrasted with Roman Catholic or other Christian traditions of spirituality.

circles, Bible reading (including devotions at the beginning of meetings), or Christian symbolism in the design of rooms.

Even though helping can be experienced as a Christian spiritual event, it does not have to be interpreted in this classic way. In diaconal practice, quite different forms of spirituality are practiced by employees, including reiki, guided meditation, breathing exercises, singing bowls, healing stones, experiences of silence, other esoteric practices, or Native American rites.[6] These forms of spirituality point to a different understanding of spirituality as a "basic anthropological constant" because the human is "a spiritually gifted and a spiritually seeking being."[7]

If spirituality is founded anthropologically, human needs rather than the content of Christian tradition is decisive for spiritual practice. In this view, the speech of the spirit (*spiritus*) does not refer to the spirit of God but rather to the human spirit, in opposition to human physicality.[8] This understanding seems to underlie current everyday use of the term and denotes a certain basic mood of the human spirit, which expresses itself in an inner restlessness and the desire to experience transcendence: "Perhaps all longing is the muffled waiting for the ground of life."[9] The human longing for wholeness in life and for something greater than the visible world is one of the reasons for the diversity of spiritual practices. Likewise, individual needs for contemplation, stillness, and harmony with oneself and one's environment can be taken up by diverse spiritual offerings that correspond to the desires of the individual for wholeness and meaning in life. The content of such an understanding of spirituality remains vague and indefinite, so that spirituality becomes a "container term" largely independent of content.[10] The appeal that such spiritual offerings have for many people, including those working in *diakonia*, shows not only a high need for a connection beyond everyday life – which apparently can only be answered to a limited extent by Christian offerings – but also a different understanding of spirituality than that arising from Christian faith.

This contrast becomes particularly clear regarding the orientation of spirituality. Spiritual practices in the sense of "wellness for the soul" (relaxing, discovering oneself anew, realigning oneself) take up sensual experiences that enable an escape from the everyday world and thus contribute to recovery from its stresses and strains to reflect on the essentials. They question traditional Christian forms of spiritual life, which are often cognitively dominated, especially in academic discussions. At the same time, they reveal a striking

---

[6] Coenen-Marx, *Geist Gottes*, 47.
[7] Arndt Götzelmann, "Spiritualität als Bildungsaufgabe: Religiöse Dimensionen der Personalentwicklung und Unternehmenskultur im Gesundheits- und Sozialwesen," in *Bildung* vol. 1, ed. Wilhelm Schwendemann, 5–20 (Freiburg: FEL-Verlag, 2005), 10.
[8] Jens Martin Sautter, "Spiritualität lernen. Glaubenskurse als Einführung in die Gestalt christlichen Glaubens," in *Beiträge zur Evangelisation und Gemeindeentwicklung*, vol. 2 (Neukirchen-Vluyn: Neukirchner, 2005), 47.
[9] Fulbert Steffensky, "Suche nach spiritueller Erfahrung," *Neue Wege: Beiträge zu Religion und Sozialismus* 99, no. 7/8 (2005): 222, https://doi.org/10.5169/seals-144524.
[10] Sautter, "Spiritualität lernen," 48.

contrast to Christian spirituality. The focus on leaving everyday life behind in an effort to relax the soul ultimately promotes a theological dualism, which leads to a spiritual realm of the world, as created by the Spirit and oriented toward God, and, separately from this, a material realm of a "world apparently not created by the Spirit and not oriented toward God."[11] Christian spirituality, by comparison, refers explicitly to the body–soul wholeness of a human being. The physical dimension is just as much under the determination of God's Spirit as the soul dimension. Therefore, Christian spirituality is not about leaving behind the everyday world with its constraints, but about shaping it according to God's will.

One can interpret diverse spiritual practices as phenomena that point to underlying questions, yet without being able to engage immediately in the search for the answers and offers that are given in the Christian faith. It could be a matter of approaching God through a third and alternative spiritual path as it sometimes becomes visible in the request for intercessory prayer; for example, praying for sick people who are not able to pray themselves. In this sense, the manifold forms of "diffuse" spirituality can be taken up in a Christian perspective as a question about the presence of God. Finding an appropriate answer to this question in forms of Christian spirituality, which could initiate people's access to God through Jesus Christ, remains a challenge also within *diakonia*.

The Spiritual Basis of Diaconal Action

The relation of spirituality – here taken up in a Lutheran perspective – and helping action is provisional. On the one hand, Lutherans understand spirituality as a gift, the result of divine action, rather than instrumental.[12] In this respect, nothing can be achieved through spirituality – either in the sense of a disposition for God's grace or in view of the coming of God's kingdom. Christians are indeed called to pray for spiritual gifts, but only in the sense of joining God's movement on Earth. As Martin Luther interpreted the second petition of the Lord's Prayer, "God's kingdom comes of itself even without our prayer; but we ask in this prayer that it may also come to us."[13] In this spiritual attitude of reception and openness to God's action, diaconal action can avoid presenting its own commitments as testimony to its spirituality.[14] The experience of justification *sola gratia* frees us to prove our faith in our concrete lives; yet, it prevents us from overestimating our own spiritual aspirations.

On the other hand, a Christological anthropology, grounded in the event of the cross, perceives the neighbor in the specific sense as a human being in whom

---

[11] Friedrich Mildenberger, "Evangelische Spiritualität: Bemerkungen zur Studie einer Arbeitsgruppe der EKD," *Zeitschrift für Evangelische Ethik* 25 (1981): 310–11.
[12] Hans-Martin Barth, *Spiritualität*, Ökumenische Studienhefte/Bensheimer Hefte 74 (Göttingen: Vandenhoeck & Ruprecht, 1993), 52.
[13] Kirchenamt der EKD, *Die Bekenntnisschriften der evangelisch-lutherischen Kirche*, ed. im Gedenkjahr der Augsburgischen Konfession 1930 (Göttingen: Vandenhoeck & Ruprecht, 2010), 538.
[14] Peter Zimmerling, *Evangelische Spiritualität. Wurzeln und Zugänge* (Göttingen: Vandenhoeck & Ruprecht, 2003), 16.

Christ meets us.[15] It sees the nakedness of Christ in the naked beggar and the hunger of Christ in the hunger of the fellow human being, orienting the Christian act of helping as an event at eye level between two human beings encountering each other as siblings in Christ. All forms of superordination and subordination, which can easily arise in an asymmetrically structured helping event (insofar as one person is dependent on the support of the other), are therefore to be countered. The tendency toward a universal ethos of helping is only one of the resulting orientations of diaconal action, which commits to help every person in need, regardless of religious, ethnic, or other differences.[16]

If every fellow human being comes into view as sibling in Christ, a further consequence is that no one may be excluded from community with God. Every human being is allowed to come in one's own being-as-it-is, without first having to fulfil certain requirements. In the trusting response to God, a person experiences this unconditional being-as-one. One of the great gifts, according to the Christian faith, is precisely that God has always met people where they are and given them the Spirit to recognize God. "We do not need to search for God ourselves; for we are found before we search."[17] If a person entrusts oneself to God, the spiritual search can find its goal in God.[18] As children of God, accepting and trusting in God's good intentions, life gains freedom and scope – freedom from all constraints of self-fulfillment or self-initiation, and the scope to perceive and engage with the other person. On this basis, the attitude of free attention to the other can be established, which is significant for human helping because it is able to protect against the instrumentalization of the helping action and intentions that run counter to the welfare of the other.[19]

Lutheran spirituality receives its mission of shaping life from the Reformation attitude to affirm and be responsible for the world, rediscovering the family, professions, and society as fields for a worshipful conduct of life.[20] The "real" Christian life does not take place primarily in the meditative realm of worship, as much as this is a constitutive part of it, or under monastic models, as helpful as these may be, but in everyday life and the locations where the believer is

---

[15] Michael Wolter, "Ethisches Subjekt und ethisches Gegenüber. Aspekte aus neutestamentlicher Perspektive," in *Diakonie in der Stadt. Reflexionen, Modelle, Konkretionen*, ed. Heinz Schmidt and Renate Zitt (Stuttgart: Kohlhammer, 2003), 50.

[16] On this universal ethos, see Gerd Theißen, "Die Bibel diakonisch lesen. Die Legitimitätskrise des Helfens und der barmherzige Samariter," in *Diakonie – biblische Grundlagen und Orientierungen. Ein Arbeitsbuch (VDWI 2)*, eds Gerhard K. Schäfer and Theodor Strohm (Heidelberg: HVA, 1998), 376–401.

[17] Steffensky, *Suche nach spiritueller Erfahrung*, 224. God's Spirit bears witness to our spirit that we are God's children (Rom 8:16).

[18] "... for You have made us for Your sake, and our hearts are restless until they rest in You." Augustine, *Confessions: A New Translation*, trans. Peter Constantine (New York: Liveright, 2018), 1 [1.1].

[19] See the four basic threats to helping activities in Theißen, "Die Bibel diakonisch lesen," 376ff.

[20] Zimmerling, *Evangelische Spiritualität*, 284.

placed.[21] There is no false opposition between the spiritual, on one side, and the everyday, on the other.

The same applies to *diakonia*.[22] Christian spirituality is realized in one's professional action as a social worker, nurse, therapist, assistant, and so on. God is present and works through the Spirit in the everyday accomplishments of professional action. All helping can be a medium of the Creator's devotion.[23] God has turned to people without restriction and shares not only individual areas of life with them but is present in all the ups and downs of human life. Christian spirituality is therefore not something spiritualized, but the shaping of faith in lived life.[24]

From this fundamental orientation toward God's will for this world and the coming of God's kingdom, there emerges attention to the development of this world that manifests itself as an attitude of vigilance for social responsibility. This corresponds to a commitment "in the fullness of tasks, questions, successes, and failures,"[25] which also contradicts a one-sided orientation toward other social models, such as success, beauty, strength, and so on, because these values undermine humanity and place weak people on the sidelines.[26] Christian spirituality promotes an inner sensorium, through which "life-serving" can be distinguished again and again from the "life-damaging." It raises its voice against the commercialization of life and protests the "economization of the soul."[27] It pays attention to the bent reed, practices solidarity with the weak, and recognizes God in mercy. In the famous words of the French bishop Jacques Gaillot: "He who immerses himself in God reappears next to the poor."[28] Christian spirituality therefore always includes a diaconal dimension. It cannot be separated from solidarity with the disadvantaged and marginalized of this world.

Forms of Christian Spirituality in *Diakonia*

Spirituality teaches reverence and compassion for life, opening up a different relationship to the created world and what is being done to it. According to

---

[21] Barth, *Spiritualität*, 51.
[22] Barth, 51. See also Dietrich von Oppen, *Der sachliche Mensch. Frömmigkeit am Ende des 20. Jahrhunderts* (Stuttgart: Kreuz-Verlag, 1968).
[23] Günther Thomas, "Behinderung als Teil der guten Schöpfung? Fragen und Beobachtungen im Horizont der Inklusionsdebatte," in *Behinderung – Profile inklusiver Theologie, Diakonie und Kirche*, eds Johannes Eurich and Andreas Lob-Hüdepohl (Stuttgart: Kohlhammer, 2014), 87.
[24] Wolfgang Huber, "'In deinem Lichte schauen wir das Licht': Quellen und Perspektiven christlicher Spiritualität," *Evangelische Kirche in Deutschland*, 22 October 2005, http://www.ekd.de/vortraege/huber/051022_huber_urach.html.
[25] Dietrich Bonhoeffer, *Widerstand und Ergebung. Briefe und Auszeichnungen aus der Haft* (München, 1961), 248.[name of publisher needed?]
[26] Gottfried Claß, "Aspekte diakonischer Spiritualität," in *Diakonische Konturen. Theologie im Kontext sozialer Arbeit*, eds Volker Herrmann and Heinz Schmidt (Heidelberg: Universitätsverlag, 2003), 289.
[27] Huber, "'In deinem Lichte'," 1.
[28] Jacques Gaillot as cited by Steffensky, *Suche nach spiritueller Erfahrung*, 225.

Leonardo Boff, "Spirituality is that attitude which puts life at the center, and defends and promotes life against all the mechanisms of death, desiccation, or stagnation."[29] Spirituality denotes an attitude that honors the things of life as gifts and does not dispose of them thoughtlessly or as if they were self-evident, simply subjecting them to one's own ends. Fulbert Steffensky described spirituality as "shaped attention."[30] Shaping the world is preceded by attention to the traces of God that are discovered in the world.[31] This attentiveness in everyday life, which Steffensky called the "vestibule of explicitly religious spirituality,"[32] must be practiced and trained to discover God's traces within the world's daily routines.

A spiritual attitude of mindfulness can help to perceive the neighbor, pay attention to vital signs, and look for possibilities to support the affirmation of life. This attitude of mindfulness becomes even more important as technical procedures shape medical and nursing contexts, overshadowing direct contact with the patient. Communal forms are also helpful for practicing spirituality, which can also be rediscovered in *diakonia*.[33] For spiritual forms not to become rigid, they need to be appropriated and communicated in creative ways. Even reading aloud together, telling stories, singing, and role-playing biblical texts open up new dimensions involving body and soul, the whole person, especially in diaconal work. Much can be learned from newer forms of spirituality, even when for Christian spirituality the orientation is to the Christ event. Forms can be practiced, but spirituality cannot be forced. It "develops of its own accord and always eludes targeted influence."[34] For this reason, the moment must always become transparent to God's presence with the individual. Spirituality lives in this sense between everyday routines and God's moments.

Even if Christian spirituality is about the formation of a specific inner attitude, it does not aim mainly at experiences of one's own inwardness. Especially in *diakonia*, spirituality will instead consider the dimension of the body. It sees the whole person in one's corporeality; that is, it tries to perceive a person in the form of one's lived life and, from there, to respond to one's needs. Diaconal care involves more than care of the body or calming the mind. To care for a person means entering a relationship with others, perceiving them as persons in their very being. It grants them the right to be needy and gives them in their neediness what is needed, what helps them, and what does them good. This can happen in a twofold way: being touched by the other person leads to reflecting on one's own life by becoming more aware of the elementary things of life and, in many cases, rediscovering how one lives one's own life.[35]

---

[29] Leonardo Boff, *Ecology and Liberation: A New Paradigm*, trans. John Cumming (Maryknoll, NY: Orbis, 1995), 36.
[30] Steffensky, *Suche nach spiritueller Erfahrung*, 225.
[31] Steffensky, 226.
[32] Steffensky, 226.
[33] Axel von Dressler, *Diakonie und Spiritualität. Impulse aus der Welt der Kommunitäten* (Neukirchen-Vluyn: Vandenhoeck & Ruprecht, 2006).
[34] Götzelmann, *Spiritualität als Bildungsaufgabe*, 18.
[35] Coenen-Marx, *Geist Gottes*, 55 and 58.

Being touched by the other person can also, however, lead one to isolate oneself. "Any real contact with a flesh and blood person makes us vulnerable."[36] A natural reaction to this is to build up protective mechanisms and build walls around one's own vulnerability, because – especially in the helping professions – one cannot attend to every need. Inner exhaustion and burnout would otherwise be the inevitable result. However, isolation and inner insensitivity put one in danger of missing successful encounters and no longer perceiving the traces of God in everyday life. The challenge is not to succumb to the purposelessness of life itself under the given conditions. Particularly in diaconal processes as driven by organizational pressure for efficiency, the necessary moment of pausing and perceiving is difficult to maintain. The free space for relationships must be fought for again and again or at least be consciously produced under time pressure.

There are various approaches that have been tested in practice to form a "Christian spiritual corporate culture."[37] It is a responsibility of management to shape organizational culture spiritually through a culture of interruption, reflection, existential communication, prayer, and so on.[38] These practices can open space for individual employees to deepen their diaconal activities spiritually.

Prospects

Christian spirituality in *diakonia* will have to concentrate on keeping religious forms of language and meaning present as indispensable resources in diaconal fields of action – otherwise *diakonia* is in danger of losing its transcendent character with reference to God.[39] In this context, it should be considered to what extent spirituality can be part of the study of *diakonia*.[40] Through dual training, diaconal students study social work as well as enroll in a theological class for two additional semesters. Within these theological studies, classes on spirituality can be offered that combine both theological reasoning and practical exercises in spirituality. Students need to be exposed to forms and rites of spirituality from a Christian perspective, since they often have not been introduced to them yet. This basic class could be followed by a class in a certain type of diaconal work where students are exposed to, for example, caring for an older adult with bodily needs. This practical experience can then be reflected upon regarding one's own understanding of the vulnerability of life, the frailty of human bodies, and the essence of life. Additionally, students may join diaconal communities, providing a common spiritual home during their course of studies that often continues during their professional work.

---

[36] Sam Keen as cited by Coenen-Marx, *Geist Gottes*, 58.
[37] Reber, *Christlich-spirituelle Unternehmenskultur*. [page ref?]
[38] Beate Hofmann, *Diakonische Unternehmenskultur: Handbuch für Führungskräfte* (Stuttgart: Kohlhammer, 2010), 459–66.
[39] Isolde Karle, "Perspektiven der Krankenhausseelsorge: Eine Auseinandersetzung mit dem Konzept des Spiritual Care," *Wege zum Menschen* 62, no. 6 (December 2010): 552, https://doi.org/10.13109/weme.2010.62.6.537.
[40] I owe the following suggestions to Heinz Schmidt.

Diaconal organizations are challenged to provide space for their staff members to pause and reflect in a guided way on the events of everyday life – to relive them, to recall them anew – in the presence of God. This everyday work provides opportunities for further training in spirituality, through many different forms, both traditional and new, including those from other cultural circles. Religious tradition, language, and forms may be remote for many, yet they open opportunities to break through into everyday life and meditate existential experiences. This offers opportunities for both sides – those who help and those who receive help – as routine processes are interrupted again and again. New perception becomes possible, and thus a reciprocal relationship can be opened up, promoting the dimension of caring that is essential for diaconal action.

Works Cited

Augustine. *Confessions: A New Translation*. Translated by Peter Constantine. New York: Liveright, 2018.

Barth, Hans-Martin. *Spiritualität*. Ökumenische Studienhefte/Bensheimer Hefte 74. Göttingen: Vandenhoeck & Ruprecht, 1993.

Boff, Leonardo. *Ecology and Liberation: A New Paradigm*. Translated by John Cumming. Maryknoll, NY: Orbis, 1995.

Bonhoeffer, Dietrich. *Widerstand und Ergebung: Briefe und Auszeichnungen aus der Haft*. München: 1961.

Claß, Gottfried. "Aspekte diakonischer Spiritualität." In *Diakonische Konturen: Theologie im Kontext sozialer Arbeit (VDWI 18)*, edited by Volker Herrmann and Heinz Schmidt, 277–91. Heidelberg: Universitätsverlag, 2003.

Coenen-Marx, Cornelia. "Dem Geist Gottes Raum geben: Spiritualität als diakonische praxis pietatis." In *Spiritualität in der Diakonie: Anstöße zur Erneuerung christlicher Kernkompetenz*, edited by Beate Hofmann and Michael Schibilsky, 47–61. Stuttgart: Kohlhammer, 2001.

Dressler, Axel von. *Diakonie und Spiritualität: Impulse aus der Welt der Kommunitäten*. Neukirchen-Vluyn: Vandenhoeck & Ruprecht, 2006.

Götzelmann, Arnd. "Spiritualität als Bildungsaufgabe: Religiöse Dimensionen der Personalentwicklung und Unternehmenskultur im Gesundheits- und Sozialwesen." In *Bildung* Vol 1, edited by Wilhelm Schwendemann, 5–20. Freiburg: FEL-Verlag, 2005.

Hofmann, Beate. *Diakonische Unternehmenskultur: Handbuch für Führungskräfte*. Stuttgart: Kohlhammer, 2010.

Huber, Wolfgang. "'In deinem Lichte schauen wir das Licht': Quellen und Perspektiven christlicher Spiritualität, Festvortrag zum 25jährigen Jubiläum des Stifts Urach." Evangelische Kirche in Deutschland, 22 October 2005. http://www.ekd.de/vortraege/huber/051022_huber_urach.html.

Karle, Isolde. "Perspektiven der Krankenhausseelsorge: Eine Auseinandersetzung mit dem Konzept des Spiritual Care." *Wege zum Menschen* 62, no. 6 (December 2010): 537–55. https://doi.org/10.13109/weme.2010.62.6.537.

Kirchenamt der EKD. *Die Bekenntnisschriften der evangelisch-lutherischen Kirche,* herausgegeben im Gedenkjahr der Augsburgischen Konfession 1930. Göttingen: Vandenhoeck & Ruprecht, 2010.

Luther, Martin. "Von der Freiheit eines Christenmenschen [On the Freedom of a Christian]." In *Weimarer Ausgabe 7/38* (1987): 20–38.

Mildenberger, Friedrich. "Evangelische Spiritualität: Bemerkungen zur Studie einer Arbeitsgruppe der EKD." *Zeitschrift für Evangelische Ethik* 25 (1981): 309–16. https://doi.org/10.14315/zee-1981-0143.

Oppen, Dietrich von. *Der sachliche Mensch. Frömmigkeit am Ende des 20. Jahrhunderts.* Stuttgart: Kreuz-Verlag, 1968.

Reber, Joachim. *Christlich-spirituelle Unternehmenskultur.* Stuttgart: Kohlhammer, 2013.

Sautter, Jens Martin. "Spiritualität lernen: Glaubenskurse als Einführung in die Gestalt christlichen Glaubens." In *Beiträge zur Evangelisation und Gemeindeentwicklung,* vol. 2. Neukirchen-Vluyn: Neukirchner, 2005.

Steensland, Brian, Xiaoyun Wang, and Lauren Chism Schmidt. "Spirituality: What Does it Mean and to Whom?" *Journal for the Scientific Study for Religion* 57, no. 3 (2018): 450–72. https://doi.org/10.1111/jssr.12534.

Steffensky, Fulbert. "Suche nach spiritueller Erfahrung." *Neue Wege: Beiträge zu Religion und Sozialismus* 99, no. 7/8 (2005): 221–28. https://doi.org/10.5169/seals-144524.

Theißen, Gerd. "Die Bibel diakonisch lesen: Die Legitimitätskrise des Helfens und der barmherzige Samariter." In *Diakonie – biblische Grundlagen und Orientierungen. Ein Arbeitsbuch (VDWI 2),* edited by Gerhard K. Schäfer and Theodor Strohm, 376–401. Heidelberg: HVA, 1998.

Thomas, Günther. "Behinderung als Teil der guten Schöpfung? Fragen und Beobachtungen im Horizont der Inklusionsdebatte." In *Behinderung – Profile inklusiver Theologie, Diakonie und Kirche,* edited by Johannes Eurich and Andreas Lob-Hüdepohl, 67–97. Stuttgart: Kohlhammer, 2014.

Wolter, Michael. "Ethisches Subjekt und ethisches Gegenüber: Aspekte aus neutestamentlicher Perspektive." In *Diakonie in der Stadt. Reflexionen, Modelle, Konkretionen,* edited by Heinz Schmidt and Renate Zitt, 44–50. Stuttgart: Kohlhammer, 2003.

Zimmerling, Peter. *Evangelische Spiritualität. Wurzeln und Zugänge.* Göttingen: Vandenhoeck & Ruprecht, 2003.

PART 4

Diaconal Studies and Formation

Chapter 17

Diaconal Studies in an Interdisciplinary PhD Programme in Norway

Annette Leis-Peters

In January 2013, the first PhD student started her research within the framework of the "Diaconia, Values and Professional Practice" programme at Diakonhjemmet University College. As of autumn 2023, approximately seventy-five PhD scholars were enrolled in the programme; about seven of them complete their thesis every year. The PhD programme was established at Diakonhjemmet University College, a faith-based Norwegian higher education institution educating deacons and other professionals in the fields of health care and social work, such as nurses, social workers, and occupational and family therapists. In 2016, this institution became VID Specialized University, a merger between several higher education institutions training professionals in the same field and having the same faith-based roots. As of autumn 2023, the new institution had about six thousand students and about six hundred employees on five campuses (Oslo, Bergen, Stavanger, Sandvika, and Tromsø), with additional de-centralized study programmes at Helgelandskysten (the western coastline area in the middle of Norway). The capital letters VID in the name of the university are an abbreviation for Scientific (*Vitenskapelig* in Norwegian), International, and Diaconal. This PhD programme is one of two within this university, the second doing research in theology and religion.

The Nordic countries, together with German-speaking countries, are the strongholds of a more conscious and everyday use of the term *diakonia* and are thus a likely region to establish PhD programmes with such a profile.[1] However, there are no other comparable endeavors that locate themselves explicitly within the framework of *diakonia* in the Nordic region, and increasing secularization makes it less and less likely that similar initiatives will emerge. Unlike the church–state separation in North America, most of the Nordic countries are historically characterized by a state–church system; that is, state and Lutheran church have been closely interlaced for the almost 500 years following the

---

[1] The Swedish researchers Erik Blennberger and Mats Hansson wrote about the difficulty of defining *diakonia*. In the Nordic context, "Diaconia refers to social activities carried out within or in connection with a Christian community/organisation." Erik Blennberger and Mats J. Hansson, "Vad menas med diakoni?" ["What is meant by diakonia?"], in *Diakoni: tolkning, historik, praktik* [*Diakonia: Interpretation, History, Practice*], eds. Erik Blennberger and Mats J. Hansson (Stockholm: Verbum, 2008), 24, translated by the author. This definition does not cover the subject area of the PhD programme, but it emphasizes that *diakonia* can take place both in congregations and in faith-based welfare organizations.

Lutheran Reformation in the sixteenth century. With the establishment of Lutheran national churches, all inhabitants became Lutherans and the king their formal head. Consequently, freedom of religion was introduced relatively late, and 90 percent of all residents were members of the national Lutheran churches until the 1980s. Against this background, and using the PhD programme in "Diaconia, Values and Professional Practice" as an example, this chapter: 1) describes the Nordic context for *diakonia* and diaconal studies, 2) looks at the history of origin of the PhD programme, 3) enquires about decisive preconditions for the emergence of the PhD programme, and 4) gives a short overview of the content and the PhD projects of the programme. The chapter concludes by discussing future opportunities and challenges of interdisciplinary PhD programmes related to diaconal studies.

Diakonia in the Nordic Region

The Nordic region of Greenland, Iceland, the Faroe Islands, Finland, Sweden, Norway, and Denmark is characterized by unique features of religion and welfare – and thus also *diakonia*. On the one hand, *diakonia* is a proper term in all Nordic languages, and the deacon is an established occupational profile at the intersection between churches and health care, care, and welfare services in the Nordic area, though expressed differently in different countries. On the other hand, the Lutheran Nordic countries comprise one of the world's most secular regions.[2]

This situation is partly explained by the introduction of a strong welfare state during the twentieth century that replaced the role of the Lutheran state churches in providing an overarching social canopy.[3] Compared to other contexts, Nordic civil society organizations including diaconal actors – such as deacons, congregations, or faith-based health and welfare organizations – have only a very limited share in the provision of health and welfare services.[4] Instead, the welfare system is based on a strong state and public sector that is trusted by the citizens – the type that political scientist Gøsta Esping-Andersen labelled the social-democratic welfare regime. This type of system has a universal approach to welfare that aims at providing the same services and benefits to all citizens from

---

[2] Inger Furseth, ed., *Religious Complexity in the Public Sphere: Comparing Nordic Countries* (Cham, Switzerland: Palgrave Macmillan, 2018); C. Haerpfer et al., eds., *World Values Survey: Round Seven – Country-Pooled Datafile Version 5.0* (Vienna: JD Systems Institute & WVSA Secretariat, 2020), https://doi.org/10.14281/18241.1; Pew Research Center, "Eastern and Western Europeans Differ on Importance of Religion, Views of Minorities, and Key Social Issues," 29 October 2018, https://www.pewresearch.org/religion/2018/10/29/eastern-and-western-europeans-differ-on-importance-of-religion-views-of-minorities-and-key-social-issues/.

[3] Jörg Stolz, "Secularization Theories in the Twenty-First Century: Ideas, Evidence, and Problems," *Social Compass* 67, no. 2 (June 2020): 282–308, https://doi.org/10.1177/0037768620917320.

[4] Karl Henrik Sivesind and Jo Saglie, eds., *Promoting Active Citizenship: Markets and Choice in Scandinavian Welfare* (Cham, Switzerland: Palgrave Macmillan, 2017), https://link.springer.com/book/10.1007/978-3-319-55381-8.

cradle to grave in the large and sparsely populated Nordic countries.[5] Such a comprehensive approach could only be achieved by giving the public sector and, more concretely, the municipalities the central role in funding, producing, and controlling welfare services.[6]

This system has undergone recent transformation. Two developments strengthened the (potential) role of diaconal actors in the Nordic welfare states. During the last three decades, the public-sector-dominated Nordic welfare systems opened gradually for private non-profit and for-profit actors. This political change was mainly motivated by arguments emphasizing that civil society should complement the public sector system with more diversity and added value. However, opening the system resulted in more for-profit providers, not more non-profit organizations offering publicly funded welfare services. After having acted in a public sector-dominated system for decades, diaconal organizations and other non-profit welfare actors found themselves in a position of economic and ideological weakness.[7] Within these frameworks, they could only sustain themselves and survive as actors within the welfare system by becoming inconspicuous; that is, by running the services as much as possible like the public providers.[8] This made it difficult for them to switch to a competition *modus* and to compete with for-profit organizations, public providers, and each other.

The second transformation with relevance for *diakonia* is the end of the age of the state church. After the Reformation, the Nordic countries established Lutheran state churches, in which the king was the formal head of the church. In the period of the strong, public-sector-dominated welfare system, there was no room for establishing alternative welfare services – not even for the largest churches in the countries, which are Lutheran. As state churches, the Lutheran churches were almost completely funded by tax money paid by every citizen. Offering alternative church welfare services in addition to the public ones would have implied that the same tax money financed two sets of welfare services. Only after the economic separation of the state and the Lutheran church was this

---

[5] Gøsta Esping-Andersen, *The Three Worlds of Welfare Capitalism* (Princeton: Princeton University Press, 1990).

[6] This system is based on full employment, limiting the ability of working women and men to contribute voluntary hours to the social field. In the health and welfare sector, most employees are women.

[7] Per Selle, "Frivillighetens marginalisering" ["The Marginalisation of Voluntarism"], *Tidsskrift for velferdsforskning* [*Journal for Welfare Research*] 19, no. 1 (March 2016): 76–89, https://doi.org/10.18261/issn. 2464-3076-2016-01-05.

[8] Selle, 76–89; Annette Leis-Peters, "Hidden by Civil Society and Religion? Diaconal Institutions as Welfare Providers in the Growing Swedish Welfare State," *Journal of Church and State* 56, no. 1 (Winter 2014): 105–27, https://doi.org/10.1093/jcs/cst134; Ingunn Moser, "Diakoniinstitusjoner som laboratoriefabrikker for morgendagens velferd?" ["Diaconal Institutions as Laboratory Factories for Tomorrow's Welfare?"], in *Nestekjærlighet på anbud. Diakonale virksomheters identitet i moderne velferdssamfunn* [*Love for Your Neighbour on Tender: Diaconal Agencies' Identity in Modern Welfare Societies*], ed. Harald Askeland (Oslo: Frekk, 2022), 142–60.

meaningful and possible.⁹ No longer being a state church nurtured the hope within the Nordic Lutheran churches, particularly in Sweden, to become more important welfare actors. So far, this hope has not yet materialized.¹⁰ Therefore, it becomes a fascinating question why an interdisciplinary PhD programme within the framework of diaconal studies could emerge from a context with limited church and diaconal involvement in the field of welfare, care, and health care.

Creating the PhD Programme

A decisive precondition for the establishment of this PhD programme is the higher education policy in Norway, which enables university colleges to offer PhD education. In other countries, this a privilege that is still reserved for full universities. To be awarded this right, university colleges need to go through a complicated accreditation process. It usually takes several years after defining a field of expertise for a PhD programme to receive official approval. It is the responsibility of the applying institution to convince the evaluation committee that the PhD arises naturally from and belongs to a self-evident trajectory with the bachelor's and master's programmes that the university college already has in its portfolio.

Diakonhjemmet University College developed from the Norwegian Home of Deacons (*Det norske Diakonhjemmet*), established in 1890.¹¹ At that time, Norway was one of the poorhouses of Europe. Poverty, diseases, and misery accumulated in the bigger cities as many people from the rural areas migrated there. Kristiania, as Oslo was called until 1925, was thus a hotspot of social hardship. The Norwegian Home of Deacons was founded as a Christian response to the many social needs piling up in the city. The idea was that well-trained men could reach out to people in need in the slums of Kristiania, as the situation was considered too dangerous for deaconesses. In addition to theology, the male deacons required preparation in health care, social work, and administration. The diaconal institution established a training hospital that was not primarily designed to provide health care on site but to serve as a place for diaconal

---

[9] Anders Bäckström, *Svenska kyrkan som välfärdsaktör i en global kultur: En studie av religion och omsorg* [*The Church of Sweden as Welfare Actor in a Global Culture: A Study of Religion and Care*] (Stockholm: Verbum, 2001).

[10] See, for example, Stig Linde, *Välfärd och kyrkan: Underlag för reflektion* [*Welfare and Church: A Basis for Reflection*] (Uppsala: Svenska kyrkan, 2016); Miriam Hollmer and Anders Bäckström, "Svenska kyrkan och välfärden. En undersökning av attityder" ["The Church of Sweden and the Welfare: A Study of Attitudes"], in *Välfärdsinsatser på religiös grund: Förväntningar och problem* [*Welfare Engagement on Religious Basis: Expectations and Problems*], ed. Anders Bäckström (Skellefteå: Artos & Norma, 2014), 31–62. In Norway, politicians have asked for more civil society involvement in publicly funded welfare services since the 2010s. For diaconal institutions, though not as much for congregations, this was a motivation to redefine their role as a more active contributor to the welfare system.

[11] See chapter by Dyrstad in this volume.

training. The practical learning in the hospital equipped the deacons to meet difficult health and social challenges in their work on the margins of society.

At the time of applying for a PhD programme in 2011, the bachelor's and master's programmes offered at Diakonhjemmet University College still mirrored these roots of preparing young people for working with groups in society struggling with health and social challenges. The programmes ranged from nursing, social work, occupational therapy, and social pedagogics[12] on the bachelor's level to family therapy, value-based leadership, social work, elder care, and diaconia on the master's level. To persuade the accreditation committee, Diakonhjemmet University College had to demonstrate that the knowledge and research base of these programmes were connected, binding together the different bachelor's and master's programmes in a natural way through unique, cutting-edge expertise. This expertise could not be located exclusively in one of its health or welfare programmes. Compared to public higher education institutions, Diakonhjemmet University College was far too small to compete with research on the forefront of any of these larger fields. However, none of the public institutions possessed expertise in the field of diaconal studies. *Diakonia* thus became the missing link that not only represented the common historical roots but also created a connection between different professional traditions and knowledge areas in welfare, health care, and care. Building the PhD programme around diaconal studies not only made the proposal distinct from other interdisciplinary initiatives but also provided it with a distinctive value that only a faith-based institution could represent.

Why Norway, of All Nordic Places?

Within the Nordic countries, Norway is not the only likely location for the emergence of an interdisciplinary PhD programme in diaconal studies. Sweden employs more deacons, and within the Lutheran Church of Sweden, the ministry of the deacon is older and better anchored.[13] In Finland, deacons are highly organized and widely appreciated, as exemplified during the COVID-19 crisis.[14] In the Evangelical Lutheran Church in Finland, each congregation is required by law to employ a deacon. Finland is also the only Nordic country to publish a scientific journal in the field of diaconal studies.[15] However, there are three critical factors that provided favorable preconditions for the establishment of an interdisciplinary PhD programme related to diaconal studies in Norway. These

---

[12] This profession specializes in working with people with disabilities.

[13] In comparison to many other churches in the world, Nordic Lutheran churches are highly professionalized and very well funded (through church taxes). Most of their activities are led by employees with professional training, ranging from priests to church musicians and from catechists to deacons.

[14] Lise-Lotte Hellöre, "When Diaconia Became an Exhausted Millionaire: Experiences from the Coronavirus Pandemic in Finland," *Diaconia: Journal for the Study of Christian Social Practice* 12, no. 2 (September 2021): 117–36, https://doi.org/10.13109/diac.2021.12.2.117.

[15] *Diakonian tutkimus: Journal for the Study of Diaconia*, https://journal.fi/dt.

factors are linked to the Norwegian higher education policy and the educational policy of the Lutheran majority church, the Church of Norway.

The first important precondition is that Norway allows not only full universities but also university colleges (and specialized universities) to apply to administer PhD programmes when fulfilling certain criteria. This, for example, is not the case in Finland. The second significant prerequisite is the relative openness of Norwegian educational policy to fund faith-based higher education institutions and programmes with profiles that could be perceived as denominational, such as programmes in *diakonia*. In this respect, the contrast to Sweden is obvious, where religion is increasingly understood as part of the private sphere, keeping the public sphere secular and religiously neutral, not least of all in the area of education.[16] For example, VID Specialized University has a sister university in Sweden, Marie Cederschiöld University, that has a similar history and educational portfolio and is owned by diaconal institutions. Their comparable interdisciplinary and interprofessional PhD programme is named "The Human in a Welfare Society," omitting any reference to diaconal studies.

Equally important is the decision of the Church of Norway in 2004 to require a master's degree in *diakonia* for all employees who want to become a deacon in the Church of Norway.[17] Within the church context, this means that deacons are now supposed to be educated at the same high level as priests. Their formal competence should consist of a bachelor's degree in preparation for a welfare, health care, or pedagogical vocation complemented by a master's degree in *diakonia*. For higher education, the decision implied that the Church of Norway needed a master's programme in *diakonia*. In response, two higher education institutions created such a programme, competing for the approximately thirty students who might have an interest in becoming a deacon every year.[18]

This was very beneficial for research about *diakonia*, or the emerging field of diaconal studies, in at least three respects. First, the establishment of master's programmes in *diakonia* necessitated that employees develop competence on the forefront of *diakonia* research. It also makes it attractive for early career researchers to direct their research focus toward *diakonia*. Second, the master's programme requires a thesis; that is, master's students are obliged to conduct an independent research project corresponding to six months of full-time study. With this work, they contribute to a research corpus about *diakonia* in Norway

---

[16] Linnea Lundgren, *A Risk or a Resource? A Study of the Swedish State's Shifting Perception and Handling of Minority Religious Communities between 1952–2019* (Stockholm: Ersta Sköndal Bräcke University College, 2021), https://esh.diva-portal.org/smash/get/diva2:1584388/FULLTEXT01.pdf.

[17] This decision also affected the educational requirements of deacons in other, smaller churches in Norway. Among them, The United Methodist Church in Norway was the first to introduce similar demands for becoming a deacon.

[18] In 2013, MF Norwegian School of Theology, Religion and Society and Diakonhjemmet University College joined forces and offered a joint master's programme in *diaconia*. A third higher education institution, the Faculty of Theology at the University of Oslo, offered a master's programme in Professional Ethics and Diaconia. However, this master's programme was not adapted to the professional demands that the Church of Norway had defined for deacons.

and thus to the establishment of a research area. Last but not least, now that students are able to complete their studies with a master's in *diakonia*, it is logical to continue with a PhD in the area of diaconal studies.

In this context, it is again interesting to compare the Norwegian and the Swedish situations. In Sweden, the mandatory specialization for becoming a deacon is offered in a church education center without any formal connection to the Swedish higher education system. This means that fully educated deacons have no qualification on a master's level, which makes it impossible for them to enter a PhD programme at the completion of their education. In Norway, the master's in *diakonia* also made the PhD possible in different sense. By building a master's programme in *diakonia* that had theological content but that remained independent from theology as a discipline, the PhD in "Diaconia, Values and Professional Practice" became independent from its traditional location within the discipline of practical theology and gained the opportunity to develop in an interdisciplinary setting.

The Construction of an Interdisciplinary PhD Programme

To construct an interdisciplinary area for PhD research, the concept of *diakonia* needs to be made relevant both within and beyond church settings and theological discourses.[19] In the "Diaconia, Values and Professional Practice" PhD programme, this relevance is established by connecting *diakonia* to the concepts of values and professional practice. This integration is apparent in the programme description, learning outcomes, and PhD projects.

Programme Description

Understanding *diakonia* as professional practice underlines that diaconal work has taken place in different ways historically and currently. *Diakonia* goes on in different churches and various welfare, health care, and care services through the activities of faith-based (diaconal) organizations or individuals who live out their faith in professional social commitment. Seeing *diakonia* through the prism of professional practice gives an opportunity to reflect on the roots of the diaconal movement in the nineteenth century that are shared by many professions in the fields of social work, education, health care, and care.

Values motivate all professional and voluntary work in the social field, including *diakonia*. Values are also at stake in each human encounter, notably in those characterized by power imbalances, like the relationships between users and providers of social, care, or health services.

> The PhD programme Diaconia, Values and Professional Practice is dedicated to studies of professional practice in public sector and civil society institutions, in health care and social/welfare services, churches and faith- and value-based organizations. It applies diaconia and values as the main perspectives, and it works

---

[19] Unlike students in full-scholarship programmes in Norway, PhD students in many other countries need to pay tuition fees. Thus, it might be less important in Norway than in other countries that a programme of study equips them with marketable job skills.

with an interdisciplinary approach as an innovative contribution to the research field of diaconal studies.[20]

Reflection on values thereby connects *diakonia* with all agents in this field and highlights the values of the specific Christian tradition upon which *diakonia* is based.

Learning Outcomes

The standardized time for finalizing a PhD in full-time studies is three years in the Norwegian educational system. Half a year is dedicated to PhD courses. The rest of the time is used for PhD research. In its current version, the programme description of the PhD programme encompasses twelve learning outcomes, half of which are general learning outcomes relevant to various PhD programmes in humanities and social sciences and half of which define the anticipated expertise in the research field of *diakonia*, values, and professional practice.

In the area of "Knowledge," it is expected that the candidate:

- is in the forefront of knowledge in the intersection of the academic fields of Diaconia, Values and Professional Practice.
- has a thorough understanding of scientific theoretical issues relevant to the professional field of the research project, and how these are transformed into and have implications for studies of professional practice.

In the area of "Skills," it is expected that the candidate:

- can act proficiently regarding methodological and ethical challenges in the study of professional practice and conduct research with professional and ethical integrity.
- can challenge established knowledge and contribute to the development of new knowledge, new theory, new methods, and new interpretations within the field of Diaconia, Values and Professional Practice.

In the area of "General Competence," it is expected that the candidate:

- can identify and cope with ethical issues, with emphasis on challenges related to user perspective and power in professional relationships.
- can identify and consider needs for change and innovation in the field of practical studies and take the initiative for and conduct developmental projects.[21]

The learning outcomes emphasize the study of *diakonia* as (professional) practice within the methodological and theoretical context of professional studies and with the ambition of contributing to better practices. Theology is not mentioned explicitly but can be understood as part of the framing.

PhD Projects

By the end of December 2023, seventy-four PhD scholars were enrolled in the PhD programme and an additional thirty-three had completed their dissertations.

---

[20] VID Specialized University, "Programme Description, PhD Programme in Diakonia, Values and Professional Practice (English version)," 1, https://www.vid.no/en/plans/programme-description-phd-programme-in-diakonia-values-and-professional-practice-english-2018-2019/.

[21] VID Specialized University, "Programme Description," 2.

Diaconal Studies 215

While all projects were committed to the interdisciplinary research area of the programme, more than two thirds had a clear emphasis on a single disciplinary or professional tradition. The remaining third intentionally combined different disciplinary approaches or professional backgrounds in the project (see Figure 17.1).

PhD Dissertations: Diaconia, Values, and Professional Practice	Completed	Ongoing
Emphasis on Health Studies	10	25
Emphasis on Social Work	8	13
Emphasis on Leadership Studies	3	6
Emphasis on *Diakonia*	3	10
Combination of Disciplines and/or Professional Traditions	9	20

Figure 17.1: PhD Dissertations: Diaconia, Values, and Professional Practice

Behind the numbers hide a huge variety of projects. They range, for instance, from "Care for dying persons and their relatives in palliative care services in nursing homes" or "The other person is the turning point: A qualitative study of the experiences of patients with depression, shame, and professional relationships in mental health care" in the field of health studies, to a topic like "Public childcare as a social mission of solidarity and a lifelong project" in social work. They include investigations about "Opening and closing doors. Managing at the multicultural workplace. A case study of cultural diversity and inclusion in nursing homes" in leadership studies or "Soup, soap, salvation: Developing faith-based practices in secularized societies" in diaconal studies. Typical examples for projects that involve several disciplines or professions are studies about the lifeworld of people with disabilities or on practices of values- or religious education in school or higher education.[22]

The PhD programme brings together different projects and works constantly to create a consistent research area relevant for all projects. The two compulsory courses "Diaconia, Values and Professional Practice" (same name as the study programme) and "Philosophy of Science and Research Ethics" play a key role in establishing this area across disciplines and professions. Also creating consistency are regular meetings, conferences, and paper presentations across different disciplines.

---

[22] For an overview of ongoing PhD projects in the programme, see VID Specialized University, "PhD Projects at Centre of Diakonia and Professional Practice," https://www.vid.no/en/research/phd-projects-at-center-of-diakonia-and-professional-practice/.

Opportunities and Challenges for Interdisciplinary PhD Research

Looking back on ten years of interdisciplinary PhD research in *diakonia* draws attention to specific opportunities and challenges for an interdisciplinary PhD programme that includes *diakonia* as a central concept.

Opportunities

First, locating diaconal professionalism and the ministry of the deacon in the context of professional practice provides new knowledge about *diakonia* and strengthens the professional status of deacons in the church hierarchies, where priests often dominate as first among equals. This dominance is difficult to dissolve insofar as *diakonia* is "only" considered as part of "practical" theology (a discipline that has evolved for the education of priests over centuries). The interdisciplinary research context highlights how *diakonia* as knowledge field and professional practice is part of and influenced by several knowledge traditions, including theology (among others), and should therefore be recognized in churches as a unique competence.

Second, an interdisciplinary PhD programme in *diakonia* has the potential to connect research in *diakonia* directly to cutting-edge knowledge areas in fields of practice that are crucial for diaconal work inside or outside the church, such as social work, disability studies, care studies, leadership studies, value studies, or health studies. These interdisciplinary connections have important methodological and theoretical implications. Research about diaconal practice can be inspired by innovative methods developed in the social sciences or health studies; for example, participatory approaches that are more developed and widespread in these fields of research than in theology. Various theologies of *diakonia* can be challenged and developed by discussing contributions from social theory and philosophy, for example, and vice versa.

Third, placing the study of *diakonia* in relation to the study of professional practices in welfare, health, and care services emphasizes questions, perspectives, and methods beyond those normally studied in theological settings. The PhD programme with this rich background can contribute to broadening and widening the field of diaconal studies.

The interactions among scholars in the PhD programme have finally shown that theological approaches and perspectives from Christian/faith-based social practice can be of interest for scholars who have different ideological viewpoints but similar social agendas. An interdisciplinary PhD programme that explicitly includes *diakonia* thus serves as a platform for communication and collaboration with scholars from other disciplines that is enriching both for them and the field of diaconal studies.

Challenges

The major but very productive challenge after ten years of work with the PhD programme in "Diaconia, Values and Professional Practice" is the experience that the concept of *diakonia* remains contested, both internally and generally. For example, the work of revising the PhD syllabus in 2018 was organized as a participative process involving teachers, supervisors, and PhD students in the programme. During the revision, the name of the PhD programme was challenged in several rounds. In particular, the concept of *diakonia* was perceived to be problematic by some of the students and teachers. Disagreements about the concept of *diakonia* as part of the PhD research area at the same time nurtured valuable reflections about the core of the PhD programme. In 2018, the discussions were concluded with the confirmation of *diakonia* as a key concept for the research area. However, this was only an intermediate step in a continuing conversation about the role of the concept of *diakonia* in the PhD programme.[23]

Three circumstances illustrate the vulnerability of the concept of *diakonia*. First, small research fields like diaconal studies are often perceived as too narrow and run the risk of being swallowed by overarching, more generic research areas, such as theology/religion on the one hand or professional practice on the other hand. Ongoing secularization in the Nordic countries gives a Christian concept like *diakonia* a marginal position and thus a high risk of being subsumed.

Secularization is a second risk factor for perpetuating *diakonia* as a relevant concept in an interdisciplinary research programme. In the Nordic countries, it has become increasingly difficult to communicate a specifically Christian term as the platform for collaboration. The term itself can be experienced as excluding and limiting; for example, when applying for public research funding or when attracting new PhD scholars who might be discouraged by a concept they do not know or misunderstand.

Against this background, one can see promise for mutual understanding in the empirical turn of practical theology that has resulted in a growing interest in faith practices, including diaconal ones. So far, however, this turn has not achieved increased attention for *diakonia* as an area of expertise within practical theology. This constitutes the third risk; namely, that diaconal studies might be dissolved into the larger and more general study area of faith-based practices.

It remains to be seen how the field of diaconal studies will develop internationally in the future. Hopefully, the scholars who complete their PhD in the "Diaconia, Values and Professional Practice" programme can contribute to the future discussion.

Works Cited

Bäckström, Anders. *Svenska kyrkan som välfärdsaktör i en global kultur: En studie av religion och omsorg* [*The Church of Sweden as Welfare Actor in a Global Culture: A Study of Religion and Care*]. Stockholm: Verbum, 2001.

Blennberger, Erik and Mats J. Hansson. "Vad menas med diakoni?" ["What is meant by diakonia?"]. In *Diakoni: Tolkning, historik, praktik* [*Diakonia: Interpretation, History, Practice*], edited by Erik Blennberger and Mats J. Hansson, 13–27. Stockholm: Verbum, 2008.

Esping-Andersen, Gøsta. *The Three Worlds of Welfare Capitalism*. Princeton: Princeton University Press, 1990.

---

[23] The syllabus is undergoing a new round of revision during 2024, most likely causing changes in formulations with regard to *diakonia*.

Furseth, Inger, ed. *Religious Complexity in the Public Sphere: Comparing Nordic Countries*. Palgrave Studies in Religion, Politics, and Policy. Cham, Switzerland: Palgrave Macmillan, 2018.

Haerpfer, C., R. Inglehart, A. Moreno, C. Welzel, K. Kizilova, J. Diez-Medrano, M. Lagos, P. Norris, E. Ponarin, and B. Puranen, eds. *World Values Survey: Round Seven – Country-Pooled Datafile Version 5.0*. Vienna: JD Systems Institute & WVSA Secretariat, 2020. https://doi.org/10.14281/18241.1.

Hellöre, Lise-Lotte. "When Diaconia Became an Exhausted Millionaire: Experiences from the Coronavirus Pandemic in Finland." *Diaconia: Journal for the Study of Christian Social Practice* 12, no. 2 (September 2021): 117–36. https://doi.org/10.13109/diac.2021.12.2.117.

Hollmer, Miriam and Anders Bäckström. "Svenska kyrkan och välfärden. En undersökning av attityder" ["The Church of Sweden and the Welfare: A Study of Attitudes"]. In *Välfärdsinsatser på religiös grund: Förväntningar och problem* [*Welfare Engagement on Religious Basis: Expectations and Problems*], edited by Anders Bäckström, 31–62. Skellefteå: Artos & Norma, 2014.

Leis-Peters, Annette. "Hidden by Civil Society and Religion? Diaconal Institutions as Welfare Providers in the Growing Swedish Welfare State." *Journal of Church and State* 56, no. 1 (Winter 2014): 105–27. https://doi.org/10.1093/jcs/cst134.

Linde, Stig. *Välfärd och kyrkan: Underlag för reflektion* [*Welfare and Church: A Basis for Reflection*]. Uppsala: Svenska kyrkan, 2016.

Lundgren, Linnea. *A Risk or a Resource? A Study of the Swedish State's Shifting Perception and Handling of Minority Religious Communities between 1952–2019*. Stockholm: Ersta Sköndal Bräcke University College, 2021. https://esh.diva-portal.org/smash/get/diva2:1584388/FULLTEXT01.pdf.

Moser, Ingunn. "Diakoniinstitusjoner som laboratoriefabrikker for morgendagens velferd?" ["Diaconal Institutions as Laboratory Factories for Tomorrow's Welfare?"]. In *Nestekjærlighet på anbud. Diakonale virksomheters identitet i moderne velferdssamfunn* [*Love for Your Neighbour on Tender: Diaconal Agencies' Identity in Modern Welfare Societies*], edited by Harald Askeland, 142–60. Oslo: Frekk, 2022.

Pew Research Center. "Eastern and Western Europeans Differ on Importance of Religion, Views of Minorities, and Key Social Issues." 29 October 2018. https://www.pewresearch.org/religion/2018/10/29/eastern-and-western-europeans-differ-on-importance-of-religion-views-of-minorities-and-key-social-issues/.

Selle, Per. "Frivillighetens marginalisering" ["The Marginalization of Voluntarism"]. *Tidskrift for velferdsforskning* [*Journal for Welfare Research*] 19, no. 1 (March 2016): 76–89. https://doi.org/10.18261/issn.2464-3076-2016-01-05.

Sivesind, Karl Henrik, and Jo Saglie, eds. *Promoting Active Citizenship: Markets and Choice in Scandinavian Welfare*. Cham, Switzerland: Palgrave

Macmillan, 2017. https://link.springer.com/book/10.1007/978-3-319-55381-8.

Stolz, Jörg. "Secularization Theories in the Twenty-First Century: Ideas, Evidence, and Problems." *Social Compass* 67, no. 2 (June 2020): 282–308. https://doi.org/10.1177/0037768620917320.

VID Specialized University. "PhD Projects at Centre of Diakonia and Professional Practice." https://www.vid.no/en/research/phd-projects-at-center-of-diakonia-and-professional-practice/.

VID Specialized University. "Programme Description, PhD Programme in Diakonia, Values and Professional Practice (English version)." https://www.vid.no/en/plans/programme-description-phd-programme-in-diakonia-values-and-professional-practice-english-2018-2019/.

Chapter 18

A Norwegian Case for Formation in the *Diakonia* Curriculum

Kristin Husby Dyrstad

Along with the knowledge and skills of theology, health, and social care, the formation of diaconal identity has traditionally been emphasized in Norwegian *diakonia* education. The students in previous generations lived together in a community, sharing meals, devotionals, studies, hospital practice, celebrations, and everyday life. They were collectively ordained and admitted as members of the deacon, deaconess, or parish sister association.[1] A former student in his eighties remembers how the old deacons proudly received their deacon badge and were conscious that they were deacons.[2] He described the educational institution as a Home "with a big H."[3] Today's master's students live in private homes. Some of them will be ordained, others not. They have various educational backgrounds combined with the diaconal.

To serve as a deacon is considered a profession in Norway. In a long-term comparative study of professions, researchers found that "What counts as meaningful student formation?" has often fallen into the background in times of specialization and professionalization.[4] How and when did the space for diaconal formation change in Scandinavian deacon training? Looking into archival material, the late 1960s to the mid-1980s appears to be a transition phase.

---

[1] Ordained is here a translation of the Norwegian term *vigslet*. *Vigsling* does not equal either ordination or consecration but, in line with Meland and Pädam, we use the term ordination. Roar Meland, "The Deacon in the Church of Norway," in *The Ministry of the Deacon: Anglican-Lutheran Perspectives*, eds. Gunnel Borgegård and Christine Hall (Uppsala: Nordic Ecumenical Council, 1999); Tiit Pädam, *Ordination of Deacons in the Churches of the Porvoo Communion: A Comparative Investigation in Ecclesiology* (Uppsala: Kirjastus TP, 2011).

[2] The deacon badge, a Johannite cross, was introduced in 1899 to place deacon service in a historical tradition and to protect against "false deacons": persons without diaconal education. The Johannite cross had been used by the ancient Crusaders who practiced nursing and Christian acts of love in the Holy Land. Harry Moen, *Kallet og tjenesten: streif fra den mannlige diakonis historie i Norge [The Calling and the Service: Impressions from the History of the Male Diakonia in Norway]* (Oslo: Det norske Diakonforbund).

[3] In-depth interview with a male deacon trained at Diakonhjemmet in the 1960s, conducted by Kristin Husby Dyrstad, 31 March 2022. This citation and all other citations from the Norwegian source material are translated by the author.

[4] William M. Sullivan and Matthew S. Rosin, *A New Agenda for Higher Education: Shaping a Life of the Mind for Practice*, Jossey-Bass Higher and Adult Education Series (San Francisco: Jossey-Bass, 2008), xix.

Significant developments within the welfare professions, the higher education system, and the Church of Norway impacted the institutions of diaconal education. This chapter investigates how curricular changes in this period impacted the formation of diaconal identity.

This investigation proceeds through a case study of Diakonhjemmet (the Deacon's Home) in Oslo. I examine definitions, aims, and study programme changes. Since its establishment in 1890, Diakonhjemmet has offered holistic deacon education and has intended to work broadly on behalf of the Evangelical Lutheran Church.[5] The training qualifies workers primarily for caritative work in institutions, organizations, and churches.[6] Until 1968, when Diakonhjemmet accepted women into the programme, only men were deacons (whereas women were deaconesses or parish nurses). They were all trained as nurses. In 1971, the institution was divided into a nursing school (*Diasyk*), a social work school (*Diasos*), and a theological school (*Diatas*).[7] The three schools, recognized as colleges by governmental authorities around 1980, were supposed to collaborate on a four-year programme of diaconal education.[8] This chapter investigates this collaborative project, emphasizing the space for formation.

Methodology, Theoretical Perspectives, and Outline

The history of Diakonhjemmet as a pioneer in Norwegian health and social education – and an original contributor to diaconal thinking in the Lutheran majority church – was researched extensively by Gunnar Stave.[9] His primary focus was the institution's identity and integration into the public welfare system. Kari Martinsen studied the first Norwegian deaconess training and compared it with Diakonhjemmet.[10] Sven-Erik Brodd, among others, described how the

---

[5] Until 1972, Diakonhjemmet was the only Norwegian institution that offered deacon training. Other institutions provided training for deaconesses and parish sisters.
[6] In contrast, for example, to the Anglican or Roman Catholic tradition, where deacon ministry is mainly associated with priestly liturgical service. Stephanie Dietrich, "Diakontjenesten i et økumenisk perspektiv" ["The Ministry of Deacons in an Ecumenical Perspective"], in *Diakonen – kall og profesjon [The Deacon: Calling and Profession]*, eds. Dietrich et al. (Trondheim: Tapir akademisk, 2011), 135.
[7] *Diatas* is an abbreviation for Diakonhjemmet's theological school with administrative subjects. The main subjects are theological and thus the school is referred to as a theological school.
[8] *Diasos* was approved as a college in 1979, *Diatas* in 1980, and *Diasyk* in 1981.
[9] Gunnar Stave, *Mannsmot og tenarsinn: Det norske Diakonhjem i hundre år [Courage and Servant Mind: The Norwegian Diakonhjemmet for One Hundred Years]* (Oslo: Samlaget, 1990); Gunnar Stave, "Identitet og integrasjon: ein studie av ein diakonal institusjon med særleg vekt på ideologien, identiteten og integrasjonen i det offentlege velferdssystemet" ["Identity and Integration: A Study Of A Diaconal Institution with Particular Emphasis on Ideology, Identity and Integration in the Public Welfare System"] (Trondheim: Norwegian University of Science and Technology, 1996).
[10] Diakonissehuset was established in 1868. Kari Martinsen, *Freidige og uforsagte diakonisser: et omsorgsyrke vokser fram, 1860–1905 [Courageous and Daring Deaconesses: A Caring Profession Develops: 1860–1905]* (Oslo: Aschehoug/Tanum-Norli, 1984).

Mother Houses were gradually transformed into centers of diaconal education in Sweden, similar to Norway, in the 1960s and 1970s.[11] Kjell Nordstokke and Stephanie Dietrich are central contributors to understanding the emergence of *diakonia* as an interdisciplinary science.[12] The challenge of interdisciplinarity is crucial when we study the formation of diaconal identity. The deacon's role and identity in Norway and Sweden have been marked by unclarity from a theological and ecclesiological perspective and as a profession in the labor market.[13] Diaconal studies often emphasize theological, ecclesiological, and sociological perspectives, while my angle is primarily pedagogical and historical.

Methodologically, this study interprets source material from the Mission and Diakonia Archives (MDA) at VID Specialized University.[14] The main sources are reports and programme statements by the executive board at Diakonhjemmet, admission rules, study plans, and anniversary booklets.[15] These documents represent the institution's official educational policy. Minutes from board meetings and comments from teachers and directors in the magazine *Hilsen fra*

---

[11] Sven-Erik Brodd, "The Deacon in the Church of Sweden," in *The Ministry of the Deacon: Angican-Lutheran Perspectives*, eds. Gunnel Borgegård and Christine Hall (Uppsala: Nordic Ecumenical Council, 1999).

[12] Kjell Nordstokke, "The Study of Diakonia as an Academic Discipline," in *Diakonia as Christian Social Practice: An Introduction*, eds. Dietrich et al. (Oxford: Regnum Books International, 2014). Stephanie Dietrich, Kari Karsrud Korslien, and Kjell Nordstokke, *Diakonen – kall og profesjon [The Deacon: Calling and Profession]* (Trondheim: Tapir Akademisk, 2011). Stephanie Dietrich et al., "Introduction: Diakonia as Christian Social Practice," in *Diakonia as Christian Social Practice: An Introduction*, eds. Dietrich et al. (Oxford: Regnum Books International, 2014).

[13] Meland, "The Deacon in the Church of Norway"; Anders Bäckström, "Diakoner med annan arbetsgivare än Svenska Kyrkan" ["Deacons with Employers Other than the Church of Sweden"], in *Diakoni och samhälle [Diakonia and Society]*, ed. Thomas Ekstrand (Uppsala: Diakonivitenskapliga Institutet i Uppsala, 2001); Helene Teglund, "Diakoner med tjänst utanför Svenska Kyrkan" ["Deacons with Service Outside the Church of Sweden"], in *Diakoni och samhälle [Diakonia and Society]*, ed. Thomas Ekstrand (Uppsala: Diakonivetenskapliga Institutet i Uppsala, 2001); Katarina Olofsgård, "Professionell eller perspektivbärare? Om diakoners yrkesidentitet" [Professional or Perspective Carrier? About Deacons' Professional Identity] (Magistergrad Ersta Sköndal Högskola, 2003); Olav Helge Angell, "Diakoniforståing og identitet hos diakonar i Den norske kyrkja" [Diaconal Understanding and Identity among Deacons in the Church of Norway], in *Diakonen – kall og profesjon [The Deacon: Calling and Profession]*, eds. Dietrich et al. (Trondheim: Tapir Akademisk, 2011); Olav Fanuelsen, "Diakoner i Den norske kirke- et historisk tilbakeblikk" [Deacons in the Church of Norway – a historical retrospective], in *Diakonen – kall og profesjon [The Deacon: Calling and Profession]*, eds. Dietrich et al (Trondheim: Tapir Akademisk, 2011); Marianne R Nygaard, "Diakoners profesjonsvilkår i Den norske kirke" [Deacons' professional conditions in the Church of Norway], Tidsskrift for Praktisk Teologi 28, no. 2 (2011).

[14] VID is a merger of several Norwegian diaconal educational institutions, including Diakonhjemmet University College.

[15] "Executive Board" is a translation of the Norwegian *hovedstyret* and "director" a translation of *forstander*.

Diakonhjemmet [*Greetings from Diakonhjemmet*] give a deeper understanding of curricular changes and internal discussions. Textbooks by teachers in *diakonia* education also serve as source material. To guide the interpretation of the written sources and provide more insight into the theme of identity formation, I have added some oral sources by conducting three in-depth interviews with former students.

Based on how the terms appear in the archival sources, this chapter does not differentiate between *diakonia* education and deacon education, speaking interchangeably of diaconal identity, deacon identity, and professional deacon identity. I apply a broad understanding of the term *diakonia* curriculum and include more informal elements connected to "upbringing in the Home" before the 1970s. The term *formation* refers to the process of change students undergo, personally and spiritually, in their outlook, behavior, ideals, goals, and interpretation of experiences.[16] Exploring the space for formation in interdisciplinary *diakonia* education, I find it fruitful to relate to the Carnegie Foundation's studies, which compare the education of clergy to professionals in engineering, law, medicine, and nursing.[17] The Carnegie studies use the concept of apprenticeship, historically a part of all professional training, not as a "slavish imitation of master teachers" but as three "high-end apprenticeships": a cognitive or intellectual apprenticeship, a practical apprenticeship of skill, and an apprenticeship of identity formation.[18] I also derive theoretical perspectives from the project "From Vocational to Professional Education," with contributors from the Scandinavian and North American contexts.[19]

The structure of this chapter consists of three sections, exploring changes in definitions, aims, and study programmes in *diakonia* education around 1970–1980. At the end of each section is a discussion of how curricular changes have impacted the space for formation. The conclusion reflects on how the findings can contribute to the further development of diaconal studies.

I find that Diakonhjemmet, in the shift from a home model to a more academic model of *diakonia* education, terminated traditional formative elements without replacing them with new ones. Curricular development gave priority to an expanded theological knowledge base in line with academic standards in other disciplines and the desire to distance itself from a pietistic focus on practical *diakonia* and Christian personalities. Although the ability to reflect critically was strengthened, there was a general weakening of formative elements. Increased ambiguity about what should be regarded as diaconal methods and practices

---

[16] Patricia Benner, *Educating Nurses: A Call for Radical Transformation*, Preparation for the Professions Series, vol. 3 (San Francisco, CA: Jossey-Bass, 2010); Molly Sutphen and Thomas de Lange, "What is Formation? A Conceptual Discussion," *Higher Education Research and Development* 34, no. 2 (2015), https://doi.org/10.1080/07294360.2014.956690.
[17] Charles R. Foster et al., *Educating Clergy: Teaching Practices and Pastoral Imagination* (San Francisco: Jossey-Bass, 2006); Sullivan and Rosin, *A New Agenda for Higher Education*; Benner, *Educating Nurses*.
[18] Benner, *Educating Nurses*, 25; see also Foster et al., *Educating Clergy*, 5.
[19] Jens-Christian Smeby and Molly Sutphen, *From Vocational to Professional Education: Educating for Social Welfare* (London: Routledge, 2015).

negatively influenced the possibility of diaconal identity formation. Future *diakonia* education in Scandinavia, North America, and other contexts can learn from this Norwegian case that the goal of identity formation and the implementation of practical and formative elements should be emphasized when curricula are developed. Focusing on programme coherence and meaningful relationships between the three types of apprenticeship can contribute to this.

Curricular Changes and Diaconal Formation, 1970–1980

The 1981 programme statement on *diakonia* and *diakonia* education constitutes a fruitful starting point for this case study.[20] The executive board initiated changes in response to debates in the 1970s between Diakonhjemmet's three schools: nursing, social work, and theology. Although the theological school had a special responsibility for diaconal teaching, all three schools were to be collaborators in the institution's *diakonia* education.

Definitions of Diakonia Shift from Individual Calling to Church-Centeredness

Definitions of *diakonia* used in curricular documents provide insight into the institution's education programme in different periods. In this section, I compare the 1981 definition to earlier ones, each representing different views of *diakonia* and the church.

The short 1981 version is: "*Diakonhjemmet* understands diakonia as the church's care for people in need."[21] Further clarifications state:

> Diakonia is the ministry of the church. In diakonia, it is the church that acts. "Church" is understood in the Lutheran Confession as the community of all believers united around Word and Sacrament. The church as the subject of diakonia is therefore represented first by the organized church (the church and Christian organizations with diaconal objectives) and second by individual Christians who, in their vocations, seek to help people in need.[22]

Diakonhjemmet underlined the organized church as the primary actor for *diakonia* and individual Christians as the secondary actor. This reflects an attempt to balance the conflicting views on *diakonia* competing in the 1970s and early 1980s. The three schools agreed to describe *diakonia* as the church's care for people in need. However, the social work school's 1981 plan stated that "church" meant "not only the Church of Norway but also Christian organizations and the individual Christian person."[23] The plan elaborated, "Diaconal care encompasses all human beings and is directed towards all aspects of human social problems, both material and spiritual."

On the other hand, the theological school's new syllabus book for diaconal studies in 1980 emphasized that "the Christian congregation provides the horizon

---

[20] MDA, *Hilsen fra Diakonhjemmet*, no. 4 (1981), 2–9.
[21] MDA, *Hilsen fra Diakonhjemmet*, no. 4 (1981), 7–8.
[22] MDA, *Hilsen fra Diakonhjemmet*, no. 4 (1981), 7–8.
[23] MDA, "Diasosplan," 27 May 1981, 3.

for diakonia."²⁴ The school stressed that *diakonia* springs from the Eucharist and is meant to serve the church community. Although Diakonhjemmet's director, Rolf Lein, was critical of what he called "strong forces within Norwegian diakonia" who wanted to "limit diaconal work to the church," he agreed to strengthen the definition's emphasis on the organized church. A backdrop for this was the desire to increase the focus on *diakonia* and the number of deacon positions in the Church of Norway.²⁵

The individual Christian, referred to as the secondary actor of *diakonia* in the 1981 definition, was considered primary until the 1970s. In an admissions form used in the late 1960s, the applicant had to answer, "What has moved you to become a deacon?" and "Are you aware that deacon means servant, and are you willing to serve where God places you?"²⁶ A pietistic view of *diakonia* inherited from the founders had characterized Diakonhjemmet's education since 1890, as we find in Thorleif Nordseth's 1943 introductory book on diaconal service.²⁷ Nordseth, director of the programme, defined *diakonia* as the "ministry of Jesus' hands" and the deacon as the "Servant of Jesus Christ."

The students learned that *diakonia* is "primarily about personalities, Christian personalities." It was not important where the deacon worked but that he had "the right deacon mind." Diakonhjemmet's broad view of the church was explained in these words at its 50ᵗʰ anniversary: "Of course we want to serve the congregation, but we are in Wichern's spirit when we also joyfully enter into community life wherever it is possible to be light and salt – in hospitals, in prisons, wherever there is a way."²⁸ From its establishment, *diakonia* education was for "those who felt called in the spirit of Christ's love to do the service of mercy among the sick, poor, and needy."²⁹

Until 1969, all graduating students were collectively ordained (in Norwegian, *vigslet*) before they entered various work in society, including Christian congregations or organizations.³⁰ After 1969, only those who went to church

---

²⁴ Alf B. Oftestad, *En bok om kirkens diakoni [A Book about the Church's Diakonia]* (Oslo: Luther, 1980), 37.
²⁵ The first specific deacon positions in the Church of Norway were established in 1974. Before this, deacons who worked in parishes of the Church of Norway were mainly employed in the position of *klokker* or *klokkerdiakon* (pastor's assistant), responsible for visiting the sick and assisting the pastor in congregational work.
²⁶ MDA, "Opptakelsesskjema. Det Norske Diakonhjem. Diakonelever." Admission form from the 1960s.
²⁷ Thorleif Nordseth, *Innføring i tjenesten. En liten håndbok for diakoner [Introduction to the Service: A Little Handbook for Deacons]* (Oslo: Det Norske Diakonhjem, 1943), 44ff.
²⁸ The German pioneer Johann Hinrich Wichern, who established the Rauhes Haus in Hamburg for the training of deacons in 1833 and was later called the father of male *diakonia*, was a source of inspiration for Diakonhjemmet. Thorleif Nordseth, *Det Norske Diakonhjem 1890–1940. Festskrift utgitt av Styret ved Thorleif Nordseth Diakonhjemmets Forstander* (Oslo: Det Norske Diakonhjem, 1940), 12.
²⁹ MDA, "6. Beretning om Det Norske Diakonhjem. For 1895. Ved Hjemmets Forstander," 1896.
³⁰ In the Church of Norway, the term *ordinasjon* has traditionally been used only for pastors because of the theological understanding of the Augsburg Confession, Article 5,

positions were ordained and could call themselves deacons. Forty years later, a long-term teacher at the theological school reflected on the development in the 2000s: "The church-centered paradigm has made a major breakthrough, although much remains before deacon ministry is established in every congregation, as was the dream."[31]

To what extent did the more church-centered *diakonia* definition at Diakonhjemmet impact the space for formation? The basis for discussion is limited until we look at how educational aims and study plans changed around 1980, but there are some tendencies. When the perspective of individual calling was removed or lessened in the definition, the emphasis on personal and spiritual growth could easily diminish in deacon training, especially since teachers at Diakonhjemmet opposed the pietistic heritage in various ways. Theological teachers in the 1970s called for a clearer ecclesiology for *diakonia*, rooted in the sacraments and avoiding secularizing tendencies. The social work school, on the other hand, was concerned with social analysis and client-centeredness. The institution's reduced emphasis on the "deacon mind" and the student's relationship with God, combined with a stronger focus on the congregation and social analysis, contributed to a loss in the apprenticeship of identity formation.

From Holistic to Diverse Educational Aims

How did the 1981 aims for the overall *diakonia* education differ from earlier educational goals at Diakonhjemmet?[32] This question is explored without reference to the specific educational purposes of the three schools. The 1981 statement declares:

> *Diakonhjemmet's* aim is to qualify Christian women and men for diaconal service and diaconal work in church and society. It consists of qualification as a nurse or

---

that there is only one *embete* or *ministerium ecclesiasticum* (office), defined by its function; to preach the gospel and distribute the sacraments, belonging to the pastor. In this interpretation, deacons have been considered part of lay ministry through *vigsling*, not *ordinasjon*. Nevertheless, in the 1970s and after, there have been continuous theological discussions about whether the Augsburg Confession, Article 5 can be understood as a threefold ministry of pastors, deacons, and catechists. Swedish deacons have been ordained since 1999. The Norwegian liturgies have not been clear as to whether deacons are part of the *ministerium ecclesiasticum* (or only the pastors), although there came significant signals when deacons could wear a stole from 2011. Lars Østnor, *Kirkens tjenester med særlig henblikk på diakontjenesten [Church Ministry with a Particular Emphasis on Deacon Ministry]* (Oslo: Luther, 1978); Stephanie Dietrich, "Forståelsen av diakonitjenesten i Den norske kirke" [The Understanding of Diaconal Ministry in the Church of Norway], in *Diakonen – kall og profesjon [The Deacon: Calling and Profession]*, eds. Dietrich et al. (Trondheim: Tapir Akademisk, 2011).

[31] "The Act on Deacon Ministry" was adopted by governmental authorities on 31 May 1985. Kai Ingolf Johannessen, "Diakontjenestens plassering i kirken" [The Position of the Deacon Ministry in the Church], in *Diakoni – en kritisk lesebok [Diakonia: A Critical Textbook]*, eds. Johannessen et al. (Trondheim: Tapir Akademisk, 2009), 40.

[32] MDA, "Diakoni og Diakoniutdanning ved *Diakonhjemmet*. Ved Hovedstyret," 27 October 1981, 9.

social worker combined with a theological education. The overall aim of the education at *Diakonhjemmet* is to train diaconal candidates who can enter as deacons in the church's own work. It is also an important goal to train diaconal candidates for service in positions in society at large. The education as a whole aims to qualify for positions in a) congregation and church, b) diaconal institutions/organizations, c) society's health and social services.

On several points, this formulation of purpose differs from the one from the late 1960s. First, it says, "Christian women and men," while in 1968, the phrase was "believing young men," corresponding with the admission policy.[33] Second, the aim of qualifying diaconal candidates for "the church's own work" was prioritized in 1981, compared with the 1971 expression that Diakonhjemmet "aims to educate young believers, in the spirit of Christ's love, to do diaconal service in church and society among people in need."[34] Third, while the 1968 programme consisted of uniform training in "nursing school and teaching in diaconal subjects," starting in 1971, students chose between nursing (*Diasyk*) or social work (*Diasos*) combined with theological education (*Diatas*).[35]

After the split into three schools, what was earlier called "diaconal subjects" is now described as "theological education." None of the three schools had *diakonia* in its name. Nevertheless, *diakonia* was intended to permeate all educational purposes and activities. The educational committee stated in 1971:

> One should not use the term "diaconal education" for the theological and practical/ecclesiastical subjects, because nursing and social worker education is also part of the education for becoming a deacon. After this, the committee uses "deacon education" or "diaconal education" for the *entire* education, while the parts are described as nursing and social worker education and theological and administrative education.[36]

The aim of a coherent *diakonia* education was emphasized in 1971 and 1981, building on Diakonhjemmet's previous experience of being a "small, familial institution where everyone knew each other."[37]

This goal was, however, difficult to fulfil for several reasons. First, when the campus was modernized and expanded in the late 1960s to deal with a larger number of applicants, the interaction between students, teachers, director, and other employees (like the head deacon and the house father) became more fragmented.[38] Fewer students lived on campus. The theological school asked for

---

[33] MDA, *Hilsen fra Diakonhjemmet*, no.s. 7–8 (1968), 18.
[34] MDA, "Plan og Opptaksvilkår for Det Norske Diakonhjem." Study admissions in autumn 1971 and spring 1972.
[35] Students enrolled between 1968 and 1971 were all trained as nurses, social workers, and deacons through a five-and-a-half-year programme.
[36] MDA, "Innstilling om Teologiske og Administrative Fag i Diakonutdanningens 1. og 2. Avdeling," 1971.
[37] MDA, "Diakonhjemmet i dag – Tilbakeblikk og Fremsyn Høsten 1975," Rolf Lein, 5 June 1975, 1.
[38] Sigurd Heiervang, *Tro og tjeneste. Et festskrift ved Det Norske Diakonhjems 75-års-jubileum [Faith and Service. For the Celebration of Diakonhjemmet's 75th Anniversary]* (Oslo: Det Norske Diakonhjem, 1965), 28–33.

teaching facilities closer to the other schools.[39] They considered greater physical distance as a limitation for a coherent education.

A second challenge was the increased professionalization and academization of nursing and social work. Sweden and Norway, representing the Nordic welfare model, forefronted the academic drift from vocational education to higher education in the post-war period.[40] Diakonhjemmet, among the pioneers in Norwegian nursing, considered nursing and, later, social work useful tools in diaconal work.[41] They adjusted the curricula to be a part of the governmental authorization system.[42] However, around 1980, the theological school noted that "one has not been able to prevent what was feared, namely that nursing education and social work education would become a goal in itself."[43] Diaconal institutions found that preparation for the professional diaconal role was more demanding than the role connected to the students' first profession.[44] About half of the students left Diakonhjemmet as nurses or social workers before completing their *diakonia* education.[45]

The third obstacle involved discussions on how to view *diakonia* compared to social work, considering Luther's teaching on the two kingdoms, the temporal and the spiritual. Hard fronts arose at the institution, especially between the schools of social work and theology, after the rector of the social work school, in his role as a politician on leave from Diakonhjemmet, voted for a new and more liberal Norwegian abortion law in 1975.[46] Despite the complex challenges that Diakonhjemmet faced in the 1970s and into the 1980s, they continued to fight for coherence, expecting that all three schools must take up "questions connected to the relationship between nursing/social work and Christian faith/diakonia."[47]

---

[39] MDA, "Målsetting og Arbeidsoppgaver 1975 – Diatas," 3.
[40] Smeby and Sutphen, *From Vocational to Professional Education*.
[41] MDA, "14 ende Beretning om Det Norske Diakonhjem for 1903," 6.
[42] Governmental authorities have played a crucial role in education, approval of competence, and determining framework conditions for professions in Europe compared with, for instance, the United States; Jan Messel, *Profesjonsutdanninger i sentrum: fra jordmorutdanning til OsloMet 1818–2018 [Professional Education in the Centre: From Midwife Training to OsloMet 1818–2018]* (Oslo: PaxForlag A/S, 2022), 77. Diakonhjemmet's nurse education was publicly approved in 1950 and the social work education approved in 1968.
[43] MDA, "Utdrag av 'Eksternt Opptak – Komitéens Innstilling,' Executive Board Meeting," 2 December 1978, 6.
[44] Bäckström, "Diakoner med annan arbetsgivare än Svenska Kyrkan" [Deacons with Employers other than the Church of Sweden], 4.
[45] All students were required to enrol in the entire diakonia course. However, a practice developed whereby many of them applied to quit before entering the "theological year." MDA, *Hilsen fra Diakonhjemmet* no. 1 (1980).
[46] MDA, "Det Norske Diakonhjem, Forstanders Oppsummering av Situasjonen foran Behandlingen av Diakonhjemssaken i Hovedstyrets møte 25. oktober 1977," Rolf Lein, 13 October 1977.
[47] MDA, "Diakoni og Diakoniutdanning ved Diakonhjemmet. Ved Hovedstyret," 27 October 1981, 9.

How was the space for forming diaconal identity impacted by these difficulties? At the root of the coherence problem was Diakonhjemmet's attempt to negotiate between the aim of formation for Christian service and formation as one aspect of the qualification for an occupation. Nordseth expressed in the 1940s: "We never get tired of emphasizing deacon work as an act of calling, even though it obviously has to be regarded as an occupation also."[48] The professional perspective gradually grew stronger, as the educational committee stated in 1981 that "it is important for the quality of diakonia education that each subject area has a content that can gain public approval."[49]

Diakonhjemmet's choice to be part of the authorization system entailed curricular adjustments to strengthen theoretical, practical, and formative elements in nursing and social work. Nursing programmes are often effective in forming professional identity through situated coaching and experiential learning.[50] Social work training at Diakonhjemmet emphasized student interaction with professionals from the field.[51] The apprenticeship of identity formation was more accessible to nurses or social workers than deacons.

The hybrid deacon profession, without a system of public authorization, was vulnerable and struggled to find its place in a time of secularization and specialization. The state increasingly assumed responsibility for welfare services that *diakonia* had earlier pioneered. Interdisciplinary collaboration and cross-professional community building, which could have strengthened the formation of diaconal identity, were hindered by internal conflicts. The theological school questioned which identity the students were being educated for when the connection to the "father house" and the formation process for deacon service was weakened.[52] Their main strategy was to strengthen the theological knowledge base.

Academizations of Study Programmes

After exploring and discussing changes in definitions and aims, especially regarding the formative elements, we next must consider the study programmes. Although the plans of the schools of nursing and social work included diaconal perspectives, we limit ourselves to the development at the college of theology (*Diatahs*), considered the central school in forming diaconal identity.[53] The college operated with one plan (T-0) for theological teaching during the students' first three years and another for the fourth "theological year."

---

[48] Nordseth, *Det Norske Diakonhjem [The Norwegian Diakonhjem]*, 50.
[49] MDA, "Diakoni og Diakoniutdanning ved Diakonhjemmet. Ved Hovedstyret," 27 October 1981, 9.
[50] Benner, *Educating Nurses*, 11.
[51] MDA, "Diasos Reform. Diakonhjemmets Sosialskole," 1972, and "Diasosplan," 27 May 1981.
[52] MDA, "Utdrag av 'Eksternt Opptak – Komitéens Innstilling,' Executive Board Meeting," 2 December 1978, 6.
[53] When *Diatas* was approved as a college in 1980, the abbreviation was changed to *Diatahs*. The "h" stands for Høyskole or College.

The educational committee in the early 1980s decided to keep the previous educational model.⁵⁴ However, they stressed that revisions and modifications were critical, considering the large number of students who dropped out of the programme before they became diaconal candidates.⁵⁵ After several years of interdisciplinary committee work, the revised plan for theological teaching was finalized in 1984.⁵⁶ The T-0 programme for nursing consisted of worldview/ethics, nursing ethics, philosophy of religion, New Testament, practical *diakonia*, and spiritual counselling. The T-0 programme for social workers provided general theology and biblical knowledge, theological doctrine and philosophy of religion, ethics, spiritual counselling, and *diakonia*.⁵⁷ The fourth year of full-time theological study consisted of five subject areas.⁵⁸ The main subject, *diakonia*, covered the theological basis for *diakonia* (*diakonikk*) and practical *diakonia*, which addressed "various aspects of the church's diaconal work" and allowed for deepening through elective subjects. The other areas were Bible (Old and New Testament) theological-systematic subjects (dogmatics, philosophy of religion, ethics, and *diakonikk*), practical ecclesiastical subjects (spiritual counselling, preaching, and practical *diakonia*), and historical subjects (church history with denominational knowledge, history of *diakonia*, and religious studies).

In 1985, full-time theological study was opened for external applicants with appropriate basic training to increase the number of *diakonia* students. It was then termed a one-year diaconal study programme, which points to a more independent academic *diakonia* programme. Diakonhjemmet introduced a master's degree in Diakonia in 1995 and an international master's degree in "Diakonia and Christian Social Practice" in 2011.⁵⁹

To what extent did the 1984 programme differ from the earlier ones? The theological subjects were essentially the same as in the 1970s and earlier. However, the syllabus and the content attained a more advanced theoretical level. Since the establishment of the theological school in 1971, a new generation of academically strong theologians gradually raised the standard to the university level.⁶⁰ In their view, *diakonia* education lacked theological depth due to the

---

⁵⁴ MDA, "Utdanningsutvalgets Innstilling om Utdanningsmønsteret ved Det Norske Diakonhjem," 13 January 1982.
⁵⁵ In 1979, fifty diaconal candidates graduated (thirty-eight nurses and twelve social workers) out of more than one hundred registered, according to MDA, *Hilsen fra Diakonhjemmet*, no. 1 (1980), 8.
⁵⁶ MDA, "Innstilling om den Teologiske Undervisning. Det Norske Diakonhjem. Teologisk/Administrativ Høgskole," 1984.
⁵⁷ Both programmes comprised 150 hours in three years and were thematically linked to nursing or social work and, in the fourth year, theological study.
⁵⁸ MDA, "Ett Års Diakonistudium," 1985. Information booklet from Diakonhjemmet.
⁵⁹ In 1995, the Norwegian "Hovedfag," equivalent to a master's degree, was established in collaboration with the Faculty of Theology at the University of Oslo. In 2004, Diakonhjemmet launched their own master's in Diakonia.
⁶⁰ MDA, "Innstilling om Teologiske og Administrative Fag i Diakonutdanningens 1. og 2. Avdeling" (1971), 2–3.

previous focus on Christian personalities and practical-diaconal work.[61] By the early 1980s, the college of theology had developed a scholarly *diakonia* environment that was unique both nationally and internationally.[62] Emphasis on the theoretical came at the expense of the practical, as students missed practical-diaconal experience and teachers who were "deacons from the field."[63] Diakonhjemmet became increasingly aware of this problem as the 1984 programme strengthened the practical-diaconal teaching and introduced the possibility of choosing subjects of specialization.

However, there were different opinions and ambiguity as to what should be termed diaconal practice from the late 1960s onwards. In 1979, the rector of the nursing school claimed that "much of the uncertainty associated with the concept of *diakonia* must be seen in relation to the lack of contact with a diaconal field of practice and a poor systematization of methods in practical diakonia."[64] From his perspective, qualifying for diaconal work was the responsibility of the theological school. Hence, it was problematic that the theological teaching was primarily theoretical. On the contrary, the theology teachers argued that nursing was the most important practical-diaconal subject in *diakonia* education (Norwegian *diakonia* in the 1970s was still heavily associated with nursing).[65] They underscored that nursing education was not just a part of *diakonia* education but was itself *diakonia* education, together with the instruction at the theological school.

In the same period, the more church-centered definitions and aims of *diakonia*, together with the decision that only those who entered church positions could be ordained, meant that more students requested practice periods in the Church of Norway.[66] It was not clear what was considered diaconal methodology in church work. While former deacons were all educated as nurses and cared for sick people in the parish, the choice between nursing and social work, together with the introduction of government home helping services in 1969, called for a new deacon role.[67] Those deacons trained as social workers struggled to find ways to work through networking and community building. They felt they had a "different kind of identity" than the traditional nurse deacons, who visited people alone and entertained at senior get-togethers, as one source described it.[68] One

---

[61] Oftestad, *En Bok om kirkens diakoni [A Book about the Church's Diakonia]*, 40.
[62] MDA, *Hilsen fra Diakonhjemmet*, no. 1 (1980), 11.
[63] MDA, "Uttale frå Studentane ved Diatahs om Diakonutdanninga." Letter to the Executive board from the student boards; SU-Diatahs, SU-Diasos, and SU-Diasyk.
[64] MDA, Letter from Arild Skåra at Diakonhjemmets Sykepleierskole (Diasyk), March 1979.
[65] MDA, "Det Norske Diakonhjem, Diatahs, Lærerråd, Respons på Ny Skoleplan for Diasyk," 1980.
[66] Students in earlier years could ask to have a practice period in a Church of Norway parish, but it was also common to have all practice periods in hospitals, diaconal institutions, and private care.
[67] MDA, "Departementet for Familie -og Forbrukssaker. Retningslinjer for Statsstøttede Hjelpeordninger for Hjemmene," 7 January 1969.
[68] In-depth interview with a female social worker and deacon trained at Diakonhjemmet in the 1980s, conducted by Kristin Husby Dyrstad, 28 March 2022.

strategy to support students in their diaconal identity formation involved employing teachers at the school of theology who were social workers or nurses with additional theological education.

Conclusion

When the institution transitioned from a home model to a more profession-based model, the development of diaconal identity became more difficult. The older home model taught obedience and knowledge transfer, lacking emphasis on critical thinking.[69] More recent ideals for higher education include the ability to question, criticize, and examine one's own and other's contexts.[70] The strengthened knowledge base, research profile, and discussion between stakeholders at Diakonhjemmet in the 1970s and 1980s increased the critical competence of *diakonia* students. However, there was ambiguity about what was to be regarded as diaconal methods and practice, even as research played a strong role in granting identity within the professions.[71] Despite the formation of more critical professionals, the overall conclusion was that Diakonhjemmet terminated traditional formative elements connected to campus life, calling, and collective ordination without replacing them with new ones during this period of growth and academization. The space for formation was not sufficiently redeveloped for new times.

What can future *diakonia* education in Scandinavia, North America, and other contexts learn from this Norwegian case? When the Norwegian Association of Deacons celebrated its 100th anniversary in 2015, Dag Rakli, a former student and teacher from Diakonhjemmet, asked whether the current space for formation could have been larger if formation had been defined as an overarching concept in *diakonia* education all the way along.[72] After exploring historical sources, my conclusion aligns with his view and that of the Carnegie research proposal that higher education institutions should define their educational mission to include formation in addition to the intellectual and practical aims.[73] Like theological preparation for pastoral ministry, preparation for diaconal ministry involves questions of meaning, purpose, and identity to a larger extent than preparation for most other occupations. The young academic field of diaconal studies

---

[69] Central values in the "upbringing" in the Home were order, cleanliness, respect, obedience, and willingness to serve. Nordseth, *Det Norske Diakonhjem [The Norwegian Diakonhjem]*.

[70] Bernt Gustavsson, *Bildningens dynamik: framväxt, dimensioner, mening [The Dynamics of Education: Emergence, Dimensions, Meaning]* (Gothenburg: Bokförlaget Korpen, 2017); Sullivan and Rosin, *A New Agenda for Higher Education*, xvi.

[71] Bäckström, "Diakoner med annan arbetsgivare än Svenska Kyrkan" [Deacons with Employers other than the Church of Sweden], 8.

[72] Dag Rakli, "Diakoni og Dannelse" [Diakonia and Formation], in *Det Norske Diakonforbund – gjennom 100 år [The Norwegian Association of Deacons: Through a Hundred Years]*, ed. Leiv Sigmund Hope (Oslo: Det Norske Diakonforbund, 2015), 30.

[73] Sullivan and Rosin, *A New Agenda for Higher Education*; see also Foster et al., *Educating Clergy*, 5.

naturally emphasizes expanding the knowledge base and raising the scientific level in its effort to grow. Nevertheless, when new curricula are developed, the goal of identity formation and implementation of practical and formative elements must be given attention, not hidden deep within the planning documents.

One way to strengthen the formative elements is to focus explicitly on coherence. Diakonhjemmet's curricular history shows that the institution persistently aimed at coherence in its interdisciplinary *diakonia* education and refused to abandon this goal, although they struggled to succeed. Current research on educational programmes in academic and professionalized contexts highlights the importance of developing programme coherence among different parts of the curriculum and between theory and practice.[74] For students to experience coherence, teachers in diaconal theological education should have experience in the field of diaconal practice, not only theoretical competence. When new pedagogies for *diakonia* are constructed, attention must be given to: 1) the interaction and integration between students and teachers, 2) balance between classroom learning and contextual placements, 3) the relationship between faith and academic knowledge, and 4) the connection between education for diaconal studies and the "first" profession for which students are trained. History has shown us that the willingness to adapt to new contexts and needs is strong in the diaconal field, which is promising for future curriculum development.

Works Cited

Angell, Olav Helge. "Diakoniforståing og identitet hos diakonar i Den Norske Kyrkja" [Diaconal Understanding and Identity among Deacons in the Church of Norway]. In *Diakonen – kall og profesjon [The Deacon: Calling and Profession]*, edited by Stephanie Dietrich, Kari Karsrud Korslien, and Kjell Nordstokke, 187–204. Trondheim: Tapir Akademisk, 2011.

Benner, Patricia. *Educating Nurses: A Call for Radical Transformation*. Preparation for the Professions Series, vol. 3. San Francisco, CA: Jossey-Bass, 2010.

Brodd, Sven-Erik. "The Deacon in the Church of Sweden." In *The Ministry of the Deacon. Anglican–Lutheran Perspectives*, edited by Gunnel Borgegård and Christine Hall, 97–140. Uppsala: Nordic Ecumenical Council, 1999.

Bäckström, Anders. "Diakoner med annan arbetsgivare än Svenska Kyrkan" [Deacons with Employers other than the Church of Sweden]. In *Diakoni och samhälle [Diakonia and Society]*, edited by Thomas Ekstrand, 1–10. Uppsala: Diakonivitenskapliga Institutet i Uppsala, 2001.

Dietrich, Stephanie. "Diakontjenesten i et økumenisk perspektiv" [The Ministry of Deacons in an Ecumenical Perspective]. in *Diakonen – kall og profesjon [The Deacon: Calling and Profession]*, edited by Stephanie Dietrich, Kari Karsrud Korslien, and Kjell Nordstokke, 127–51. Trondheim: Tapir Akademisk, 2011.

---

[74] Smeby and Sutphen, *From Vocational to Professional Education*.

———. "Forståelsen av diakonitjenesten i Den Norske Kirke" [The Understanding of Diaconal Ministry in the Church of Norway]. In *Diakonen – kall og profesjon [The Deacon: Calling and Profession]*, edited by Stephanie Dietrich, Kari Karsrud Korslien, and Kjell Nordstokke, 111–26. Trondheim: Tapir Akademisk, 2011.

Dietrich, Stephanie, Kari Karsrud Korslien, and Kjell Nordstokke, eds. *Diakonen – kall og profesjon [The Deacon: Calling and Profession]*. Trondheim: Tapir Akademisk, 2011.

Dietrich, Stephanie, Knud Jørgensen, Kari Karsrud Korslien, and Kjell Nordstokke. "Introduction: Diakonia as Christian Social Practice." In *Diakonia as Christian Social Practice: An Introduction*, edited by Stephanie Dietrich, Knud Jørgensen, Kari Karsrud Korslien, and Kjell Nordstokke, 1–9. Oxford: Regnum Books International, 2014.

Fanuelsen, Olav. "Diakoner i Den Norske Kirke – et historisk tilbakeblikk" [Deacons in the Church of Norway: A Historical Retrospective]. In *Diakonen – kall og profesjon [The Deacon: Calling and Profession]*, edited by Stephanie Dietrich, Kari Karsrud Korslien, and Kjell Nordstokke, 87–96. Trondheim: Tapir Akademisk, 2011.

Foster, Charles R., Lisa E. Dahill, Lawrence A. Golemon, and Barbara Wang Tolentino. *Educating Clergy: Teaching Practices and Pastoral Imagination*. Preparation for the Professions Series Vol. 1. San Francisco: Jossey-Bass, 2006.

Gustavsson, Bernt. *Bildningens dynamik: framväxt, dimensioner, mening [The Dynamics of Education: Emergence, Dimensions, Meaning]*. Gothenburg: Bokförlaget Korpen, 2017.

Heiervang, Sigurd. *Tro og tjeneste. Et festskrift ved Det Norske Diakonhjems 75-års-jubileum [Faith and Service. For the Celebration of Diakonhjemmet's 75th Anniversary]*. Oslo: Det Norske Diakonhjem, 1965.

Johannessen, Kai Ingolf. "Diakontjenestens plassering i kirken" [The Position of the Deacon Ministry in the Church]. In *Diakoni – en kritisk lesebok [Diakonia: A Critical Textbook]*, edited by Kai Ingolf Johannessen, Kari Jordheim and Kari Karsrud Korslien, 29–43. Trondheim: Tapir Akademisk, 2009.

Martinsen, Kari. *Freidige og uforsagte diakonisser: et omsorgsyrke vokser fram, 1860–1905 [Courageous and Daring Deaconesses: A Caring Profession Develops, 1860–1905]*. Oslo: Aschehoug/Tanum-Norli, 1984.

Meland, Roar. "The Deacon in the Church of Norway." In *The Ministry of the Deacon: Anglican–Lutheran Perspectives*, edited by Gunnel Borgegård and Christine Hall, 59–96. Uppsala: Nordic Ecumenical Council, 1999.

Messel, Jan. *Profesjonsutdanninger i sentrum: fra jordmorutdanning til OsloMet 1818–2018 [Professional Education in the Centre: From Midwife Training to OsloMet 1818–2018]*. Oslo: PaxForlag A/S, 2022.

Moen, Harry. *Kallet og tjenesten: streif fra den mannlige diakonis historie i Norge [The Calling and the Service: Impressions from the History of the Male Diakonia in Norway]*. Oslo: Det norske Diakonforbund, 1977.

Nordstokke, Kjell. "The Study of Diakonia as an Academic Discipline." In *Diakonia as Christian Social Practice: An Introduction*, edited by Stephanie Dietrich, Knud Jørgensen, Kari Karsrud Korslien, and Kjell Nordstokke, 46–61. Oxford: Regnum Books International, 2014.

Nordseth, Thorleif. *Innføring i tjenesten. En liten håndbok for diakoner [Introduction to the Service: A Little Handbook for Deacons]*. Oslo: Det Norske Diakonhjem, 1943.

———. *Det Norske Diakonhjem 1890–1940 [The Norwegian Diakonhjem 1890–1940]*. Oslo: Det Norske Diakonhjem, 1940.

Nygaard, Marianne R. "Diakoners profesjonsvilkår i Den norske kirke" [Deacons' Professional Conditions in the Church of Norway]. Tidsskrift for Praktisk Teologi 28, no. 2 (2011): 32–46.

Oftestad, Alf B. *En bok om kirkens diakoni [A Book about the Church's Diakonia]*. Oslo: Luther, 1980.

Olofsgård, Katarina. "Professionell eller perspektivbärare? Om diakoners yrkesidentitet" [Professional or Perspective Carrier? About Deacons' Professional Identity]. Magistergrad. Stockholm: Ersta Sköndal Högskola, 2003.

Pädam, Tiit. *Ordination of Deacons in the Churches of the Porvoo Communion: A Comparative Investigation in Ecclesiology*. Uppsala: Kirjastus TP, 2011.

Rakli, Dag. "Diakoni og Dannelse" [Diakonia and formation], in *Det Norske Diakonforbund – gjennom 100 år [The Norwegian Association of Deacons: Through a Hundred Years]*, edited by Leiv Sigmund Hope, 26–31. Oslo: Det Norske Diakonforbund, 2015.

Smeby, Jens-Christian, and Molly Sutphen, eds. *From Vocational to Professional Education: Educating for Social Welfare*. Routledge Research in Higher Education, vol. 7. London: Routledge, 2015.

Stave, Gunnar. "Identitet og integrasjon: ein studie av ein diakonal institusjon med særleg vekt på ideologien, identiteten og integrasjonen i det offentlege velferdssystemet" [Identity and Integration: A Study of a Diaconal Institution with Particular Emphasis on Ideology, Identity and Integration in the Public Welfare System]. Trondheim: Norwegian University of Science and Technology, 1997.

———. *Mannsmot og Tenarsinn: Det Norske Diakonhjem i Hundre År [Courage and Servant Mind: The Norwegian Diakonhjemmet for One Hundred Years]*. Oslo: Samlaget, 1990.

Sullivan, William M., and Matthew S. Rosin. *A New Agenda for Higher Education: Shaping a Life of the Mind for Practice*. The Jossey-Bass Higher and Adult Education Series. San Francisco: Jossey-Bass, 2008.

Sutphen, Molly, and Thomas de Lange. "What Is Formation? A Conceptual Discussion." *Higher Education Research and Development* 34, no. 2 (2015): 411–19. https://doi.org/10.1080/07294360.2014.956690.

Teglund, Helene. "Diakoner med tjänst utanför Svenska Kyrkan" [Deacons with Service Outside the Church of Sweden]. In *Diakoni och samhälle [Diakonia and Society]*, edited by Thomas Ekstrand, 11–77. Uppsala: Diakonivetenskapliga Institutet i Uppsala, 2001.

Østnor, Lars. *Kirkens tjenester med særlig henblikk på diakontjenesten [Church Ministry with a Particular Emphasis on Deacon Ministry]*. Oslo: Luther, 1978.

Chapter 19

Investment in Diaconal Flourishing in The Episcopal Church

Lori Mills-Curran

In the last fifty years, widespread ecumenical consensus has been achieved that a call to serve the needs of the suffering world in the name of God is constitutive of Christian baptismal identity.[1] Scripture and tradition support this view, and denominations affirm its importance under a variety of titles: charity, outreach, Inner Mission, and so on. Whether fulfilling the responsibilities of this baptismal call to serve the world earns grace or is the fruit of it, there is ecumenical agreement that pursuing it is a responsibility of all the baptized. In recent years, the ecumenical world has increasingly utilized the Greek term *diakonia* to denote this work.

The Episcopal Church (US) distinguishes between the baptismal call to the work of *diakonia* and the diaconal call to the ordained leadership role.[2] It affirms a baptismal call to *diakonia*, asking each baptismal candidate to "seek and serve Christ in all persons" and to "strive for justice and peace."[3] Its 1979 rite of examination for diaconal ordination articulates the deacon's special vocation: "At all times, [the deacon's] life and teaching are to show Christ's people that in serving the helpless they are serving Christ himself."[4] It is now common for Episcopal authority to assert that deacons are essential stewards of the church's mission of *diakonia*. Diaconal leadership in and witness to the importance of fulfilling this responsibility is primary.

This chapter outlines how The Episcopal Church's denominational practices concerning the ordained diaconate do not adequately support deacons in this task of resourcing the people's call to *diakonia*. Of most concern are theological assumptions about ordained diaconal identity that undergird diaconal practice: that this order needs little organized support for its work; that provision of such supports can be left to each diocese; that deacons may be expected to fund their ministry supports from personal wealth; that diaconal support needs are quite similar to those of priests; and that certain social resources on which deacons have relied in the past will remain available to the next generation of deacons.

---

[1] *Baptism, Eucharist and Ministry*, Faith and Order Paper No. 111 (Geneva: World Council of Churches, 1982), Ministry III.C, para. 31.
[2] The Episcopal Church denotes the Province of the Anglican Communion headquartered in the United States of America. It includes eleven nations, not all of which are in North America.
[3] *The Book of Common Prayer and Administration of the Sacraments and Other Rites and Ceremonies of the Church* (New York: Church Publishing, 1979), 293–94.
[4] *Book of Common Prayer* (1979), 543.

Also of grave concern is a shadow legacy of unexamined racist and sexist influences on diaconal identity, which may extend invisibly to diaconal practice today. This chapter invites readers to consider how these factors influence Episcopal diaconal identity itself, and how that identity continues to be interpreted in ways that subject deacons to unique vocational stresses, attenuate their effectiveness, discourage vocations, and ultimately impede *diakonia*.

An Unexamined Economic Legacy

Much Episcopal reflection about ministry supports for deacons assumes that deacons wish such support to be similar to the professional compensation and associated benefits provided to priests. That is not the contention here.[5] At issue here is diaconal identity itself and whether a prior era's system of ministry supports, primarily designed for another order with another mission, is serviceable for diaconal needs today.

Episcopal concern for priestly ministry supports originated early in the twentieth century, stemming from the conviction that failure to provide them impeded the spread of the Gospel. Advocates argued that without them "the Church ... was guilty not only of neglect but of abuse."[6] By the mid-twentieth century, a model emerged: the priest was provided pension and medical insurance funded through parish assessments dispatched to the Church Pension Fund. Although parish compliance was made mandatory (after an early voluntary system had largely failed), it was uneven for some time. The Pension Fund expended great effort to educate participants about entitlements and increased benefits (carefully within the limits of good financial practice) to include life insurance, spiritual and psychological supports, financial advice, and investment opportunities for active participants from a variety of ministry settings.[7]

The Pension Fund was also deputized by General Convention to fulfil certain denominational functions, including serving as the official Recorder of Ordinations.[8] Each diocesan bishop was and remains responsible for transmitting

---

[5] While Episcopalians are usually startled to learn that most deacons across the globe are compensated professionals, Episcopal deacons are normally non-stipendiary volunteers, educated locally without seminary-based educational requirements. Any argument that urges professional compensation for deacons must grapple with the question of educational preparation.

[6] Harold C. Martin, *Outlasting Marble and Brass: The History of the Church Pension Fund* (New York: The Church Hymnal Corporation, 1986), 50, quoting James Hall McIlvaine in 1907.

[7] Priests working in roles traditionally seen as extensions of ministry (school, prison and hospital chaplaincy, nonprofit roles) are included through special arrangement with episcopal permission. The Pension Fund has recently become proactive in reaching out to priestly seminarians with educational and well-being resources funded by external grants.

[8] The General Convention is the institutional authority for Episcopal doctrine and practice.

ordination information to the Pension Fund, where its research department analyses the data to inform denominational planning.

Prior to 1952, all deacons were considered transitional – an "inferior order" of the traditional *cursus honorum* – apprentices on their way to the priesthood.[9] But from 1952 to 1970, slightly over 500 deacons who did not anticipate becoming priests were ordained specifically to help with the Baby Boom pastoral workload. These "perpetual deacons" were trained privately by a priest to help with liturgy, pastoral care, and sacramental preparation. With ordination restricted to an older age than that of priests, these volunteers were deployed for life to one parish and could not change dioceses. Their ordinations were generally not recorded.

This new identity for deacons as perpetual volunteer clerics created questions. Creating an order of unassessed clerics suggested vacillation in the Pension Fund's commitment to clerical financial support. The denomination made a way for the needed labor to be accepted: it adopted a canon that required perpetual deacon candidates to vow that they would not seek priesthood and would support themselves from personal wealth or secular employment.[10] These ministry conditions created the impression that the Episcopal diaconate is a retirement ministry, which is still widely assumed today.[11]

The perpetual deacon canon was short lived. As part of a widely documented post-World War II ecumenical phenomenon, the Episcopal diaconate was re-envisioned in the late 1960s in yet a new way. A new diaconal identity (often referred to as the vocational diaconate) was adopted at The Episcopal Church's 1970 General Convention. This diaconate's contours differed from both the transitional apprentice-priest diaconate and the newer model of perpetual volunteer assistant for one church. It envisioned deacons with a distinctively servant-oriented identity and is the model of the diaconate most Episcopalians are familiar with today. This vision came to full fruition with the changes made to diaconal vows in the 1979 Prayer Book.

An Unexamined Gender Legacy

But throughout the 1970s, the effort to create this new servant-oriented diaconal identity was entangled in arguments over women's ordination to the Episcopal priesthood. Some supported opening the ordained diaconate to women only because it confined them to a servant role suitable for their nature, a "religious

---

[9] *The Book of Common Prayer and the Administration of the Sacraments and other Rites and Ceremonies According to the Use of the Protestant Episcopal Church in the United States of America Together with the Psalter or Psalms of David* (New York: Church Pension Fund, 1929), 535.

[10] Susanne Watson Epting, *Unexpected Consequences: The Diaconate Renewed* (New York: Morehouse, 2015), 21.

[11] According to the most recent Church Pension Fund estimate, the average age of deacons is about seventy years of age.

extension of the ideal of true womanhood."[12] Other advocates, including most Episcopal deaconesses, envisioned a compensated order with a ministry focus in the world different than that of a pastor.[13] Still others, advocates of women's priesthood, accepted a female diaconate only as a transitional step to their final goal. At the General Convention in 1970, these varied advocates succeeded in opening an ordained diaconate to women and abolishing the category of consecrated Episcopal deaconesses.[14]

The new servant-oriented women deacons would be professionally educated (with standards similar to priests and deaconesses), could be compensated, and were eligible for pensions.[15] But until 1979, the Prayer Book continued the reference to the diaconate as an inferior order, and supporters of women's priestly ordination re-emphasized the subservient aspects of the deacon's servant identity.[16] In addition, acceptance of the new deacons implied a bishop's willingness to ordain women; thus, some bishops abstained.[17]

These debates complicated widespread adoption of the renewed diaconal identity and appear to have delayed thoughtful reflection on diaconal ministry needs as such. Although the church had opened the possibility of a different diaconate as a stipendiary position for women, the old canon lived on. Almost all vocational deacons continued as volunteers. Dioceses continued to fail to record diaconal ordinations. Deacons employed in church entities were told they were employed in a lay capacity and ineligible for clergy pension benefits.[18] As

---

[12] Pamela W. Darling, *New Wine: The Story of Women Transforming Leadership and Power in the Episcopal Church* (Cambridge, MA: Cowley, 1994), 108.

[13] Episcopal deaconesses were a 100-year-old consecrated and celibate vocation with extensive networks of women-led formation and training. They had long sought access to ministry supports but had not attained them. See chapters by Bailey and Noyes in this volume.

[14] Interestingly, deaconesses consecrated with the laying on of hands were "grandmothered" into the new identity without additional rites. This choice may prove significant for current discussions pertaining to the expansion of exchangeability of consecrated deacons of the Evangelical Lutheran Church in America with Episcopal deacons. See chapter by Budde in this volume.

[15] The 1970 Deacons' Canon allowed former deaconesses to continue in the pension plan provided for them mid-century, to remain in their pre-existing self-organized plan, or, revealingly, to access "some other pension plan ... providing better guarantees of a dependable retirement income." Women deacons ordained after 1971 were to be included in the Pension Fund available to other professionally trained clerics, despite the fact that priesthood was not anticipated for them. "Constitution and Canons Together with the Rules of Order," The Episcopal Church, Office of the General Convention, 1970, Title III, Canon 50, section 7, p. 94, https://www.episcopalarchives.org/governance-documents/constitution-and-canons.

[16] See chapter by Bailey in this volume.

[17] Under a "conscience clause" arranged by the House of Bishops soon after adoption of the 1976 canon allowing women's priesthood, bishops who dissented were allowed to abstain from such ordinations indefinitely. This practice was disallowed in 1997.

[18] These practices have been and remain common; however, they contravene canon law and have no basis in Pension Fund regulations. Since a few vocational deacons had crept into compensated employment, canon law was changed in 1990 to require all

the Pension Fund provided a wider variety of ministerial supports, the contrast between priests' well-organized, assessment-funded denominational supports and those provided to deacons became greater. A definitive new theology, which obscured the need for providing ministry supports for deacons, grew up as well.

An Unexamined Theological Legacy

As the issue of women's priestly ordination calmed, deacon numbers increased. However, there remained significant practical impediments to deacon access to ministry supports. Many dioceses assumed that inclusion in local priestly supports was sufficient.[19] And as the servant-identified deacons consolidated the contours of the renewed identity on the ground, much was made of their *individual* call to kenotic self-emptying.

The 1979 Prayer Book revisions of diaconal ordination vows lent credibility to this theology. While it had abandoned the 1928 Prayer Book's language of "inferior order," this Prayer Book continued to exhort deacons to be "modest and humble."[20] The value of deacons to the church was often explained as intrinsically vested in diaconal humility. Advocates of the new diaconate held that deacons were called to "personify the servant character of the entire church."[21] The deacon "as symbol ... represents the infinite in finite forms as a human being" and should expect the "suffering inherent in such tension."[22] Following the scholarship of the day, the seven ministers set aside in Acts were assumed to be humble table waiters. This theology has significantly informed diaconal identity and spirituality and remains strong among Episcopal deacons today.

The emphasis on humility as the defining feature of diaconal identity was called into question, however, through new biblical research in the 1990s. John N. Collins showed that the scriptural platform upon which the church's new servant-identified diaconal theology relied was a mistranslation. Tracing every available contemporaneous use of *daikon-* root words, Collins demonstrated that biblical diaconal identity had little to do with humble servanthood. It was better interpreted as "authorized agent" or "envoy."[23] Collins's work provided a

---

compensated deacons to be assessed if they made above certain mandatory minimums. "Constitution and Canons," 1988, Title III, Canon 6, section 10, 67.
[19] Neither the cost of events, such as required clergy conferences, nor their inconvenience to persons employed outside of the church was generally considered.
[20] *Book of Common Prayer* (1979), 545.
[21] John E. Booty, *The Servant Church: Diaconal Ministry and the Episcopal Church* (Wilton, CT: Morehouse, 1982), 80.
[22] Booty, 80. This kenotic diaconal identity influences many aspects of diaconal experience, including restrictions on deacon use of common symbols of clerical authority (clothing and titles). Debates also flourished about deacons voting as clerics in church councils; practice is still inconsistent, despite adoption of a 2006 canon intended to settle the debate. See "Constitution and Canons," 2022, Title III, Canon 7, section 4(e).
[23] John N. Collins's published contributions on this subject are both technical and voluminous. A relatively accessible recent summary of his insights is found in *Diakonia*

welcome tool for deacons to make sense of diaconal identity through the lens of liberation theology. They were eager to make the most of their new call, first identified in the 1979 Prayer Book: "to interpret to the Church the needs, concerns, and hopes of the world."[24] They began to identify their "prophetic voice."[25]

Implications for diaconal ministry supports were severe. As Episcopal deacons moved out of the parish to exercise their special prophetic voice in service and advocacy for the poor and marginalized, the natural supports flowing to the beloved perpetual deacons and their families in their settled placements vanished. The 1979 rite called deacons "to a special ministry of servanthood directly under your bishop."[26] This language affected diaconal placement practices, as bishops began to deploy deacons as their special envoys. On a practical level, this meant that deacons might have little input as to where they were placed or their length of assignment. Terms of one to three years were common.

For a retired couple, or a single deacon, this new requirement was manageable. But the new prophetic diaconal identity also had increasing appeal to the young, and the minimum age for ordination was eventually reduced to twenty-four years of age. Young deacons were much more likely to have children in the home but often had to choose between denying their spouse and children consistent Christian community with its proper formation or leaving them behind. Unless they had economic privilege, they continued their secular employment. Piling identity upon identity (liturgical assistant, servant in the parish, advocate for the poor) increased deacon stress.

Discussion of the economic impact of the diaconate on earning capacity, or even trying to claim ministry expenses, was often deemed inappropriate in diaconal circles, indicative of poor commitment.[27] Some deacons now worried that their prophetic voice might be muted if they became financially entangled with the church in any way. Such assumptions may also underlie how even relatively inexpensive denominational or diocesan supports for deacons have been slow to develop. Many bishops developed excellent local programmes of support, but practices were always dependent on each (new) diocesan bishop's assumptions about diaconal identity and needs – and subject to the demands of a busy bishop's schedule.

As the renewed diaconate gained acceptance, the membership-funded Association for Episcopal Deacons assumed leadership in articulation of best

---

Studies: Critical Issues in Ministry (Oxford: Oxford University Press, 2014), 3–36. The Episcopal Church was an early adopter of Collins's insights since it was promulgated by Ormonde Plater in his seminal diaconal text, *Many Servants: An Introduction to Deacons* (Lanham, MD: Cowley, 1990).

[24] *Book of Common Prayer* (1979), 543.

[25] Susanne Watson Epting, *Prophetic Voice of the Deacon*, Monograph Series 19 (Providence, RI: North American Association for the Diaconate, 2008).

[26] *Book of Common Prayer* (1979), 543.

[27] This implicit shaming of deacons about financial concerns fragments the diaconal community and is deeply resented by deacons of lesser means.

practices for deacon support and formation.[28] As early as 1978, the Association applied for grants to fund research on deacon formation and wellbeing. It published theological monographs and built systems of support and training for deacon supervisors. Aware of inconsistent diaconal recording practices, the Association employed staff to serve as a de facto diaconal Recorder for twenty years. By 2003, the Association advocated successfully for a new canon, informed by thirty years of diaconal practice, proposing formation practices from a diaconal rather than seminary-oriented priestly perspective and recommending a model for diocesan support structures.[29] In 2008, the Association again secured funding for academic research about diaconal practice.[30] In 2017, after convening practitioners and scholars to develop them, the Association released implementation standards for the new formation canon.[31]

The burdens of making themselves and their ministry needs visible to their denomination continue largely to be borne by deacons themselves. Somehow, whether deacons are considered servants or prophets, the ministry support considerations related to diaconal identity remain the same. Whether out of servant humility or respect for their prophetic voice, deacons' lack of access to any well-established denominational supports, or indeed comprehensive denominational attention to their needs at all, seemed theologically correct.

An Unexamined Racial Legacy

In the summer of 2020, Episcopalians in the United States watched as George Floyd's death fired Christian consciences anew to support anti-racism efforts. Many dioceses initiated or buttressed efforts to unearth the ways in which the church has been complicit in institutionalized racism.[32] Research indicates that

---

[28] Previously known as the North American Association for the Diaconate, the Association was founded in 1974 to advocate for the acceptance of the order. (As of January 2024, two dioceses remain without deacons.) As noted above, standards for diaconal formation in 1970 had envisioned professional formation similar to priests, satisfying both deaconesses and advocates for women's priestly ordination. The standard was widely remarked as unfair to a *volunteer* vocation.

[29] "Constitution and Canons," 2006, Title III, section 7, "Of the Life and Work of Deacons." The canon recommends appointment of an archdeacon to oversee deacon affairs, formation of a deacons' council of practitioners and theologians to develop policy and formation, regularly gathering the deacons' community for education and mutual support, and required post-ordination mentoring. The number of dioceses implementing these recommendations is unknown.

[30] "Deacons and Their Ministries in the Episcopal Church: As Reported by Deacons in 2008 & 1978," Draft 2, 19 March 2009, https://www.episcopaldeacons.org/uploads/2/6/7/3/26739998/deaconsministries.pdf.

[31] Association for Episcopal Deacons, *Competencies for Deacons 2017*, rev. 2018, https://www.episcopaldeacons.org/uploads/2/6/7/3/26739998/cmptnc17rv1-18.pdf. See also chapter by Lytle in this volume, describing how these competencies are guiding one seminary's provision of diaconal formation.

[32] "Episcopalians Confront Hard Truths about the Episcopal Church's Role in Slavery, Black History," The Episcopal Church, 28 February 2018,

the Episcopal response to early abolitionist arguments about the Bible's acceptance of slavery was vastly problematic.[33] This knowledge had undergirded the denomination's support for civil rights in the 1960s and lends energy to today's vigorous anti-racism efforts. Yet, racist legacies continue to shadow diaconal identity today.

Episcopal clerics of color have faced innumerable hurdles in ministry. Among them was systematic use of the inferior order of the diaconate to constrain Black men's ministries. "Most Southern bishops advised black ministerial candidates to aspire only to deacon's orders [and] not only relegated black men to a 'perpetual colored (*sic*) diaconate' but tacitly encouraged them to seek full ordination in other denominations."[34]

The life of Peter Williams Cassey (1831–1917) illustrates how diaconal status was used. Ordained in 1863 as a "missionary deacon" (in the euphemism of his day), Cassey was an abolitionist, educator, church planter, and rector of several churches. He sought priestly ordination but was rejected in three dioceses for overtly racist reasons, despite Episcopal support.[35]

Cassey's achievements were memorialized in 2018 by inclusion in The Episcopal Church's list of saints.[36] The significance of his case is that even though his illustrious career was accomplished as a deacon, he was memorialized *as a priest*. The mistake was only rectified in 2022, when a successor diocese of one of the three that had rejected Cassey's application for priesthood brought it to the attention of the General Convention. The easy utilization of the deacon's inferior identity as a tool of racism was still invisible well into the twenty-first century.

Much more work is needed for The Episcopal Church to reflect on how these former practices resonate with people of color and how they influence diaconal discernment today. "Colorblindness" to the economic and institutional implications of officially long-abandoned policies must be addressed in the church as well as in the nation.[37] Failing to apprehend the racial implications of former diaconal identities is no longer a viable denominational posture.

---

https://www.episcopalchurch.org/racialreconciliation/episcopalians-confront-hard-truths-about-the-episcopal-churchs-role-in-slavery-black-history/. Well into the twentieth century, The Episcopal Church had parallel interior structures for Black people. Black bishops also did not have authority equal to whites.

[33] Gardiner H. Shattuck Jr., *Episcopalians and Race: Civil War to Civil Rights* (Lexington, KY: University Press of Kentucky, 2000), 7–55.

[34] Shattuck, 16–17.

[35] "C010: Amending Biographical Information for the Feast of Peter Williams Cassey and Annie Besant Cassey," Virtual Binder 2022, The 80th General Convention of The Episcopal Church, https://2022.vbinder.net/resolutions/123?house=HD&lang=en.

[36] "The Lectionary Page: Lesser Feasts and Fasts, 2022, April 16," https://lectionarypage.net/CalndrsIndexes/TxtIndexLFF.html.

[37] One issue needing exploration is assessing the effect of racial restrictions on Native American deacons. See, for example, the Bishop of South Dakota's suggestion that pensions of such "missionary deacons" be half that of whites. Martin, *Outlasting Marble and Brass*, 279n5.

Next Steps

Responding to the recent decline in full-time priestly employment in the church, the Pension Fund significantly broadened eligibility for clerical participation in 2018.[38] These changes effectively swept most deacons into benefit eligibility – if they receive any compensation at all. The implications have only slowly percolated through the Episcopal community, with many deacons becoming aware for the first time of the benefits offered.[39] Could a practical means be found to allow deacons access to some of the robust supports provided by the Pension Fund? By law, the Pension Fund cannot provide services of any kind to unassessed individuals. The Diocese of Vermont was the first to adopt a diocesan resolution requiring churches to provide a minimal sum of assessed compensation to all deacons as a means of overcoming this barrier.[40]

Advocates of these resolutions still envision a diaconate in which most deacons earn a living primarily from non-church sources. None of the current resolutions ask for generalized diaconal compensation at a market rate. Instead, these resolutions advocate for something completely different than The Episcopal Church has ever had – a share of the resources gathered through the thrift of their forebears, creatively distributed through old structures to serve the specific needs of a new model of lifelong ministry.[41] Minimal compensation resolutions are most accurately understood as mechanisms by which the church uses current systems to attend to the spiritual and financial planning needs of a new model of lifelong ordained ministry while respecting the legal constraints governing the old system. Current practice envisions only one model for the embrace of a lifelong ministry, even as another lifelong ministry with different contours has come into its own.

The Episcopal Church could devise other models to assume some level of denominational responsibility for diaconal wellbeing.[42] However, minimal

---

[38] The Church Pension Group eliminated mandatory minimum compensation for pension eligibility and adopted a definition of "employment" much broader than that of employment law.

[39] In the process, many discovered that their ordinations were never recorded. The Pension Fund has been extraordinarily attentive to this issue since 2015. Their success was such that the Association discontinued its role as de facto diaconal Recorder in 2023.

[40] Usually $25/month plus $4.50 in assessments is requested. For resolution text, see Deacons of the Diocese of Vermont, "Amendment to Resolution Establishing Minimum Clergy Compensation Regarding Compensation to Deacons," n.d., https://www.episcopaldeacons.org/uploads/2/6/7/3/26739998/vt20-dcnresltn.pdf.

[41] Some deacons do advocate for similar compensation, but others argue our practice of local deacon formation is a preadaptation to current trends in which seminary-based, twentieth-century training standards are proving unsustainable, with bivocational ministry becoming the new norm.

[42] The Pension Fund provides grant-funded programming to unassessed seminarians and could do so for deacons. The denomination could partner with the Association for Episcopal Deacons or the charity Fund for the Diaconate to assess needs. General Convention testimony in 2024 solicited such financial support, according to Maureen Hagen, personal communication, 1 February 2024.

compensation arrangements offer one significant advantage: they render the denomination's deacons fully *visible*. Two factors obscure deacon visibility within the denomination: the lingering number of unrecorded deacons and the low number of deacons active in the Pension Fund. It is only through disciplined recordation and the provision of active pension status that the needs of deacons will become visible to The Episcopal Church in a comprehensive way. This is because The Episcopal Church uses its Recordation and Pension Fund active participation databases as the sources of information for its well-established and professionally staffed research department. Its research conclusions are authoritatively accepted throughout The Episcopal Church to inform denominational priorities. Thus, while alternative models of providing for diaconal needs might be effective, they would not accord deacons the visibility necessary for inclusion in long-range denominational planning. Considering deacons in such planning will allow The Episcopal Church to assess the unique needs of the lively emerging community of younger deacons. Although many still assume the diaconate is a retirement ministry, the order has great appeal among the young, who worry about the diaconate's financial impact on their family's finances.

Young deacons anticipate a cloudy future for the many social supports that enabled the previous generation of deacons to accept a diaconal call. They share a well-founded concern about the viability of Social Security and Medicare. In their experience, employer-provided retirement assistance is minimal: fixed-benefit plans are unknown, and matching funds for savings are minimal or non-existent. Many are making their way in the gig economy or at cash-strapped nonprofits with limited medical insurance. Home ownership and children seem beyond financial possibility, and student debt overshadows all discernment. From this perspective, the benefits to be secured from long-term minimal active participation in the Pension Fund (professionally managed investment opportunities, small pensions, and subsidized, high-quality spiritual and personal ministry supports) are deemed significant. In sum, young deacons experience the current Episcopal diaconate as functionally reserved for the wealthy.

The number of Episcopal deacons is growing apace, and the primary goal of this chapter is to render their struggles visible. Deacons incarnate what the "nones" want the church to become: less hierarchical, frugal with the church's resources, freed to focus on the world's needs, resolved to equip the people of God for hopeful service, and deeply committed to the belief that God will provide for the church if baptismal servanthood is faithfully grasped. The diaconate can be an even more powerful tool in the hands of a holy God if The Episcopal Church implements a theology of deacon identity that renders deacons and their needs visible. Then the church can conscientiously design diaconal practice as it is needed today rather than perpetuate inapplicable models or unworthy past legacies. Only then will deacons, and the *diakonia* deacons are called to steward on behalf of the church, flourish as God desires.

Works Cited

Association for Episcopal Deacons. *Competencies for Deacons 2017*. Rev. 2018. https://www.episcopaldeacons.org/uploads/2/6/7/3/26739998/cmptnc17rv1-18.pdf.

The Book of Common Prayer and Administration of the Sacraments and Other Rites and Ceremonies of the Church. New York: Church Publishing, 1979.

The Book of Common Prayer and the Administration of the Sacraments and other Rites and Ceremonies According to the Use of the Protestant Episcopal Church in the United States of America Together with the Psalter or Psalms of David. New York: Church Pension Fund, 1929.

Booty, John E. *The Servant Church: Diaconal Ministry and the Episcopal Church*. Wilton, CT: Morehouse, 1982.

"C010: Amending Biographical Information for the Feast of Peter Williams Cassey and Annie Besant Cassey." Virtual Binder 2022. The 80th General Convention of The Episcopal Church. https://2022.vbinder.net/resolutions/123?house=HD&lang=en.

Collins, John N. *Diakonia Studies: Critical Issues in Ministry*. Oxford: Oxford University Press, 2014.

"Constitution and Canons Together with the Rules of Order." The Episcopal Church, Office of the General Convention. 1970, 1988, 2006, 2022. https://www.episcopalarchives.org/governance-documents/constitution-and-canons.

Darling, Pamela W. *New Wine: The Story of Women Transforming Leadership and Power in the Episcopal Church*. Cambridge, MA: Cowley, 1994.

"Deacons and Their Ministries in the Episcopal Church: As Reported by Deacons in 2008 & 1978." Draft 2, 19 March 2009. https://www.episcopaldeacons.org/uploads/2/6/7/3/26739998/deaconsministries.pdf.

Deacons of the Diocese of Vermont. "Amendment to Resolution Establishing Minimum Clergy Compensation Regarding Compensation to Deacons." n.d. https://www.episcopaldeacons.org/uploads/2/6/7/3/26739998/vt20-dcnresltn.pdf.

"Episcopalians Confront Hard Truths about the Episcopal Church's Role in Slavery, Black History." The Episcopal Church. 28 February 2018. https://www.episcopalchurch.org/racialreconciliation/episcopalians-confront-hard-truths-about-the-episcopal-churchs-role-in-slavery-black-history/.

Epting, Susanne Watson. *Prophetic Voice of the Deacon*. Monograph Series 19. Providence, RI: North American Association for the Diaconate, 2008.

———. *Unexpected Consequences: The Diaconate Renewed*. New York: Morehouse, 2015.

"The Lectionary Page: Lesser Feasts and Fasts, 2022, April 16." https://lectionarypage.net/CalndrsIndexes/TxtIndexLFF.html.

Martin, Harold C. *Outlasting Marble and Brass: The History of The Church Pension Fund*. New York: The Church Hymnal Corporation, 1986.

Plater, Ormonde. *Many Servants: An Introduction to Deacons*. Lanham, MD: Cowley, 1990.
Shattuck, Gardiner H. Jr. *Episcopalians and Race: Civil War to Civil Rights*. Lexington, KY: University Press of Kentucky, 2000.
World Council of Churches. *Baptism, Eucharist and Ministry*. Faith and Order Paper No. 111. Geneva: World Council of Churches, 1982.

Chapter 20

A Competency-Based, Mentor-Assessed Path for Diaconal Formation

Julie Anne Lytle

Episcopal deacons within the United States are typically older (over 55 years), white, and financially well off. While most bishops say they want to attract younger people to diaconal ministry, traditional models of preparation are not conducive to millennials and gen-z lifestyles. The Episcopal Church faces membership declines and the subsequent reduction of finances and staff, ageing clergy, and shrinking enrolment of candidates for ordained ministry. Potential students struggle to balance a desire for theological education, the likelihood of a move to a residential campus and the losses it can spawn (especially home, income, and community), and the probability of significant debt. To address these challenges, a group of Episcopal dioceses are collaborating with an Episcopal Seminary, Bexley Seabury, to initiate a paradigm shift. With an ever-expanding list of new digital technologies, many post-pandemic users' have increased their comfort using computers to connect with family, church, and work. This development prompts school administrators and diocesan leaders to explore distributive learning, fueling the development of an innovative new model of theological education and diaconal formation.

This chapter introduces the Deacons Formation Collaborative and the innovative competency-based, mentor-assessed, diaconal preparation process its members launched in October 2023. It establishes the context that nurtured the Collaborative's emergence and explores four particular currents that influenced decisions and design: the expansion of competency-based theological education (CBTE) and more learner-centric educational models; the introduction of competencies for ministry and discipleship; Bexley Seabury's transformation to a seminary-beyond-walls that prepares all the baptized for ministry; and shifting diocesan financial and human resources expanding opportunities for collaboration. It describes the curriculum, which requires collaboration between a seminary and a diocese, as well as insights gleaned while trying to design and provide a cost-effective, student-directed, time-flexible diaconal preparation for students to prepare in and for their contexts. The chapter concludes by establishing how this process encourages a common diaconal theology, consistent formation requirements across The Episcopal Church, and sensitivity to the needs of dioceses with few postulants and/or limited resources.

Contextual Currents and Planting Seeds

The seeds of the Collaborative were planted when I was hired as an associate professor to direct Bexley Seabury Seminary's distributive and lifelong learning initiatives in 2018. My conviction that digital and educational technologies could be harnessed to provide those seeking theological education and ministerial formation with the needed and desired resources no matter where the learner or the resources were located matched the school's desire to transform into a seminary-beyond-walls. We initiated a year of listening to hear where the Spirit was calling us.

In January 2019, a group of deacons and deacon educators met in "the Deacons Summit" to consider whether and how Bexley Seabury could support deacons and deacon formation in The Episcopal Church. The deacons and deacon educators were interested especially in education and formation tailored to prophetic witness in the world – but only if the school demonstrated that it was committed to *diaconal* formation. Rather than participate in offerings designed for those preparing for priestly ordination, they were hungry for resources that used a diaconal lens.

They also wanted to ensure that our offerings were flexible, affordable, accessible, and adaptable. While these goals are common in distributed learning environments, Collaborative members wanted to define them in ways that express their significance within the diaconal community. *Flexible* ensures that students can start when they are ready (multiple admissions points) and will fit within one's life that likely includes commitments to family, church, work, and self. Unfortunately, many programmes make students wait until the start of a school year no matter when they were welcomed as a postulant and often have required monthly physical gatherings for two or more years. *Affordable* seeks to break patterns established by the non-stipendiary model of diaconal ministry that typically attracts only those who are financially secure and/or retired. *Accessible* touches a variety of aspects including geography, culture, language, education, technology, and other support systems – aspects that disproportionally affect participants from marginalized communities. *Adaptable* allows for personalization and customization, recognizing a student's prior learning and enhancing preparation to serve in a chosen context. The group also wanted to be assured that deacons would be valued as contributors to the school's governance and instruction. These principles established a foundation for Bexley Seabury and its partners to create a competency-based, mentor-assessed, personalized diaconal formation process as well as a platform for sharing resources.

Competency-Based Theological Education (CBTE)

Competency-based education (CBE) emerged in the 1960s and 1970s as educators embraced a more learner-centric model of education. Rather than a teacher-driven, scope-and-sequence set of academic content or courses, students master outcomes identified for defined results, typically at a self-defined pace. These shifts reflect what we know about adult learning, which typically is more effective when students: are involved in planning and evaluating their learning experiences; integrate what they are learning with prior life experience; identify connections between their personal and professional lives; and find learning applicable in practical ways.¹ Although there is no universally accepted definition, a correlation of theory and practice is at the heart of CBE and can be traced to the 1862 Morrill Land-Grant Acts, which "provided the basis for an *applied education* oriented to the needs of farm and townspeople *who could not attend the more exclusive and prestigious universities and colleges of the eastern United States.*"² Shifts during the Industrial Age introduced skills-focused training to equip learners for the demands and needs of particular jobs. Multiple learning theories converged into what we now generally call CBE.

An article by J. Gervais provides an excellent introduction to the theoretical foundations of CBE, based on the contributions of behaviorists, functionalists, and humanistic theorists. These include:

- the introduction of measurable learning objectives linked with assessments that shift curricular focus from content-centered to student-centered learning;
- correlations between a student's ability to learn and an instructor's quality of teaching;
- the introduction of "mastery learning" and the argument that most students (90 percent) can master what is taught;
- studies on instruction delivery and self-paced learning;
- the introduction of learning modules to break down learning outcomes into specific activities that prepare a student to demonstrate proficiency;
- the shift from group learning to individualized learning that adapts to a student's ability, learning style, and learning pace; and
- the introduction of backward design as a curriculum development approach that starts with the end in mind (what will the learner need upon completion), identifies the components for reaching that end, then creates a path that outlines the steps for a learner to prepare.³

These qualities have driven a brisk spread of CBE programmes, particularly those geared toward specific career outcomes, as educators and corporate leaders seek to make learning more accessible, equitable, and financially attainable.

Not surprisingly, the growing embrace of competency-based outcomes has influenced conversations not only about secular education but also about theological education. In 2015, the Association of Theological Schools began studying emerging

---

¹ German educator Alexander Kapp introduced andragogy in 1833 to refer to adult learning by using "the Greek word for man leading or teaching (*andra*) instead of the Greek word for child (*peda*)." American educator Malcolm Knowles (1913–1997) popularized andragogy and developed the foundational theories of this "art and science of helping adults learn." Malcolm Knowles, *The Modern Practice of Adult Education: From Pedagogy to Andragogy* (Chicago: Follet, 1980), 43.
² Frank W. Clark, "Characteristics of the Competency-Based Curriculum," in *Competency-Based Education for Social Work: Evaluation and Curriculum Issues*, eds. Morton L. Arkava and E. Clifford Brennen (New York: Council on Social Work Education, 1976), 23, emphasis added.
³ J. Gervais, "The Operational Definition of Competency-Based Education," *The Journal of Competency-Based Education* 1, no. 2 (June 2016): 98–106, https://doi.org/10.1002/cbe2.1011.

educational models, including CBE, for forming religious leaders. Member schools referred to it as Competency-Based *Theological* Education (CBTE) to recognize that while mastery of knowledge is necessary, so is personal and pastoral formation. CBTE emphasizes learning over classroom time, mastery of professionally oriented competencies, well-planned learning activities or assessments (class-based or not, online or onsite) that students may complete at their own pace, and a community of learning in which regular and substantive interaction occurs between qualified faculty and students.[4] Even though The Episcopal Church's standards for diaconal education and formation are not governed by the Association for Theological School's degree standards, and most Episcopal dioceses do not require deacons to complete an academic degree, the Association's insights about CBTE are benefitting everyone engaged in ministry preparation.

Anglican and Episcopal Competencies for Ministry and Discipleship

A competency-based view of preparation for Episcopal diaconal ministry was evident in the North American Association for the Diaconate's guidelines for diocesan diaconate programmes as early as the late 1980s.[5] In 1997, the North American Association's president, Susanne Watson (Susanne Watson Epting after her 2001 marriage), renewed a commitment to develop guidelines for diaconal formation; she wanted to assist dioceses that lacked deacon formation and was concerned that unique diaconal training in each diocese inadvertently created "a diocesan order, rather than an order for the whole church."[6] When the Anglican Communion primates established the Theological Education for the Anglican Communion workgroup in 2001 to provide guidelines for the theological education, Watson Epting was invited to join.

Between 2003 and 2006, the group's task force created a holistic model of intellectual, practical, emotional, and spiritual formation.[7] Embracing an outcomes-based model for education, they led a shift from a focus on what a person needs to know to what competencies a learner needs to gain in order to fulfil this or that task/job/vocation. Five "Ministry Grids" identify competencies

---

[4] "'Let's Begin with the End in Mind': Competency-Based Theological Education," in *Educational Models and Practices Peer Group Final Reports*, Association of Theological Schools, 151–58, https://www.ats.edu/files/galleries/peer-group-final-report-book.pdf.

[5] Keith McCoy, "Draft Formation Guidelines Move Forward," *Diakoneo* 21, no. 5 (1999): 7. The National Center for the Diaconate was created in in 1974, evolving into the North American Association for the Diaconate in 1986 and adopting the name Association for Episcopal Deacons (AED) in 2011 when the Anglican Deacons Canada founded their own community. See "Deacons' Organization Announces New Name," The Episcopal Diocese of Texas, 26 April 2011, https://www.epicenter.org/article/deacons-organization-announces-new-name; and "A Brief History of AED and the Episcopal Diaconate," Association for Episcopal Deacons, https://www.episcopaldeacons.org/history.html.

[6] Susanne Watson, "Formation of Ministering Christians," *Diakoneo* 21, no. 5 (1999): 9.

[7] Susanne Watson Epting, *Unexpected Consequences: The Diaconate Renewed* (New York: Morehouse, 2015), 100.

for bishops, priests and transitional deacons, vocational deacons, licensed lay ministers, and lay people. These grids uniquely identify competencies for different periods of ministry and discipleship: during the discerning and selection process; at the point of licensing, commissioning, or ordination; and during one's tenure.[8] The primates hoped each of the Anglican Communion provinces would embrace these competencies and refine them for their own contexts.

The 2015 General Convention of The Episcopal Church affirmed the Ministry Grids as a "Framework for Competent Ministry" (2015-A081).[9] In 2017, the Association for Episcopal Deacons (AED) completed a long-running effort to publish *Competencies for Deacons*. A revised edition was released in 2018 incorporating initial feedback from dioceses. This version helps to guide diaconal preparation in Episcopal dioceses.[10]

Bexley Seabury's "Continuum of Theological Education"

At Bexley Seabury, the listening sessions I conducted in 2018–2019 included a critical review of our mission, "to form lay and clergy leaders to proclaim God's mission in the world." School representatives acknowledged that our offerings designed for those preparing for priestly orders did not sufficiently meet the needs of students preparing for lay leadership and diaconal ordination. To truly prepare individuals *in* their context *for* their context, Bexley Seabury launched initiatives to respond to the particular needs of each order.

These changes occurred incrementally and began by identifying appropriate competencies for each order. The document *A Christian Life of Faith: Signs and Thresholds along The Way*, provided the structure for a library of short courses for lay people.[11] These courses launched in January 2021 and are available on the school's lifelong learning website.[12] Two CBTE programmes were launched in 2023: the Mentor-Assessed Path MDiv pilot programme, which prepares students to demonstrate Bexley Seabury's accredited MDiv competencies, and the Collaborative's diaconal preparation process, which meets the AED competencies. The resulting series of programmes establish a continuum of theological education designed to meet learners

---

[8] "Ministry Grids," Anglican Communion, https://www.anglicancommunion.org/theology/theological-education/ministry-grids.aspx.

[9] The minutes commend that "all dioceses use them as instruments for guiding the ongoing formation of leaders in the Church" and "as a framework for effective assessment of those preparing for ordination." *Journal of the General Convention of The Episcopal Church*, Salt Lake City (New York: General Convention, 2015), 399–400, https://www.episcopalarchives.org/sites/default/files/publications/2015_GC_Journal.pdf.

[10] "AED's Competencies for Deacons," Association for Episcopal Deacons, https://www.episcopaldeacons.org/deacon-competencies.html.

[11] Julie Lytle, ed., *A Christian Life of Faith: Signs and Thresholds along The Way: Competencies for Laity: Claiming, Engaging, Sustaining, Cultivating/Catalyzing Faith*, 18 November 2020, https://tinyurl.com/ChristianLifeFaith.

[12] "Pathways for Baptismal Living," Bexley Seabury Seminary, https://www.bexleyseabury.edu/pathways.

where they are and support them as they build confidence and gain credentials to respond to their call (Figure 20.1).

Continuum of Theological Education/Opportunities for Lifelong Learning

Personal enrichment, Licensures, Certificates, Graduate degrees, pre- and post-grad continuing education/electives for all four orders: lay, deacon, priests, and bishops

Spirituality, Discernment, and Vocation	Fundamentals of Faith:	Church Imperatives	Electives—Living your Faith in the Church and in the World	Diaconal Formation	Diploma in Anglican Studies	Master of Divinity	Doctor of Ministry
(4 months)	Five course Series • Foundations • Engaging God's Story • Theo/Ethics • History/Polity • Prayer/Worship	• Becoming Beloved Community • Doctrine of Discovery • Understanding Addiction • Supporting Recovery	• See full library of offerings at Pathways website	Mentor-Assessed, AED Competency-Based Deacons Formation process created by Deacons Formation Collaborative	(Certificate Programs)	• Course-assessed model • Mentor-assessed model (MA options)	• In Congregational Development
Discernment for all. Asks how God is speaking. Not discernment for ordained ministry.	Four-week courses, Can take individually, First three prerequisites for preaching license						
Two-Plus-Two blending two years of courses on Pathways for Baptismal Living and two years of courses at Sitting Bull Indigenous College to prepare Indigenous learners for graduate study.							Audit/Non-credit Options including travel/immersion experiences

Figure 20.1: Continuum of Theological Education

From Local Formation to Collaboration

Between 1978 and 2008, the number of Episcopal deacons in the United States swelled from 600 to 2600. During this period, there was a significant increase in the number of people preparing for diaconal ordination in diocesan schools or programmes: 41 percent in 1978 compared to 87 percent in 2008.[13] Diocesan schools for diaconal formation and diocesan schools of ministry that include diaconal formation typically developed because a bishop desired to prepare postulants locally. Sometimes this was to ensure a particular emphasis within a deacon's self-understanding[14] or to ensure that The Episcopal Church's canonical changes differentiating diaconal preparation from priestly education occurred.[15] Anecdotal references critique seminaries as "ivory towers" ill-equipped to prepare diaconal postulants for their home contexts and rebuff them for attempting to "sell" what they have (courses designed for preparing priests) instead of developing programmes with a diaconal lens. Although I had an eight-year history of collaborating with and supporting deacons as executive director of the Episcopal Province of New England, many archdeacons and deacon directors initially were reluctant to explore seminary-based collaborations because I was perceived as a seminary representative. This hesitation shifted to openness about potential collaboration as dioceses became more confident in Bexley Seabury's commitment to tailor resources for each order.

The Deacons Formation Collaborative

The Collaborative is the culmination of conversations initiated in October 2021 when Bexley Seabury hosted a second Deacons' Summit. Twenty-one archdeacons, commissions on ministry representatives, formation directors, vocations officers, ministry developers, standing committee members, and representatives from four schools for ministry gathered to determine whether the seminary, dioceses, and other theological schools with resources and capacity could partner to support dioceses in need of diaconal preparation programmes. After exploring potential barriers – varied theologies of the diaconate, different curricular priorities, divergent models of assessment, and the impact of bishop changes – the majority of the group agreed to collaborate in developing a model

---

[13] "Deacons and Their Ministries in the Episcopal Church: As Reported by Deacons in 2008 & 1978," PEALL (Proclaiming Education for All) Task Force, The North American Association for the Diaconate, The Mission Leadership Center, and The Evangelism and Congregational Life Center of the Episcopal Church, January 2009.

[14] Ormonde Plater identified seven diaconal "waves" and the formation and preparation inferred from their roles and contexts in the history of The Episcopal Church. Ormonde Plater, *Many Servants: An Introduction to Deacons*, rev. ed. (Lanham, MD: Cowley, 2009).

[15] The 2003 General Convention of the Episcopal Church instituted canons to ensure programmes have a diaconal focus and include study of "Diakonia and the diaconate," human awareness and understanding, spiritual development and discipline, and practical training and experience. Watson, "Formation of Ministering Christians," 87–88.

of diaconal preparation using AED competencies to meet the canonical diaconal ordination requirements of The Episcopal Church.

With support from a 2023 Constable Grant, the Collaborative was created to provide a process for making diaconal formation and theological education available to a greater diversity of students in The Episcopal Church as well as to create a platform for sharing resources to support diaconal formation. Ad hoc subcommittees established the contours of the emerging preparation process with work reviewed by periodic gatherings of the larger body. We agreed upon a set of characteristics to guide development:

- **Competency-Based.** The AED Competencies for Deacons (revised 2018) grounds the formation process, which is designed to help each person form a diaconal identity, build skills, and expand knowledge for their particular ministry and context.
- **Mentor-Assessed.** A three-mentor team ensures educational, denominational, and vocational perspectives are integrated as students and mentors collaborate to understand programme requirements, develop a personalized learning plan, progress through asynchronous and hybrid learning experiences, and demonstrate proficiency.
- **Context-Aware.** A diaconal lens informs student perspectives as they become more critically reflective, pastorally responsive practitioners and apply insights gleaned in their local setting.
- **Personalized.** Learning paths are customizable to meet each student's educational needs, vocational goals, and to acknowledge sensitively and fully the gifts and knowledge individuals have already cultivated.
- **Self-Paced.** Detached from prescribed schedules, students can dedicate as much time to the programme as their situation allows, pacing their learning to the ebb and flow of changing demands in their personal and professional lives.
- **Accessible.** Learning Paths are available synchronously and asynchronously online.
- **Affordable.** Costs can be distributed through a monthly subscription that in many cases is shared with diocesan and parish sponsors.

These characteristics shape the student experience and guide member decision making.

Defining appropriate ways to share resources and responsibilities has been central to establishing the Collaborative as a partnership between dioceses and Bexley Seabury Seminary. Affectionately described as a "Yours, Mine, and Ours" approach, we delineated specific roles and responsibilities of the diocese and school as well as roles and responsibilities they share. Bexley Seabury provides learning experiences, monthly integration seminars, and academic mentors, as well as mentor training and support; dioceses ensure selected participants meet canonical requirements, identify diocesan mentors, and provide opportunities for local formation and contextualized learning. Together, they tailor learning experiences to meet diocesan needs and ensure that those preparing for diaconal ministry meet local requirements (Figure 20.2).

Deacons Formation Collaborative (DFC)			(Potentially) Shared Diocese and DFC	Diocesan Formation
Learning Community (All those preparing for diaconal ordination)	Individual with Mentor Team	Mentors		
Online Rolling Admission Online Matriculation Gather May - Retreat/ Graduation	Enrolling/ Orienting	Enrolling/ Orienting	Invitation – What/Who is a Deacon COM/Discernment Group training, esp. explaining Competency-Based Mentor Assessed Process	Discernment of Call Nomination to Postulancy Social History, Behavioral Screening, Life History, Criminal/Background Check, Med/Psych Evaluation, etc.

Weekly Options: Check-in Chapel: Learner Led – Prayer -- Various forms /Compline	Engagement of team developed & assessed Standard/Customized Paths:
	• Engaging Holy Scriptures
	• Diakonia and the Diaconate
	• Deacons as Theologians and Diaconal Theology
	• Living The Life of a Deacon:
	  ○ Organizing and Advocacy
	  ○ Engaging God's People
	  ○ in the Pulpit, the Parish and the World
	• Christian History and Anglican/Episcopal Church History & Tradition
	• Wellness &Maintaining a Vibrant Spiritual Life
			• Constitution & Canons
			• Title IV & mandated reporting
			• Church-wide imperatives
			• Becoming Beloved Community
			• Doctrine of Discovery
			• Safeguarding God's People
			• Understanding Addiction/ Recovery Allies
				Diocesan Based Training on local customs and governance (vestments & clergy wear, placement & letters of agreement, etc.)
				
				Doing social justice – On the ground study of what it means in our context.
				
				Prep for Ordination (Vows, etc.)

Monthly Formation: - Diaconal Lens Integration BSSF Community-wide Conversations: BBC, Town Meetings, etc. Supervised Ministry Experience	Monthly time to reflect on Field Placement/ Learning Community experience (case studies) Weekly zoom webinar – fellowship, prayer, deacons spotlight, continuing educ.	Monthly Mentor Support Meetings	Experiential Learning (Supervised Ministry/Field Placement and/or Clinical Pastoral Education) Ministry Reflection Group	Community activities & events (physically gathered) Diocesan Convention CPE, if required
Annual Review	Growth and Integration Review			Letter to bishop
Commencement - Ritual Celebration of Completion	Certificate for each Demonstration of Diaconal Competencies			

Figure 20.2: The "Yours, Mine, and Ours" Approach for Diaconal Preparation

This approach encourages deep relationships and establishes opportunities for wisdom sharing among programme participants, within diocesan contexts, and across the church. This is particularly true within the student and mentor team who travel the curricular path from orientation and prior learning assessment through core competency paths and demonstration of degree proficiencies in a capstone process (see Figure 20.3).

Student's Path

Path To Proficiency			Planning Your Adventure	Follow your Charted Learning Path Meeting Regularly with Mentors as Ready & for Annual Review	Capstone Project	Celebration!
Application to the DFC Program	Interview & Acceptance	Orientation Activities	Student & Mentors Meet	**Cyclic Activities** Complete Standard/Customized Paths & Summative Assessments; Participate in Anglican Formation Zoom Sessions & Onsite Retreats; Participate in Supervised Ministry Placement & Reflect with Supervisor; Annual Review with Mentors	Student & Mentors Meet	

Mentor's Path

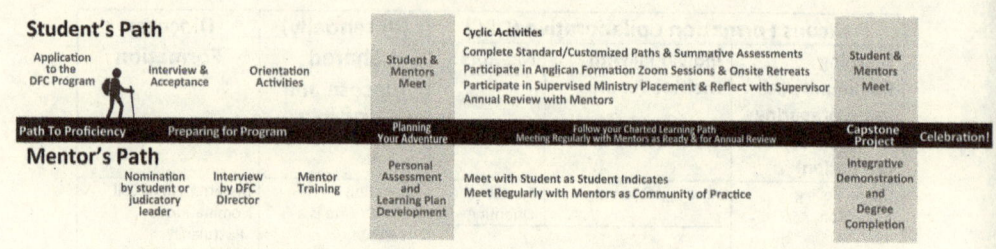

			Personal Assessment and Learning Plan Development	Meet with Student as Student Indicates; Meet Regularly with Mentors as Community of Practice	Integrative Demonstration and Degree Completion	
Nomination by student or judicatory leader	Interview by DFC Director	Mentor Training				

Figure 20.3: Signposts along Student's and Mentor's Paths to Degree

The curriculum is designed to facilitate student integration of content/knowledge, craft/application, and character/identity formation through six interwoven elements:

1. **Eight Core Competency Paths:** self-paced student engagement of personalized learning paths to prepare and demonstrate proficiency: Engaging Holy Scriptures; Diakonia and the Diaconate; Deacons as Theologians and Diaconal Theology; Living The Life of a Deacon in the Pulpit, the Parish, and the World; Living the Life of a Deacon: Engaging God's People; Living the Life of a Deacon: Organizing and Advocacy; Church History, Anglican/Episcopal History & Tradition; and Wellness & Maintaining a Vibrant Spiritual Life.
2. **Supervised Ministry Experience**: engagement in ministry and reflection with a supervisor in a local context, typically in one location for the duration of one's programme.
3. **"Deacon Talking"**: participation in a weekly cycle of web conferences that include prayer and worship, highlights of a current deacon's ministry, and ministry education that integrates students within the wider Episcopal diaconal community.
4. **Diocesan/Local Formation**: regular engagement in diocesan-defined activities, typically with the bishop and/or other diocesan deacons in local context.
5. **Integration and Growth Review**: regular review of student progress to integrate knowledge, wisdom, and skills gained through the programme into a life of ministry, service, and ongoing formation; self-awareness and self-regulation, articulating spiritual and vocational development in contextually appropriate ways; demonstration of rootedness and growth in regular, ongoing spiritual practices both personally and communally; intercultural engagement and global awareness that exhibit curiosity and openness to engagement with diverse persons, communities, and contexts; and the capacity, desire, and commitment to lifelong learning.
6. **Capstone Project**: student's mentor-assessed, final demonstration of proficiencies to complete the programme.

At the heart of the programme is the **Relational Learning Process** that students and mentors engage as they progress through each of the eight competency paths and demonstrate integrated learning in a capstone project. Each competency has a defined "standard path" that outlines a way for students to engage significant resources and activities to prepare to demonstrate their proficiency. Unlike traditional courses where a teacher defines the content and process for engaging it, the Relational Learning Process is unique in providing the student and mentors an opportunity to personalize and contextualize learning by adapting or recreating their path. This provides a means to recognize a student's wisdom, prior training, and experience as well as to tailor the learning process to particular ministry goals.

The process has three distinct phases. In the first phase, *Defining the Path*, students and mentors reflect on what proficiency in a competency means, define what needs to be done for assessment, assess the student's prior learning and experience, identify growth areas and resources, and define a path to prepare to demonstrate the competency. In the second phase, *Following the Path*, students engage learning experiences at their own pace; periodically meeting with mentors to review progress, ensure development of knowledge, skills, and personal aptitudes; and, as necessary, make adjustments. This is an iterative process culminating in a decision to follow a "standard path" provided by the seminary, adapt the standard path, or create one's own path. The last phase, *Demonstrating Proficiency*, occurs when the student and mentors agree that the student is ready to demonstrate proficiency by completing a Summative Assessment Review. While each step in the process builds on the steps that come before it, the process is not meant to be rigid or linear. Steps may be revisited to support development in a competency. When the student and mentors agree that the student has sufficiently demonstrated proficiency in the eight competencies, the student completes a capstone project to demonstrate their holistic and comprehensive integration of content, craft, and character,

Insights Gleaned

Nine students from three dioceses – California, Minnesota, and Montana – started the Collaborative pilot preparation process on 25 October 2023. Another 15–20 students are expected to start in 2024. Though it is too early to draw conclusions, there already are insights to be gleaned from these early adopters, particularly in comparison to a cohort of students who started a similar mentor-assessed pilot path to earn a Master of Divinity in January 2023.

A collaborative approach establishing partnerships between a seminary and diocese, as well as across dioceses, shows signs of mutual benefit. Initial responses from dioceses have been positive. A Memorandum of Understanding delineates roles and responsibilities for each partner and joint operations have sparked outside-the-box solutions. Diocesan staff already knew students in their discernment process and were readily able to identify appropriate mentors when the student was affirmed by their Commission on Ministry. Students with diocesan recognition are motivated to move through the preparation process. Bexley Seabury provides students and mentors access to library resources and technology supports typically not available in diocesan settings, while students and mentors are expanding Bexley Seabury staff's and faculty's understanding of diaconal ministry and establishing relationships that will benefit all ministries in the future.

A more unified understanding of and approach to diaconal ministry is emerging in The Episcopal Church. The diaconal waves catalogue the sources that promote confusion when describing a deacon or diaconal ministry in The Episcopal Church. With evidence of an emerging new wave, the Association for Episcopal Deacons, diocesan archdeacons, and deacon directors are trying to promote a unified view of deacons for the twenty-first century. The Collaborative, by its nature as a multi-diocese collaboration and shared preparation processes, is cultivating a common understanding of deacons among our students and helping to eliminate the risk of creating a "diocesan order," as previously identified by Watson Epting.

A more diverse student population is possible. The inaugural group of Collaborative students are, on average, younger and represent a variety of cultural groups. Some of the students have identified the student-directed online nature of the programme as the element that makes diaconal preparation possible. Additionally, two dioceses decided to cover the cost of diaconal formation so that finances are not a barrier.

A holistic approach to diaconal preparation, integrating "content, craft, and character," provides immediately applicable resourcing. In addition to satisfying adult learning needs, students appreciate the opportunity to articulate *all* the training and experience, not just the academic preparation, that they bring to their process. This holistic approach to diaconal preparation also responds to the concern that identified "two fifths of the deacons in 2008 apparently wish they had more assistance in integrating 'book' knowledge with their learning how to carry out various diaconal ministries."[16]

Sustained training and communication are critical for the expansion of this type of education and formation. Adults interpret through the lens of their experience. Because most adults have been formed by instructor-led educational systems, they typically perceive the "standard path" as a course with modules to quickly "check off" rather than a starting point for conversation about what each member of the student–mentor team brings and how that will inform, form, and even transform each of them, especially the student.

Intentional iterative design provides "safe fails" for individuals engaged in personal formation as well institutions that provide diaconal formation. Far too many variables exist for individuals and institutions to consider when designing a theological education and ministry formation process. Expecting a student and mentor team, or a programme planning team, to identify the exact configuration of components a learner needs to be prepared for ministry in their given context is unrealistic. Instead, when a student or institution finds that an assumption did not satisfy their need, a process allowing "safe fails" acknowledges our humanity and establishes a means to adjust.

Competency-based theological education inherently forms lifelong learners. Though more demanding initially, the Collaborative's Relational Learning Process inculcates participants as lifelong learners and mitigates limitations inherent even in the most flexible programmes and processes. By design, the Relational Learning Process teaches students a method to review their

---

[16] "Deacons and Their Ministries in the Episcopal Church," 10.

experience and ministry goals, identify areas of growth, determine ways to engage that growth area, and define ways to assess proficiency. Judicatories may adopt ministry or competency grids, like those provided by the Anglican Communion, that identify "signs and thresholds" for personal and professional ministry discernment over various phases of discipleship.

Conclusion

The Collaborative's approach to diaconal preparation is innovative, adaptable, and contextually responsive. Its inherently collaborative "Yours, Mine, and Ours" approach maximizes diocesan and seminary contributions and mitigates potential hurdles, particularly when staff, students, and financial resources are thin. Its Relational Learning Process democratizes diaconal formation, empowering students as agents of their learning and co-creators tailoring their activities and resources for their ministry and ministry context. This relationality is the most significant contribution of the Collaborative and a mentor-assessed model of diaconal formation.

Works Cited

Anglican Communion. "Ministry Grids." https://www.anglicancommunion.org/theology/theological-education/ministry-grids.aspx.

Archdeacon/Deacon Directors. "Principles Common to Quality Deacon Formation Programs." Association for Episcopal Deacons, 2009. https://www.episcopaldeacons.org/uploads/2/6/7/3/26739998/principlestoformtn.pdf.

Association for Episcopal Deacons. "AED's Competencies for Deacons." https://www.episcopaldeacons.org/deacon-competencies.html.

Association for Episcopal Deacons. "A Brief History of AED and the Episcopal Diaconate." https://www.episcopaldeacons.org/history.html.

Bexley Seabury Seminary. "Pathways for Baptismal Living." https://www.bexleyseabury.edu/pathways.

Clark, Frank W. "Characteristics of the Competency-Based Curriculum." In *Competency-Based Education for Social Work: Evaluation and Curriculum Issues*. Edited by Morton L. Arkava and E. Clifford Brennen, 22–46. New York: Council on Social Work Education, 1976.

"Deacons and Their Ministries in the Episcopal Church: As Reported by Deacons in 2008 & 1978." PEALL (Proclaiming Education for All) Task Force, The North American Association for the Diaconate, The Mission Leadership Center, and The Evangelism and Congregational Life Center of the Episcopal Church. January 2009.

"Deacons' Organization Announces New Name." The Episcopal Diocese of Texas, 26 April 2011. https://www.epicenter.org/article/deacons-organization-announces-new-name.

Epting, Susanne Watson. *Unexpected Consequences: The Diaconate Renewed*. New York: Morehouse, 2015.

Gervais, J. "The Operational Definition of Competency-Based Education." *The Journal of Competency-Based Education* 1, no. 2 (June 2016): 98–106. https://doi.org/10.1002/cbe2.1011.

Journal of the General Convention of The Episcopal Church, Salt Lake City. New York: General Convention, 2015. https://www.episcopalarchives.org/sites/default/files/publications/2015_GC_Journal.pdf.

Knowles, Malcolm. *The Modern Practice of Adult Education: From Pedagogy to Andragogy*. Chicago: Follet, 1980.

"'Let's Begin with the End in Mind': Competency-Based Theological Education." In *Educational Models and Practices Peer Group Final Reports*, Association of Theological Schools, 151–58. https://www.ats.edu/files/galleries/peer-group-final-report-book.pdf.

Lytle, Julie, ed. *A Christian Life of Faith: Signs and Thresholds along The Way: Competencies for Laity: Claiming, Engaging, Sustaining, Cultivating/Catalyzing Faith*. 18 November 2020. https://tinyurl.com/ChristianLifeFaith.

McCoy, Keith. "Draft Formation Guidelines Move Forward." *Diakoneo* 21, no. 5 (1999): 7.

Plater, Ormonde. *Many Servants: An Introduction to Deacons*. Rev. ed. Lanham, MD: Cowley, 2009.

Watson, Susanne. "Formation of Ministering Christians." *Diakoneo* 21, no. 5 (1999): 9.

Chapter 21

Theology of Liberative Service

Mary Elizabeth Moore

The heart of the diaconate is service, a calling for all Christians to serve God and the wellbeing of the world. It is also a calling for deacons to inspire, lead, and support the service of all. This chapter explores a theology of the diaconate and liberative service, marked by compassion, justice, and peace. These liberative features are far-reaching and particular. *To be compassionate* is to extend loving attention and care to every being in God's creation. *To be just* is to upturn destructive systems and ensure thriving for people facing poverty, slavery, mental illness, racial discrimination, vulnerabilities of political violence, and ecological destruction, *and* to ensure thriving for oceans, forests, and wildlife. *To sow peace* is to cultivate communities of reconciliation, reparation, and restoration. Here I offer theological constructs and missional directions for *diakonia* and diaconal ministries, concluding with educational proposals.

The focus of this chapter is on *liberative* service, expressed in transformative values, actions, and social structures. Liberation requires solidarity and mutuality among humans and other beings aimed toward enduring liberation. Practices of solidarity and mutuality have been emphases of *diakonia* since the late 1970s.[1] *Diakonia* is not service in which people with power do works of charity or benevolence for those with less power; it is rather liberative service enacted by peoples and communities. I chose the term "liberative" over liberating because it is an active, participative concept, rather than a colonizing one; it points to the larger social context and all the relationships that contribute to the liberation of human and more-than-human beings, the whole planet, and cosmos. My goal is to enhance the prophetic and transformative wholeness of service.[2]

Prophetic, transformative goals are increasingly part of the global diaconal movement. Dietrich Werner and Matthew Ross, for example, map the accents in

---

[1] See, for example, the preparatory consultation and publication before the Sixth Assembly of the World Council of Churches in 1983: World Council of Churches, *Contemporary Understandings of Diakonia: Report of a Consultation* (Geneva: WCC, 1982), esp. 1–8.

[2] The choice of "liberative" is not an insistent one, but it conveys my emphasis on the holistic, mutual, and transformative qualities of diaconal service, echoing the "social and prophetic dimension of the church's mission" advocated in: World Council of Churches and ACT Alliance, *Called to Transformation: Ecumenical Diakonia* (Geneva: WCC, 2022), 44. I myself have used "liberating service" in the recent past: Mary Elizabeth Moore, "Liberating Service: In Christian Community and Diaconal Ministries," *The World is My Parish: Festschrift for the Rev. Dr. Norma Cook Everist, Emerita Professor, Currents in Theology and Mission* 49, no. 2 (April 2022): 7–12, http://currentsjournal.org/index.php/currents/issue/view/68.

diakonia and draw out themes of social responsibility in Hebrew and Christian scriptures, as in Luke 4:18 with its accent on "good news to the poor," "freedom for the prisoners," "sight for the blind," and setting "the oppressed free."[3] Tracing the history of the church's *diakonia*, they conclude by accenting the prophetic nature of the diaconate, which "offers deliverance from injustices and oppression. When the church fails to offer its witness and to be prophetic, the reaction of the world will be indifference and apathy."[4]

Diakonia, or *service*, has long been the primary focus of the diaconate, with less attention given to its local, global, and ultimate purposes.[5] The term *diakonia* has often been interpreted as simple service for the community, though some have called attention to the complexity of its meanings and inadequate translations of biblical words with the *diak-* root; still others have challenged the dominant interpretations and connotations of service.[6] An excellent review of these issues is found in Ben Hartley's chapter in this volume, in which he addresses the limits of "social service" as an inclusive understanding of *diakonia*, as well as the accent on being humble. In recent years, global conversations have expanded on the meaning of *diakonia*, reflected in works by people in the Global South, Asia, and the Pacific, who write extensively about "eco-diakonia."[7] Abednego Nkamuhabwa Keshomshahara offers a plea for eco-diakonia, recognizing that "eco" deals "with the relations of organisms to one another and to their physical surroundings" and "*diakonia*" calls people "to render social services to the needy on behalf of God while at the same time advocating for vulnerable people by negating the causes of miseries in the world." Eco-diakonia

---

[3] Dietrich Werner and Matthew Ross, "Terminologies, Learning Processes and Recent Developments in Ecumenical Diakonia in the Ecumenical Movement," in *International Handbook on Ecumenical Diakonia*, eds. Ampony et al. (Oxford: Regnum Books International, 2021), 8–11, esp. 10.

[4] Werner and Ross, 8–25, esp. 24, quoting World Council of Churches and ACT Alliance, *Called to Transformation*, 32.

[5] Three US examples emerge from Episcopal and United Methodist contexts. See: James Monroe Barnett, *The Diaconate: A Full and Equal Order*, rev. ed. (Valley Forge, PA: Trinity Press International, 1995, 1979); Rosemary Keller, Gerald Moede, and Mary Elizabeth Moore, *Called to Serve: The United Methodist Diaconate* (Nashville: Board of Higher Education and Ministry, The United Methodist Church, 1987); Ben L. Hartley and Paul E. Van Buren, *The Deacon: Ministry through Words of Faith and Acts of Love* (Nashville: General Board of Higher Education and Ministry, The United Methodist Church, 1999).

[6] WCC and ACT Alliance, *Called to Transformation*, 15–16, 31–33, 43–45; John N. Collins, *Diakonia: Re-Interpreting the Ancient Sources* (New York: Oxford University Press, 1990); Renate Kirchhoff, "Main Biblical Themes of Diaconia from European Perspectives," in *International Handbook on Ecumenical Diakonia*, eds. Ampony et al., 26–30; Moore, "Liberating Service."

[7] Dietrich Werner et al., eds., *International Handbook on Creation Care and Eco-Diakonia: Concepts and Perspectives from the Churches of the Global South* (Oxford: Regnum Books International, 2022), https://www.ocms.ac.uk/free-book-resources/.

thus "deals with protection, care, cure and advocating against any harm coming to God's creation."[8]

Welcoming this concept, Jürgen Moltmann accents a spirit of gentleness in eco-diakonia, and Mathews George Chunakara focuses on God's vision and the community's role as "agents of God's grace for the healing and transformation of the world."[9]

Questions still arise. Is *diakonia* a form of subjugating self to others in a spirit of humility, or does it have roots that go deeper than these hierarchical images?[10] Does it spread service wider than a deacon's immediate world? I propose here that *diakonia* is a way of being and acting in the world. It is rooted not only in biblical and historical understandings of *diakonia* but also in central Christian teachings of love for God and neighbor, and its reach extends to the whole of God's creation.

This discussion clearly shows that the diaconate is both a ministry of transformation and a ministry that is itself being transformed over time. During the same periods in which diaconal understandings and practices were expanding, the whole field of missiology was also changing, often with similar questions. In 1991, David Bosch published *Transforming Mission*, which pointed beyond a homogenous world permeated by colonialism, apartheid, and modernity to a radically changed world that requires a paradigm shift.[11] More recent writings reflect the continuing shifts, especially as people write from diverse contexts in the world.[12]

Theology of Liberative Service

Service is giving one's life and all one's efforts for the good of all – the flourishing of human beings and of every being in the universe, every corn plant

---

[8] Abednego Nkamuhabwa Keshomshahara, "The Ecclesial Mandate of Eco-Diakonia in the Mission of God: An African Lutheran Perspective," in *International Handbook on Creation Care and Eco-Diakonia*, eds. Werner et al., 25. Keshomshahara is a bishop of the Evangelical Lutheran Church in Tanzania. See also: Mathews George Chunakara, "Eco-Justice and Eco-Diakonia – An Imperative for Creation Care: Perspectives and Initiatives from CCA," in *International Handbook on Creation Care and Eco-Diakonia*, eds. Werner et al., 356–68. CCA is the Christian Conference of Asia.
[9] Jürgen Moltmann, "Words of Greeting," in *International Handbook on Creation Care and Eco-Diakonia*, eds. Werner et al., xiii; Mathews George Chunakara, "Words of Greeting," in *International Handbook on Creation Care and Eco-Diakonia*, eds. Werner et al., xvi–xvii. Moltmann is Professor Emeritus of Systematic Theology, University of Tübingen. Chunakara is General Secretary of the Christian Conference of Asia.
[10] See chapter by Yip in this volume.
[11] David Bosch, *Transforming Mission: Paradigm Shifts in Theology of Mission* (Maryknoll, NY: Orbis, 1991).
[12] Dana L. Robert, *Faithful Friendships: Embracing Diversity in Christian Community* (Grand Rapids, MI: Eerdmans, 2019); John Paul Isaak, "A Missio-African Discourse on Eco-Diakonia," in *International Handbook on Creation Care and Eco-Diakonia*, eds. Werner et al., 53–59. Isaak has been a professor, theological school rector, and political leader in his native Namibia and in parts of Europe.

and flower, rock and stream, insect and moose, atom of air and grain of sand. Liberative service is loving the Lord your God with all your heart, soul, mind, and strength and loving your neighbor as yourself (Mark 12:29–31, Matt 22:37–39, Luke 10:25–28). It is a calling to all people – to live for God, self, and neighbor. Such love is not servitude but a generous outpouring of love for God and God's creation. Biblical references to neighbor expand the word to anyone and everyone you encounter or anyone whose life you affect, consciously or unconsciously. That is *everyone*, even the stranger or enemy.

Following the love commands in Luke 10:25–37, the questioning lawyer asks, "'And who is my neighbor?'" (10:29, NRSV). Jesus does not respond with descriptions and directives but with the story of a Samaritan who stopped to help an injured man by the side of the road. Jesus does not list the qualities of the injured man that qualify him for being a neighbor; instead, he describes the actions of the Samaritan caregiver. He then asks the lawyer who he thinks is the neighbor. The lawyer replies, "'The one who showed him mercy.'" Jesus responds, "'Go and do likewise'" (10:37). The meaning of neighbor lies in the act of caring – Latin *caritas*, Greek *agape* – both connoting unconditional love. We will thus find neighbors wherever people act in love.

Global writings interweave love and *diakonia*. Renate Kirchhoff engages key texts on *diakonia* and then turns to the love commands. She notes that, in Leviticus 19:18b, "love" is a translation of the Hebrew *ahab*, an attitude that motivates beneficial actions toward one's neighbor.[13] In court proceedings, *ahab* protects human rights for both foreigners and Israelites. In Luke's love texts, Kirchhoff emphasizes that the lawyer is asking Jesus to define the characteristics of a neighbor, implicitly asking what makes a person worthy of being a neighbor. Jesus shifts the focus to the helping action itself.[14]

Similarly, John Paul Isaak emphasizes that, in both biblical and African traditions, love of God cannot be separated from love of neighbor. He connects the African concept of *ubuntu*, recognizing that *diakonia* takes place within co-humanity and community.[15] Panti Filibus Musa adds an ecological emphasis, noting that "Lutherans understand earth-keeping as part of, and expression of, our love for God and our neighbor."[16] Stretching even farther, Keshomshahara sees eco-diakonia as critical to Christian faith and discipleship, expressing love for all God's creation.[17]

These texts and their histories of interpretation are anchors for Christian *diakonia*, though they do not speak explicitly to diaconal ministries. By grounding Christian life in love, however, they do ground the ministries of the whole body. Jesus' neighbor story happened on the road; it portrays love responding to need, wherever it is. It magnifies the importance of the ministry of

---

[13] Kirchhoff, "Main Biblical Themes of Diaconia," 29. Kirchhoff is a professor of New Testament and Protestant welfare studies in Freiburg, Germany.
[14] Kirchhoff, 30. Jesus is addressing "the people who have the ability to help."
[15] Isaak, "A Missio-African Discourse on Eco-Diakonia," 57–58.
[16] Panti Filibus Musa, "Words of Greeting," in *International Handbook on Creation Care and Eco-Diakonia*, eds. Werner et al., xix. Musa is Archbishop of the Lutheran Church of Christ in Nigeria and President, Lutheran World Federation.
[17] Keshomshahara, "The Ecclesial Mandate of Eco-Diakonia," 25.

all Christians and points indirectly to the need for diaconal callings that connect the church's ministry with the world and with strangers and outcasts.

A deacon's call is to offer such direct service and to empower others in services of love, both inside and outside the church, in local settings and on the road. Diaconal ministries extend to people we know, do not know, and barely know and to people in situations of trauma, oppression, illness, ease, or chaos.[18] If we take seriously the biblical texts related to the non-human natural world, we also extend our ministries to trees and streams, ants and bees; every being in the universe. Deacons are neighbors who inspire love and acts of love in and with the whole community of creation.

By attending to the love commands and the question "who is my neighbor?" we come to deeper understandings of service, the historical and theological heart of diaconal ministries. Service appears in multiple biblical texts, such as the commissioning of seven disciples to serve the people and the subsequent martyrdom of Stephen, one of the seven (Acts 6:1–6, 8–10, 7:54–60). We can also turn to the early church and the role of deacons in managing the church's finances and service to those who were poor, outcast, or ill. We can follow the service ministries of deacons and widows through the early church and succeeding centuries and in recent decades of diaconal renewal. Service is the persistent theme, embodying love for and with the community. Pope Francis describes deacons as "custodians of service for the church."[19] Such service is liberative because it frees people to see themselves as worthy before God. Deacons listen and travel as neighbors, advocates, and co-workers for freedom. Neither paternalistic nor colonizing, it is a ministry of accompaniment with neighbors – individuals, eco-communities, and societies.

The dangers are real that service will become an act of domination, marked by giving to others what *we* think they need or, more troubling, establishing attitudes and structures that foster perpetual domination of those we serve. Liberative service overturns such control if it is grounded in Jesus' value of loving God and neighbor. Yet another biblical value fosters liberative service. This is the value of laying down your life for your friends, as Jesus advocates in John's Gospel: "'This is my commandment, that you love one another as I have loved you. No one has greater love than this, to lay down one's life for one's friends'" (15:12–13, NRSV). The command is an invitation to love others as friends, not to be servants or slaves to others, but to form relationships of mutuality and action, "to do as I command you" (15:14), to "go and bear fruit" (15:15b). Jesus' words describe his relationships with his followers and their relationships with one another and the larger world: "I do not call you servants ["slaves" in Greek] any longer, because the servant does not know what the master is doing; but I have called you friends, because I have made known to

---

[18] On trauma-informed response, see chapter by Stephens in this volume.
[19] Pope Francis, "Address of His Holiness Pope Francis to the Permanent Deacons of the Diocese of Rome, with their Families," presented in the Hall of Benediction, St. Peter's Basilica, Vatican City, 19 June 2021, https://www.vatican.va/content/francesco/en/speeches/2021/june/documents/20210619-diaconi.html.

you everything that I have heard from my Father" (15:15a). Jesus describes a relationship that is intimate, mutual, and liberative, to the end "that you may love one another" (15:17).

Why is liberative service critical for deacons? It is service that frees, equips, and empowers others. It is grounded in love for others, not because they are downtrodden, needy, or "lesser than," but because they are friends. Such service frees others to know they are genuinely loved, frees them to love others, and creates opportunities for mutual liberation. Deacons thus minister with people living on the streets, in prisons, in abusive homes. They minister in eco-farming, habitat protection, solar energy innovations, health care for people in poverty, advocacy for people with disabilities, policy development to reduce fossil fuel dependence, holistic care for people with mental illness, forest and ocean protection, and training of law enforcers in non-violent interventions. Further, these ministries create opportunities for others to participate in liberation.

Marks of Liberative Service

The diaconal movement is ecumenical, joining Christians from every branch of the Christian church's tree and beyond. It serves the whole inhabited world, or the ecumene. Ecumene derives from the ancient Greek *oikouménē*, and that from *oikos*, or household; thus, the ecumene is our home. It is no longer limited to Planet Earth but extends to the cosmos, our even larger home.

The ministry of deacons is most frequently described ecumenically as word, service, compassion, justice, and peace.[20] Ioan Sauca emphasizes the connections of eco-diakonia with the World Council of Churches' (WCC) accent on Justice, Peace, and the Integrity of Creation, launched in the Sixth Assembly in Vancouver (1983) and continued in conciliar processes, a global convocation in Korea (1990), and the more recent Pilgrimage for Justice and Peace, which includes ecological challenges. Sauca sees the eco-diakonia movement as adding

---

[20] These words appear in different combinations in diverse communions, but they are widely shared. I have addressed them recently in posing a liberating vision of diaconal ministries, having identified five values that are broadly shared in ecumenical theologies, as well as the relationship of liberating service with the sacraments and sacramentality. Moore, "Liberating Service," 7–12. These emphases are also pervasive in recent literature on radical discipleship and on the diaconate. See Darryl W. Stephens, *Bearing Witness in the Kin-dom: Living into the Church's Moral Witness* (United Methodist Women, 2021); WCC and ACT Alliance, *Called to Transformation*, 53–66, 68–69, 111–12; Wanda Deifelt and Beate Hofmann, "Towards a Comprehensive Concept of Diaconia: Care, Transformation, Empowerment, Advocacy and Conviviality," in *International Handbook on Ecumenical Diakonia*, eds. Ampony et al., 53–61; Ignatius Swart, "The Transformative Power of Diakonia – Theological Reflections from South Africa," in *International Handbook on Ecumenical Diakonia*, eds. Ampony et al., 62–67; Cornelia Coenen-Marx, "The Transformative Power of Diaconia – An Eight-Headed Hydra," in *International Handbook on Ecumenical Diakonia*, eds. Ampony et al., 68–72.

to the WCC emphases of the past forty years.[21] Interestingly, the renewal of diaconal ministries in Roman Catholic and Protestant churches took place during the same period, especially the 1980s and 1990s, suggesting a link between the church's central values and the shaping of ministry. The continuing focus on love-centered liberative service is seen in the 11th Assembly theme, "Christ's Love Moves the World to Reconciliation and Unity" (2022).[22] Liberative service manifests itself in three marks.

Compassion. Shanda is a deacon, and most people do not know her name. She spends her days visiting children, young people, and elders who live in health care facilities. Shanda sits with people as they are told about yet another escalation in their disease, as they struggle against loneliness, as they face abandonment by family and friends. She is a compassionate presence, who spends her days among the tombs with people who are still very much alive, no matter their disabilities, diseases, and suffering.

Compassion is extending passion (loving concern) to the whole community, attending to and caring for every being in God's creation. Compassion is far more than being "nice," which might be nothing more than following rules of socially acceptable manners. Compassion is grounded in being with and listening closely to others; it leads to respectful behavior, and it also leads to ardent advocacy. Compassion is feeling the feelings of other beings, whether fellow humans or a drought-dried river or whales in search of a livable habitat with enough food to survive and enough quiet to communicate with one another. Standardized caring for people in hospitals and nursing facilities can never respond to their deepest yearnings; superficial caring for rivers and whales can never be sufficient to know their realities and threats. To be liberative, diaconal service needs to be soaked in compassion.

Justice. Jason is a deacon dedicated to building racial-ethnic justice in his community through education and policy development. Other deacons are immersed in work for human rights, justice for LGBTQIA+ peoples, homeless ministries, public housing initiatives, health care for underserved populations, community ministries with children, urban agriculture, environmental protection, and wellbeing economics projects. The projects vary, as do the contexts and needs, but they share a goal of justice, contributing to the thriving of all peoples and the whole planet.

The ministry of deacon has always been involved in practical concerns, even in the early church when deacons managed the community's funds and ensured the equitable distribution for charitable and life-supporting ministries of the church. The emphasis on justice has carried through the history of the diaconate across denominations and parts of the world. Deaconess movements in the Philippines, African countries, and the United States have been dedicated to justice, focusing on health care, education, care and advocacy for the poor, and struggles for just public policies. These traditions are carried today by deacons

---

[21] Ioan Sauca, in *International Handbook on Creation Care and Eco-Diakonia*, eds. Werner et al., xxii. At the time of writing, Sauca was Acting General Secretary of the World Council of Churches.
[22] Sauca, xxiii.

in many different roles, denominations, and locales. The diaconal goals of justice are critical to liberative service, whether deacons serve as social workers, doctors, nurses, teachers, caregivers, community and church musicians, or directors of missional service in their local parishes.

Peace. The liberative service of deacons is also embodied in its mission of just peacebuilding, which seeks reconciliation, reparation, and restoration. Some of these ministries are enacted in local churches, community organizations (such as schools or police departments), international negotiation teams, interreligious organizations, or global sites of conflict. Intertwined with compassion and justice, peacemaking is liberative service that embodies love for friends; the "other" is reframed from enemy or neglected stranger to neighbor and friend.

Friends are people whom the church knows as beings of worth to be loved and engaged with dignity. Stretching the liberative vision still further requires that deacons befriend the whole of God's creation. For example, evidence abounds that ants have complicated communication systems that alert forests to dangers, and that trees communicate and share nourishment through their root systems so as to strengthen an entire forest and the most fragile beings in it. For deacons to be peacemakers, our love needs to include the entire universe as interrelated friends who depend on one another to flourish.

Conclusions for Diaconal Studies

If the mission of deacons is to give our lives for our friends, and to engage in liberative service, our work is never done – neither is the joy of being together in service for the flourishing of God's creation. The mission of deacons is wide-ranging and complex but is guided by the love of Jesus for his friends. Our diaconal mission is to love and to inspire, equip, and empower the whole church in ministries of love. The educational practices that I describe as sacramental teaching form one important guide for diaconal education.[23]

The theological education of deacons is an underdeveloped challenge, though some models exist. I highlight qualities that contribute to vital diaconal education. First, the diaconate is related to the *diakonia* of the whole church and should therefore take place in relation to the laity and persons preparing to be elders, presbyters, and priests. Second, the diaconate is a global, ecumenical order. Education needs to engage with the broad range of deacons, and communities of deacons, preferably in ecumenical and globally engaged settings. Third, deacons, deaconesses, and diaconal ministers are ministers of transforming love, and their education needs to give them opportunities to grow as whole persons – spiritual beings, relationship builders, community leaders, visionaries, and wise practitioners.

---

[23] Sacramental teaching includes expecting the unexpected, remembering the dismembered, seeking reversals, giving thanks, nourishing life, reconstructing community, and repairing the world. Mary Elizabeth Moore, *Teaching as a Sacramental Act* (Cleveland: Pilgrim, 2004).

Such education includes the knowledge of ages and cultivates student visions and capacities to serve in the specialized ways to which they are called. Diaconal education needs to be soul-shaping, opening our eyes and ears and arms to the liberative call of God and the underlying call of the whole community to love God and neighbor. Deacons are agents of love and liberation who inspire and open doors for the whole body to liberative action. Education is their field of opportunity to study, reflect, deepen spiritually, and actively engage in transformative service. Most important, diaconal education inspires bold visions of liberation in God's creation.

Works Cited

Barnett, James Monroe. *The Diaconate: A Full and Equal Order,* Rev. ed. Valley Forge, PA: Trinity Press International, 1995, 1979.

Bosch, David. *Transforming Mission: Paradigm Shifts in Theology of Mission.* Maryknoll, NY: Orbis, 1991.

Chunakara, Mathews George. "Eco-Justice and Eco-Diakonia – An Imperative for Creation Care: Perspectives and Initiatives from CCA." In *International Handbook on Creation Care and Eco-Diakonia*, edited by Werner et al., 356–68. Oxford: Regnum Books International, 2022.

Chunakara, Mathews George. "Words of Greeting." In *International Handbook on Creation Care and Eco-Diakonia*, edited by Werner et al., xvi–xvii. Oxford: Regnum Books International, 2022.

Coenen-Marx, Cornelia. "The Transformative Power of Diaconia – An Eight-Headed Hydra." In *International Handbook on Ecumenical Diakonia*, edited by Ampony et al., 68–72. Oxford: Regnum Books International, 2021.

Collins, John N. *Diakonia: Re-Interpreting the Ancient Sources*. New York: Oxford University Press, 1990.

Deifelt, Wanda and Beate Hofmann. "Towards a Comprehensive Concept of Diaconia: Care, Transformation, Empowerment, Advocacy and Conviviality." In *International Handbook on Ecumenical Diakonia*, edited by Ampony et al., 53–61. Oxford: Regnum Books International, 2021.

Hartley, Ben L., and Paul E. Van Buren. *The Deacon: Ministry through Words of Faith and Acts of Love*. Nashville: General Board of Higher Education and Ministry, The United Methodist Church, 1999.

Isaak, John Paul. "A Missio-African Discourse on Eco-Diakonia." In *International Handbook on Creation Care and Eco-Diakonia*, edited by Werner et al., 53–59. Oxford: Regnum Books International, 2022.

Keller, Rosemary, Gerald Moede, and Mary Elizabeth Moore. *Called to Serve: The United Methodist Diaconate*. Nashville: Board of Higher Education and Ministry, The United Methodist Church, 1987.

Keshomshahara, Abednego Nkamuhabwa. "The Ecclesial Mandate of Eco-Diakonia in the Mission of God: An African Lutheran Perspective." In *International Handbook on Creation Care and Eco-Diakonia*, edited by Werner et al., 25–34. Oxford: Regnum Books International, 2022.

Kirchhoff, Renate. "Main Biblical Themes of Diaconia from European Perspectives." In *International Handbook on Ecumenical Diakonia*, edited by Ampony et al., 26–30. Oxford: Regnum Books International, 2021.

Moltmann, Jürgen. "Words of Greeting." In *International Handbook on Creation Care and Eco-Diakonia*, edited by Werner et al., xiii. Oxford: Regnum Books International, 2022.

Moore, Mary Elizabeth. "Liberating Service: In Christian Community and Diaconal Ministries." *The World is My Parish: Festschrift for the Rev. Dr. Norma Cook Everist, Emerita Professor, Currents in Theology and Mission* 49, no. 2 (April 2022): 7–12, http://currentsjournal.org/index.php/currents/issue/view/68.

———. *Teaching as a Sacramental Act*. Cleveland: Pilgrim, 2004.

Musa, Panti Filibus. "Words of Greeting." In *International Handbook on Creation Care and Eco-Diakonia*, edited by Werner et al., xix. Oxford: Regnum Books International, 2022.

Pope Francis. "Address of His Holiness Pope Francis to the Permanent Deacons of the Diocese of Rome, with their Families." Presented in the Hall of Benediction, St. Peter's Basilica, Vatican City, 19 June 2021. https://www.vatican.va/content/francesco/en/speeches/2021/june/documents/20210619-diaconi.html.

Robert, Dana L. *Faithful Friendships: Embracing Diversity in Christian Community*. Grand Rapids, MI: Eerdmans, 2019.

Sauca, Ioan. "Words of Greeting." In *International Handbook on Creation Care and Eco-Diakonia*, edited by Werner et al., xxii. Oxford: Regnum Books International, 2022.

Stephens, Darryl W. *Bearing Witness in the Kin-dom: Living into the Church's Moral Witness*. Nashville: United Methodist Women, 2021.

Swart, Ignatius. "The Transformative Power of Diakonia – Theological Reflections from South Africa." In *International Handbook on Ecumenical Diakonia*, edited by Ampony et al., 62–67. Oxford: Regnum Books International, 2021.

Werner, Dietrich, Daniel Beros, Eale Bosela, Lesmore Ezechiel, Kambale Kahongya, Ruomin Liu, Grace Moon, Marisa Strizzi, eds. *International Handbook on Creation Care and Eco-Diakonia: Concepts and Perspectives from the Churches of the Global South*. Oxford: Regnum Books International, 2022. https://www.ocms.ac.uk/free-book-resources/.

Werner, Dietrich, and Matthew Ross. "Terminologies, Learning Processes and Recent Developments in Ecumenical Diakonia in the Ecumenical Movement." In *International Handbook on Ecumenical Diakonia*, edited by Ampony et al., 8–25. Oxford: Regnum Books International, 2021.

World Council of Churches. *Contemporary Understandings of Diakonia: Report of a Consultation*. Geneva: WCC, 1982.

World Council of Churches and ACT Alliance. *Called to Transformation: Ecumenical Diakonia*. Geneva: WCC, 2022. https://www.oikoumene.org/resources/publications/ecumenical-diakonia.

Index of Names

Asuncion, Filomena (Lumen), 150, 154–56, 158
Avis, Paul, 51, 59
Ayres, Anne, 163
Baluntong, Glofie, 150–51, 158
Bertheau, Caroline, 31
Black, Eveline, 175, 180–81
Bodelschwingh, Friedrich von, 15, 55
Booth, Edith, 167
Bosch, David, 267
Brodd, Sven-Erik, 222
Calvin, John, 55
Cassey, Peter Williams, 246
Chunakara, Mathews George, 267
Collins, John N., 2, 24, 29, 52–57, 59–60, 68, 124–25, 243
Copeland, M. Shawn, 129
Crain, Margaret Ann, 48
Dietrich, Stephanie, 223
Donovan, Mary S., 163
Douglas, Kelly Brown, 126
Duterte, Rodrigo, 153
Elliot, Neil, 185
Esping-Andersen, Gøsta, 208
Fliedner, Friederike (Münster), 15, 31
Fliedner, Theodor, 15, 30, 55, 162
Floyd, George, 70, 245
Flynn, John, 32
Francis, Pope, 269
Gaillot, Jaques, 200
Grant, Jacquelyn, 125–26
Guild, Caroline Elizabeth, 175–76, 180–81
Hartley, Ben, 266
Herman, Judith, 134–35, 139
Hiatt, Suzanne, 160–61, 166–67
Horsley, Richard, 128
Howson, John Saul, 162–63
Isaak, John Paul, 268
Jesus, 2, 19, 29–31, 40, 53–54, 63–64, 91, 94–97, 101, 104, 107–9, 111–12, 114, 123–31, 136, 149, 152, 186, 192, 268–70, 272
Johnson, Susanne, 75, 77, 80–84
Keshomshahara, Abednego Nkamuhabwa, 266, 268
Killerman, Sam, 116
King, Martin Luther Jr., 111
Kirchhoff, Renate, 268
Kundtz, David, 118
Lein, Rolf, 226
Litao, Rubylin, 150, 153–54, 158
Loehe, Wilhelm, 15
Luther, Martin, 55, 106–7, 196, 198, 229
Mahohoma, Takesure, 112

Marcos, Ferdinand Sr., 154–55
Matthews, Betty, 32–35
Mercedes, Anna, 128
Minard, Catherine, 175–76, 180
Moltmann, Jürgen, 56, 267
Muhlenberg, William A., 162–63
Müller, Julia, 77
Murray, Pauli, 161, 167
Musa, Panti Filibus, 268
Nordseth, Thorleif, 226, 230
Passavant, William, 15
Paul, apostle, 29, 59n28, 111, 133, 196
Peter, apostle, 186
Phoebe, 29
Piccard, Jeanette, 161, 165–67
Pieterse, Hendrik J.C., 75, 77–79, 83
Powell, Ruth, 36
Rolland, Francis William, 32
Rolland, William Strothert, 32
Ross, Matthew, 265
Roxburgh, Alan, 36
Russell, Letty, 104
Sauca, Ioan, 270, 271n21
Schaber, Peter, 76–77
Schlager, Bernard, 118
Schreiter, Robert, 142
Schultz, Rima Lunin, 164–65
Sieveking, Amalie, 31
Solberg, Mary, 127
Southgate, Horacio, 177
Stave, Gunnar, 222
Stephen, 60, 269
Steffensky, Fulbert, 201
Stringfellow, Horace and family, 175, 178
Thalheimer, M.J., 33
Townes, Emilie, 127
Tyler, Adeline Blanchard, 173, 175–82
Tyler, John, 176
Villalon, Marie Sol, 150–52, 158
Werner, Dietrich, 265
West, Traci, 135
Westhelle, Vítor, 128
Whittingham, William Rollinson, 162, 175–76, 181
Wichern, Johann Hinrich, 15, 31, 55, 226
Zielinski, Frances, 162, 165–68

Subject Index

accompaniment, 15, 19–21, 105, 136, 141, 150–2, 269
accountability, 18, 58, 107, 137, 187, 192–93
activism, 102, 149, 155–56
advocacy, for the diaconate, 34, 70, 242–43, 245, 247; for women priesthood, 160–62, 167, 242; social, 1–2, 4, 18, 35, 40–41, 47, 102, 116–17, 120, 138, 140, 150–54, 191, 244, 260, 266–67, 269–71.
apprenticeship, 65, 224–25, 227, 230
Augsburg Confession, 196, 226–27n30
Australia, 31–36
baptism, 19, 30, 35, 42, 44–46, 59, 64, 105, 109, 185, 239, 248
bearing witness, 133–34, 139–40, 142–43
Bible, 29–30, 52–55, 68, 90–91, 96, 113–14, 124–25, 186–87, 197, 201, 231, 243, 246, 266–69
bishop, 19–21, 30, 41–43, 45–46, 63, 93, 112–13, 159–62, 164–66, 168, 175–76, 187–88, 191, 200, 240, 242, 244, 246, 257
Book of Common Prayer, 39, 45, 175, 239, 241–44
Canada, 178, 185–87, 189

capitalism, 80, 84, 155
Catholic, 21, 31, 39, 69–70, 93, 155, 163–67, 191, 271
Central House for Deaconesses, 164n30, 167
charity, 31, 75, 78–79, 83, 95–96, 113, 177–80, 239, 265, 271
children, 31–31, 53, 66, 115, 117–18, 175–78, 181–82, 215, 244, 248, 271
Christendom, 16, 19, 22, 29
Christ, 19–20, 40, 45, 59, 65–66, 91, 96–97, 101–2, 104, 106–9, 111–12, 123–24, 126–31, 175, 196, 199, 201, 226, 239
Christology, 64, 198
Church of Norway, 212, 222, 225–26, 232
Church of Sweden, 211
clericalism, 18–19
collaboration, 1, 11, 93–94, 102, 106, 138, 153, 174, 177, 189, 216–17, 222, 225, 230, 251–52, 257–59, 261–63. See also partnership
community development, 23, 78, 81–82, 190. See also conviviality
compassion, 2, 34–37, 43, 65–70, 83, 102, 112–15, 133, 136–37, 150–53, 156–57, 179, 265, 270–72

compensation, 30, 47–48, 163, 240, 242, 247–48
consensus model, 189–90
conviviality, 18, 134, 138–41, 143
COVID-19, 1, 66, 92, 124, 131, 150, 211
creation care, 21–22, 25, 44, 63–64, 71, 94, 96, 108, 131, 133, 137–38, 140, 142, 265, 267–73
culture, 30, 33, 53–54, 60, 69–70, 80–81, 103, 114–15, 127, 131–32, 138, 174, 185, 189, 202, 215, 260
curriculum, diaconal, 25, 71, 102, 222, 224–25, 229–30, 234, 251, 253, 257–60. See also diaconal studies
cursus honorum, 241
daily life, 3, 4, 15, 20–21, 25, 105
deacon, 2–3, 15–16, 18–21, 24, 29–30, 34–37, 39–48, 52–55, 57, 59–60, 63–71, 96, 102–3, 105, 107, 111–20, 123, 126, 130, 159–62, 164–68, 173–77, 179, 182, 188–90, 207–8, 210–13, 216, 221–24, 226–28, 230, 232–33, 239–48, 251–52, 254–55, 257–60, 262, 265, 269–73
deaconess, 15–16, 18, 20–21, 31–35, 37, 43, 46, 59, 63–64, 68, 105–7, 111, 140–1, 149–58, 159, 161–68, 173–76, 178–82, 210, 221–22, 242, 272

de-subjugation, 124, 126–32
diaconal community, 101, 102n2, 106n12, 202, 244n27, 252, 260
diaconal identity, 3, 25, 39, 52, 165, 168, 221–25, 230, 233, 239–46, 258. See also vocation
diaconal practice (praxis), 1, 18, 23, 25, 36–37, 75, 77–78, 80, 83–84, 90–94, 131–40, 143, 153, 197, 216, 232, 234, 239–40, 245, 248
diaconal studies, 1, 3–5, 18, 21–22, 24–25, 36–37, 47, 60, 71, 75–76, 83–84, 107, 208, 210–17, 223, 225, 233–34, 272–73. See also education, diaconal.
diaconate, 1–2, 15–21, 31, 33–35, 37, 39–46, 48, 51, 54, 59–61, 63, 70–71, 101, 105n8, 106n12, 107, 111, 115, 131–33, 159–62, 164–68, 176, 182, 186–89, 192–93, 239, 241–44, 246–48, 254, 257, 265–67, 271–72
diaconate of all believers, 2, 15, 17, 19–21, 37, 39, 44–45, 48, 105n8, 131–33, 272
Diakonie, 31, 51, 162
diapraxis, 17, 134, 137, 140, 143
dignity, 18, 34, 44, 75–77, 80, 83–84, 126, 137–41,

143, 150, 156–57, 195, 272
disabilities, 103–4, 116–17, 211n12, 215–16, 270–71
discernment, 107, 120, 191, 246, 261, 263
disciples, 35, 54, 60, 63–65, 101, 186, 269
discipleship, 1, 18–19, 23, 53, 59, 111, 114, 138, 251, 255, 263, 268, 270n20
diversity, 23, 60, 114, 116, 120, 149, 197, 209, 215, 258
dualism, 198
Dutch Reformed Church, 78
ecclesiology, 17–20, 30, 39, 51, 55, 102, 223, 227
eco-diakonia, 22, 24–25, 265–68, 270
education, 3, 31, 76–77, 89, 118–19, 154–55, 177, 253, 271–72; Christian (religious), 75, 117–18, 177, 215; diaconal, 25, 46–47, 60, 71, 89, 102, 207, 212–13, 221–34, 240n5, 251–52, 254, 260, 272–73; higher, 207, 210–15, 222, 227–29, 232–34, 252; theological, 1, 3–4, 25, 71, 101, 216, 224, 228, 233–34, 252–58, 262.
elder. See presbyter
emissary, 2, 24, 40, 52–58, 60, 124
empowerment, 17–18, 68, 78–79, 83, 89–91, 94–98, 115, 133, 137, 142–43, 150
environment, 34–35, 134, 150, 156, 271. See also creation care; eco-diakonia
episcopate, 41, 45, 160
ethics, 31, 57, 131, 133–39, 143, 195, 214–15, 231
Eucharist, 46, 68, 95, 226
eunuch, 60, 114
evaluation, 91, 94, 137, 186, 190–91, 210
evangelism, 23, 47
exchangeability of deacons, 39, 41–44, 47–48, 242n14
faith, 11, 18, 23, 29–30, 36, 46, 78, 81, 84, 89–93, 96, 106–7, 111–14, 116, 125–26, 137, 140, 149, 151, 155–57, 161, 180, 182, 186, 189–90, 192, 195–200, 207–8, 211–13, 215–17, 229, 234, 268
farmers, 152, 155
finances, 22, 47–48, 68–70, 79, 93, 120, 149, 163, 174–75, 177, 188, 190, 195, 209, 211n13, 212, 217, 239–45, 247–48, 251–53, 262–63, 269, 271
Finland, 208, 211–12
flourishing, 71, 112, 130, 133, 139, 142–43, 267, 272
foot washing, 53, 186
formation, 31–32, 34, 36–37, 47–48, 65, 81, 177, 192, 201, 221–25, 227, 230,

233–34, 244–45, 251–52, 254, 257–60, 262–63
freedom, 34, 68, 102, 126, 154, 196, 199, 208, 266, 269
friend(ship), 58, 107–8, 112, 115, 118–19, 155, 157, 174–75, 181, 269–72
full communion, 39–41, 43, 46–47
gender, 23, 33, 93, 113–14, 116, 118, 120, 141–42, 159, 174, 241. See also non-binary; transgender
Germany, 1–3, 15, 30–31, 33, 55, 64, 90, 102, 162, 179, 195
Gospel, 21, 36, 46, 58–60, 63, 65–67, 77, 97, 101–2, 105, 112, 240, 269
grace, 19, 34, 64, 103, 105, 107–9, 111–12, 141, 149, 187, 196, 198, 239, 267
grassroots, 81, 187–91
Hanover Report, 42, 102
Harris Memorial College, 150
healing, 17, 40, 42, 44, 63–64, 92, 95, 97, 111, 114, 118–20, 124, 130–32, 134–35, 137, 141–42, 189, 197, 267
health, 58, 77, 82, 92–93, 95, 117–18, 120, 124, 128–29, 143, 155, 180–81, 190, 192, 195, 207–8, 210–13, 215–16, 221–22, 228, 270–71

hierarchy, 18–19, 89, 92, 101, 106, 123, 125, 128, 159–61, 165, 174, 186, 188–89, 216, 248, 267
holy orders, 159–68, 174
Holy Spirit, 20, 40, 42, 48, 68, 97, 107–9, 188, 191–93, 196
homophobia, 113–14
hospital, 31–32, 113, 136, 173, 176, 179, 181–82, 210–11, 221, 226, 271
hospitality, 18, 30, 105, 112–13, 115, 119–20, 189
human rights, 33–34, 76, 117, 119, 136, 138, 140, 149–50, 152–54, 156, 201, 246, 268, 271
humility, 29, 58–59, 123, 157, 243, 245, 267
immigrants. See migrants
inclusion, 24, 30, 81, 93, 102, 104, 112–19, 131, 192, 243, 246, 248, 266
inferior order, 241–43, 246
Inner Mission, 55, 195, 239
integral mission, 23
interdependence, 76, 84, 112
interdisciplinary, 23, 134, 210–17, 223–24, 230–31, 234
justice, 1–2, 16–18, 25, 34–35, 37, 40, 43–44, 47, 52, 63, 65–71, 81, 94, 101–2, 105–6, 108, 111–12, 114, 119, 124–26, 131–32, 134, 136–40, 142–43, 149–56, 158, 162, 182, 186, 192–93, 195, 265–66, 270–72

kenotic self-emptying, 243
koinonia, 104, 111–17, 120
laity, 43–46, 58, 63–65, 67, 69, 103–5, 112, 114, 159–60, 163–64, 166, 168, 227, 242, 255, 272
Lambeth Conference, 46, 164–66
laying on of hands, 42, 45–46, 113, 242n14
leadership, 2–4, 24–25, 36, 47, 58, 67–69, 97, 102, 116, 154, 159, 161, 163, 165, 168, 186–92, 211, 215–16, 239, 244, 255
LGBTQIA+, 93, 111, 113–20, 141–42, 271
liberation, 21, 69, 78, 92, 133, 136, 150, 155–56, 265, 270, 273
liberation theology, 2, 56, 78, 90, 93, 133n3, 135, 138n27, 244
liberative service, 56, 93, 133, 138–39, 141, 143, 265, 267–73
liturgy, 20, 39, 42–46, 63, 65–66, 68, 115, 133, 165–66, 168, 227n30, 241, 244
love command, 44, 64, 71, 111–12, 136, 150, 186, 195–96, 267–70
Lutheran World Federation, 17, 22, 94–95, 137–38, 141
Marie Cederschiöld University, 212
martial law, 154–55
martyr, 150, 154–56, 269

memory, 124, 126–27, 129–31, 139–40, 142
migrants, 33, 90, 136, 142, 150–52, 157
ministry of the baptized, 19–21, 35, 37, 65, 101, 105, 225, 268–69
missio Dei, 37, 66, 71
mission, 1–2, 4, 15–21, 23–25, 29, 32, 34–37, 39–40, 42–45, 47, 52, 55, 58–59, 63–67, 70–71, 84, 89, 94, 97, 112, 124–26, 136, 138, 142, 158, 163, 186–87, 199, 215, 239–40, 246, 255, 265, 267, 272
moral agency, 18, 68, 70, 76, 80, 83–84, 93, 96–98, 126–27, 130, 133–37, 141, 143
Mother House, 31, 223
neighbor, 2, 15, 21, 23, 44, 59, 64, 67, 71, 84, 107–9, 112, 136, 141–42, 175, 179, 186, 195–96, 198, 201, 267–69, 272–73
neighborhood, 19, 36–37, 81–82, 103, 178
Niagara Report, 41
non-binary, 114, 116, 118, 142
nonprofits, 67, 118, 209, 248
Norway, 3, 207–8, 210–13, 221, 223, 229
nursing, 3, 31–32, 96, 174, 179, 182, 201, 211, 215, 222, 224–25, 228–32, 271
ordination, 39, 42, 44–46, 58, 64–66, 69–70, 133,

159, 161, 165–68, 175, 221n1, 233, 239, 241–47, 252, 255, 257–58
organizational culture, 185, 189, 202
paradigm, 4, 16, 19, 21, 23–24, 75, 80–81, 83–85, 136, 227, 251, 267
partnership, 21, 37, 78, 81, 83, 85, 102, 106, 152, 195, 258. See also collaboration
pastoral care, 21, 67, 112, 118, 196, 241
patriarchy, 69–70, 92, 166
peace, 17–18, 35–37, 94, 97, 102, 105, 107, 113, 136–37, 150, 153, 180, 239, 265, 270, 272
pensions, 47, 161–63, 165, 167, 240–43, 247–48
perpetual deacon, 161, 166, 241, 244, 246. See also vocational deacon
persecution, 102, 108, 151, 155–56
Philadelphia Eleven, 159–62, 165
Philippines, 149–56, 271
poor, 30–31, 35, 55, 59, 75–85, 103, 105, 113, 124–25, 127, 130, 133, 136–38, 149–56, 158, 175, 177–78, 181, 200, 210, 226, 244, 266, 269, 271
poverty, 1, 22, 30, 34, 75–78, 84, 89–90, 92–93, 98, 106, 129, 150–51, 153, 155–56, 210, 265, 270

power, 19–20, 40, 69, 78, 80–81, 84, 97, 101–2, 104–6, 133, 136–37, 143, 152, 157–58, 174, 186, 193, 213–14. See also empowerment; moral agency
powerful, 34, 48, 60, 68, 71, 76, 80, 85, 103, 128–31, 137–38, 142, 149, 152, 155, 160, 265
practical theology, 4, 75, 83, 213, 217
praxis, 25, 36–37, 77, 83, 90–93, 129, 133–34, 136, 138–40, 143. See also diaconal practice (praxis); diapraxis
prayer, 46, 65, 101, 107, 115, 152–53, 157, 178, 181–82, 192, 196, 198, 202, 260
preaching, 60, 63, 65–66, 75, 77–78, 83, 115, 227n30, 231
presbyter (ordained elder), 19, 43–46, 60, 63–67, 69–71, 120, 189, 272
Presbyterian Church of Australia, 31–33
priesthood of all believers, 19. See also ministry of the baptized
prison ministry, 30, 106, 113, 176, 226, 240
professionalization, 195, 221, 229
prophetic role, 2, 17, 23, 35, 37, 40, 56, 60, 65, 68, 78, 83, 105–6, 136–37, 142,

149, 152, 156, 244–45, 252, 265–66
queer, 111, 113–20
race 117, 124–26, 131–32, 135, 140, 142, 161, 176, 178–79, 246. See also white (race)
racism 70, 128, 131, 137, 245–46
reconciliation, 2, 17, 40–42, 46, 64, 89–90, 94–95, 97–98, 105–6, 108, 111, 119, 124, 130–34, 136–37, 141–43, 186, 189, 192, 265, 272
Reformation, 199, 208–9
revitalization, 1, 3, 15, 20–21, 24–25, 37, 39, 71, 81, 83–84, 131, 161
sacrament, 21, 33, 42–46, 65–66, 69, 105, 174, 178, 185, 196, 225, 227, 241, 270n20, 272
separation of church and state, 70, 207, 209
servant leadership, 2, 58, 102, 159, 161, 165, 168
servanthood, 2, 35, 80–81, 101, 106, 112, 123–26, 159, 243–44, 248
servitude, 125, 127–28, 268
sexism, 70, 92, 103, 113–14, 160, 240
social service, 3–4, 15, 25, 51–56, 60, 80, 95, 106, 136–37, 156, 176, 195, 228, 266
social work, 3, 30–31, 47, 52, 66, 96, 106, 165, 174, 200, 202, 207, 210–11, 213, 215–16, 222, 225, 227–33, 272
solidarity, 2, 3, 17, 25, 40, 89–90, 98, 104, 115, 119, 127, 129–30, 133, 136–40, 142–43, 150, 152, 195, 200, 215, 265
Son of Man, 29, 101, 124
South Africa, 75, 77–78, 112
spirituality, 1, 19, 33, 47, 66, 95, 111, 115–16, 118, 128, 134, 139–40, 143, 150, 156, 158, 161, 174–78, 180–81, 187–90, 192, 195–203, 224–25, 227, 229, 231, 240, 243, 245, 248, 254, 257, 272–73
state church, 208–10
stewardship, 96, 189–90, 239
storytelling, 54, 127, 150–51, 155, 181, 187–88, 268
suffering, 2, 15, 18, 25, 32, 34–35, 81, 90–92, 96–98, 102, 105, 107–8, 124–26, 128–31, 133, 135–43, 151–52, 155–56, 158, 176, 179–80, 239, 271
survival, 71, 76, 134–35, 151, 153, 157, 181, 187, 209, 271. See also victim-survivors
sustainability, 106, 187, 189–90
Sweden, 58, 208, 210–13, 223, 229
theological education, 1, 3–4, 25, 71, 101–2, 228,

233–34, 251–55, 258, 262, 272
theology of ministry, 15–16, 19, 21, 24, 44, 161
trafficking, 152
transformation, 2–3, 16–18, 25, 31, 36, 40, 64–65, 76, 84, 89–90, 92, 94–95, 97–98, 137, 142, 149. 209, 267
transgender, 111, 114–16, 118–19
transitional diaconate, 44, 160, 168
trauma, 1, 22, 114, 119, 133–35, 139–43, 269
Trevor Project, 117–18
Trinity, 20, 104, 107
ubuntu, 268
unhoused persons, 66–67, 71, 95, 103–4, 106, 271
Uniting Reformed Church, 78
victims, 35, 58, 114, 124, 135, 141, 150, 152–54, 158, 189, 192
victim-survivors, 133–37, 139, 141–42
VID Specialized University, 207, 212, 223
violence, 35, 93, 97, 102, 128, 135, 149, 153, 179, 265
vocation, 3, 18–21, 24, 31, 39, 43–45, 47, 54–55, 58, 60, 66, 107, 133, 151, 164, 176, 212, 225, 229, 239–42, 245n28, 247n41, 254–55, 257–58, 260

vocational deacon, 39, 43–44, 47, 176, 241–42, 255. See also perpetual deacon
voice, 40, 81, 83, 92, 127, 200
vulnerability, 129, 187, 202, 217, 230, 265
vulnerable, 35, 37, 67, 108, 158, 202, 266
war on drugs, 149–150, 153–54
weddings, 115
welcome, 30, 33, 36, 95, 103, 112–13, 116–18, 120, 135, 141, 149, 152, 157, 181, 189–90, 192
welfare, social, 31, 55, 195, 208–13, 216, 222, 229–30
white (race), 69–70, 103, 117, 125–26, 130, 137, 140, 186, 246, 251
women, 19, 30–33, 64, 69, 92, 103–4, 107, 125–26, 135, 140–41, 150–153, 159–68, 173–80, 182, 209n6, 222, 241–43
Word and Sacrament, 21, 33, 43–45, 174, 196, 225
Word and Service, 34, 43–45, 63, 101
World Council of Churches, 3, 16–17, 22, 39, 51–52, 58, 270–71
worship, 16, 21, 29, 42, 45, 48, 60, 95, 104–5, 149, 156, 192, 199, 260
youth, 115, 117–18, 153, 157, 191

Contributors

Valerie Bailey is chaplain to the college at Williams College, Massachusetts, and a priest in The Episcopal Church (US).

Jessica Bickford is a deacon in the Anglican Church of Canada – Diocese of Montreal and co-founder of Phoenix Community Projects, where she serves as the executive director.

Sandra Boyce is president of Diakonia World Federation and a member of the Uniting Church in Australia.

Mitzi J. Budde is professor emerita at Virginia (Episcopal) Theological Seminary and a deacon in the Evangelical Lutheran Church in America.

Margaret Ann Crain is professor emerita of Christian Education and Deacon Studies at Garrett-Evangelical Theological School and an ordained deacon in The United Methodist Church.

Norma P. Dollaga is a deaconess in the Philippines Annual Conference of the Manila Episcopal Area of The United Methodist Church, appointed to Kapatirang Simbahan Para sa Bayan (KASIMBAYAN)/Ecumenical Center for Development.

Kristin Husby Dyrstad is a deacon in the Evangelical Lutheran Church of Norway, working on a PhD at VID Specialized University about the history of deacon education.

Johannes Eurich is extraordinary professor for practical theology at Stellenbosch University, South Africa, director of the Institute for Diaconal Studies at Heidelberg University, Germany, and chair of The International Society for the Research and Study of Diaconia and Christian Social Practice (ReDI).

Norma Cook Everist is Professor of Church and Ministry, Emerita, Wartburg Theological Seminary, Iowa, and a deaconess and pastor in the Evangelical Lutheran Church in America.

Benjamin L. Hartley is an associate professor of Mission and World Christianity at Seattle Pacific University and an ordained deacon in The United Methodist Church.

Annette Leis-Peters is a professor of Sociology of Religion and Diaconal Studies and programme coordinator for the PhD programme in Diaconia, Values and Professional Practice at VID Specialized University in Norway.

Julie Anne Lytle is an associate professor and director of Distributive and Lifelong Learning Initiatives at Bexley Seabury Seminary Federation, Chicago.

Lori Mills-Curran is former executive director of the Association for Episcopal Deacons and founding executive director of ProGente Connections, an ecumenical immigrant advocacy ministry in the Boston area.

Mary Elizabeth Moore is Professor Emerita of Theology and Education and Dean Emerita of the School of Theology, Boston University, and a deacon in The United Methodist Church.

Craig L. Nessan is the William D. Streng Professor for the Education and Renewal of the Church and a professor of Contextual Theology and Ethics at Wartburg Theological Seminary, Iowa.

Daphne B. Noyes is a deacon in The Episcopal Church (US) and recipient of research grants from the Episcopal Women's History Project and the Historical Society of the Episcopal Church.

Dionata Rodrigues de Oliveira is the diaconal advisor of Nordeste Gaúcho Synod and is the Community of Deacons coordinator for Igreja Evangélica de Confissão Luterana no Brasil.

Darryl W. Stephens teaches at Lancaster Theological Seminary, Pennsylvania, and is a deacon in The United Methodist Church.

Ignatius Swart is a full professor in the Department of Religion and Theology at the University of the Western Cape, South Africa, and a member of the Dutch Reformed Church.

Leo Yates Jr. is an adjunct professor at Wesley Theological Seminary and a United Methodist deacon serving in pastoral ministry.

Man-Hei Yip is an assistant professor of Systematic Theology at Wartburg Theological Seminary, Iowa.